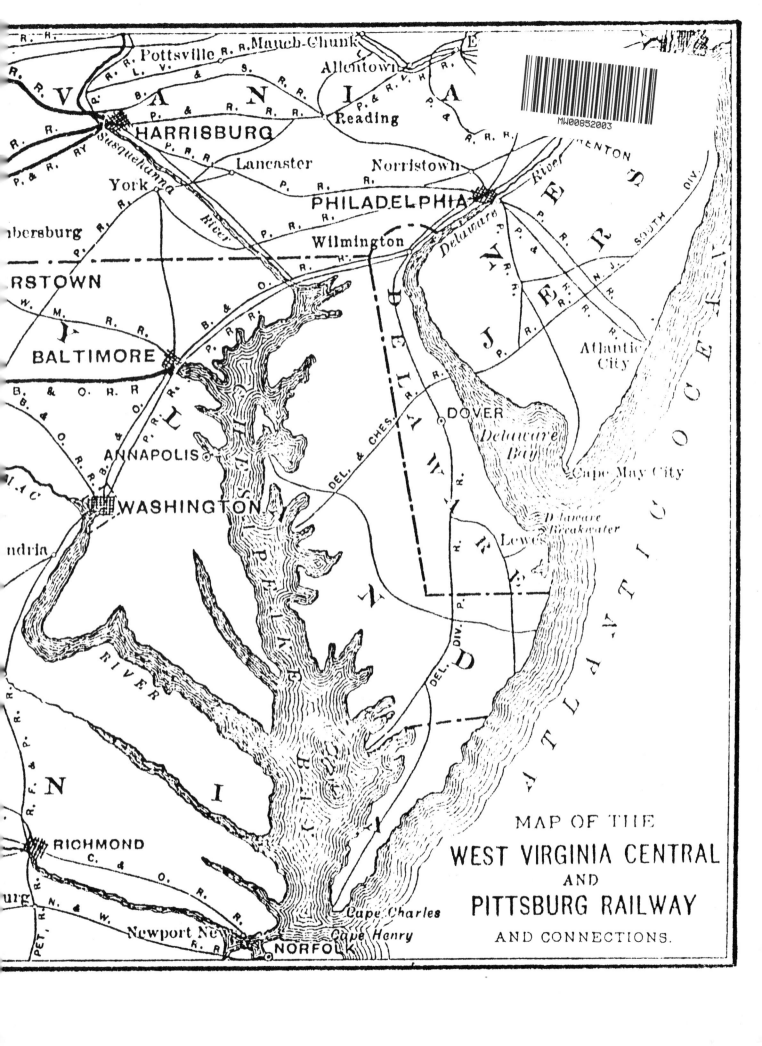

MAP OF THE
WEST VIRGINIA CENTRAL
AND
PITTSBURG RAILWAY
AND CONNECTIONS.

The West Virginia Central and Pittsburg Railway

A Western Maryland Predecessor

by

Alan Clarke

Author of
"West Virginia's Coal and Coke Railway"

2003
TLC Publishing Inc.
1387 Winding Creek Lane
Lynchburg, Virginia 24503-3776

Table of Contents

West Virginia Central No. 41 on turntable at Thomas
Collection of Rob Whetsell

Library of Congress Control Number: 2003103900
ISBN 1-883089-87-5
Layout & Design by Sue Evans, Lynchburg, Va. 24501
Printed by Walsworth Publishing Company, Marceline, MO 64658

Front Endsheet: *Map of the West Virginia Central and Pittsburg Railway and connections.*

During the 1980's, the author was involved in a project to photograph stone bridges throughout the U. S. One of the first photographed, in July 1981, was the stone railroad arch at Craven Run near Elkins, West Virginia (Fig. 1). In 1981, it was still in regular use, although its significance was not realized at the time. In February 1990, a notice appeared in the railroad press of a new railroad utilizing an abandoned stretch of track along the Elk River in West Virginia. The original railroad, the Coal and Coke Railway, had built a number of stone arches, so it seemed an appropriate time to take a look at the history of the line.

Fig. 1. Stone arch at Craven Run near Elkins, July 1981

The search for information soon led to the West Virginia Room of West Virginia University Library and the collected papers of Henry Gassaway Davis, the president of the C. & C. Although Davis had started to build the C. & C. in 1902, it was soon obvious that Davis's first railroad, the West Virginia Central and Pittsburg Railway, was also worthy of attention.

The West Virginia Central had its origins in 1866, but no work was done until 1880. The line worked its way up the North Branch of the Potomac River to reach a coalfield at Elk Garden, the first coal being shipped in October 1881. Davis and his associates had grander ambitions. Although Davis had got his start in the timber business, it was the mining and selling of coal that attracted him. He knew that there was an insatiable demand for coal and coke in Pittsburgh and the cities of the east coast. Many schemes were proposed, surveys conducted and railroads built to meet this demand. By 1902, the West Virginia Central stretched from Cumberland to Huttonsville and Belington and was pushing towards Durbin and a junction with the Chesapeake and Ohio Railway.

The West Virginia Central led to a boom in the areas through which it passed. Many new towns sprang up around the lumber mills and coal mines, but as first the timber was exhausted and then the coal was worked out, a decline set in, hastened by the abandonment of the very railroads that had brought life to the area in the first place.

It is this story, the story of railroad and industrial expansion followed by decline, which forms the basis of this book.

The name of the principal railroad, the West Virginia Central and Pittsburg Railway, illustrates one of the problems encountered when writing about this era. Throughout the Davis ownership of the West Virginia Central and Pittsburg, the "Pittsburg" was never spelled with an "h," although this changed somewhat after 1902, as can be seen in Fig. 138. Similarly, the names of towns and rivers also changed over time, e.g. Tygart's lost its "apostrophe s" and became Tygart Valley River. To ensure consistency, the modern spelling as found on the current U. S. G. S. maps will be used. However, the names of companies will be spelled as their owners intended, e.g. Tygarts River Lumber Company.

Some sections of the West Virginia Central remain in use, while other sections have disappeared beneath roads or dams or have been converted to trails. Many of the towns and industries have disappeared also, or are shadows of their former selves. It is worth noting, however, that the arch at Craven Run, which started this whole project, survived abandonment by the railroad and a road widening scheme, and can still be seen on the east side of Rt. 219, approximately one half mile north of the junction with Rt. 33.

It is the hope of the author that this book will keep alive the memories of a fascinating railroad, its towns and industries, and an exciting era in West Virginia's history.

Acknowledgements

The West Virginia Central and Pittsburg Railway was well photographed during its later years as part of the Western Maryland Railway, but its earlier years were not so well recorded. However, thanks to the help of a great many people in West Virginia and elsewhere, a large number of photographs were obtained and many fascinating items of West Virginia Central memorabilia were received. To all those who helped in any way, I wish to extend my sincere thanks – without you this book would not have been possible. Photographs were provided by the following individuals: William Metheny, Paul C. Mullins, Donald Rice, Alice Wisner, Harold K. Vollrath, Don Henderson, Richard Dye, Jane Barb, Rob Whetsell and John King. Illustrations that are not credited are in the author's collection.

The following individuals and organizations also provided photographs and information: T. Robert Shives, Western Maryland Railway Historical Society; William McNeel, Pocahontas County Historical Society; James and Alice Philips, Tucker County Historical Society; Library of Congress; Debra Basham, West Virginia State Archives; L. Susan Tolbert, National Museum of American History; Railroad Museum of Pennsylvania; James L. Schoonover, Davis Trust Company; University of Notre Dame Archives; David Pfeiffer; National Archives and Records Administration; DeGolyer Library, Southern Methodist University; Association of American Railroads; Robert W. Brendel; Delaware State Archives; Carnegie Library of Pittsburgh; National Park Service; City of Cumberland; Maryland State Archives; Milton Hart, Westernport Heritage Society, and finally the staff at the West Virginia Room of West Virginia University Library including Kathleen Kennedy, Christy Venham, David Bartlett and Delilah Board. My thanks also to T. Robert Shives for help with the manuscript, Ann Miller Mooney for proof reading, David Dillon for his excellent diagrams, and Ann Turpyn, who continues to be a much abused librarian.

Finally, a special thanks to my wife, Pat, for help with the typing and her encouragement and patience during the writing of this book.

On June 20, 1863, West Virginia became the thirty-fifth state of the Union. The reasons for the separation of West Virginia from Virginia were many and complex, not the least of which were the economic problems of western Virginia, caused by years of neglect by the state government in Richmond.

The area that was to become West Virginia was mainly populated by small farmers and the cottage industries that supplied them. The only areas where even a rudimentary industry had developed were the Charleston region, where the presence of brine had led to the formation of a salt industry, and Wheeling, which had the beginnings of an iron based industry. These towns were successful only because of the ready availability of rivers to transport goods to market. The remainder of the region was cut off from any suitable means of land or water transportation and without such transportation, development was virtually nonexistent.

It generally had been recognized early in the 19th Century that the prosperity of the states lying along the eastern seaboard depended on the exploitation of the lands to the west. On March 2, 1807, the United States Senate directed the secretary of the treasury to prepare a report describing the roads and canals that were in existence and how they could be improved by Congress. The secretary, Albert Gallatin, submitted his report on April 4, 1808, which recommended the federal government's involvement in developing such projects. The report reviewed those canals and turnpikes that already had been built. This showed that the states in the northeast had been very active in building turnpikes, but south of the Potomac River "...few artificial roads have been undertaken." Turnpikes were beginning to spread westwards from Alexandria, Virginia, and one or two minor roads commenced at Richmond.

One result of the report was the construction of the National Road from Cumberland westwards, which reached Wheeling in 1818, hastening the development of the town. The National Road was originally planned to go to St. Louis on the Mississippi River, but only reached Vandalia, Illinois, before it was made obsolete by the railroads.

In 1816, the General Assembly of Virginia created "The Fund for Internal Improvement", and established a Board of Public Works to administer the fund. The Board appointed a principal engineer to oversee the various canal and turnpike projects. By 1848, three turnpikes crossed the mountains into what is now West Virginia. The first of these to be constructed was the Kanawha Turnpike running from Covington to Charleston, which was reached in 1827. This was followed by the Northwestern Turnpike in 1838, which linked Winchester and Parkersburg. The final turnpike, the Staunton and Parkersburg, was authorized in 1838, but not completed until 1847.

The most significant project for the Board was the James River and Kanawha Canal designed to link Richmond and Charleston with a system of canals, turnpikes and river improvements. The canal reached Buchanan in 1851, but was never a commercial success.

Although the turnpikes in western Virginia helped to develop towns such as Clarksburg, Weston and Buckhannon, they did not bring to the interior regions the economic development which their promoters had promised, and which the inhabitants still needed.

The 1850's saw an increase in interest by Richmond in improvements in western Virginia, when more money was made available for turnpike construction. The effort was, by now, too little and too late, as attention had turned to the railroads as a means of opening up the underdeveloped areas of the country. The Baltimore and Ohio Railroad, which had started construction as early as 1828, had reached Cumberland, Maryland, in November 1842, and the Ohio River at Wheeling in 1852. Of greater significance to what was to become West Virginia, was the Northwestern Virginia Railroad, a B. & O. subsidiary, which connected with the B. & O. at Grafton and reached the Ohio at Parkersburg in 1857.

On the same day that the B. & O. started building in Baltimore, a canal was started on the banks of the Potomac River in Washington. The canal, the Chesapeake and Ohio Canal, was projected to follow the Maryland side of the Potomac to Cumberland, and from there to Pittsburgh. Progress was slow and the canal did not reach Cumberland until 1850. Because the railroads were by then a clearly superior form of transportation, the canal was never built beyond Cumberland. In its early days, the canal played an important role in moving a large tonnage of coal, which the railroads were not yet equipped to handle. Later, when the railroads could move large amounts of coal, cheaper rates on the canal gave mine owners a choice of transportation.

In Virginia, the Louisa Railroad, chartered in 1836, was the first railroad to head west from the vicinity of Richmond. The name was changed to the Virginia Central Railroad in 1850 to reflect this ambition and by the start of the Civil War, the railroad had reached Clifton Forge. No further construction occurred during the war years. At the end of the war, the railroads built in Virginia and West Virginia are shown in Fig. 2. In 1867, the name of the Virginia Central was changed to the Chesapeake and Ohio Railroad when the company decided to build to the Ohio River. Early in 1869, C. P. Huntington became interested in the new road and was able to secure funds to complete the line to the Ohio River in 1873.

On February 28, 1878, the General Assembly of Virginia approved an act incorporating the Richmond and Alleghany Railroad to build a line along the James River Canal to Lynchburg. A year later a second act transferred the property of the canal company to the R. & A. The company was empowered to build to the West Virginia state line via Jackson River or Craig's Creek. The route was completed to Clifton Forge in 1881. No additional construction towards West Virginia was undertaken, and the R. & A. was taken over by the C. & O. in 1890.

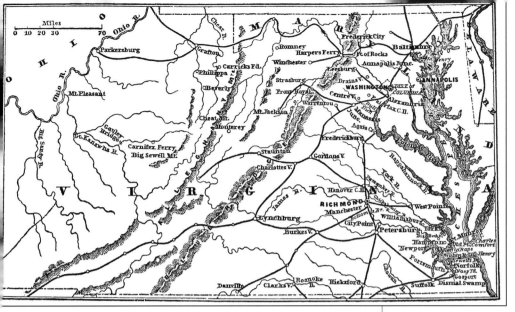

Fig. 2. Railroads in Virginia and West Virginia at the time of the Civil War

Even with the completion of the B. & O. and the C. & O. through West Virginia, there were still vast stretches of country that were inaccessible to the new railroads, hindering the development of the new state. Among the most inaccessible of areas were the Appalachian Mountains, consisting of a long series of ridges running from the B. & O. at Cumberland in the north, to the C. & O. in the south. The area had long been known to contain vast amounts of timber and was thought to contain coal as it was the southerly extension of the Georges Creek coalfield west of Cumberland. From the north the region was penetrated by the North Branch of the Potomac River, and from the south by the Greenbrier River. Other rivers such as the Cheat, Tygart Valley and the Elk and their many tributaries, drained the western flanks of the mountains.

The North Branch of the Potomac had been considered by the B. & O. as a possible route westward in 1848, and it had been surveyed by the chief engineer, Benjamin H. Latrobe. The route had been abandoned in favor of the Savage River line, which was shorter and did not require a tunnel. In a letter written in 1870, Latrobe did mention that, "The route along the North Branch would be highly favorable for a coal road, with descending grades to the B. & O. at Piedmont."

Apart from hunters and explorers, the region lay undisturbed. One intrusion was made when Judge Dobbin of Baltimore built a lodge on the Blackwater River near the falls. The lodge became quite famous and was visited by many people anxious to see the falls and to hunt and fish in the area (Fig. 3). The lodge was reached by a trek of 25 miles from the B. & O. at Oakland, Maryland. One nameless individual who visited the area, wrote the following on his return to civilization:

"Some day, not too long distant, the sordid ambitions of the speculator will enter these forests and fell the magnificent timber and despoil the scene of its unrivalled grandeur and beauty. Perhaps the iron horse will go snorting round the cliffs and gorges of these mountains where now the wild beast skip and play in undisturbed security."

Although the article was undated, its author was correct

when he prophesied the arrival of the "iron horse." However, the speculator who was to be most closely identified with the region was not a person of "sordid ambition" as expected. Henry Gassaway Davis (Fig. 4.) was convinced he was bringing the benefits of civilization to a forgotten area and at the same time conveying its resources to those who needed them. A few years later he wrote, (although the words are perhaps not entirely his own): "Speculation following the Civil War took Eastern capital to the West. Immigration was large, and naturally sought the unsettled lands, which the Government offered at a nominal price to those who would occupy them. Trans-continental railroads, with branches in all directions, were projected and built, and the gold and silver of the Western Mountains beckoned men on. Iron furnaces were fed from the ore of Lake Superior; Pennsylvania, Ohio and Illinois provided the fuel to keep them going. Michigan and Wisconsin largely supplied the lumber markets. Texas and adjoining States kept busy the looms in woolen mills. All avenues of industrial wealth led to the West. They passed by and through the State of West Virginia, and those who traveled these roads little knew, and took little note of the wealth of opportunity through which they were passing, waiting to be gathered. The tide of Western development having reached its flood, began to ebb, and when the light of inquiry was turned upon the fields of investment at home they found treasures neglected. The Alleghenies were as rich in coal and timber as the Rockies were in the precious metals. The heart of the wealth of the Alleghenies is in West Virginia, and its throbbing has just begun with the awakening of its industrial life."

West Virginia Central and Pittsburg Railway Company, 1899

Henry Gassaway Davis was born in Baltimore, Maryland, on November 16, 1823. His father, Caleb Davis, was a merchant in Baltimore owning a grocery and feed store, and a farm at Woodstock, Maryland. Either because of business reverses in Baltimore, or because he sensed favorable opportunities along the new railroad,

Fig. 3. The falls of the Blackwater

Fig. 4. Henry Gassaway Davis
West Virginia and Regional History Collection,
West Virginia University Library

the B. & O., which was being built near Woodstock, Caleb Davis moved his family to the farm. He obtained contracts for grading along the line of the B. & O. but these did not prove profitable, and the family was plunged into bankruptcy.

Soon after, the elder Davis became incapacitated, leaving Henry, at the age of 14 or 15, to support the family. Davis went to work on a plantation owned by George Howard, who had served as governor of Maryland a few years earlier, and was friendly with the Davis family. He rose to become manager, but left in 1842 to become a brakeman on the B. & O. Within a year, he became freight conductor, and in this position he came to the attention of Thomas Swann, the president of the B. & O. Swann was impressed by Davis, and moved him up into passenger service. In this capacity, he became acquainted with some of the dignitaries who used the line, such as Henry Clay, who is credited with getting Davis interested in politics.

At the age of 24, Davis was promoted to division superintendent, and became President Swann's right hand man. In his new capacity, Davis was reported to be convinced that trains could run safely at night, a practice that previously had not been tried. He persuaded Swann to allow a test of his theory, which proved to be successful. As division superintendent, his salary was $100.00 per month, enough for him, at the age of 30, to think of getting married. In 1853 he married Katherine Anne Bantz. They had five children, Hallie, Henry, Kate, Grace and John T. Henry, the eldest son, died at sea in 1896; John T. Davis was to become involved in many of his father's business interests. The year 1853 also saw Davis ask for a transfer to become agent for the B. & O. at Piedmont in what is now West Virginia.

Davis had been aware for some time of the potential of the lands in this region in terms of timber and coal. He had been buying land out of his salary for as little as 50 cents to $1.50 per acre. He was helped in this when his father-in-law died in 1854, leaving Davis a substantial sum. During this period, Davis, along with two of his brothers, William and Thomas, set up a company, H. G. Davis and Company, which engaged in general trading in the Piedmont area, and also branched out into cutting and sawing lumber and eventually into coal mining. The business proved highly successful, so much so that Davis resigned from the B. & O. to devote his full time to the company. During the Civil War, the company flourished, receiving contracts from both the B. & O. and the U. S. Government for the supply of horses, lumber and coal.

With the cessation of hostilities in 1865, Davis was able to invest the considerable sums he had earned during the war in further land purchases. At the same time he was able to embark on

his political career when he was elected to the West Virginia House of Delegates as the representative of Hampshire County as a "Union-Conservative", later becoming a Democrat. This success enabled him to secure the passage of the act to incorporate the Potomac and Piedmont Coal and Railroad Company.

The act incorporating the railroad was passed on February 26, 1866. Listed as the incorporators were H. G. Davis, T. B. Davis, W. R. Davis, W. J. Armstrong, J. Phillip Roman, James Boyce and R. G. Reiman, and these individuals became directors of the new company. The purpose of the company was listed as the "mining of coal, the building of manufactories, saw mills or furnaces, the burning of brick, the manufacturing of lumber and the buying and disposing of same, together with the right to buy and sell real estate, and the transportation of coal and other products of its mines and property to market,…" These activities, with the possible exception of the manufacture of bricks, were to be the mainstay of Davis's business interests for the next fifty years.

The railroad was granted permission to build from any point on the B. & O. along the North Branch of the Potomac River, to its mines and lands in Mineral, Grant, Tucker and Greenbrier counties. The road could also be extended to the town of Piedmont and to a connection with the Loudoun and Hampshire Railroad, or any other railroad.

Davis did not appear to be in any hurry to use his new franchise, as his lumber business at Deer Park in Allegany County, Maryland, seemed to keep him busy. Davis had purchased several thousand acres of land at Deer Park in 1867, laid off the town and built a summer house there. During this time he was still purchasing lands in Maryland, particularly in an area of Garrett County known as Strawberry Plains. An 1870 newspaper report noted that the mill produced twenty tons, or 10,000 board feet of lumber per day. To supply the mill, 13 miles of 3.1/2 foot gauge tramroad were built into the woods using 1.1/2 x 1.1/2 inch flat iron rails laid on oak stringers. On the steeper sections, T rails were used. Surprisingly for an ex-railroad man, Davis preferred horses to steam engines for hauling his cars, although he was reported to be using small locomotives at his mines.

Davis did pay several visits to the Elk Garden area, some 12 miles up the North Branch, in the years 1868 and 1869, and he purchased some land there in June 1869. He also visited the Canaan region and reported finding seams of coal about six feet thick. At the end of 1869, Davis and a partner, Major Alexander Shaw, were looking for coal around Elk Garden but with little success. On October 4, 1870, Davis noted in his diary that, "prospects are bad but we still have hopes." Perhaps because of his lack of success in finding coal, Davis then considered the North Branch with a view to building a boom and floating down lumber. By July 1871, Davis noted that he now owned 40,000 acres of good timber lands along the North Branch and that it would require between $70,000 and $100,000 to set up a boom and mill.

In the spring of 1872, Davis negotiated the purchase of two tracts of land, the Merrill tracts, totaling 5,696 acres. The land stretched south from the Fairfax Stone along the North Fork of the Blackwater River and included the site of the present town of Thomas. Davis paid $1.25 per acre for the land.

Davis was not the only individual with plans for the North Branch. John Swan, who was the heir to some 17,000 acres of land on the Maryland side of the river known as Swan's Potomac Manor, had the land resurveyed in 1869. Impressed by the resources, in 1872 Swan had the Maryland legislature amend an 1853 act, which had created the Manor Mining and Manufacturing Company. This company had been empowered to build a railroad along the North Branch, but had done nothing since incorporation, and apparently did nothing of consequence after the amendment.

At the same time the West Virginia legislature passed an act creating the North Branch Railroad, which was authorized to build to a connection with the C. & O., but again nothing came of the effort.

Other railroads during this period had grandiose plans to build from Virginia across the mountains into West Virginia to exploit coal, timber and iron ore resources of the state. One of the first was the Washington, Cincinnati and St. Louis Railroad, which was chartered on March 15, 1872. The company proposed to build a narrow gauge line from Washington, through Rockingham County, Virginia, to the North River Gap and into West Virginia. Although the railroad actually did some grading it ceased all work in 1874. The North River Gap was to interest other potential railroad builders.

Next on the scene was the Washington and Ohio Railroad, to which a number of counties lying along the proposed route made subscriptions, payment being dependant upon the railroad reaching the county limits. Newspaper reports at the time, heralding the arrival W. & O., did draw attention to the coal seams along the Buckhannon River that were reported to be 12 feet thick. The W. & O. was actually a new name for an old railroad, the Alexandria, Loudoun and Hampshire Railroad, which had been chartered in 1853, and was projected to run to Keyser in Hampshire County. By the start of the Civil War, the road had reached Leesburg (Fig.). In 1870, the company was authorized to extend west to the Ohio River, and hence changed its name to the Washington and Ohio Railroad Company. In 1878, the company was in bankruptcy, a fact that was to play a minor role in Davis's future plans.

This was followed by the Shenandoah Valley and Ohio Railroad, which actually let some contracts for work near Franklin, West Virginia, before disappearing in 1874.

In 1874, an ambitious proposal for a double track freight railroad, the Potomac and Ohio Railroad, was made to the U. S. Senate Committee on Transportation. Again this proposal mentioned the valuable coalfields of West Virginia, this time on the Elk and Gauley rivers, but nothing was to come of the proposal.

A final proposal came in October 1874 and was to influence Davis if only by the choice of its name. The West Virginia Central Railway, like its counterparts, was designed to run from Charleston to Harrisonburg and then to either Aquia Creek or to West Point, both locations lying on the Potomac River.

Davis's efforts to build a railroad at this time also were on hold although his interest in the Elk Garden coalfield had not lessened. In September 1874, Davis received a report on two plots of land in the region, amounting to 684 acres, which were being offered for sale. William M. Owens, county surveyor for Allegany

County, Maryland, reported that the land contained 323 acres of the 14-foot seam of coal known as the "Big Vein." This was estimated to be able to produce 4,000,000 tons of coal. To get the coal to market, a tramroad and incline plane could be built either to the proposed North Branch Railroad, or to the B. & O. at Piedmont for a cost of approximately $100,000. Opening the mines and building houses for the miners and necessary workshops was estimated to cost an additional $40-50,000. It was estimated that coal could be delivered to the B. & O. at Piedmont for $1.05 per ton. Davis must have been impressed by the arguments as he purchased both plots. Davis also was interested in coalfields elsewhere in the state, and in December, he purchased 1149 acres of coal lands in Barbour and Taylor counties for $51,722, with Alexander Shaw taking a one fourth interest.

In November 1874, Davis took a trip to Randolph and Barbour counties to look at coal seams in the area. His interest may have been prompted by the enthusiastic accounts of these coalfields published by the proprietors of the railroads, which hoped to exploit them. Davis however was not impressed, even though a vein of coal at Roaring Creek in Randolph County was reported to be 11 feet thick. Davis noted in his diary, "Upon the whole I do not think as well of the Randolph and Roaring Creek coal deposits as I had been led to think." Davis's opinion of this coal was to change radically.

On November 13, 1874, Davis reported that work had started on a mill at West Piedmont and that he had purchased timber on some 25,000 acres of land belonging to Swan's Potomac Manor. The total amount spent on the mill and river improvements to this time had been $70,000.

Perhaps because of all this activity, the capital stock of the P. & P. C. & R. was increased on December 11, 1874.

During this time Davis did not neglect his political interests. In the years following the Civil War, the West Virginia Legislature was made up of many conflicting factions stemming from the war, which made it difficult to develop the sound institutions needed for the new state. Davis survived the conflicts and served one year as a delegate. In 1868, he was elected to the State Senate, and was reelected in 1870. During his time in the State Senate, he had become one of its leaders and was elected to the U. S. Senate on January 31, 1871 for a six-year term. He was reelected on January 28, 1877 for a second term that expired in 1883.

During his time in political office, Davis was to meet many people who later would be associated with him in his various business enterprises. One such individual was Stephen B. Elkins (Fig. 5), who was to marry Davis's eldest daughter, Hallie, on April 14, 1875. This was the second marriage for Elkins. His first wife, whom he had

Fig. 5. Stephen B. Elkins
West Virginia and Regional History Collection, West Virginia University Library

married in 1866, died before he entered Congress.

Elkins was born in Ohio on September 20, 1841, but early in his life moved to Missouri. He attended the University of Missouri, graduated in 1860 and began a career as a schoolteacher, which was interrupted by the Civil War. After serving on the Union side, he was discharged and moved to New Mexico. Here he studied law and became a member of the bar in 1863, and was also elected to the New Mexico Legislature. Elkins became active as a title attorney in land sales and amassed a small fortune. With this beginning, he then moved to the purchase of lands in his own right. In 1867 he was appointed attorney general for the territory and six years later, he was elected as a Republican to the U. S. Congress. He served two terms in Congress as a non-voting member, since New Mexico had not yet acquired statehood. Elkins introduced a bill to give New Mexico statehood in 1875, but this was defeated, much to Elkins's chagrin. With this defeat and faced with the continuation of his non-voting status, he lost interest in Congress and refused a third term. After his two terms in Congress Elkins set up a law practice in Washington, but in 1878, he moved to New York. He was still actively involved in politics, having been appointed a member of the Republican National Committee in 1875, later becoming its chairman.

The year 1875 was important for Davis for reasons other than his daughter's marriage. The year also saw the start on railroads that actually would be built and have some influence on Davis's plans.

The Buckhannon Delta on April 25 carried an announcement that a narrow gauge railroad would be built up the Tygart Valley River from Grafton to Philippi. Although no name was mentioned for the proposed road, this was the first notice of what was to become the Grafton and Greenbrier Railroad. No further word was heard about progress until 1881.

Further west, the Weston and West Fork Railroad was organized in 1875 to run from Clarksburg to Weston, although again there would be a delay before construction started in 1877. Financial problems caused a suspension of the work in 1878, but it was rescued by Johnson Newlon Camden. Camden was another of Davis's associates with a long history of mixing business and politics. Davis, Elkins and Camden were perhaps the three business and political leaders who were most responsible for shaping the new state of West Virginia after the Civil War.

Camden was born on March 6, 1828 at what is now Jacksonville, West Virginia. He became interested in the law and was admitted to practice in 1850. Ten years later he became involved in drilling for oil along the Little Kanawha River east of Parkersburg. In 1863, a raid by the Confederates destroyed his oil operations along the river, but he rebuilt the company after the war. He also became the leader of the Democratic Party in the state in 1868, but lost a bid for governor in 1872. By 1872, Camden's oil business was declining in the face of the monopolizing tactics of John D. Rockefeller and the Standard Oil Company. The Panic of 1873 caused further problems for Camden and he sold out to Standard Oil in 1875. For the next few years, in the words of Camden's biographer, he became Rockefeller's "right hand man" in West Virginia. Camden was elected to the U. S. Senate on January 19, 1881, his first victory in an election. With his election, Camden effectively withdrew from the oil business.

Camden became interested in the Weston and West Fork Railroad in 1878, and organized the Clarksburg, Weston and Glenville Railroad to operate the W. & W. F. A year later, the W. & W. F. transferred all its property and leases to the new company. Camden wrote to Davis on August 6, 1879, asking him to subscribe to bonds of the company. The first train over the new railroad was to reach Weston on September 1, 1879. Another company, the Buckhannon and West Fork Railroad was organized in April 1883, to build a railroad from Buckhannon to Weston. All of these companies merged on February 6, 1890, to become the West Virginia and Pittsburgh Railroad with Camden as its president. The new railroad was to extend south to Pickens in 1892 and to Richwood in 1899.

Throughout 1875, Davis was kept busy by his activities on the North Branch. In April, he purchased additional coal acreage, known as the Armstrong lands, for $25,000. Floods in August brought down logs to the boom at West Piedmont enabling Davis to declare, "the enterprise on the North Branch a success." At this time, the money spent on the project had reached $100,000. By September, the country was feeling the effects of a depression caused by, according to Davis, "tight money." This had started with the Panic of 1873 and had grown steadily worse. The effects were felt in the operations of Davis and Company; Davis noted that "coal and lumber trade less now than before." Davis was sufficiently optimistic to take another trip up the North Branch to examine coal lands around Stoney River and Difficult Run. A four-foot vein of coal was found on Difficult Run and an eight-foot vein on Stoney River.

The year 1876 was important politically for Davis as he actively campaigned in West Virginia for the national Democratic ticket, and also for his own reelection to the U. S. Senate, which occurred in January 1877. The only item of business that Davis considered worthy of note was a flood on the Potomac River when he hoped to float between 25,000 and 30,000 logs to West Piedmont. Unfortunately the flood was greater than anticipated; the boom was breached and the onrushing logs destroyed a bridge belonging to Davis, followed by the county road bridge. The combined mass then destroyed one span of the Cumberland and Pennsylvania Railroad bridge at Piedmont. Davis estimated that he had lost 15,000 or 20,000 logs with an estimated financial loss of $30,000. There is no indication as to who paid to replace the destroyed bridges.

By 1877 there was no improvement in the financial condition of the country and Davis was still complaining about poor business. His total expenditure on the mill and boom at West Piedmont by now amounted to $115,000. The mill could produce 25,000 to 40,000 feet of lumber, lath and shingles each day, but because of high freight rates, he was not able to do as much business as was possible. He wrote to the general freight agent of the B. & O. suggesting rates from Piedmont of $3 per ton to Baltimore, $2.50 to Frederick, and $2 to Martinsburg. These last two towns were important as they had connections to the Pennsylvania Railroad. Davis complained that he was being charged more to ship a car of lumber from Deer Park to Baltimore than it cost to ship a similar car from Indiana. Davis returned to this problem in a letter to John Garrett, the president of the B. & O. Although he recognized the current financial difficulties in the country accounted for much of the decrease in manufacturing and farming along the B. & O., he also blamed high local freight rates charged by that company. Davis claimed it cost more to send freight 100 miles on the B. & O. than it did from Chicago to Baltimore (900 miles). Davis concluded by asking for a revision in local freight rates before the matter was brought before the legislature.

Whatever Garrett thought of this proposal is not known as he was beset by more urgent problems at this time. The B. & O., along with the other trunk lines, had announced a 10 percent wage reduction to take effect on July 16. For a first class fireman earning $1.75 per day, this represented a loss of 17 cents. When the cut went in effect, the firemen on the B. & O. at Baltimore struck and also prevented freight trains from leaving the city. Later in the day, firemen at Martinsburg joined the strike. Davis noted the onset of the strike in his diary and was to follow it closely for the next two weeks. The New York Times called the strike "foolish" and called on the B. & O. to "resist intimidation of this lawless character." Rioting occurred in Baltimore on July 20 leading to a loss of life. On July 21, Pittsburgh became the scene of a battle between strikers and the militia, in which about 20 people were killed and much railroad property destroyed. Davis noted that women and children were included among the dead. By now the New York Times had become just a little more sympathetic towards the strikers when it noted that some railroad workers earned little more than subsistence wages, but even then questioned why the railroads should be expected to pay more if men could be found willing to work. By now the strike was total throughout the Northeast and the Midwest. By the end of the month some freight trains were beginning to operate on the B. & O., protected by troops and using replacement firemen. Keyser was to remain the last stronghold of the strikers who were allied with striking coal miners and Chesapeake and Ohio Canal boatmen. By August 2, the strike was over.

Davis made no comment on the strike in his diary other than to record its progress. For Davis the strikers were a "mob" although later he was to claim to be a friend of both capital and labor.

With peace restored to the railroads, Davis's attention again turned to Elk Garden where he attempted to buy more coal lands but this time was unsuccessful. In November, another flood on the Potomac swept 10-15,000 logs into the boom at West Piedmont although a few escaped.

The year 1877 had been a disastrous one for the nation's railroads not only because of the strike, but also because of a decrease in earnings, which in turn reduced the amount of new construction. By 1878, the situation finally improved with nearly 3000 miles of new railroad being built. Davis however, still held back from starting any construction on the P. & P. C. & R. and does not seem to have been active in buying more coal lands.

In April 1879, the New York Times carried an announcement that the narrow gauge Pittsburg Southern Railroad, running from Pittsburgh to Washington, Pennsylvania, had been sold by the sher-

iff in Washington County for $55,000. The road, which had been completed a few months earlier, was to be of considerable interest to Davis in 1880.

In the fall, Davis was back on the North Branch, examining timber he owned on the Potomac Manor lands around Three Forks Run. He observed that all the timber had been cut from the Right Prong and that cutting was occurring on the middle fork and that good timber remained to be cut on the Left Prong. He also noted that he was going to build another mill some 2.1/2 miles from Swanton. A month later he noted in his diary he was looking at coal veins in the region around Wilsons but gave no indication where this was located.

By January 1880, Davis was ready to start thinking about railroad building. The year 1879 had been a very good year for new railroad construction nationally with some 4,563 miles of track being laid, indicating a high degree of confidence in the future by the railroad owners, a confidence that Davis obviously shared.

Davis's first step was to contact the B. & O. to discuss rates on coal for the new line. His partner, Alexander Shaw who was president of the Cumberland and Elk Lick Coal Company, proposed the board of the P. & P. C. & R. be constituted as follows: H. G. Davis, Thomas B. Davis, S. B. Elkins, A. Shaw, his brother John Shaw, and W. L. Roberts.

At this time Elkins was still living in New York and was not directly involved in the scheme, but he did have some thoughts as to the future plans of the company even though the first shovel of earth had not yet been turned. He was aware of the proceedings of a meeting of the board of directors of the R. & A. held on January 25, 1880, at which the board had decided to build up the Jackson River to the West Virginia state line. Elkins wrote to Davis on January 26, mentioning the decision of the R. & A., and recommending that Davis should build to meet the R. & A. Elkins also recommended building a railroad down the Tygart Valley River to a junction with the B. & O. at Grafton. This would give direct access to Wheeling, which, according to Elkins, was "becoming an important manufacturing center and will probably want iron and iron ore from along our line." Elkins also considered the possibility of building down the Cheat River to Pittsburgh, but thought the Tygart Valley line superior as it passed through more coalfields. The thorny question as to whether the railroad company or a separate company should own the coal lands, he tactfully left for Davis to decide.

The annual meeting of the P. & P. C. & R. was held on January 27 at which time Davis was elected president. It also was agreed to deed more coal lands to the company in spite of Elkins's reservations. A report from W. E. Porter, the resident engineer, was presented on the cost of a narrow gauge road to Elk Garden.

An encouraging report was published about this time by the mine inspector for Maryland, Owen Riordan, who noted that the railroad would soon be built and that it would exploit "the best blacksmith coal in the world."

The P. & P. C. & R. was not the only company looking at these resources. The Pittsburg Southern had been energized by its new owners and was actively looking at the coal and iron ore deposits of West Virginia and Virginia. It was claimed that the 13 blast furnaces operating in the Pittsburgh area required 750,000 tons of ore a year and this demand was not being met from existing fields. The proposed narrow gauge line was to be built to Grafton via Morgantown, and then up the Tygart Valley River and the Greenbrier River to the ore fields of Greenbrier and Pocahontas counties. Unfortunately, even though the new route had many supporters including the governor of West Virginia, it never reached its destination and was purchased by the B. & O. in 1883.

On March 20 came the first announcement that the P. & P. C. & R. might finally be getting ready for construction when an order was placed for wheelbarrows with E. J. Fredlock of Piedmont. The start date was given as April 1, although actual construction did not begin until April 20.

Davis noted on April 24 that he was buying an additional 4,900 acres on Stoney River, "if the title is good."

Stephen B. Elkins was officially invited to become associated with the P. & P. C. & R. by Alexander Shaw in a letter dated May 11, 1880. Shaw mentioned that the company already owned 200 acres of surface land and 273 acres of Big Vein coal and a similar amount of small vein. Davis and Shaw together proposed to deed to the company an additional 1912 acres that would include 485.1/2 acres of Big Vein coal. Shaw estimated that the Big Vein land would yield 20,000 tons of coal per acre and produce an estimated $1,260,000 in revenue. Shaw wrote that it was proposed to issue $3,000,000 in stock and that Elkins could have $500,000 at $12.50 per share or $62,500. Elkins was given the option of deeding some land that he already owned to the company giving a cash requirement of $26,500. The company would then own 12,000 acres and have $89,000 cash on hand. Shaw estimated the total cost to build the road and open the mines at $125,000 leaving $36,000 to be raised. Shaw concluded by saying, "the price will yield handsome profits."

On May 20 the company started to advertise for men to work on construction, at least 200 being required, and by July 8 it was reported that construction was well under way.

Davis and his brother, Thomas, walked over the new route from Bloomington to Elk Garden on September 1, accompanied by the members of their engineering staff. The party included James Parsons, the resident engineer, and the superintendent, W. E. Porter. Porter had been an engineer on the B. & O. during the Civil War, where he was involved in repairing the damage to that road in West Virginia as a result of Confederate raids. James L. Randolph, chief engineer of the B. & O. also accompanied the group. Davis noted that five miles were graded and that 200 men were at work.

Davis, Elkins and Alexander Shaw met on September 15 to organize the company. At the meeting the idea of extending the road must have come up as Davis wrote to Charles P. Manning saying that they were going to build from the B. & O. to the C. & O. via the North Branch and the Greenbrier River. Manning had worked on the Alexandria, Loudoun and Hampshire Railroad when it was planning an expansion west, and was familiar with the country.

Davis, along with Thomas Davis, Elkins and Randolph, visited Elk Garden on October 1 to decide on the location of the inclined plane. Three possible routes were available. Davis's preferred

route was for a plane from opening No. 1 down Barkers Ridge to Deep Run about two miles from the North Branch. This was the route finally selected and Porter and Parsons were informed that land had been purchased on Deep Run and to "locate your line up the Run."

Davis and Alexander Shaw went over the road on October 20 and reported 200 men still at work. A few days later, Davis wrote to the Superintendent of the Census and reported that the road to Elk Garden was under construction and was two-thirds graded. The gauge was 3.1/2 feet and it was to be laid with 40 pound per yard steel rail. The finish date was put at July 1, 1881.

In November, Davis asked William Pinkney Whyte, a senator from Maryland, and the company's attorney in that state, to review the charter of the P. & P. C. & R. to see if there were any problems. Whyte thought that because no elections for directors had occurred between 1873 and 1879, this could be considered grounds for forfeiture. Special legislation would be required to overcome this problem. This gave Davis good reason to rethink the whole project. Davis later wrote to Whyte suggesting that the original charter be amended to change the name to the West Virginia Central Railroad and to build through Pocahontas and Randolph counties. In addition, he wanted to be able to build along the Cheat, Tygart Valley or Greenbrier rivers to a connection with the C. & O., W. & O. or the R. & A. Finally he requested that the capital be increased to $1,000,000

An account of the construction expenditures on the new road was submitted to Davis on November 20. This showed that from April 1 to November 1, $33,605 had been spent. It also was noted that the company was losing men because of the severity of the weather.

On November 24, Elkins wrote to Davis about a meeting he had with T. E. Sickels who had been an engineer on the Union Pacific Railroad. Davis had expressed an interest in building a pulp mill along his new road, and Elkins had asked Sickels for information on such a facility. Elkins had also discussed the extension of the P. & P. C. & R. south and had asked Sickels to report on the feasibility of such an undertaking. Sickels must have impressed Davis and Elkins, as he was to become a director and consulting engineer for the project. Elkins also mentioned a meeting with the president of the R. & A. on November 23. The R. & A. was now thinking of building to Lexington, but was still interested in joining up with Davis to secure a line to Pittsburgh. There also was a possibility of a line being built through West Virginia to Columbus, Ohio.

Davis asked for one final report from Professor Fountaine at the University of Virginia, who had been recommended by Governor Mathews of West Virginia. Fountaine was not too much help, as he had no knowledge of the practicality of building a railroad through the region, but was impressed by the amount of timber that could be harvested.

Thus, by the end of 1880, the idea of extension to both the R. & A. and to Pittsburgh was very much in Davis's mind.

The new year, 1881, found Davis in a highly optimistic mood. He noted in his diary on January 1, that, "our coal and lumber trade is good." On January 3, he wrote to John Garrett and William

Keyser of the B. & O. explaining that he was going to extend to the C. & O. and was thinking of converting to standard gauge. He concluded by asking about freight rates so that he could begin to plan.

Davis also asked Porter for an estimate on converting the road to Elk Garden to standard gauge. Porter responded that it would cost $13,026.26 to build a mile of standard gauge line compared to $8,689.60 for narrow gauge. However, it was noted that a standard gauge engine at $10,000 could do the work of two narrow gauge engines at $14,000, and that the operating cost of the standard gauge line per day would therefore be lower.

Elkins had another meeting with Sickels on January 27, after Sickels had met with Parsons to discuss the proposed route. It was agreed that this was not the time of year to go prospecting and even in summer, travel would be difficult in the area between Stony River and the Cheat River because of thick laurel growth. Elkins mentioned that the Washington and Ohio Railroad had surveyed the area around what is now Elkins, and the R. & A. had surveyed from that point over to the Greenbrier. Elkins suggested that if Davis could use his influence to obtain copies of these surveys, it would speed up matters.

Two weeks later, Elkins became aware of plans for a railroad to be built down the Monongahela River. He wrote to the president of the Alleghany Valley Railroad to see if he knew anything about the new road. He was informed that the new road was the Pittsburgh, Virginia and Charleston Railroad, which was controlled by the Pennsylvania. It was recommended that Elkins consider a connection with the Pittsburg Southern, which was shortly to be extended to Waynesburg, for a route to Pittsburgh although an independent route would be better.

The amended charter for the new railroad was received by Davis early in the new year from Whyte. Davis then submitted it to Robert White, the attorney general for West Virginia. White had reservations about the constitutionality of the charter, and also whether the legislature would agree to the generous provisions which had been in the original charter, as there was growing anti-railroad sentiment in both houses. To gather support for the bill Davis wrote to a number of members of both houses, and the act to amend the charter was passed on February 23, 1881, essentially in the form wanted by Davis. The act also included the provision for the new railroad to extend to Pennsylvania although that had not been part of Davis's original proposal. The name for the new company was the West Virginia Central and Pittsburg Railway. Although the report of the proceedings spelled Pittsburgh with an "h", the new company never used this spelling in any of its correspondence, documents etc., or on its passenger cars.

A day or two before the passage of the West Virginia Central bill through the West Virginia legislature, Davis wrote once more to Garrett and Keyser of the B. & O. Davis pointed out that it was imperative that they come to an agreement about rates, as a decision had to be made between narrow and standard gauge for the new line. He also mentioned that he had an agreement with the C. & O. Canal, and that the decision of the B. & O. would determine how much coal went by rail. On February 23, Davis received a letter from M. H. Smith, the general freight agent for the B. & O., stating that the company would accept Davis's suggestions in regard to rates.

Thus February 23, 1881 was to be an important day for Davis. The legislature had passed the charter for his new railroad, and he had a favorable agreement with the B. & O. for rates. Surprisingly, with all this attention focused on West Virginia, Davis spent time in early February in the Connellsville, Pennsylvania, coalfield with Porter. He noted in his diary that he was interested in purchasing between 600 and 800 acres in the field. He later noted that he had purchased 1150 acres at $233 per acre.

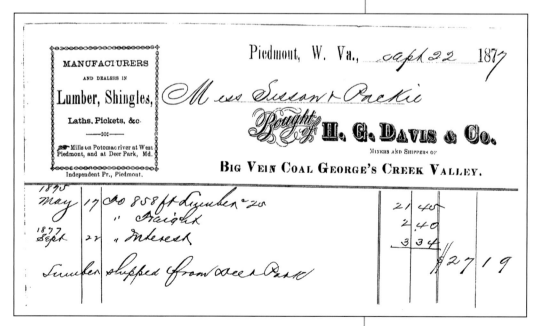

Fig. 6. H. G. Davis & Co. account, 1877
West Virginia and Regional History Collection,
West Virginia University Library

The West Virginia Central and Pittsburg Railway – the road to Elk Garden

With the approval by the B. & O. to offer the favorable freight rates sought by Davis, the decision to change the gauge of the railroad was soon made. One of the first steps taken, was to determine how the new road would pass under the B. & O.'s stone viaduct across the North Branch near Bloomington. James Randolph suggested on March 16, 1881, that an excavation could be made behind the bridge's east abutment, and after some modifications, the abutment would serve to support one end of a steel girder bridge. The embankment could then be dug out and a new abutment built on the east side to support the girders and to permit two West Virginia Central tracks to pass through. Randolph thought two tracks would be necessary to allow for better arrangements for the interchange of traffic at West Virginia Central Junction. The estimated cost of the work was $18,390.

The Patapsco Bridge and Iron Works, which had received the order for a bridge to be built near Bloomington, was notified on March 16 by Davis of the gauge change. Davis wanted the bridge redesigned to accommodate the heavier standard gauge trains. Although the bridge company had completed the preliminary drawings it was willing to go ahead with the changes in the hope that further business would come its way.

On April 6, Davis received a report from Porter on the expenditures during March and which showed the following:

For grading	$1,582.40
Removing slips	631.60
Cutting timber on right-of-way	291.35
Cutting crossties	95.95
An additional 1150 crossties	172.50
Material	305.43
	477.73
	3,079.23

Porter noted that 225 men were at work and making fair progress in spite of the stormy weather.

Davis received a report on April 11 from George H. Moffett, who had been sent by Davis to explore the iron ore fields along the proposed line of the road in the Greenbrier valley. Moffett also complained about the poor weather hampering his explorations. He reported first on the deposits east of the Allegheny Mountains and south of Traveler's Repose. He claimed that there were large deposits of ore near Warm Springs in Bath County, Virginia, and further south, large ore deposits in Alleghany County were being worked by the Low Moor company. On the west side of the mountains, "is an iron field in quality and quantity equal to any other in the United States." The field started at Green Bank and extended 40 or 50 miles to Anthony's Creek in Greenbrier County. One ore, brown hematite, was reported to occur in veins 12 to 50 feet thick.

Also about this time, Davis received the report from Sickels on the proposed extensions south to the R. & A. and north to Pittsburgh. The southern route would take a line up the North Branch, over to the Blackwater River and down this to the Cheat River. A branch of the Cheat would then be followed to its headwaters, and then across the summits to the boundary between West Virginia and Virginia. Sickels reported that three possible routes existed to Pittsburgh:

1. by the Tygart Valley River and the Monongahela River
2. as before but to Uniontown where two existing railroads connected with Pittsburgh
3. by the Youghiogheny River to Confluence and then to Pittsburgh

Sickels claimed it would cost $3,100,00 to build to the Virginia line, which would include equipment and housing. The traffic for the new line would be "bituminous coal and iron ore from the inexhaustible deposits on the line of the road, and of lumber from the primeval forest which extends its entire length." Mention was also made of the interest of the Pittsburgh iron makers in the ore deposits in West Virginia. Sickels thought the new road in its first year would haul 800,000 tons of coal an average of 20 miles, and 150,000 tons of iron ore an average of 75 miles. In addition, lumber, mail and passenger revenues would put the total expected earnings at $1,106,850. If the operating expenses were put at 60 percent, this left $442,700 for the payment of interest and dividends.

Back on the road steady progress was being made. Porter asked Davis on April 18, to order the wheels for the wheelhouse on the plane at Elk Garden. He expected these would take time to obtain and did not wish the work to be delayed. On April 25, Porter recommended that laborers be paid $1.25 per day so that the company could attract a better quality of worker. Men currently looking for work according to Porter, were "not worth a dollar a dozen." Davis's response is not known, but he was not noted for being generous to his employees. By July, Davis was prepared to pay $1.25 for an 11-hour day for good men.

On April 18, Davis wrote to the Baldwin Locomotive Works in Philadelphia and the Grant Locomotive Works in Paterson, New Jersey, asking for the price on a locomotive for June delivery. He also needed a 3.1/2 foot gauge locomotive for use on the track between the mines and the plane. These letters were followed by a similar letter to Porter of Pittsburgh. Grant could not deliver before February 1882, and Baldwin required at least a year, but did refer Davis to E. H. Wilson and Company of Philadelphia, dealers in second hand standard gauge locomotives. Davis also contacted the Danforth Locomotive and Machine Company of Paterson, New Jersey, which was able to deliver a 4-4-0 locomotive in September if the order was placed immediately.

E. H. Wilson informed Davis that they had an 1869 4-4-0 built by the Rogers Locomotive Works on sale for $4,200. The engine had just been overhauled and received new flues. Davis replied that he would take it for $4,000 cash on the B. & O. tracks at Baltimore ready to run. Wilson refused to take a lower price and, possibly because of the time spent bargaining, the locomotive that was finally delivered to Davis in June was not the engine originally described by Wilson. The engine was an ex-Philadelphia and Reading Railroad 4-4-0 No. 367. This engine had originally been built by the New Jersey Locomotive and Machine Works in 1856 and ran on the Catawissa Railroad as their No. 14 (Fig. 7), before becoming part of the Reading. The locomotive was delivered to the B. & O. in Baltimore in June, but required some minor repairs before being sent forward to Piedmont. The B. & O. billed Davis for $13.37 for this repair and the cost of a mechanic to ride on the engine to Piedmont. The final cost of the engine to Davis was $4251.37.

Fig. 7. Catawissa Railroad No. 14
Collection of Robert W. Brendel

Davis returned to Danforth's proposal on June 9 and asked for specifications and cost for a freight locomotive. Danforth proposed a 2-8-0 consolidation type, weight 96,400 pounds and with 20"x24" cylinders. Danforth claimed the engine could haul 700 net tons on 52-foot grade and 260 net tons on a 150 foot grade. The price was $14,000 and a December delivery could be expected. Danforth later guaranteed a February delivery if the order was placed immediately. An order was placed by Davis on June 30. He later specified that the engine should have one pump and one injector, and bolted on tires as used by the B. & O. The engine was to be given the number "2" and could be delivered any time after November 1.

At about the same time, the first combined passenger, baggage and mail car for the railroad was being built at the Mt. Savage shops of the Cumberland and Pennsylvania Railroad. Davis was asked in June whether he wanted a stove and candle lights in the car, but his response is not recorded, and no other information on this car is available.

In June, considerable thought was given to the financial and organizational structure of the railroad. At a meeting on June 18, the capital of the company was increased from $3,500,000 to $6,000,000. A second meeting was held in Baltimore on June 25 at which Davis gave a report on the progress to that time. Davis reported that nine miles were ready for ties and rails, and that 1,200 tons of 56 pound rail at $65 per ton had been received. One engine and several freight cars were ready for use. He also mentioned the favorable reports that had been received from iron and coal experts from along the line of the road to the Greenbrier, and gave every indication that this was where the road was headed. It was mentioned that Augustus Schell, a New York financier, and William Pinckney Whyte would act as trustees should it be decided to issue bonds to finance construction. At the meeting, Davis was elected president of the company and Elkins vice president. The board of directors consisted of Elkins, Schell, Camden, Alexander Shaw, Sickels, Thomas B. Davis, William Keyser of the B. & O., James G. Blaine and W. H. Barnum who were both senate colleagues of Davis, and John A. Hambleton, a Baltimore banker.

Meanwhile, back on the railroad, Porter reported on July 2 that track was laid as far as the B. & O.'s Bloomington bridge and ties had been distributed beyond the bridge. The work on the west abutment was expected to be completed that day, which would then allow work to commence on the opposite side. The new engine was also reported to be doing well. It left Piedmont every morning at 6.00 A.M. carrying construction workers and returned at 6.00 P.M. The engineer on No. 1 at this time was Ream Keller. Porter summarized his report by noting that he was "encouraged by the progress of the work."

Davis asked the C. & P. to build eight or ten hoppers of 30,000 pound capacity. The price was to be cost plus ten percent. He also asked for an inexpensive car, half passenger and half baggage, to be used during the construction of the road.

Davis and Elkins took a three day trip to the area around Fairfax Stone and the Blackwater River starting on July 5. They examined several coal seams including one near Dobbin House that was eight feet thick. They spent one night at Dobbin House which Davis noted was now disused. A second trip was made by Davis, Elkins and Camden accompanied by two other senators, Bayard of Delaware and Johnson of Virginia. The party traversed the whole route to White Sulphur Springs taking ten days. Sickels and Parsons also went over the entire road leaving on July 12 and expecting to take eight days. Davis ordered George Moffet to meet them along the way and to examine the iron ore fields. He was ordered to purchase up to 50,000 acres of the best of the field at about $1.00 per acre.

The participants must have been impressed by their visit, as at a Board of Directors meeting held on August 4, a decision was made to extend the road to meet either the C. & O. or the R. & A. It also was agreed to borrow $3,600,000 as a first mortgage on the

Fig. 8. A $1000 First Mortgage Bond of the West Virginia Central and Pittsburg Railway

road. To do this, $3,600,000 of bonds were to be issued (Fig. 8) and used at a rate of $5,000 per mile to finance construction of the road. The first issue, of $1,000,000, was handled by John A. Hambleton and Company of Baltimore. To facilitate the sale of the bonds, a prospectus had been prepared by Elkins which detailed the work that had been done to Elk Garden and the expected cost to build to the Virginia state line, some $3,072,750. The resources of coal, iron ore and timber along the proposed route were considered, and favorable reports from Riordan, Parsons and others were given. Even comments from Governor Matthews of West Virginia in support of the Pittsburg Southern were used, as they pertained to Tucker, Randolph, Pocahontas and Greenbrier counties. The prospectus did include a map (Fig. 9), which showed the line extending beyond the Fairfax Stone.

Favorable reports continued to come in from Riordan and Moffett on the coal and iron ore resources. Parsons reported on the progress of surveying parties working on the upper reaches of the North Branch, and also the efforts being made to find a route down the Blackwater or across to Red

Fig. 9. Map of the North Branch of the Potomac and the West Virginia Central and Pittsburg Railway
West Virginia and Regional History Collection, West Virginia University Library

Creek and then down to the Cheat River.

It was announced on August 1, that Captain John Sheridan would be general superintendent of the mines, and that Benjamin Thomas was at work making the openings at Elk Garden. Sheridan had previously been superintendent at the Atlantic and Georges Creek Coal Company and Thomas came from the Shaw Brothers mine at Meyersdale in Pennsylvania. The tramroad was being graded from the mine to the plane, and H. K. Porter of Pittsburgh, were at work on the engine for use on the tramroad. A sawmill was in use at the site cutting lumber for houses and a barn for 30 horses.

Four hundred men were reported to be at work on August 8, at which time it was reported that track was laid along half of the route to Deep Run. It was expected that coal would start moving from Elk Garden by the middle of October. By August 19, the track was within one mile of Deep Run, and the ironwork for the new bridge at Bloomington had arrived in Piedmont. The new bridge, and the B. & O.'s viaduct, as they appeared in 1957, are shown in Fig. 10.

On August 10, it was noted that contracts for the construction of the next 20 miles would be let soon, and on August 15, an announcement was made requesting bids for grading and masonry to be delivered to the company's office by September 10, 1881. The work was to be finished by June 1, 1882.

By August 2, Davis was asking Danforth when Engine No. 2 would be delivered, and he also directed a similar question to H. K. Porter relative to the narrow gauge engine. He claimed that he would be ready to ship coal in September and the lack of this engine would cause a delay. Davis again, on August 18, asked Danforth if the engine could be delivered by October, and also asked for a bid on another locomotive for April 1882 delivery. When the price quoted was $1,500 more than for No. 2, he thought there must be some mistake. Davis was finally assured that Engine No. 2 would be delivered in time for the formal opening of the road.

Davis also contacted Charles F. Mayer, president of the C. & P., to see if the Mt. Savage shops could build an engine. He later decided against the purchase of another "light engine" and asked Mayer, on September 12, to bid on an engine "to be as good as the combination engine built by Baldwin, Danforth or Pittsburgh." To be on the safe side, he also asked Pittsburgh to bid on a locomotive

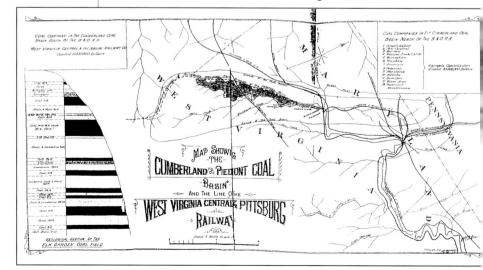

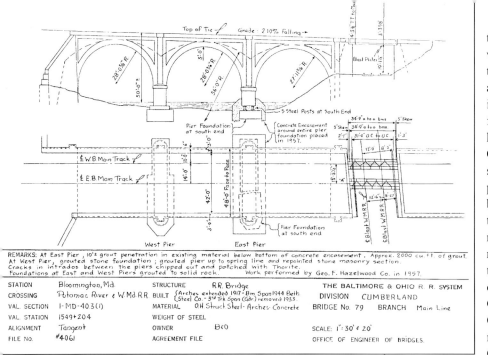

STATION	Bloomington, Md.	STRUCTURE	R.R. Bridge	THE BALTIMORE & OHIO R.R. SYSTEM
CROSSING	Potomac River & W.Md.R.R.	BUILT	{Arches extended 1917-Bm.Span 1944 Beth. {Steel Co.-3rd Trk Span (Gdr) removed 1933.	DIVISION CUMBERLAND
VAL. SECTION	1-MD-403(1)	MATERIAL	O.H.Struct Steel-Arches-Concrete	BRIDGE No. 79 BRANCH Main Line
VAL. STATION	1549+204	WEIGHT OF STEEL		
ALIGNMENT	Tangent	OWNER	B&O	SCALE: 1":30' & 20'
FILE NO.	#4061	AGREEMENT FILE		OFFICE OF ENGINEER OF BRIDGES.

REMARKS: At East Pier, 10' grout penetration in existing material below bottom of concrete encasement. Approx. 2000 cu. ft. of grout. At West Pier, grouted stone foundation; grouted pier up to spring line and repointed stone masonry section. Cracks in intrados between the piers chipped out and patched with Thorite. Foundations at East and West Piers grouted to solid rock.   Work performed by Geo. F. Hazelwood Co. in 1957.

Fig. 10. B. & O. viaduct and the West Virginia Central bridge, circa 1957

for delivery next August, and contacted E. H. Wilson and Company to see if it had anything.

At the end of August, Riordan was looking at coal seams in the vicinity of Dobbin House but was finding only small seams. This seems to have convinced Davis not to purchase land in the area, as on September 5 he wrote to Robert A. Dobbin withdrawing his offer to purchase the Dobbin Manor tract.

On the same day he wrote to Alexander Shaw noting that the track would be laid to the foot of the plane in a day or two and that the grading of the plane would be finished at the same time. Earlier Davis had visited Elk Garden and on his return had written to Shaw asking him to hurry the delivery of fastenings and spikes.

At about this time, Davis became aware that the Manassas Gap Railroad in northern Virginia might be for sale. The railroad had been chartered in 1850 to run from Manassas to Harrisonburg. Work had started in 1851 and by 1854, the line had reached Strasburg and four years later, it terminated at Harrisonburg (Fig. 2). The Manassas Gap Railroad, like a number of its peers, had visions of crossing the mountains to the coalfields of Hampshire County, but the Civil War put an end to these dreams. After the Civil War, the railroad became part of the Orange and Alexandria Railroad, which finally emerged as the Virginia Midland in February 1881.

Davis asked Porter to submit a report on the Manassas Gap Railroad, detailing the potential for profit and the expense required to connect the line to the coalfields. Parsons was also instructed to survey a line from Strasburg to the coalfields.

Perhaps because of his new interest in an east-west line, on September 21 Davis again wrote to Dobbin expressing an interest in purchasing land north and east of the Blackwater River and Glade Run, "upon which your father built the house."

However, it was to be the southern extension that was to be Davis's first priority. On September 17, he complained to Porter

that the expenses were too high and to cut the workforce to 100 men. He also complained about the number of picks and wheelbarrows lying around the work and asked Porter to prepare an inventory. Davis also wrote to Robert Garrett, first vice president of the B. & O., saying that he hoped to start shipping freight and passengers on October 1, and suggesting that the two companies should share the cost of constructing a depot and platform at the junction. The junction was later to be named West Virginia Central Junction. One of the winning contractors, John Humbird, was reported to be ready to start on the first seven miles from Deep Run on September 24. As a sign that the promised advantages of civilization were on their way, Davis asked the Assistant Postmaster General to establish post offices at West Virginia Central Junction, Elk Garden and Deep Run. The name of the latter place was changed to Shaw on October 14.

The first timetable for the new road was included in Davis's letter books, dated October 1, 1881. Trains were scheduled to leave Sand House at the end of the line at 8:00 A.M. and 2:30 P.M. Return trains from West Virginia Central Junction were scheduled for 9:00 A.M. and 3:30 P.M. Fares from the Junction were 10 cents to Pine Swamp, 15 cents to Warnocks, 25 cents to Deep Run and 30 cents to Sand House. No charge was to be made of less than ten cents; other charges were to be in the same proportion as those above. Freight rates were as follows;

All packages weighing less than 50 lb. to any station . . . .15 cents

All packages weighing between 50 and 100 lb. to any station . . .
. . . . .20 cents

All packages weighing between 100 and 300 lb. to any station . .
. . . . .25 cents

All freight weighing over 300 lb. and less than a carload, ...
. . . . .one cent per 100 lb. per mile.

Full car load to Deep Run and Sand House $5.00

Porter reported on October 5 that 112 miles of new construction would be required to connect Strasburg with the coalfields to give a total distance from Alexandria of 200 miles. This was 14 miles less than the distance from Cumberland to Baltimore. He estimated the cost to put the road in order and to buy necessary equipment at $250,000. To this had to be added a rental of $25,000 for the first year. The gross earnings were put at $124,000, which, after deducting operating expenses and interest payments, would leave a profit of $8,880. However, if the road were connected to the coalfields near Fairfax Stone, the expected profit for the first year would be $65,000.

Parsons, in his report dated October 10, proposed a line starting at Stony River and following Surry Creek to Petersburg. The South Branch of the Potomac would then be followed to Moorefield; South Branch Mountain would be crossed by Bakers Run and Lost River to Cacapon and Wardensville. The last stage was to follow Cedar Creek to Strasburg. The W. & O. had surveyed an alternate route from Cacapon to Winchester. Parsons estimated that if a maximum grade of 80 feet to the mile were used, the road could be built for $1,224,000, but if a couple of sections of a 100 foot grade were used, approximately $100,000 could be saved. Parsons submitted a rough map to Davis on October 31 showing the proposed route (Fig. 11).

Davis ordered additional hoppers from the C. & P. on October 12, and a few days later he expressed an interest in a locomotive to be built by the C. & P. for $13,500. The first combination car, built by the C. & P. for the West Virginia Central, was delivered on October 14 and was reported to be "very handsome."

At about the same time he wrote to Dobbin saying that he had been unsuccessful in purchasing the Dobbin Manor lands, although he later ordered James E. Moore to purchase land between the Fairfax Stone and the Blackwater for no more than $1.50 per acre. A few days earlier he had instructed Fred J. Knight to examine the country between Moorefield and the Valley of Virginia and report on the iron ore deposits.

The road was opened for traffic on October 19, and the first coal was shipped from Elk Garden on October 20. Davis noted in his diary that both the mine and the mill were doing well. He also noted "we pay 50 cents for digging coal." The road was formally opened on November 2, when Davis and a large party of dignitaries left Cumberland at 8.00 A.M. and traveled over the C. & P. to Piedmont and then to West Virginia Central Junction. Here the party transferred to a West Virginia Central train to Elk Garden. The party included Elkins, Bayard, Alexander Shaw, Hambleton, Governor William Hamilton of Maryland and Richard C. Kerens. Kerens had been involved with Elkins during his time in New Mexico and was currently involved in railroads, banking and politics in St. Louis. Not included in the party was Arthur Pue Gorman, who was Davis's cousin, and senator from Maryland. Although Gorman had been an early investor in the West Virginia Central, he thought it necessary to return his stock when he was reelected president of the C. & O. Canal for a term that expired in June 1882. Davis had secured a large reduction in rates from the canal company, and Gorman did not want to "find myself in a position which would give evil-disposed persons an opportunity to criticize my course and to possibly jeopardize the interest of both your company and the canal." In spite of the favorable agreement mentioned by Gorman, all of the coal shipped during the first week from Elk Garden, left Cumberland via the B. & O.

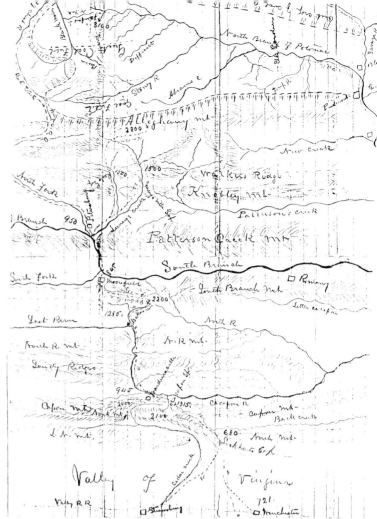

Fig. 11. Map by James Parsons showing the possible route to Strasburg, Virginia. October 31, 1881
West Virginia and Regional History Collection,
West Virginia University Library

North Branch and the Blackwater. He noted that the "coal and timber is even beyond expectation."

Knight reported to Davis on October 23 on the results of his explorations. He mentioned that two furnaces had been in operation in the area, one known as the Capon Iron Works was some five miles north of Wardensville, the second was the Crack Whip Furnace which had not been used for some 40 years. Both furnaces produced between 25 and 30 tons of iron per week from deposits that had long been covered over. However it was believed that beds of hematite of between 12 and 15 feet thick existed.

Davis received more encouraging news from Riordan on October 29, when he reported that he had found a vein of excellent coal some three feet thick near the Blackwater Falls, along the Kent Road. Riordan attached a rough map to his letter which showed the position of the vein relative to the Falls and to Dobbin House (Fig. 12).

Encouraged by all this good news, Davis gave some thought to

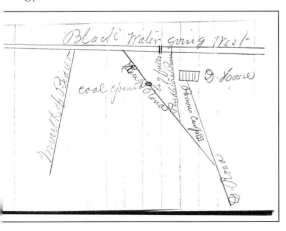

Davis accompanied by some of his guests from the previous day, took a trip to the area between the

Fig. 12. Riordan's map of the Blackwater Falls area
West Virginia and Regional History Collection,
West Virginia University Library

building a railroad from the coal fields of the Blackwater to either Winchester or Strasburg and to lease the Manassas Gap Railroad. The new railroad was to be called the "Coal and Iron Railway" and Davis estimated the cost at $4,100,000. The capital stock was to be $6,000,000 of which Davis, Elkins, Blaine and Schell would take $4,500,000. "Friends of the W. V. C. & P. would receive $750,000," according to Davis's notes.

Davis also decided to order an engine from the C. & P. and the order was placed on November 16 for $13,500. On the same day, Davis received a bill from the C. & P. for three gondolas ($1,938.06) and three hoppers ($1,569.48). Davis thought the bill excessive and was not too pleased a few weeks later to hear that the cars were found to have a problem with overheating axle boxes and would not "hold tallow."

Towards the end of November, Davis was urging Porter to hurry along the engine house and wye at Shaw, and also stressing to the B. & O. the necessity for a depot at the Junction. He also instructed Parsons to consider the Maryland side of the North Branch for the extension to the summit. Parsons had earlier in the month led a party to survey a line up Laurel Fork to a meeting with the Greenbrier.

Davis had come to an understanding with John S. Barbour, president of the Virginia Midland Railway concerning surveys carried out by H. D. Garden of the Virginia Midland. Garden surveyed a route from Strasburg to Moorefield a distance of 63 miles, and costing an average of $28,000 per mile to build. The difficulty would be in crossing South Branch Mountain where the cost per mile would be $40,500. Barbour thought the results were more promising than expected given the rough topography of the country. Davis had agreed to pay the cost of the survey corps, and this amounted to $1,097.90. Garden later did a horseback survey of a different route between Strasburg and Moorefield, but the route was 42 miles longer although the grades were easier. The new route was claimed to run through vast fields of iron ore that had a metallic content between 40 and 45 percent. Some small furnaces in the area were already using this ore and selling the finished iron in Pittsburgh at $36-38 per ton. Garden summed up his surveys by concluding the first route was preferable.

At the end of December, Garden, now surveying for the R. & A., was in the region of the headwaters of the Elk and Gauley rivers looking for a possible route to Charleston. He also mentioned a meeting in Charleston with Major Campbell of the Baltimore, Cincinnati and Western Railroad, which was planning to build up the Elk from Charleston. Garden hoped to get some information on that company's plans.

On December 22, Davis wrote to Barbour and told him he was not interested in leasing or purchasing the Manassas Gap Railroad. He was still interested in the Washington and Ohio Railroad and received a copy of a valuation report made by its past president, Lewis McKenzie, putting the value of the road at $725,000. The road was sold a month later to the Baltimore, Cincinnati and Western for $592,000, but Davis did not make a bid.

One final note of the year was a letter from Davis to Porter on December 26, telling him to use sheathing from the mill at Piedmont for the engine house at the Junction in an effort to save money for a possible expansion to Piedmont in 1882.

Thus by the end of the year, the groundwork for the future of the West Virginia Central was laid. The extension to the head of the North Branch was under construction, and explorations to all points of the compass had convinced Davis that a profitable expansion could be made.

Fig. 13. The B. & O. viaduct at Bloomington, circa 1911. The West Virginia Central bridge is hidden by trees at the right

Davis – the Altoona of West Virginia

A report was issued in January that outlined the progress that had been made by the new road up until January 1, 1882. In addition to the two locomotives, the report indicated that the company possessed five gondolas, two flat cars, ten iron hoppers and five other cars as well as one combined passenger and baggage car. The total cost of the rolling stock was put at $27,264.61. The mining department was shown to have the one narrow gauge engine delivered by Porter in October, and four narrow gauge cars running on nearly 1.1/3 miles of track. Since the first shipment of coal had been made on October 20, 1881, 11,372 tons of coal had been shipped up until December 31. Seventy miners were employed, and two double tenement houses and one single house had been erected in addition to blacksmith and carpenter shops and a stable. For the extension south, it was reported that 4.1/2 miles of track had been graded at an expenditure of $17,308.30. The 16 miles from the end of the first extension to the summit were still being located but it was expected that contracts for this work would be let in the spring for completion in the fall of 1883. The total cost of the extension from Shaw to the summit was estimated at $892,750. Porter, when submitting his section of the report, included the inventory that he had been asked to prepare in September, and which listed every item that was in use, including even those items that were broken, e.g. 56 broken picks and 28 broken shovels. He also listed the buildings that had been completed as being water tanks at Shaw and West Virginia Central Junction, a four stall engine house and machine shop at the Junction, one passenger and freight house at Shaw, one carpenter shop and three boarding houses.

Riordan also submitted a report to Davis of his explorations from June 1, 1881 to the present. Riordan mentioned that in the Fairfax Stone-Dobbin House area he had opened two veins of coal, one being 11 feet thick and the second four feet thick, all the veins together giving some 52 feet of coal. According to Riordan, "this is the most remarkable coal region so far discovered in this or any country, ... the whole is free of slate, bone coal or any impurities whatsoever." A second area explored lay between Dobbin House and Buffalo Creek and here veins of between three and six feet

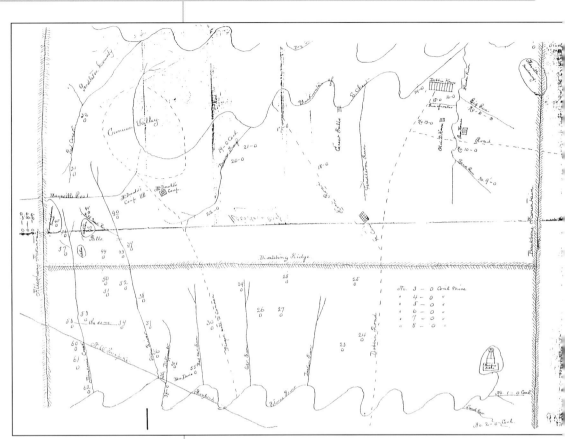

Fig. 14. Riordan's map of the Upper Potomac coal region
West Virginia and Regional History Collection,
West Virginia University Library

were found. A third area was around Stoney River and here Riordan found 15 coal seams ranging from a few inches to nine feet although some slate was found. Again Riordan attached a rough map to his report, which showed the openings he had made and the general topography of the region (Fig. 14).

Davis also received a further report from Garden on the planned extension of the R. & A. through West Virginia. Garden examined a route from Jackson River in Virginia over to the Greenbrier in West Virginia. From the Greenbrier, two possible routes existed following either the Elk or Gauley rivers to Charleston. The estimate of the Elk River route to Charleston was $5,926,000 for 263 miles, and for the Gauley route of 219 miles, the figure was $5,424,000. Garden mentioned that there were large quantities of iron ore and coal along the route as well as vast amounts of timber. What the directors of the R. & A. thought of the report is not known, but it did provide additional encouragement to Davis.

On January 10, Davis wrote to a number of car companies asking for bids on two passenger cars and on 40,000 pound gondolas. This was followed by a letter to Danforth, asking for a price and delivery time on an engine similar to No. 2. Danforth replied that such an engine would cost $15,000 for August delivery. Davis made a counteroffer of $14,500, saying that he liked the Danforth locomotives and hoped to buy more in the future. Danforth however was not interested, and Davis eventually agreed to pay $15,000 for October delivery. He may have wished to revise his ideas of Danforth's engines when it was reported that Engine No. 2 had blown off a cylinder head on January 21. Davis wrote to the C. & P. on January 25, to see if the delivery of the engine it was building could be hurried up. He was told that a delay had occurred because the Baldwin Locomotive Works, which was casting the cylinders and had promised a January 1 delivery date, could not now meet that deadline, and thus C. & P. could not promise an early delivery. Davis also was told that C. & P. was fully booked and could not take an order for another locomotive for delivery before 1883.

Parsons submitted an amended report on the line from the head of the North Branch to Winchester on January 18, as he now thought a tunnel would be necessary. He also changed the route slightly to go through Greenland Gap and then used a tunnel to get through Patterson Creek Mountain. Two alternative routes were considered using Mays Gap or Kline Gap and then to Petersburg. Parsons put the cost of the Greenland Gap route at $1,180,000 to which had to be added $383,000 to connect with the Washington and Ohio Railroad at Round Hill. The figures using the Mays Gap or Kline Gap routes were slightly higher. Parsons concluded by mentioning the large amounts of iron ore that existed along the line of the road.

Davis had other individuals survey the route and examine the Upper Potomac coalfield, including A. G. Warfield, Jr., and Raphael Pumpelly, a noted geologist. Warfield submitted a report on February 26 covering the territory between the terminus of the W. & O. to Stony River via Wardensville and Petersburg. He reported that only one tunnel would be required at Bean's Gap on the South Branch Mountain. He estimated a maximum westbound gradient of 80 feet to the mile and an average cost per mile of $25,000 for the 110 miles. Pumpelly examined the Upper Potomac region in January, but did not report in detail until March 23. He took coal samples from some of the openings made by Riordan and prepared coke from them in a laboratory. He was able to obtain an excellent coke from a seam between four and eight feet thick lying between Dobbin House and the Fairfax Stone, and also from a four-foot seam lying beneath the first. The coal gave a yield of a low sulfur coke of 71 to 74 percent. He concluded his report by estimating the Upper Potomac coalfield at approximately 250 square miles. Davis was highly pleased with the results of Pumpelly's work and a summary was reproduced in most of the Annual Reports of the West Virginia Central for the next 20 years.

Encouraged by these reports, Davis decided in late January to incorporate a railroad in Virginia to connect with his extensions in West Virginia. At Davis's request, the Virginia legislature passed an act on February 21, 1882, incorporating the Virginia and West Virginia Railroad Company, with Davis, Elkins, Schell and others listed as the incorporators. Also listed was John B. Davis, who was the elder brother of Henry and who was not usually involved in his sibling's business interests. John had become involved in business

and banking in Richmond, Virginia, and this is possibly the reason he was called on by his brother. The new company was empowered to build a railroad through the counties of Frederick and Shenandoah from the Virginia state line to Alexandria or some other point on the Potomac River. The railroad could connect with the Manassas Gap Railroad, but if it did not, it would go through Winchester.

Davis also wanted to amend the charter of the West Virginia Central to allow him to build through the counties of Grant, Hardy and Hampshire to the Virginia line, and he again wrote to legislators to seek support. He also asked that permission to build to the Ohio or Kanawha rivers be included in the amendment. The amendment passed the Senate on February 13, but it was not signed into law by the governor. Davis then started to think of creating a new railroad to be called the Coal and Iron Railway.

Although he had ordered a new engine from Danforth at the end of February, Davis decided to send his newly appointed master of machinery, F. W. Lippencott, to look at some engines that E. H. Wilson had for sale, but he did not buy any. He did receive a bid from the Jackson and Sharp Company to supply a passenger car for $3,600. Davis offered Jackson and Sharp $3,500 for the car for April delivery. Jackson and Sharp reluctantly accepted the offer on March 11. Davis later told them he needed the car to be delivered no later than April 20, and that it should be painted a "medium green." The car was eventually delivered on May 20. The numbering of the first two cars is a little uncertain. The combination car received earlier eventually became No. 2; the first passenger car becoming No. 1.

Early in March, the coal companies in the Georges Creek region announced that on March 15 the price of mining coal would be reduced from 65 cents per ton to 50 cents with similar reductions in other wages. This precipitated a strike that was to last five months. Davis did not expect any trouble at the Elk Garden mines, and he wrote to Sickels that they were now mining 650 tons per day and expected this to increase to 750 tons by April. Elkins and Shaw both thought that a second opening and inclined plane should be built at Elk Garden to increase production. Davis was not so sure and only agreed to the proposal provided Shaw would sell the increased output, estimated at about 1,200 tons per day.

At the end of March, Davis asked for bids on the next 20 miles of road of which six would be along the Maryland side of the North Branch. The bidding was not public, but rather letters were sent to reputable contractors asking them for bids with a closing date of April 15. The work was due to be completed by September 1, 1883. To cross the river, he also asked for bids on a bridge of two spans, each of 100 feet.

Construction on the first 20 miles south of Shaw was proceeding well in early April except for one contractor, Andrew Gleeson, who only had 49 men at work. It was estimated that 300 men would be required to finish the work on time. A day or two later there were 150 men at work, and Davis was assured that there would be no delay. Convinced that all was proceeding according to plan, Davis asked for bids on 2,000 tons of 56 pound rail.

During April, Parsons was still struggling through dense laurel thickets to locate the next section of the extension. He reported on

April 16 that he was within a mile of Elkins, which was the name chosen for the point where the Northwest Turnpike crossed the North Branch. Parsons reported that the alignment was good with no heavy grades. He hoped to be able to finish by the beginning of May and move his team over to Canaan and start work there. This must have been good news to Davis who had recently purchased 12,000 acres of land in the region belonging to the late Chief Justice Marshall, for five dollars an acre. He offered to divide the land among his senate colleagues and also Shaw and Camden.

He later wrote to Elkins saying he was going to deed 20,000 acres of land in the Upper Potomac area, to the C. & I. On April 13, he traveled along the proposed route of the C. & I. from Winchester to Petersburg accompanied by Windom and Sickels. He reported that the route was "as favorable as expected." A few days after his return from the trip, Sickels was reported to be sick. Davis had earlier complained to Elkins that Sickels was not spending enough time on the affairs of the company so Sickels sent his brother, Jackson, to serve in his place. Davis accepted this change with little comment.

Davis divided the work on the extension into two residencies, each supervised by a resident engineer who was to report to George W. Smith, the division engineer. Davis hired a new engineer, D. F. Adams, to be responsible for the second division, which extended to the summit, but when Adams later declined, Davis then gave Parsons responsibility for this section.

News of another railroad interested Davis in the middle of April. On April 10, the incorporators of the Grafton and Greenbrier Railroad met in Philippi to organize the company and open subscription books. The G. & G. had been slow to organize after its original charter had been issued and a new act of the West Virginia legislature was passed in March 1882 granting the company an extension until August to complete its organization. At the meeting, John W. Mason was elected president, although in May he was replaced by Samuel Woods. The meeting attracted the attention of Davis, who wrote to both Mason and Woods expressing an interest in building the line if sufficient funds could be raised from the counties and a free right-of-way obtained. Davis again wrote to Woods on May 4 indicating he would build the line if $100,000 could be raised. Davis would also raise the capital over and above the $100,000 necessary to complete and equip the line. The organizers of the G. & G. had estimated that $100,000 was all that would be required although Davis put the figure at $250,000. Davis's interest encouraged Woods and his colleagues to continue to raise money for the project and on June 20 the citizens of Grafton voted in favor of the scheme. The G. & G. decided to build their own road and by November, the line from Grafton to Philippi was under contract. This was, however, not to be Davis's last contact with the G. & G.

On May 3, Davis wrote to Danforth (now known as the Cooke

Fig. 15. West Virginia Central No. 3 on the Blackwater grade (undated)
Collection of the Western Maryland Railway Historical Society

Locomotive and Machine Company) asking them to cancel the order for the engine because of a poorer business outlook. He later reinstated the order but asked for a reduction in price, which Cooke reluctantly agreed to. The engine was delivered at the end of August. The locomotive ordered from C. & P. was delivered in early June and became West Virginia Central No. 3. (Fig. 15). The final cost of the locomotive was $13,547.37.

A few days later, on May 16, Davis wrote to Enos Anderson and asked him to build some coke ovens at Mineville for a trial of the coal. Davis was sufficiently enthusiastic about the potential for a coke business either at Elk Garden or at the Upper Potomac field, that he ordered four coke cars from the company of William Keyser, Keyser Brothers and Company of Baltimore. These were delivered at the end of May at a total cost of $500.

At the end of April, Parsons had completed a line to the summit, and by the middle of May had two groups of contractors clearing trees and brush from some six miles of the route. On the lower part, the contractors had 520 men at work. Davis wrote to Porter on May 27, telling him that 1,000 tons of rails were on the way, and that he should start track laying as soon as he received them. Parsons received orders from Davis on June 9 telling him to continue the line to the Blackwater, and to find a place for a junction with the road coming up from Winchester. The name chosen for the town to be built at this point was to be "Davis." The Railroad Gazette, on the same day, carried an announcement that contracts had been let to three contractors, Humbird, Codwise and Company, and to Adams and Kennedy, for the grading and masonry on the section to the summit.

Davis, accompanied by Elkins, Chaffee and Blaine paid a visit to Elk Garden on June 1, and Davis noted that they all were well pleased. Davis was further pleased when he was able to report to Hambleton that the net earnings for April had been $11,198.50, and for May the railroad had netted $864.69 and the mine $10,671.98 for a total of $11,536.67.

Parsons meanwhile, was having trouble locating a line to the proposed junction. He complained about the constant rain and also the numerous ridges running across the proposed route which made locating difficult. Parsons was looking for a route either from the summit or from the head of Stony River to the mouth of Beaver Creek. One member of Parsons's party, Frank G. Ruffin, Jr., was not pleased with the way the expedition was being conducted. He wrote to Davis complaining that Parsons was "totally incompetent," and the corps was a "mob of such unpleasant character … so objectionable, I have no desire to remain," and tendered his resignation. Ruffin also found Parsons's son, Frank A. Parsons, who was employed as a transitman, to be totally worthless, and that because of an error in the location of the line to Fairfax Stone, some $50 to $75,000 had been wasted. Davis was not impressed and Parsons continued his work.

By the middle of July, Parsons, although complaining about the exhausting nature of the work, had reached the pass that led into the Canaan Valley. From here he could send parties to both Stony River Mountain or to Cosners. On July 23, Parsons wrote to Davis that he hoped to finish in a couple of weeks and by the end of the month Parsons submitted a rough map of the routes surveyed (Fig. 16). He reported that two options existed: one for a junction in Canaan Valley, the second at the mouth of Beaver Creek.

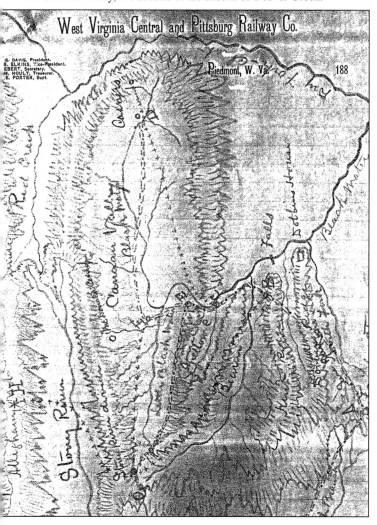

Fig. 16. Parsons's map of the Beaver Creek region (redrawn for clarity)
West Virginia and Regional History Collection,
West Virginia University Library

It was reported on July 14, that rumors of the Elk Garden miners joining the Georges Creek miners in their strike were without foundation. This proved unduly optimistic when the miners struck a few days later. Davis was not about to tolerate such an action, and discharged between 15 and 20 miners who were reported to be the leaders. By now production at Elk Garden had reached 1,000 tons daily. Production also had started from a mine at Windom owned by the Big Vein Coal Company, and by early August was reported to have reached 250 tons per day with some 40 miners being employed. The strike in the Georges Creek field finally ended on August 23, when the men returned on the coal companies' terms. The end of the strike caused problems for Elk Garden and Windom by mid-September when both mines were reported to be on half time.

At the end of July, George Smith resigned as division engineer and was replaced by A. G. Warfield.

Davis and Elkins made another trip of the road in September. On his return, Davis noted that, "We have walked or rode over the entire line."

A few days after this trip, the region was hit by a severe storm. Porter and Jackson Sickels wrote to Davis pointing out that Abram Creek had reached the level of the grade at the abutments for the new bridge, and that any attempt to reduce the opening would create problems in future floods. They both urged Davis to finalize plans for the bridge.

It was noted by the Cumberland Daily Times on September 25 that a new track had been completed to Piedmont from West Virginia Central Junction, giving the West Virginia Central direct access to Piedmont. The track, approximately three quarters of a mile in length, had been built jointly by the B. & O. and the West Virginia Central.

Piedmont had developed into an important town after the B. & O. reached there in 1851. West of Piedmont, the railroad climbed the formidable Seventeen Mile Grade to reach the summit of the Alleghenies, so the town was a logical site for the development of railroad shops and a roundhouse (Fig. 17). Two years later a railroad was built up Georges Creek to Lonaconing to serve the developing Georges Creek coalfield. This line later connected with the Cumberland and Pennsylvania Railroad and was later taken over by the C. & P.

Davis, during his first term in the West Virginia legislature, had been instrumental in passing legislation to create Mineral County from part of Hampshire County, and also securing a charter for the town of Piedmont. Although Davis maintained a voting address in Piedmont and built a house there, which still stands on Jones Street, he spent most of his time at Deer Park in Maryland.

Because of its important location on the B. & O. and its proximity to the Georges Creek coalfield, the town became an important commercial center (Fig. 18), with a population at the turn of the century of approximately 2,000.

By October 9, the track on the extension had been laid as far as Blaine, some 16 miles from Piedmont (Fig. 19). By the end of October, materials for the new inclined plane and opening had arrived at Mineville. Davis requested bids for up to 50 hoppers, similar to the current B. & O. design, of 15 ton capacity. This was

Fig. 17. The railroad yards at Piedmont (undated)

had paid $15 per acre for the land, and that it was well timbered and contained coal and was probably worth $100 per acre.

The year ended with Davis suggesting to Elkins that they build a line from Piedmont to Cumberland, and then to extend to Williamsport, the terminus of the Western Maryland Railroad. Newspaper reports at the same time suggested that a connection would be built through Cumberland to Bedford, Pennsylvania where Cornelius Vanderbilt was building the South Pennsylvania Railroad in competition with the Pennsylvania Railroad. None of these schemes came to anything immediately, but the idea of building to Cumberland was to emerge again later.

later changed to 18 tons and the number increased to 80 for April delivery. Davis went over the line again on November 14 and reported, "all moving well."

During the first two hectic years involved in building the railroad, opening mines and planning new extensions, Davis was still a U. S. senator, but his second term was due to finish in March 1883. On November 18, he sent a letter to the Wheeling Register indicating that he would not be a candidate for reelection. According to Davis, "business is more agreeable to me than politics," although he noted in his diary that, "I have no doubt of my election if I had

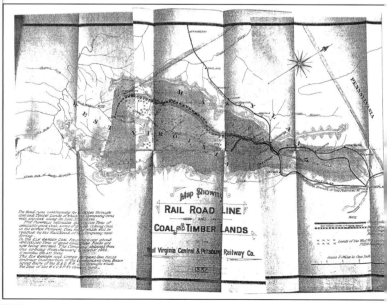

Fig. 18. Main Street, Piedmont (undated)

On January 9, 1883, the First Annual Report of the West Virginia Central and Pittsburg Railway was published. This showed that the railroad and mine together had made a profit of $87,441.84 and that 228,244 tons of coal had been mined. The report also noted that the working expenses were 48.3/4 percent of gross earnings, a figure with which Davis was very proud but hoped to reduce even further. It was also noted that 16 double and two single houses had been built at Elk Garden during the year, "all of which are now occupied by a very desirable class of residents." Work on opening No. 2 and the second inclined plane had been suspended until spring.

Davis also noted later in the year that the equipment owned by the West Virginia Central on January 1, 1883 consisted of four locomotives, one passenger car, one passenger/combination

been a candidate." It is likely that Davis would have had a hard battle to gain the nomination, and it has been suggested that Davis, by withdrawing, hoped to be drafted. Whatever his motives, Davis was not to run for elective office until 1904, although he remained active in the Democratic Party at both the state and national levels. His name occasionally surfaced as a candidate for governor, although Davis was not interested.

On December 16 it was reported that the work on the extension had been closed down for the winter. By this time, track laying had reached Abram Creek, nine miles beyond Shaw, and the 80 foot iron truss across the creek was in place. The distance to the summit from Abram Creek was 27 miles of which 20 miles were graded and ready for the tracks. The cost of the extension was estimated at $755,300 of which $455,402 had already been expended.

Davis notified Elkins on December 25, that he had purchased 845 acres in the vicinity of the mouth of Beaver Creek and that it, "is the only place to fix our town of Davis." Davis reported that he

Fig. 19. Map of the West Virginia Central and Pittsburg Railway, 1882
West Virginia and Regional History Collection,
West Virginia University Library

car, eight gondolas and 20 iron hoppers.

The first order of business in the new year, 1883, was to replace Sheridan, who had resigned as mine superintendent at Elk Garden. The new superintendent was N. W. Musgrove of Fairmont. Davis informed Porter that active work on the new plane and opening would resume in the middle of February, and it was expected to be ready by the middle of April. Davis was upset to hear that the West Virginia legislature was considering regulation of mine owners, "in the way of inspection, ventilation etc." He wrote to C. Wood Daily and George E. Price, a legislator, asking them to oppose the legislation, as such matter should be left to the managers and employees.

Davis asked Elkins to order 80 iron hoppers for $450 each from the Carlisle Manufacturing Company on January 15. This was followed in March by an order to the same company for a combination passenger and baggage car for delivery May 1 and costing $1,500.

Porter, who had received bids for the bridge across the North Branch from both Bollman and the Keystone Bridge Company, was instructed by Davis to offer Bollman $4,000 for the bridge. Bollman accepted this figure and received the contract. Porter was also instructed in February to reduce the hours worked by laborers from 11 to ten per day. However their daily rate of $1.15 was not reduced.

The drivers at the Elk Garden mine were not so lucky in March when they struck for higher pay. All the strikers were discharged and their places taken by new men.

Davis noted in his diary on March 4 that his second term in the U. S. Senate had ended on the previous day and that, " I intend to devote much of my time to the interest of the West Virginia Central Company, building the road, mining and selling coal." At the end of March, Davis noted that he was busy establishing a coal house in Baltimore and agencies in New York and Boston. This had become necessary when Alexander Shaw and Davis disagreed over the marketing of the extra coal produced at Elk Garden. Davis then decided that the West Virginia Central would be responsible for selling all of its coal in the future, a decision which upset Shaw, who would become adamantly opposed to Davis and his plans.

Although work had started on the extension at the end of February, it was the beginning of April before all the contractors had full crews at work. Because of the failure of contractor Gleeson, Porter took over the work on this part of the route, and Warfield was reported to be ready to locate a line from Fairfax Stone to the mouth of Beaver Creek. Davis expected the road to be completed to Elkins by June, and to Fairfax Stone by August. Porter doubted the track would reach Elkins before August.

Porter recommended that Davis purchase a house car for carrying supplies as the work progressed and this was ordered from Carlisle on May 12 for $510. The same company reported that the combination car ordered earlier was receiving its final coat of paint and would be shipped shortly. When the car was finally delivered it became West Virginia Central No. 3.

Davis noted on May 1 that the company was getting along very well and that 200 men, mostly colored, were at work on the extension. At a Board of Directors meeting on May 10, it was agreed to continue the road to the mouth of Beaver Creek. On June 1, Davis went over the road to Fairfax Stone and reported that the track was laid to Schell, 22 miles from Piedmont. He also noted that Riordan had found an eight-foot seam of coal, which appeared to underlie a large area of the Upper Potomac region.

In June, Davis asked B. S. Randolph, a civil engineer and geologist, to take over from Warfield who was indisposed. One of Randolph's first tasks was to review the work that had been done locating the line to the mouth of Beaver and to report on the coal in the area. Randolph recommended that a diamond drill be used to provide an exact geological map of the area.

Davis met with vice presidents Robert Garrett and Samuel Spencer of the B. & O. to discuss freight rates in June. It was agreed that the West Virginia Central would receive a rebate of 25 cents per ton on coal shipped between May 11 and June 5, 1883, and a rebate of 35 cents on coal shipped after June 5. The memorandum prepared by Davis listing these arrangements is interesting in view of an agreement made earlier in the year between the B. & O. and the Pennsylvania not to allow rebates or drawbacks. Davis had also been receiving a rebate from the C. & O. Canal and was concerned that this should continue even when the West Virginia Central started to ship coal from the wharf belonging to the Consolidation Coal Company in Cumberland. Apparently reassured, he later sent 10,000 tons of coal to Georgetown by canal at a rate of $2.80 per ton; the rate by rail would have been $3.10 per ton.

Spencer later in July accompanied Davis and Elkins on a trip to the Upper Potomac and Blackwater regions to examine coal and timber. "All are well pleased with what we have seen," according to Davis, " coal and timber are in large quantities."

Nine men of a construction gang were injured on July 26 when a charge of powder went off prematurely. A pebble had dropped into the hole that had been charged with explosive, and while attempting to remove the stone, the charge was detonated. Fortunately, no one was killed.

Davis and Elkins were over the road again in early August and noted that trains were running as far as Elkins, 32 miles from Piedmont, and that track laying was progressing south of Elkins. It should be noted that this was the original site of Elkins, and should not be confused with the present town of that name. A month later, another trip convinced Davis that the road would be finished on November 1. Davis also noted, "coal of Upper Potomac looks well."

Davis was again complaining to Garrett and Spencer about freight rates in September, particularly the rates governing the transportation of coal to New York and New England. Davis complained that he was essentially cut out of the New York market. He asked that the agreement of January 1881, which allowed for pro-rating, be put into effect. "This agreement was the chief inducement to change the gauge of our road from narrow to standard so as to better connect with your line." It was to be January 1884 before the B. & O. agreed to a rebate of 50 cents per ton on coal bound for New York.

During the fall of 1883, Davis had been busy with plans for

the extension eastward. He had engaged a couple of attorneys, Joseph Sprigg of Moorefield, and W. Dyer of Petersburg, to take care of right-of-way matters in Hardy and Grant counties respectively. Davis thought that the counties should vote a subscription to the railroad, otherwise the right-of-way should be provided free. Davis estimated the cost of the extension as follows:

Construction	No. of Miles.	Cost per mile	Total
Winchester to Wardensville	30	$21,000	$630,000
Wardensville to Bakers Run	18	20,000	360,000
Bakers Run to Moorefield	14	50,000	700,000
Moorefield to Maysville	30	20,000	600,000
Maysville to summit	13	45,000	585,000
Summit to coal field	10	30,000	300,000
Total	115		3,175,000

Equipment	Cost
Side tracks, water stations, station houses, machine shops etc.	$250,000
Engines, cars	400,000
Opening mines	100,000
Total	**$3,975,000**

The next step for Davis was to ask the secretary of state of West Virginia if the name "Coal and Iron Railway" was available. When he was assured that the name could be used he had an act passed by the legislature incorporating the railroad, which became effective April 12, 1884. The incorporators of the C. & I. were listed as Davis, Hambleton, Keyser, T. H. Garrett, Gorman, Chaffee, Enoch Pratt, Pinkney Whyte, Camden, Blaine, Elkins, Bayard and others.

Davis and his brother, Thomas, made a trip over the road on October 19, by which time track laying had reached the Big Trestle, some four miles from Fairfax Stone. Randolph was instructed to continue the road to the eight-foot vein of coal on the Glade Run of the Blackwater River, approximately one mile south of the summit. The eight-foot vein was to become known as the "Davis vein." Randolph and Riordan were both instructed to make an opening on Pendleton Run in this vein. The drilling machine recommended earlier by Randolph was delivered to Piedmont on October 5, and was later reported to be in use northwest of the Fairfax Stone. One final item during October was a letter from Davis to G. W. Harrison asking him to set up a meeting with Fredlock to discuss building a depot at Blaine.

The early organization of the West Virginia Central's operating department is not known, and Harrison's position and when he started with the company are also unknown. Certainly Thomas Davis was the general manager and Harrison occupied the position of superintendent, traffic agent and passenger agent at various times. Harrison had been with the B. & O. before the Civil War; during the war he was a captain in the Quartermaster's department.

Randolph wrote to Davis on November 23, stating that all the contractors had completed their work and that he would close out the entire work on December 1. Track laying was completed to

Fairfax summit on November 25, and Porter was then ordered to continue to a coal opening on the North Fork of the Blackwater.

Work with the boring machine in the vicinity of the Fairfax Stone had not proved satisfactory. Although an eight-foot vein of coal was discovered, it contained a lot of slate according to Davis. The machine then was moved to the vicinity of Dobbin.

Randolph meanwhile was instructed to survey a route to the east for the Coal and Iron Railway, and produced a report on December 14 indicating some improvements in the line selected by Parsons. Randolph also noted the presence of small iron furnaces along the proposed route and considered that large ore fields could be found in the vicinity. The estimated cost of a single track railroad from Winchester to the Blackwater coal region was $3,615,000. Randolph also reported on the results of an earlier survey from Manassas to the mouth of Occoquan Creek on the Potomac River, and considered the possibility of locating a coal terminal there. However, the water was only six feet deep at low tide which led Randolph to consider two other locations to the south of Occoquan Bay (Fig. 20). The first was at Freestone Point (now part of Leesylvania State Park), where the water was 11 feet deep and the second at Cockpit Point where the water was even deeper. Randolph recommended Freestone Point, and this was an idea that Davis was to return to later.

On November 4, Davis purchased a wharf on Curtis Bay in Baltimore for $10,000. The wharf had 250 feet of waterfront and five acres of land. Elkins later purchased a half interest in the

Fig. 20. Proposed extension to the Potomac River
West Virginia and Regional History Collection,
West Virginia University Library

property. Davis also explored the possibility of purchasing a couple of iron or wooden colliers built to carry between 1,000 and 1,500 tons of coal, but did not pursue his maritime ambitions immediately.

At the end of November, a railroad was being considered between Clarksburg and Morgantown, and this also was eventually to have an impact on Davis and his plans. The proprietors of the projected road, known as the Pennsylvania and West Virginia Railroad, were R. T. Lowndes, president of the company, J. T. Sands and Colonel Ben Wilson. The project seemed to have caught the attention of Davis, who wrote to some businessmen in Morgantown to discuss a railroad from that city to the B. & O. However, he did not follow up on the idea immediately. The proposed road also attracted the attention of Camden, who hoped to use it to connect with the Pennsylvania Railroad. Nothing came of the proposed Pennsylvania and West Virginia Railroad, and the scheme lapsed when the B. & O. built its own line from Fairmont and Morgantown between 1884 and 1886.

The Grafton and Greenbrier Railroad on the other hand, was advancing steadily towards its initial goal of Philippi. By December 20 track was laid to within four miles of the town, and Philippi was finally reached in January 1884. Although the trains were now running, charges were made about financial mismanagement during construction, poor engineering and general incompetence. Samuel Woods, the president, had resigned in May and had been replaced by B. F. Martin. In spite of the problems, Davis was convinced the road would extend to Beverly, and in response to a query from a citizen of that town, indicated that the West Virginia Central might connect with the G. & G. at some point.

The Carlisle Manufacturing Company received an order for 50 additional hoppers on December 5, with an option for 50 more at $375 each. An order was also placed for two boxcars at $475 each with an option for five more.

At the end of the year, Davis wrote to Robert W. Eastham, a landowner in the Canaan Valley, noting that men would not work in the area during the winter months, but he was hopeful that the work would be resumed in the spring. Eastham was encouraged to build a "sled road" through to the mouth of Beaver Creek for which Davis would pay $50. Eastham was to be useful to Davis in developing the new town of Davis, but was later to achieve a degree of notoriety, due in a small part to the West Virginia Central. The difficulty in working in the winter months was underscored in January 1884, when a heavy fall of snow brought the work to a standstill.

The first coal from a new mine at Elk Garden operated by the Atlantic and Georges Creek Consolidated Coal Company was shipped at the beginning of January 1884. This company had originally operated along Georges Creek but its mine, the Atlantic mine, worked out during 1884.

One of Davis's first tasks in 1884 was to take up with Garrett and Spencer a proposed traffic agreement for the Coal and Iron Railway and rebates on coal bound for New York. Although he was able to get a 50 cent per ton rebate, negotiations stalled on the traffic agreement question when the B. & O. issued orders not to load West Virginia Central hoppers when B. & O. hoppers were available. This was the beginning of trouble between the West Virginia Central and the B. & O. John Garrett, the president of the B. & O., who had been a close personal friend of Davis, became ill during 1884, leaving the running of the company to his son, Robert. Davis was never to enjoy the same relationship with Robert as he had with his father. John Garrett died in September 1884, and was succeeded as president by Robert. The Pennsylvania Railroad and the B. & O. were to engage in a vicious freight rate battle in March which prompted Davis again to request concessions from the B. & O. but without success.

However, Davis was still sufficiently confident to ask for bids on a new 2-8-0 locomotive from Cooke and Baldwin and also on a passenger car and a combination car from Harlow and Hollingsworth and from Jackson and Sharp, and to order 50 new hoppers from Carlisle. The order for the passenger cars was given to Jackson and Sharp for a total of $6,000 for delivery in May. When delivered, the new passenger car became No. 4; the combination car became No. 5 when it was delivered in July 1884 (Fig. 21). Baldwin was given the order for a new locomotive, which became West Virginia Central No. 5 when it was delivered (Fig. 22). Both companies agreed to take coal in partial payment, which no doubt helped them to secure the contracts and was to set a precedent for Davis's future dealings with both companies.

Davis was approached in March to see if he would sell the charter for the Virginia and West Virginia Railway, which had been incorporated in February 1882, but he decided against a sale. He was however interested in selling the mill at Piedmont and received an offer to trade the mill and boom for coal lands on Stony River, but no deal could be arranged.

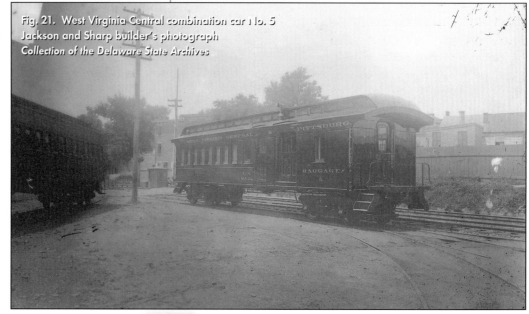

Fig. 21. West Virginia Central combination car No. 5
Jackson and Sharp builder's photograph
Collection of the Delaware State Archives

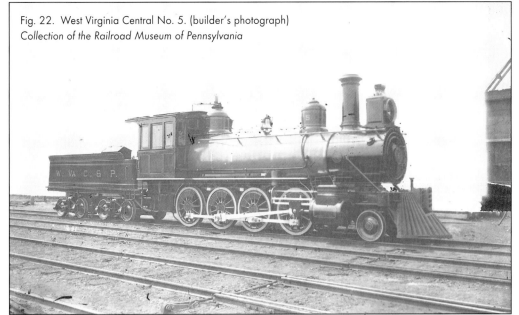

Fig. 22. West Virginia Central No. 5. (builder's photograph)
Collection of the Railroad Museum of Pennsylvania

With the better weather in March, Randolph resumed his surveys for the C. & I. In April, Davis offered Randolph a permanent position at a salary of $250 per month and asked him to survey the area around Davis.

On April 1, Davis noted that he was at work on the C. & I. and hoped soon to organize, and on April 5, he wrote to Camden and asked him if he would care to participate in the new company. Davis noted in his diary on April 10 that the C. & I., "if built would be one of the great coal roads of the country and will open up a good country, also a large lot of timber."

Trouble occurred on the new work in April when Porter lost men who quit when they were asked to work an 11-hour day. Porter was instructed to "pay them off and do not yield." Further defections occurred in May, when black workers quit but Harrison thought they could be replaced with Germans from Baltimore and blacks from Virginia. This provoked criticism of Davis as it was claimed he was bringing in blacks to influence elections and Porter was later instructed not to hire any additional black workers.

Parsons was instructed to run a line from Thomas to Davis on May 22. By the end of May Porter reported that a Y for turning engines had been completed at the summit. On July 14, with track laying nearing Thomas, Porter was told that coal from Thomas was to be shipped as soon as possible. Thomas was reached at the beginning of August and the first coal shipped on August 6. Harrison was advised on August 12, that the mine at Thomas was to be referred to as "No. 3." Davis requested that samples of coal be shipped for testing for coke making.

On August 6, Davis and Elkins, along with their wives, returned from a visit to the site of Davis. Davis noted in his diary that, "Davis is intended to be the end for the present of our W. V. C. & P. road and where we will locate our shops. Mr. Elkins, myself and others are thinking of making Davis our future home. We are clearing off the ground now." (Fig. 23). Davis thought that one day the town would be equal to Altoona in Pennsylvania, which had grown up around the shops of the Pennsylvania Railroad.

Davis was back in the area again at the end of August when he walked along the proposed route from Thomas to Davis with Porter and Parsons. He noted that work on the 6.1/2 mile extension was progressing fairly well, and that the railroad would reach Davis by November 1. At the same time he cautioned Porter to reduce expenses, as it was difficult to raise money.

Both Thomas Davis and Porter submitted reports to Davis on September 11, and both reported everything was going well. Track laying had reached a point 1.1/2 miles from Thomas and grading had reached Pendleton Run, where a trestle would be needed. Thomas Davis reported that the mines at Elk Garden and Thomas were in "good order" but thought they could reduce the price of getting out coal.

Two weeks later, Porter reported everything was still moving well and that he would be in Davis by October 31. He expected to be able to reduce the force by 150 men and six horses.

Randolph continued to look for a suitable route for the C. & I., and by the end of September submitted a final report and map to Davis on a route from the site of Davis to Moorefield (Fig. 24). Davis thought that a route through Kline Gap rather than Maysville would be shorter, but in response to a query from G. B. Roberts, president of the Pennsylvania Railroad, he had to admit that the financial outlook was not promising for building the new road.

On September 26, a B. & O. engine and cars were damaged at West Virginia Central Junction, when they derailed at an open switch. The B. & O. claimed that the switch had been left open by the crew of a West Virginia Central locomotive. The crew had used the B. & O. north track between Piedmont and West Virginia Central Junction because the West Virginia Central track was

Fig. 23. Early view of the site of Davis

DAVIS, WEST VA AT THE BEGINNING OF 1883

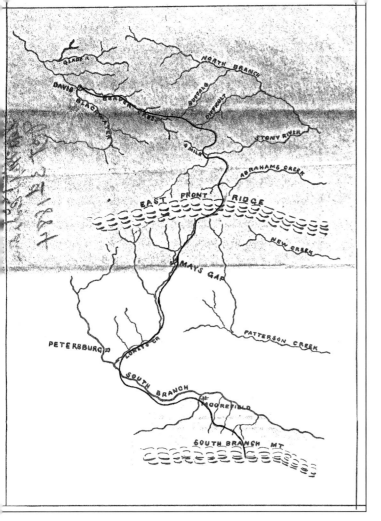

Fig. 24. Proposed route for the Coal and Iron Railway between Davis and Moorefield. The route has been darkened for clarity
West Virginia and Regional History Collection,
West Virginia University Library

blocked by a work train. Although the crew of the West Virginia Central engine had permission to use the B. & O. track, and claimed to have restored the switch, Davis was not pleased to receive a bill for $1,508.70 for the damage caused and it was still unpaid two years later.

The last rail on the extension to Davis was laid on November 1, although it was not expected to commence a regular service until the following spring.

On November 3, Camden sent Davis a copy of a contract for the purchase of 90,000 acres of land at the head of the Cherry and Williams rivers in Webster and Nicholas counties of West Virginia. The land was well timbered and thought to contain coal. Camden claimed that when he first contracted to buy the property, known as the Caperton lands, he did not know there was a problem with the title. Camden thought the legal difficulties could be resolved and asked Davis and Elkins if they would take a half interest. After some negotiations, Davis and Elkins each agreed to take a quarter share in the land.

Prices paid for coal during the fall of 1884 were very low leading the mine operators to consider reducing wages. Davis and President Mayer of the Consolidation Coal Company met in early November to discuss the situation. Mayer agreed to inform Davis

in advance when the Georges Creek operators planned to reduce wages. Davis was informed by Mayer on November 15, that a reduction in wages would occur on December 1. The new rates would be 40 cents per ton for the miners, and $1.60 per day for drivers. Other wages would be reduced by 10 percent except where the men were only earning $1 a day, which was thought to be too low to reduce. When the notice of the reduction was posted, the Georges Creek miners informed the operators that they could not accept the new scale and went on strike. Davis ordered a similar reduction at his mines to take effect on December 5. The Elk Garden miners called a meeting and demanded that all coal be weighed to determine their wages. This was refused by Thomas Davis, who told the men that if they didn't like the new scale, they would be paid off. Only a few men reported for work and Thomas Davis had notices posted warning that men who did not report for work on December 5 would be paid off. Thomas Davis was convinced the trouble would only last a couple of days. The Georges Creek miners returned to work at the new scale on December 5 and were followed by the Elk Garden miners.

The final item for 1884 was an instruction to Parsons on December 31, telling him to look for a route from Moorefield up to the Canaan Valley via the Mouth of Seneca. However, by the middle of January 1885, Davis was claiming that because of the "general want of confidence in the country," there was little prospect of the C. & I. being built.

On the West Virginia Central, one of Davis's first decisions of 1885 was to rename a station between the summit and Thomas as "William" after his brother. The station had originally been called "Cleveland." Davis also wanted to change the name of the West Virginia Central to the West Virginia Central Coal and Railway Company, and he wrote to George Price, now president of the West Virginia senate, to introduce a bill to that effect. Davis claimed the railroad was no longer heading for Pittsburgh but would head southwest through the state.

The Third Annual Report for the West Virginia Central, published on January 27, 1885, noted that three depots had been built during the previous year. One of these was the depot at Blaine, shown in Fig. 25 some 20 years later.

The Grafton and Greenbrier was also interested at this time in extending both to the southeast, towards Virginia, and also down the Elk River towards Charleston. To accomplish this second objective, a new company, the Grafton, Buckhannon and Charleston Railroad, was incorporated in September 1884 involving many of the same individuals as the G. & G. In February 1885, a stockholder's meeting was held which authorized the sale of $400,000 of bonds to extend to Huttonsville.

On February 3, Davis asked Porter to be as frugal as possible in running the road. This was followed two days later by a letter telling Porter that his salary would be reduced to $2,000 per year, and that due to the general depression of business, the road would not be extended this year.

The bleak financial situation did not prevent Davis from asking Baldwin in February to build a new passenger engine. Baldwin offered to build the engine for $6,325; Davis counter offered $6,000 and asked for delivery in May. Baldwin accepted the pro-

Fig. 25. Depot at Blaine, circa 1907.
The building on the left is the Hamill Coal and Coke Company's store

posal and the locomotive became West Virginia Central No. 6 when it was delivered (Fig. 26).

Davis also asked Jackson and Sharp in March about the cost of an officers' car to sleep between four and six people and to have cooking and heating facilities. He also ordered a combination car that was three quarters passenger and one quarter baggage for $2,150, although it was paid for in coal. This car became the West Virginia Central's No. 6.

In April, Davis wrote to a number of tannery companies to persuade them to locate a tannery along the line. One company that responded positively was the Fayerweather and Ladew Company of New York. In June, Davis wrote to H. S. Ladew suggesting either Davis or Bayard as a possible site for a tannery and that the West Virginia Central would be "both liberal and fair both for bark and transportation." Davis offered Fayerweather and Ladew 100 acres of land, at $20 per acre, for the tannery at Davis. The company expected to take 10,000 cords of bark per year for ten years of which between 3,000 and 5,000 cords would come from Davis owned land. The company would be charged $1.00 per cord for bark from Davis land and two cents per mile for delivery. After a trip over the West Virginia Central on July 14, Fayerweather and Ladew agreed to build at Davis and expected to start construction in spring 1886.

At the end of April, rumors started to circulate that the miners in the region would demand restoration of the 50 cents per ton for coal or there would be a strike. On May 5 it was reported that the Elk Garden miners had struck, with only 15 of 225 miners reporting for work. The Armstrong mines, operated by the Big Vein Coal Company, and the Atlantic mine, owned by the Atlantic and Georges Creek Consolidated Coal Company,

were also closed by the strike. The Elk Garden miners were confident they would be joined by the Georges Creek miners, but this did not happen, and by May 18, miners began to trickle back to work. On May 19, the strike ended at Elk Garden, and Davis noted that the men were anxious to return to work but that he was not going to rehire the strike leaders.

Davis and his brother visited the site of Davis on May 1, and agreed to lay off the town in lots of between 30 and 50 feet wide and 150 feet deep with a 20-foot wide alley at the back of the lots. The lots were expected to sell for $50 to $250 each.

Train service started to Davis in June, with two trains daily in each direction, one a passenger and mail and the second a mixed train of both passenger and freight cars. The service was reduced in winter to one train each way. A depot was built at Davis during 1885, and is shown in Fig. 106.

Another company that was to have an effect on the town of Davis was the J. L. Rumbarger Lumber Company, which was originally from Indiana, and already owned a mill at Dobbin. In July, the company entered into an agreement with Davis to lease between 5 and 10 acres of land to build a boom and saw mill about 1.3/4 miles from Davis, and to construct a tram road from the mill to Davis.

Davis visited the new town of Davis on July 1 and noted that building had commenced and that "the eleven foot coal is turning out good."

Fig. 26. West Virginia Central No. 6
West Virginia and Regional History Collection,
West Virginia University Library

The Coal Trade Journal, on September 23, reported on the mining activity around Elk Garden, noting that, "Like other coal fields, shipments are a little slow this year." The article noted that the tipple at Mineville, designed to handle 1,000 tons daily, was connected by a 1,450-foot double incline plane down which the loaded mine cars were transported. The cars were brought from Nos. 1 and 3 openings along a tram road of one mile in length by a Porter locomotive. The No. 2 opening had not worked since the strike earlier in the year but was capable of producing 500 tons daily. A 2,350-foot incline connected this mine to the tipple at Mineville. The Atlantic and Georges Creek Consolidated Coal Company operated near No. 2, but on the other side of Deep Creek. An incline of 1,700 feet connected with a tram road serving the mine. About 100 men and boys were employed but were only working half time. The Big Vein Coal Company at Windom was also on half time work, but during 1883 had produced 83,170 tons of coal.

During the late summer and early fall, Davis had many discussions with the B. & O. to try to obtain favorable freight rates. He was able to get reasonable rates on hides for the new tannery, and also on finished leather bound for New York. Davis also asked for favorable rates on pulpwood as he expected a pulp mill to be built at Davis. On October 13, Davis wrote at length to Robert Garrett about the unfair treatment the West Virginia Central was receiving from the B. & O. This resulted in a meeting in November between Davis and Garrett, Spencer and Chief Freight Agent Harriott of the B. & O. Davis noted that as a result of the meeting, the West Virginia Central would be treated with more consideration in the future.

Davis was not, however, to be totally dependent on vague promises from the B. & O. By the middle of September he had started discussions with the Pennsylvania Railroad about connecting with them in Cumberland. In October he was a little more optimistic of the outcome of his discussions with the B. & O. and noted, "It looks like we could settle our differences. If we cannot, we will build a road from Piedmont to Cumberland." By November 23, Davis had all but given up on the B. & O. and instructed Parsons to draw up plans for crossing the Cumberland and Pennsylvania Railroad at the mouth of Georges Creek. On November 27, Davis, Elkins and Camden met with President Roberts and Vice President Thomson of the Pennsylvania to discuss the proposed new road. "No conclusion, but talk was satisfactory," was Davis's comment.

Towards the end of December, Davis wrote to Vice President Thomson enclosing a proposed traffic agreement between the two lines and indicating that he might continue to Williamsport and a junction with the Cumberland Valley and Western Maryland railroads. He suggested that the new road receive the same treatment for freight rates as the most favored connecting road currently operating along the Pennsylvania Railroad. Davis wrote to Roberts on January 8, 1886, noting that the Piedmont to Cumberland line could be built for under $600,000. Davis suggested that the Pennsylvania give

the new road five percent of the gross revenues received by the Pennsylvania from traffic off the new road to cover the interest on $600,000 worth of bonds if the earnings did not cover the interest. The Pennsylvania also was to place $200,000 of bonds; Davis would place $400,000.

Parsons and Porter examined the route of the extension and Porter claimed he could build it for $425,000. Porter had earlier submitted his resignation to Davis, to take effect on February 1, and this was accepted on December 29. Davis wrote that if the road were built, he would be glad to have Porter's assistance.

Harrison issued a report at the end of the year, which described the industries that had developed along the West Virginia Central. The mining activities at Windom and Elk Garden were discussed as were the new mines at Davis and Thomas. The largest lumber mills were those at Dobbin, owned by the J. L. Rumbarger Lumber Company and employing 45 men, and at Wilsonia where the Fairfax Forest sawmill employed 50 men (Fig. 27). H. G. Davis and Brother operated two mills, one near Chaffee and the other two miles above Fairfax. At Davis, both the Fayerweather and Ladew and Rumbarger companies were clearing land for their operations, and the railroad had completed its shops and an engine house. Work had also commenced on the foundations for a new hotel.

Fig. 27. Advertisement for the Fairfax Forest Mills
Cumberland Daily Times, April 16, 1885

President Roberts of the Pennsylvania Railroad wrote to Davis on January 13, 1886 expressing enthusiasm for the proposed railroad to Cumberland although he expressed some reservations about accepting all of the terms suggested by Davis. The five percent set aside requested by Davis did survive and appeared in the final contract signed by Davis, Elkins and Roberts, and which was printed in the prospectus of the new railroad published in 1886. Roberts advised Davis to place a corps of engineers on the route as soon as possible to make a final survey. Roberts also had his chief engineer examine the situation in Cumberland to see if a connection could be made between the new road and the Pennsylvania Railroad in Cumberland. The Pennsylvania Railroad, through its subsidiary, the Pennsylvania Railroad in Maryland, had reached Cumberland in December 1879. The report submitted by the engineer, W. H. Brown, showed that a connection was feasible although trouble could be expected from the Cumberland and Pennsylvania Railroad and possibly the B. & O. Brown recommended a route crossing Baltimore Street in Cumberland that would give a good location for a depot, and which would then continue up the west bank of Wills Creek to the Georges Creek and Cumberland Railroad yard. Roberts asked that all information be kept confidential. Davis however was eager to start and asked John Humbird to give an estimate for grading, although on March 16, Davis told Humbird that he was not yet ready to begin.

Also on March 16, Davis wrote to the secretary of state for West Virginia asking if the name "Piedmont and Cumberland Railway" was available and also if any other railroad had been chartered to use the same route. Davis was assured that the name was available and that although two other railroads had been chartered, any rights they might have had, had long since lapsed.

With Porter no longer in the employ of the West Virginia Central, Davis needed a good engineer to take charge, and he wrote to Roberts to see if he could recommend anyone. Roberts recommended Joseph U. Crawford, who was finishing a project for the Pennsylvania, and who had previously worked on the Texas Pacific Railroad and on railroads in Japan.

On April 3, Davis received a report from two land agents, W. W. Welch and C. H. Caudy, he had employed to obtain the right-of-way. All but two of the landowners were reported to be anxious for the road to be built. He also received word that President Loveridge of the Pennsylvania Railroad in Maryland was willing to build about a quarter of the distance between his present road and the canal basin. By the middle of April, three corps of engineers were in the field surveying different segments of the route. Davis urged Roberts to build the connecting road as quickly as possible as the B. & O. was getting "anxious."

On May 6, Davis met with Roberts, Thompson and Green of the Pennsylvania and settled all the remaining questions on the contract. The Pennsylvania had agreed to take one third of any bonds not sold at par to cover the cost of the work from Piedmont to the Baltimore Street depot. The section of line from the depot to the Pennsylvania Railroad in Maryland, estimated to cost $50,000, was to be split equally between the two companies. President Roberts, accompanied by Vice President Dubarry and Chief Engineer Brown, visited Cumberland on May 13 and went over the line of the proposed road and met with Davis. Roberts noted that Cumberland was a "pretty town indeed, though it looks as if business were rather dull." The conference led to speculation that Davis was after control of the canal (a bill was before the Maryland legislature at the time to lease the canal for a railroad) and that the canal would eventually be used by the Pennsylvania as a route to Washington.

The Piedmont and Cumberland Railway was officially organized on May 10 with Elkins as president, Davis as vice president and Harry G. Buxton as secretary and treasurer, which allowed for the contract between the P. & C. and the Pennsylvania to be signed. Although Elkins was nominally the president, it was Davis who was to be the driving force behind the new road.

At the end of May, Davis and Brown of the Pennsylvania walked over most of the route. Crawford reported that he was ready to award a contract for the Potomac River crossing at West Virginia Central Junction and the bridge across Wills Creek in Cumberland to the Philadelphia Bridge Works. Crawford estimated the total cost of the new railroad at $531,000 although some locations still had to be decided. The crossing of the B. & O. in the vicinity of the 21st bridge could be made at grade, but Davis realized that the B. & O. would never permit this, and requested that the engineers meet to discuss an overhead crossing.

A notice to contractors was posted on June 11, asking for bids on the new work, with the expectation that grading and masonry would be finished by October. The work was divided into 29 sections of one mile each for bidding, but the first two, including piers and abutments for the Potomac River bridge at West Virginia Central Junction, had already been given to Porter. The awards were announced on June 24. John Humbird was awarded sections 3, 4, 5, 6 and 7; Paige, Carey and Company of Washington, D. C. was given section 8 through 15; Noland O'Reilley of Reading, Pennsylvania 16 through 21 and Kennedy Crossan of Philadelphia sections 22 through 27. Section 28 was later let to J. C. Brady. The work through Cumberland, where the route still had to be determined was not awarded at this time, although it was later given to Humbird. Crawford met with P. L. Burwell, superintendent of the C. & P., and Randolph of the B. & O., to discuss the grade crossing of the C. & P. at Westernport. It was Crawford's opinion that an overhead crossing was impractical at this point but that a grade crossing could be operated safely as it would have good visibility from all directions.

Although the P. & C. had avoided a confrontation with the B. & O. by arranging for an overhead crossing at the 21st bridge, the B. & O. still hoped to make life difficult for the new road. The P.

& C. had originally intended to cross the river into Keyser, but when the B. & O. moved a building onto the right-of-way and extended a coal trestle, Davis decided to continue on the Maryland side in spite of objections by Crawford. The final alignment of the road between Piedmont and Cumberland is shown in Fig. 28.

Fig. 28. Sketch of the Piedmont and Cumberland Railway (undated)
West Virginia and Regional History Collection,
West Virginia University Library

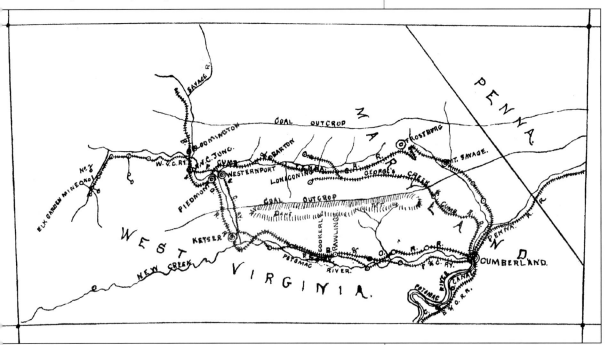

Crawford informed Davis on July 3 that he had accepted a bid from the Philadelphia Bridge Company, to supply the ironwork for seven of the planned nine Potomac River bridges and also the Wills and Georges creek bridges. The plans for the two crossings at Keyser and the crossing of the B. & O. at the 21st bridge still had not been finalized, but Crawford estimated the total cost of all bridges at $95,759. The longest bridges to be built were the six span girder bridge at West Virginia Central Junction and the seven span crossing into Cumberland. Trouble erupted in early July between Crawford and Porter who was at work on the West Virginia Central Junction bridge and the Georges Creek crossing. Crawford was not pleased with the rate at which Porter was building the piers and abutments that were to be finished by August 15 ready for the girders. Porter reassured Crawford that he would be finished in time, although Crawford was still doubtful. Crawford threatened to take the contract for the Georges Creek bridge away from Porter and give it to Humbird if Porter did not meet the deadline.

More trouble appeared in the form of an attorney, D. J. Blackiston of Cumberland, who represented several landowners along the route, including Mrs. Cookerly of Cookerly Farm, who were not satisfied with the amount of compensation offered by Davis. Blackiston had obtained an injunction to stop work until an agreement was reached. In one case, the company agreed to pay compensation in the amount of $300 per acre and the injunction was dropped. A month later, Robert Gordon, the attorney for the tenant at Cookerly Farm, indicated that some agreement had better

be reached, or, as Caudy reported on August 14, "he was disposed to be ugly." Perhaps it was not too surprising that Gordon also happened to be counsel for the C. & P. Although Davis was able to reach an agreement with Mrs. Cookerly, $2,000 being the agreed compensation, the interests of the tenant had been completely overlooked, and this was to prove costly. At this time, the problems did not appear to be any more annoying than was usual with a new railroad.

Davis had better luck with the extension beyond Baltimore Street in Cumberland. Part of the land needed belonged to the tannery owned by Fayerweather and Ladew, and they were quite willing to move some buildings for a suitable compensation, which was ultimately determined to be $4,500. The City of Cumberland passed an ordinance on July 27 granting the P. & C. the right to cross Baltimore Street at grade, to cross Market Street provided they built a bridge across the tracks, and to raise one end of a footbridge at the cement mill by 4.1/2 feet.

Humbird commenced work on the section of the railroad through Cumberland on August 13, and was reported to be at work on the foundations for the piers and abutments of the Potomac River bridge and the Wills Creek bridge. The plans for the Potomac River bridge had originally called for seven 54.1/2 foot deck girder spans, but this was changed to one deck span and three 122.1/2 foot Pratt truss spans. For Wills Creek, the plans called for five girder spans of 54.1/2 feet. Heavy rains at the end of August delayed work on both bridges. The city became concerned that construction of the Wills Creek bridge would cause flooding during times of high water, and sent the mayor and city attorney to meet with Crawford. Engineer Crawford claimed that the bridge would present less of an obstruction than presently existed, and that the railroad would do some additional excavation to improve the flow. The city was not entirely satisfied and called a special meeting of the council to discuss the matter. Representing the "Citizens and Property Holders" was Robert Gordon who was, not surprisingly, vehement in his opposition to the bridge. It was pointed out at the meeting that the railroad owned the property on either side of the creek at the site of the bridge, and therefore effectively owned the creek, the city having no easement on the stream. The matter was referred to a committee and work on the bridge continued (Fig. 29). However, the Wills Creek bridge was to become a problem again later.

Davis had also contacted L. V. Baughman, president of the C.

and O. Canal to discuss crossing the canal property and making a connection at the coal wharf. Receiving no reply, Davis tried again a few weeks later. The reason for the delay appeared to be the B. & O., which had promised the canal company that the B. & O. would purchase repair bonds if the canal company refused to allow any company but the B. & O to connect with it. Always short of money, the C. and O. canal was happy to agree. On August 26, the canal board met, and when Davis agreed to take $75,000 worth of repair bonds, the company reversed its earlier decision, and granted Davis permission to cross the canal lands and to make a connection at the coal wharf. Although the canal board had granted approval, Davis still went ahead with condemnation proceedings against the canal and its tenants, to determine the extent of damages that would be due.

The B. & O. had lost this round but was making trouble for Davis at Rawlings where the two tracks were very close together, and near the 21st bridge. P. & C. contractors were instructed to avoid the B. & O. right-of-way until an agreement was reached. An agreement was signed with the B. & O. on August 26, 1886, in which the P. & C. agreed not to approach the B. & O. tracks closer than 33 feet from the centerline. The P. & C. also agreed to build a bridge at the B. & O.'s 21st bridge and to pay $200 per acre for land needed for this purpose. It was also agreed that the P. & C. would not cross any tracks of the B. & O. at grade with the exception of the track leading to the coal trestle at Keyser. This resulted in the P. & C. building a branch into Keyser rather than building through the town and thus requiring only one bridge. The proposed grade crossing of the C. & P. at Westernport was specifically excluded from the agreement.

Davis hoped that this agreement would eliminate problems with the B. & O., but this was not to be the case, and it did not restrain the companies controlled by the B. & O., namely the Consolidated Coal Company and the C. & P., from making trouble. The first sign of new problems occurred on September 9, when the tenant at Cookerly Farm, Samuel Speelman, obtained an injunction to stop work on the farm because of damage to his crops. Davis claimed the land involved was only pasture.

With the approval of the C. and O. Canal, and following a recommendation from W. H. Brown, the original plan for a switchback on the approach to the Baltimore Street depot was abandoned in favor of a long curving approach. Brown pointed out the switchback could hold only 12 cars and the P. & C. would want to operate longer trains than this.

Not so cooperative was Charles Mayer, president of the Cumberland and Pennslyvania Railroad. After a wait of nearly two months, Mayer finally wrote to Davis refusing permission for a grade crossing at Westernport. Davis indicated that he would institute condemnation proceedings on September 15 to secure the crossing. The jury in the case visited the contested site on September 28 and returned a verdict on September 30, fixing damages at $5,000.

Also uncooperative was Lloyd Lowndes, one of the incorporators of the North Branch Railroad Company, and Alexander Shaw who owned a farm at Rawlings, both of whom were reluctant to give a right-of-way. The problem with Shaw was the start of a major confrontation between the two erstwhile partners. In this case, the right-of-way disagreement was compromised in early October.

On September 17, Davis asked Porter for an estimate on laying tracks and then decided to allow Porter to supervise the track laying on the extension. The Cumberland Times reported on September 25 that the section constructed by Kennedy Crossan had been completed and turned over to the P. & C. Not so rapidly completed was the section under construction by Paige, Carey and Company, who claimed that changes in the alignment had cost them time and money but would be finished by November 10 or 15. Crawford was able to give Davis an update on October 28 indicating all of the grading was finished except for the Paige Carey section and that approximately one sixth of the track had been laid and ballasted. Work was proceeding from both ends and also from a spur off the B. & O. at Dawson's Church allowing about two miles of track per day to be finished. All of the bridge masonry was finished, and two thirds of the bridges erected. The remaining bridges were expected to be finished by November, and Crawford was confident that trains would be running before winter set in.

The C. & P. filed an objection to the jury verdict on October 17 in the Westernport crossing case. At this time track had been laid from West Virginia Central Junction to the crossing site, and the roadbed beyond was graded and ready for track. The hearing for the C. & P. objections was set for November 4, but Davis was by now becoming rather impatient, and ordered

Fig. 29. Construction of abutments and piers for the Wills Creek bridge
Herman and Stacia Miller Collection, City of Cumberland

Porter to be ready to lay the crossing. The case was decided in favor of the P. & C. on November 6, and immediately after a passenger train had left Piedmont for Cumberland over the C. & P. tracks, Porter and a force of men installed the crossing, meeting with no opposition. A foreman and a posse of men were left on guard overnight although no problems occurred. In November, Davis had the chief signals officer of the Pennsylvania examine the crossing and make recommendations based on the Pennsylvania model in similar situations. Davis sent the plans to Mayer for

Fig. 30. Plan for the signals at the C. & P. grade crossing at Westernport
West Virginia and Regional History Collection,
West Virginia University Library

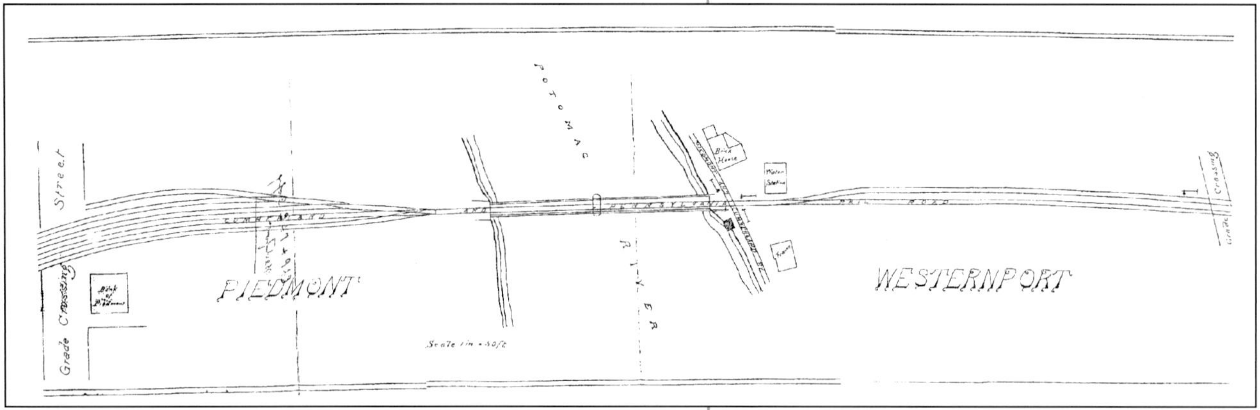

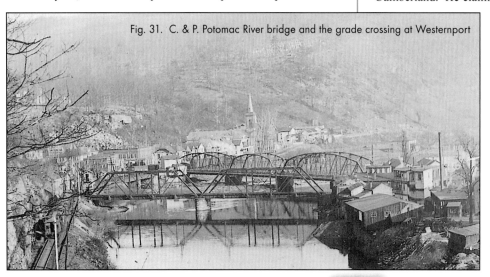

approval (Fig. 30), and on January 27, 1887 reported to Mayer that the necessary signals had been ordered. The C. & P. Potomac River bridge leading into Piedmont from the crossing, and the cabin controlling the signals can be seen in Fig. 31.

The same jury that had granted Davis the right to cross the C. & P. at grade in Westernport, decided against him in the Cookerly farm matter. It was concluded that the charter of the P. & C. did not allow it to cross the Potomac River into Maryland and that it should have remained in West Virginia until it reached Cumberland.

Davis met with Roberts on November 10, and it was decided to erect a joint depot at Cumberland at a cost of about $10,000. Bids were received early in the new year ranging from $5,625 to $6,500. The low bidder, E. J. Fredlock, was awarded the contract on January 26, 1887. The depot at Westernport was reported to be

almost finished on December 13 (Fig. 32.).

By the beginning of December, Crawford was able to report that the bridge over the B. & O., near that company's 21st bridge, was almost finished, and the cut nearby was being pushed by Paige Carey and Company. The bridge men were also busy on the bridge giving access to Keyser (Fig. 33), and work on the trestle was proceeding over the C. and O. Canal basin (Fig. 34). Final approval for the P. & C. to cross the property of the C. and O. Canal was given by the Board of Public Works of the State of Maryland on December 16, 1886. The condemnation proceedings initiated by Davis against the C. & O. Canal and its tenants were heard at the end of December and decided in Davis's favor with minimal damages.

The approaches to the bridge at 21st were finished by Paige Carey and Company on January 9, 1887 and track laying commenced immediately. A few days later, however, a large slip occurred in the cut, and Porter was compelled to operate crews day and night to remove it, although further slips kept Porter's crews busy until January 24.

A nervous watch was also being kept on the Potomac River, which was jammed with ice, and which posed a threat to the new bridges. The ice came down the river at the end of January but did no damage to either the Potomac River or Wills Creek bridges at Cumberland (Fig. 35). At the beginning of February, floods damaged a trestle near Piedmont. More slides came down near the 21st bridge on February 3, also delaying plans.

The Cumberland Daily Times reported on January 21, that Malcolm Sinclair was still fighting the condemnation proceedings for land he owned in West Virginia across the Potomac River from Cumberland. He claimed that the P. & C. was a West Virginia company that had illegally built in Maryland and it was therefore illegal for it to build in West Virginia. There is evidence that Sinclair was aided and abetted by the B. & O. in his obstructionism.

On January 31, it was reported that workmen acting for the P. & C. had torn down the fence at Cookerly Farm preparatory to laying track. One of Mayer's attorneys piously claimed, "Such things must stop or the anarchy which is so much feared will surely come," and called on Sheriff Houck to preserve the peace. The sheriff and a posse of ten men departed for the farm on February 1. On February 7,

Fig. 31. C. & P. Potomac River bridge and the grade crossing at Westernport

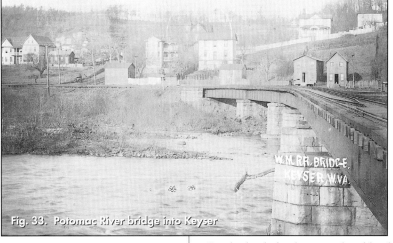

Fig. 32. The Georges Creek bridge and the depot at Westernport. The Georges Creek bridge is to the left of the Potomac River bridge, and the depot, in its original location, is on the immediate right
Collection of the Westernport Heritage Society

attorneys for the P. & C. served an injunction on the posse, which promptly withdrew. This left the field open for an invasion force, estimated at 450 men and including 200 Elk Garden miners, to take possession and lay the track, which was completed by noon on February 8. Mayer and his attorneys promptly filed to have the injunction, under which the tracks had been laid, dismissed. To prepare for any eventuality, Davis left a guard of 25 men at the farm. By February 12, Davis thought that the danger of a counterattack had passed and recommended leaving five men on guard and removing any unused rails or ties from the area. A passenger car was added to the construction train to make it a "passenger train." This train left Keyser at 7:00 A.M. and returned from Rawlings at 6:00 P.M., and it was hoped that the "passenger train" designation would help prevent a disruption of service.

Fig. 33. Potomac River bridge into Keyser

At the end of February it was reported that Mayer was organizing a gang of about 75 miners to go to Cookerly Farm and tear up the track. About 20 men were rounded up by the P. & C. officials to defend the farm, but no attack came on either February 26 or 27.

At the beginning of March, Davis was sufficiently confident that the problems were over, that he wrote to Roberts and reported that he would be ready to ship coal over the new road by April 1. The estimate for the road had increased to $720,000 due to right-of-way and legal problems. Davis also gave orders to reduce the guard at Cookerly Farm to one man, as he had spent already $265 for board for the men guarding the farm. On March 14, Davis

noted in his diary that he hoped to have trains running by April 10.

Davis's optimism was to prove misplaced.

On March 28, a special train carrying between 75 and 80 men, under the direction of W. Irvine Cross, an attorney for the B. & O., arrived at Cookerly Farm and tore up the tracks. The force remained at the farm and the battle was on.

The first reports of the incident, indicated that Sheriff Houck had accompanied the invaders but it was learned later that the sheriff only appeared on the scene after the invasion occurred. Davis's first step was to go to Hagerstown with the sheriff and persuade Chief Justice Alvey to order the withdrawal of the sheriff's posse. The good judge stated that sheriffs have no right to guard private property, and the posse was withdrawn on March 30. On the same day, an injunction was sought by Mayer, who had purchased the lease to the farm from Speelman, to prevent the P. & C. from entering the property, but this was denied. Davis also sought an injunction against Cross, the B. & O. and the C. & P.

On April 2, the battle lines were being drawn for a long siege. Cross requested that John K. Cowan, general counsel for the B. & O., grant full authority to General Agent W. F. Landers, also of the B. & O., to summon additional forces as required. To try to prevent Davis from using miners to force his way through, notices appeared throughout the mining region telling the miners not to get involved and concluding, "Do not be a cat's-paw for the benefit of a grinding monopolist who has no sympathy for you and yours."

Davis was not yet ready to resort to force. He wrote to William Read, counsel for the P. & C. in Cumberland, that he wanted no bloodshed and that he hoped to relay the track under an injunction.

On April 5, it was expected that an attack was imminent and Landers was authorized to transport between 50 and 60 men if the need arose. P. L. Burwell, general superintendent of the C. & P., also arranged to have a special engine standing by day and night to transport Sheriff Houck to Cookerly at the first sign of trouble.

Possibly because an attack never materialized on April 5, Landers request to increase the defenders to 200 men was rejected by Mayer, who thought that if an attack came it would be with a force greater than 200. If Davis used only his track crews, the farm could be defended with the existing force. A telegraph station was established at the farm, and Landers was advised to post lookouts at either end of the farm and also have someone at Piedmont and

Elk Garden to give early warning.

At the time all attention was focused on Cookerly, a judge at Keyser on April 9 gave the P. & C. permission to proceed with the condemnation of the Sinclair property provided a $5,000 bond was posted to cover any costs and damages that may ultimately be awarded. The bond was posted and the track immediately laid and an engine ran over it.

On April 14, Governor Lloyd appointed ten special police for the C. & P. and these individuals were in place at Cookerly by April 19. Davis also requested the appointment of a dozen special police, including Porter, but this did not impress Cross, who told Landers they were to be "driven from the ground like any other trespasser."

An attack was expected on April 14, when 75 men were sent to the farm to repel, as it turned out, a party of drunks from a wedding. The alarm bell at the rolling mill in Cumberland, the assembly point for reinforcements, sounded again on April 19. Telegrams flew back and forth and reinforcements were rushed to the farm. The invaders were a gang of P. & C. trackmen that attempted to lay ties, but meeting no success, withdrew without incident. Cross, later the same day, gave orders to use the ties as a stockade, and to destroy the embankments. By April 20, the danger appeared over and Mayer ordered the garrison to be reduced to 25 men. Cross also ordered Landers to ensure that none of Davis's men were allowed to remain on the disputed property, and that "no more violence be used than is necessary" in ejecting them.

Davis had requested that the P. & C. be designated as a postal route and expected that the government would protect its interests, but Cross was not impressed, and ordered any U. S. Government

officials "be forcibly driven off." Cross also ordered that the special police were to be armed with rifles, but that only blank ammunition was to be issued. The only person at the farm who was to know that the ammunition was not live was T. F. McCardell, who was in charge there. Davis was told of the presence of the guns by an informant in Cumberland.

The next move by Cross was to order that the rails and ties be removed secretly from the farm. Seven cars were loaded on April 25, but their movement was reported in the local papers. Two days later, Thomas Davis, Reed and Sheriff Houck went to Cookerly and arrested 25 men for the theft and took them to Cumberland. Among those arrested was Landers, who was held on $500 bail, and McCardell, who along with the remainder of the group, was held on $300 bail. The defendants refused to provide bail and were marched off to jail.

The next morning, the group was taken before Judge Syester who released all the prisoners. This depressed Thomas Davis who thought that after the arrests of the previous day, when the remainder of the garrison had fled, possession should have been taken of the property. With the release of the prisoners, the garrison was restored and an additional 40 or 50 guns and bayonets taken to the farm. In a move that was obviously planned to demoralize the Davis forces, a bugle was sent to Landers.

President Roberts warned Davis on May 2, that Garrett was purchasing stock in the West Virginia Central in the hope of gaining control and isolating the P. & C. Roberts hoped that the ownership of the West Virginia Central and the P. & C. was beyond the

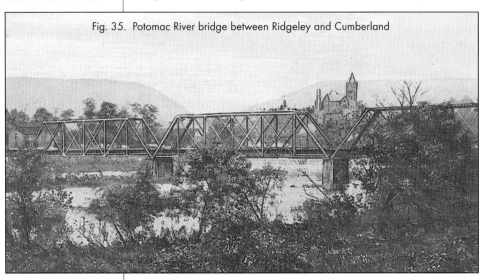

Fig. 35. Potomac River bridge between Ridgeley and Cumberland

reach of the B. & O. as he had no desire to assist in building a road that might end up with the B. & O.

On the same day an agent of Mayer obtained from the Cookerly family an assignment for all the rails, spikes, ties and bolts belonging to the P. & C. at the farm. Arrangements were made for the cars, 21 in all, to be transported to isolated sidings in the Shenandoah Valley.

Cross ordered Landers on May 14, to reduce the garrison to ten or 15 men. This information was relayed to Davis by his informant in Cumberland, but Davis made no move. Davis did inform Dailey on May 17 that he had heard that if the B. & O. lost at Cookerly, they would try the same tactics at the Sinclair property.

Perhaps feeling confident, Burwell wrote to Davis on May 26, that two freight cars belonging to the West Virginia Central were standing on the ground at Cookerly Farm. Burwell would allow Davis's men, temporarily employed by the C. & P., to remove the cars. Still Davis made no move, and on June 1 the garrison was reduced to seven men. On June 4, 20 men led by Thomas Davis attempted to lay a temporary wooden track to the two cars, but this was torn up by the defenders. McCardell, who was in charge, had only four men under his command at the time. Frustrated in not being able to lay the wooden track, Thomas Davis ordered a wire attached to the cars and they were pulled to safety using a locomotive on tracks in P. & C. territory.

Nothing much happened at the farm for the next three weeks, although McCardell and his men appeared to have been forgotten by their superiors. On June 24, he plaintively telegraphed that he and his men had nothing to eat and that along with the two families, 20 people needed to be fed immediately. McCardell ordered five pounds of cheese, five dozen eggs, pickles, 18 pounds of beef, 25 loaves, two dozen cans of peaches, one bushel of potatoes and one dozen cabbages for immediate delivery.

With McCardell reprovisioned, attention turned to the courts, specifically the Court of Appeals, where Judge Stone handed down a decision on three of the cases on June 22. Most importantly, it was decided that the P. & C. did have the right to condemn a right-of-way, but did not have the right to an injunction against Mayer. Mayer was pleased with the decision, but ordered Landers to keep a careful watch should Davis attempt to get possession. Davis, however, seemed content to let the law run its course, and filed to condemn the right-of-way immediately on hearing the court's decision. Cross telegraphed Landers on June 23 and told him that Davis was desperate, and to reinforce the farm with a large force if necessary. McCardell, on the ground, was very jittery, and reported suspicious movements by a P. & C. track gang near Rawlings. In the evening he reported lights had appeared on the ridge over the river and asked that ammunition be sent up immediately. Davis was quite confident that eventually he would gain possession and expected trains to be running within a week. Again he was to be proved a little overconfident.

Cookerly was not the only trouble spot at this time. Elkins had been trying to get a connection at Westernport with the C. & P., but was not successful. Grading for the connection was estimated to take another three weeks and so Elkins continued to negotiate.

A jury was appointed on June 27 to hear the condemnation proceedings, but Cross was still convinced Davis would attack and ordered Landers "to resist in every possible way."

Arguments in the condemnation proceedings were heard on

June 28. Cross claimed that the P. & C. was a fraudulent corporation, and that Mayer would have sold the Cookerly lease if he could have got justice in the Westernport grade crossing case. According to Cross, Mayer would vacate Cookerly if Davis would remove the offending grade crossing. The case was given to the jury on July 6 and on July 7 a verdict was reached in favor of Mayer who was awarded $17,850 in damages. Davis was not pleased and his attorneys immediately filed to have the award set aside. They claimed that inadmissible evidence had been presented to the jury, and that the sheriff was guilty of misconduct by allowing the defendants to furnish beer and whiskey to the jurors. Davis was more forthright and claimed the jury had been bribed. The reconsideration was held on July 11. The jury members were asked how they had arrived at the figure of $17,850 and it appeared that it was an average of each member's figure.

On July 12, the Cookerly Farm case ended when Mayer and Elkins agreed to compromise at $2,000. Davis informed Read and told him to prepare for a damage suite against the B. & O., the C. & P. and Mayer. Although the Cookerly problem was settled, Elkins was still after the C. & P. to allow the connection at Westernport, but presumably because of the loss of Cookerly Farm, he found the C. & P. still intransigent. Cross was also not too pleased with the result and told Landers that the P. & C. was not to approach the B. & O. closer than 19 feet from the center line of the tracks through Cookerly. He was instructed to use force if necessary to ensure compliance.

Porter was told that possession of the right-of-way would occur on July 15 and to be ready to commence track laying. Davis noted in his diary that track laying was finished on July 17 but that a few more days would be required to finish the ballasting.

The first passenger train over the new road arrived in Cumberland just after 7:00 P.M. on July 18. A large crowd of people and a band were on hand to greet the train, which was pulled by No. 6 with Jacob Barber the engineer and James Davis the fireman. The train had left Davis at 1:50 P.M. and reached West Virginia Central Junction at 5:06 P.M. A new timetable went into effect on July 18, which showed a passenger train leaving Cumberland at 6:30 A.M., reaching Davis at noon and returning to Cumberland at 7:00 P.M. A second daily service each way was provided by attaching a passenger car to a freight train. An advertisement appeared in the local newspapers announcing that freight would be accepted at the new Cumberland Central Station for all points to Davis starting on July 19. The Pennsylvania Railroad and the Georges Creek and Cumberland Railroad were already using the new station when the West Virginia Central finally arrived. The Pennsylvania had been greeted by flags and bunting when its first train arrived on May 7; the G. C. & C. had begun using the new station on May 23. The new building (Figs. 36 and 37) was still unfinished at this time as it was reported the painters did not finish their work until the end of August.

An excursion service was initiated on August 1 from Cumberland to Davis, with return tickets costing $1.25. On the first trip 200 passengers were carried in five cars.

Roberts was pleased to hear of the completion of the new road, and urged Davis to consider a connection with the

Cumberland Valley and the Western Maryland roads. A preliminary reconnaissance by a Pennsylvania Railroad engineer had shown such a route to be entirely feasible.

Problems still remained with the C. & P., which refused to make the connection at Westernport. Elkins wrote to Cross requesting that the connection be made as shippers on the West Virginia Central wanted to send mine props and lumber to points along Georges Creek. Elkins indicated that the shippers had been told that the service would start on August 14. Elkins was warned by Cowan on August 14, not to forcibly make the connection or it would lead to more litigation. Elkins agreed to wait a week. By the first week in September, the connection was finally installed but still the C. & P. remained uncooperative. Two empty West Virginia Central freight cars were placed for the C. & P. to take them to the Davis and Elkins mine 1.1/2 miles up Georges Creek, but the C. & P. refused to accept them. Davis also asked another Georges Creek mining company, the Maryland Union Coal Company, to notify the C. & P. that they

wished to ship via the P. & C. but the C. & P. still refused to move.

On or about September 22, Elkins notified Mayer that the C. & P. was in violation of an Act of Congress of February 4, 1887, in refusing to accept the cars. When Mayer still did not move, General Agent Harrison of the West Virginia Central was ordered to ready an engine to go up the C. & P. line to the Davis and Elkins mine, but there is no record that this maneuver was ever carried out. Davis finally accepted Mayer's conditions on January 5, 1888, and the first train ran across the new connection on the same day.

At a meeting of the directors of the West Virginia Central on November 21, 1887, Davis reported that he had made arrangements for the West Virginia Central to operate the P. & C. This action was approved by the directors. However, the arrangement was to be another source of friction between Davis and Shaw in a couple of years

The final act in the P. & C. drama was to be played out in court, where Davis had sued the B. & O., the C. & P. and Mayer for $400,000 damages. Davis, in turn, was sued for malicious prosecution by the three defendants, and the stage was set for another prolonged courtroom battle. The case was scheduled to be heard on February 12, 1889 in Frederick, Maryland. However, on February 9, Davis informed his attorneys that he had made an out-of-court agreement and would accept $35,000 in full settlement, the figure to be kept confidential.

Thus the long drawn out affair finally reached a conclusion, the railroad was running and everyone seemed pleased with the outcome except Irvine Cross and Alexander Shaw.

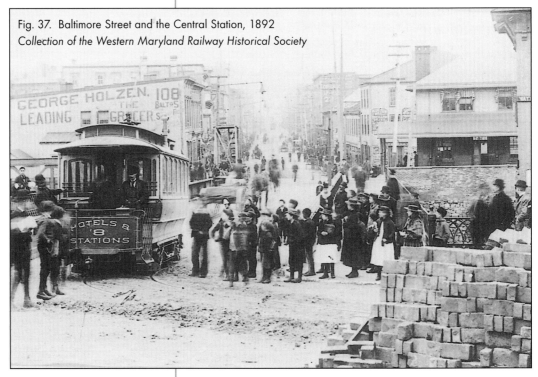

Although Davis's attention during 1886 was focused on the P. & C., he did not neglect the West Virginia Central. On the West Virginia Central, the new year, 1886, opened quietly except for a report on January 6 that a passenger train, which had left Wilsonia the previous morning, had taken 20 hours to reach Cumberland after having been delayed by landslides along the line.

Unfortunately for Davis, the quiet spell was not to last too long. At a meeting of miners in Cumberland on February 18, a demand was made that the price per ton of coal loaded be increased by ten cents in the Georges Creek, Elk Garden and neighboring fields. By March 2, when no response had been received from the operators, a strike was called for March 8. Davis wrote to the Elk Garden miners on March 6 urging them not to join the strike and that a strike, if it occurred, would lead to lost orders and even less work. Davis claimed that the coal trade was "dull and lower than at any time for years," and that the operators could not afford the advance. He did say that he would pay the increase if it was awarded by other operators. The Georges Creek miners struck on March 8, but initially the miners at the Hampshire mine near Piedmont and those at Elk Garden continued to work. The Hampshire mine closed after a couple of days when notices appeared throughout the region telling the miners to quit or face the consequences. On March 10, 100 striking miners set out for Elk Garden where the miners were still working. The strikers were forbidden to enter the company's property, and after posting some notices and exploding a few sticks of dynamite, they left peacefully. This activity had its desired effect, and by March 12, 125 Elk Garden men joined the strike. Davis noted on March 15, that the Elk Garden miners had been forced to strike by "all kinds of intimidation," and indeed 21 miners were later indicted of intimidation. By April the newspapers were reporting considerable hardship among the strikers and their families, but the strike showed no signs of ending. On May 5, 12 miners at Elk Garden attempted to return to work, but were met by a party of strikers and a fight ensued. Thomas Davis rushed to the scene whereupon the strikers turned on him and it was only by brandishing a revolver that he was able to escape unharmed. A posse led by the sheriff later arrested six strikers for the disturbance. A meeting between the operators and representatives of the Georges Creek miners took place on May 15, but no progress was made. Meetings were then held at the various mines and most miners elected to return to work at the old rate of 40 cents per ton. On May 19, miners at Georges Creek and Elk Garden returned to work.

The president of the Western Maryland Railroad, J. M. Hood, wrote to Davis on March 15, sending him a map of the W. Md's proposed extension to tidewater (Fig. 38), and also suggesting the desirability of converting the upper end of the C. & O. Canal into a railroad. This idea had occurred to other railroad entrepreneurs including Davis, but it was to be another two years before any action was taken on this idea.

Fig. 38. Western Maryland Railroad and its connections
West Virginia and Regional History Collection,
West Virginia University Library

Other railroads were considering extensions at this time. The G. & G. was again thinking of extending to Huttonsville, with a first step of reaching Belington. A contract for this work was awarded in June.

Davis was, however, busy with the P. & C., and when asked by a reporter for the Baltimore American in early June if he contemplated extending, he replied:

"Not at present; but as soon as the times are more favorable, and business will warrant it, we expect to connect with the Chesapeake and Ohio system. It is about sixty miles from Piedmont to Davis, the present terminus of the West Virginia Central road, and about 120 from Davis to the Chesapeake and we can reach a connection by going down the Greenbriar, Gauley or Elk River valleys. If the later route, which is a little the longest, be chosen, it would bring us to Charleston, the capital of the state. There is no railroad, by the way, for fifty miles on this side of the contemplated connection, and the road would run nearly its whole route through coal and iron ore territory, covered by a virgin forest of finest timber."

These routes are shown on a map produced at about this time in Fig. 39. Davis also indicated that he and Elkins planned to make Davis their home and that the new hotel, built by the railroad, would open there on June 20 (Fig. 40).

Fig. 39. Proposed extensions of the West Virginia Central and Pittsburg Railway *West Virginia and Regional History Collection, West Virginia University Library*

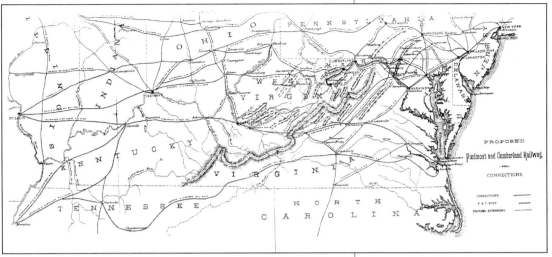

the Davis vein of coal , this did not occur until 1891.

At the beginning of August, Parsons was busy locating a line from Thomas 1.1/2 miles south along the North Fork of the Blackwater River to a mine, eventually known as the Davis mine, near Snyders Run. He reported that he would be ready to commence grading the route by the middle of August. The new mine was reported to have opened in September.

On August 21, the first of several serious accidents occurred on the Mineville branch when the boiler of Engine No. 3 exploded. No. 3 was running backwards at the time pushing several coal cars and pulling a passenger car. The explosion killed the fireman, John Bartlett, and blew the engineer, John O'Brien, some 50 feet, but he was only slightly injured. The brakeman, Timothy Caudy, escaped with a "slight scalding," and a passenger received a broken arm.

The widow of the fireman was due $400 from the relief fund, but argued that because the locomotive was faulty, and had been so since it had been received from Mt. Savage, that the railroad was negligent in allowing it to be used, and additional compensation was due. The law at the time allowed an employer to escape liability for such a mishap unless it could be proved that the company was aware of the defect but still allowed the locomotive to be used. The company's position was usually to blame the engineer for knowingly operating an unsafe locomotive. Whether Mrs. Bartlett received any additional compensation was not recorded.

Parsons received instructions on September 2, to explore the area around the headwaters of the Cheat, Elk and Greenbrier rivers, but it was to be November before Parsons was able to make the trip. In response to a question on whether he was going to build to Randolph County and connect with the G. & G., Davis was non-committal.

Later in the fall, Davis became concerned about the need for additional power and equipment when the P. & C. road opened up for business. Baldwin agreed to provide a duplicate of Engine No. 5 for $8,800 and of No. 6 for $6,750. Baldwin could deliver in January 1887 if the order was placed immediately. Later an order was placed with Jackson and Sharp for a new passenger car costing $3,400 for March delivery to be paid for in coal. Carlisle was busy building ten gondolas for $420 each for December delivery, and this order was followed by an order for a further 40 similar cars.

Davis was still very primitive even with the new hotel. Davis had visited the area again in April and was pleased to see that much progress was being made in clearing the town site. However tree stumps were everywhere giving "the town a rough and unattractive appearance," according to one newspaper. Davis hired Charles Ridgely to remove them

Fig. 40. Blackwater Hotel at Davis in 1912

at 35 cents per stump, but Ridgely soon reported that it was costing between 75 cents to a dollar to remove the large stumps and asked to be released from his contract. In an effort to make the town more attractive, Parsons was instructed to sow grass and to keep the place tidy and to prevent employees smoking. A correspondent for the Cumberland Daily Times, who visited Davis on August 11, reported that Fayerweather and Ladew had nearly completed five buildings for the new tannery and had broken ground for four more. Ten carloads of bark were already arriving daily at the tannery. In addition to the hotel, Davis now had a post office and several boarding houses and the population was reported to be approximately 500 (Fig. 41).

The same correspondent also reported that the population in Thomas had decreased to about 50 from the 300 or more that lived there when the mines were operating. Although it was expected that a shaft mine would be sunk to

Fig. 41. Housing in Davis, 1886

Parsons submitted an initial report on his visit to the Greenbrier and Gauley rivers on November 29. His report indicated that a route from Thomas to Shavers Fork, up Haddix Run to Leading Creek and down this creek to the Tygart Valley River was highly feasible. From the Tygart Valley River to the Valley Fork of the Elk River would then give a practical route to Charleston.

This news encouraged Elkins who reviewed the financial aspects of building to Beverly on the Tygart Valley River, and concluded that it was a reasonable proposition.

The end of 1886 found the prospects for the West Virginia Central to be highly favorable. The P. & C. was under construction and the possibilities for a southern extension were encouraging. Because of the prolonged miners' strike earlier in the year, coal shipments were down compared to 1885. However, the lumber business was growing and 17 mills were in operation between Piedmont and Davis, including two, at Chaffee and near Fairfax, owned by H. G. Davis and Brother. The largest mills on the road were at Dobbin, owned by the J. L. Rumbarger Company where 55 men were employed, and the mills owned by Miller and Levering. This company had purchased the timber on a 20,000-acre tract belonging to the West Virginia Central in August 1885. The tract stretched from Dobbin to Davis and the company had contracted to ship 5,000,000 board feet of lumber each year for the next five years. Two mills were located at Davis, one owned by Rumbarger and the other by A. J. Evans. The Rumbarger mill employed 75 men and produced 30,000 feet of lumber daily (Fig. 42). The

Fig. 42. Log train unloading at the millpond of the J. L. Rumbarger mill on the Blackwater River
West Virginia and Regional History Collection, West Virginia University Library

Fayerweather and Ladew tannery was also now in production and was reported to employ 400 men (Fig. 43).

The first order of business for Davis in 1887 was to recommend to Elkins and Thomas Davis that the West Virginia Central be extended to the Cheat River at an estimated cost of $200,000 and later to Beverly. Elkins, as usual, had other grandiose ideas, in this case building a line in Pennsylvania from near Harrisburg towards Cumberland using part of the defunct South Penn roadbed, which would cut 50 miles off the distance to New York. Invading the Pennsylvania's territory did not appeal to Davis and this idea was dropped.

Davis was in contact with members of the West Virginia legislature in January with a view to amending the charter of the West Virginia Central. This time Davis wanted to drop the word

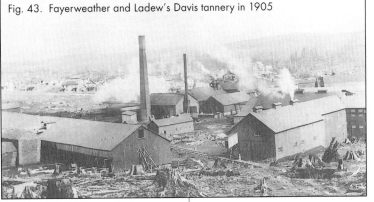
Fig. 43. Fayerweather and Ladew's Davis tannery in 1905

"Pittsburg" from the company name and to include in the charter the privilege of changing the route as necessary. There was considerable opposition to the amendments, which Davis suspected was the work of the B. & O. Although the amendment passed, it was not signed into law and hence died.

On February 16, Parsons was ordered to be ready to determine the location of the road down the Blackwater Canyon in the spring. A month later, Parsons was notified that Porter would be in charge of construction in the canyon. Porter's title was superintendent of construction when work actually started.

Davis also ordered an additional ten gondolas from Carlisle, making 50 in all, and also ordered 50 Pennsylvania Railroad model 60,000 pound coal cars at $525 each. When Jackson and Sharp wrote to say the new passenger car was ready on February 23, Davis tried to delay delivery, because of the lack of progress on the P. & C., but the car was shipped on February 28 becoming West Virginia Central No. 7. This car can be seen behind the miners and deputies in Fig. 97.

The B. & O. was also giving Davis trouble by not supplying coal cars in adequate numbers. Davis complained to Spencer, that mines with smaller outputs were receiving more cars. The Atlantic mine for example, with about one third the output of Elk Garden, consistently received more B. & O. hoppers. Davis became even more upset when he found that the West Virginia Central's own cars would, in future, count in the Elk Garden allocation.

In March, Davis received announcements from both the B. &

O. and the Pennsylvania restricting the use of free annual passes in accordance with the recently passed Inter-state Commerce Law. Passes were issued regularly by the railroads to their employees and families and to the officers of other railroads, but also to politicians, law officers, newspaper editors, freight shippers and in fact anyone who the railroad managers thought could be of assistance to them. It was claimed in congressional hearings that the Pennsylvania had issued 60,000 passes and that in some instances, as many as 20 per-cent of a railroad's passengers were being carried free. The new law prompted both the B. & O. and the Pennsylvania to limit inter-state passes to their own employees and to officers of other rail-roads. Because the P. & C. passed through Maryland and was thus engaged in interstate commerce, Davis became concerned, and asked for the return of some passes already issued, noting that it was "the proper time to relieve ourselves of this burden." Davis continued to issue passes for intrastate use as before (Fig. 44).

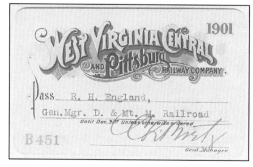

Fig. 44. Annual pass of the West Virginia Central and Pittsburg Railway

On April 12, Thomas A. Bradford, a director of the G. & G., wrote to Davis claim-ing that the B. & O. was ready to foreclose on a mortgage that they held on the road and which would give them ownership. Bradford asked Davis if he could be of any assistance in the event of a sale. Davis did not promise to take any action but confirmed that he hoped to build to Beverly.

Davis was to receive encouraging news during April of poten-tial new industries along the West Virginia Central. On April 5 a party looked over a site at Piedmont for a pulp and paper mill. Later, at the end of April, it was reported that shipments of iron ore were being made from Wilsonia, which it was hoped, would lead to a large mining industry.

The stockholders of the West Virginia Central, at a special meeting on April 28, approved of the plan to build in a southwester-ly direction towards Charleston. Davis also incorporated a new railroad at the same time, the Baltimore and Western Railway, with a capital stock of $2,000,000, and planned to run from Cumberland via Hancock to Hagerstown where it would connect with the W. Md. and the Cumberland Valley roads. These were ambitious plans when it is remembered that the P. & C. at this time was still bogged down at Cookerly Farm.

Work on the extension started immediately. On May 2, Porter was directed to clear off trees and undergrowth and commence grading one mile of line beyond the end of the present tracks, which had been located. Porter was placed in charge of construction except for the last two miles of the work, which were given to a contractor, John Doheny. The total distance of new construction was a lit-tle over eight miles. Joseph Crawford, who had been hired to work on the P. & C., was appointed consulting engineer for the new work.

By May, with the P. & C. still not finished, Davis was forced to ask Baldwin to hold up the delivery of Engines Nos. 7 and 8 until July. This was agreeable to Baldwin, which promised to ship the engines in mid-July (Figs. 45). Carlisle reported on June 4, that all but three of the 50 gondolas had been shipped. A further 50 hopper bottom gondolas were ordered from Carlisle in August.

At the end of May, Davis, Elkins and Parsons took a trip over the proposed new extension. The party left Deer Park and stayed overnight near the junction of the Blackwater and Shavers Fork. They then traveled to Beverly by way of Haddix Run and New Interest with Davis noting, "this route is quite practical for a road." The party went as far as Elk Water, 16 miles from Beverly, and were "favorably impressed by the Valley and its people."

Bradford wrote again in June reporting that he had filed an injunction to prevent the B. & O. voting the stock they had been given. Davis provided the $500 bond necessary for the injunction.

Davis contacted Charles Goldsborough in early June and offered him the post of assistant engineer on the extension at $125 per month. Goldsborough responded that he had received $200 per month on the B. & O. but would settle for $150. This was appar-ently acceptable to Davis and Goldsborough started work on June 25. Goldsborough, although officially assistant to Parsons, was responsible for the new work and reported directly to Davis.

Davis informed Garrett on June 27 of the incorporation of the B. & W., noting that the line would be easy to construct and require only two tunnels. Davis suggested that the B. & O., which had a double track main line between Cumberland and Cherry Run, haul the traffic over this section thus requiring the new road to build only 20 miles to Hagerstown. Negotiations dragged on for several months, but no satisfactory conclusion could be achieved.

Davis's interest in the B. & W. and the route towards Charleston had lessened his interest in a route from Davis east to tidewater. When he was approached by John S. Barbour to see if he would sell the charter of the Virginia and West Virginia Railroad, which had cost $2,000 to secure, he expressed an interest in a sale.

On July 20, two days after the first train ran on the finished P. & C., Davis and Elkins took an eight-day trip over the proposed southern extension. This time they were accompanied by their

Fig. 45. West Virginia Central No. 8 near Thomas circa 1890 Also in the picture is passenger car No. 11, and combination car No. 14 Collection of the Western Maryland Railway Historical Society

wives, and also by Davis's son, John T. Davis. The party journeyed in two wagons to the Tygart Valley River and Beverly, and then beyond to Mingo Flats. Here Davis noted that there was not as much timber as he had expected but that there were good grasslands. The party then went up to the watershed between the Tygart Valley River and the Elk River. Davis was encouraged by the trip and wrote in his diary, "route and resources of country better than we expected."

Goldsborough reported on the condition of the work on the extension at the end of July. The contractor, John Doheny, only had 40 men at work but expected to increase the number to 100 very shortly. Porter had 400 men at work but was reported to be paying higher wages than Doheny, which may have accounted for his problems with his men. In typical Davis fashion, Porter was ordered not to use trestles as, "I do not like trestles where they can be avoided," and to use stone culverts.

A new figure appeared on the scene in August when Elkins sold Richard C. Kerens 20 West Virginia Central six percent bonds for $20,000. Kerens was also granted an option on 80 more bonds. Kerens, of St. Louis, had been involved with Elkins in business dealings in the west and was now to become an important figure in the affairs of Davis and Elkins in the east (Fig. 46).

Davis and Elkins were along the line of the new road in the Blackwater Canyon at the end of August, this time accompanied by Joseph Crawford who had been rehired as a consulting engineer. Crawford made several minor improvements to the location particularly as regards the grades on curves and tangents. Crawford also planned the crossing of Tub Run, Big Run, Flat Rock Run and Spice Run, all of which presented interesting engineering challenges.

A party from the Pennsylvania Railroad took a trip over the P. & C. and the West Virginia Central as far as Davis. The party was led by Vice President Frank Thompson of the Pennsylvania and included Calton L. Bretz, train master of the Bedford Division, and James A. Millholland, general manager of the Georges Creek road. A few days later it was announced that Thomas Davis would resign his position as general manager of the West Virginia Central. It was reported on September 2, that Bretz had been offered the position but apparently declined. Captain George W. Harrison, was named the new superintendent of the railroad on September 13. However, Bretz, after meeting again with Davis and Elkins, wrote to Davis on October 1 saying he would accept the position if he could bring some of his own men with him and organize the railroad along the same lines as the Pennsylvania. No immediate decision was made. Other personnel changes occurred at the end of September, when Hopewell Hebb was appointed cashier, and Charles Steiner became train dispatcher.

The Pennsylvania continued to take an interest in the plans of the West Virginia Central and sent one of its engineers, Samuel Rea to examine the proposed eastern extension from Cumberland. Rea was not so confident as Davis that the route could be built easily.

Fig. 46. Richard C. Kerens
Collection of the University of Notre Dame Archives

Rea also looked at the possibility, suggested earlier by Elkins, of using the South Penn roadbed as part of a route to Harrisburg. Based on Rea's report, President Roberts recommended to Davis, that the B. & O. be used as far as Cherry Run and then a link of about four miles would be needed to connect with the Cumberland Valley. Davis had been negotiating with the B. & O. for a traffic agreement but the talks collapsed when the B. & O. entered into a period of financial instability leading to the resignation of Garrett on October 12. Garrett was succeeded as president by Samuel Spencer.

At the beginning of September, the line down Blackwater Canyon had been located across Flat Rock Run and Spice Lick Run, and Humbird was ready to commence the masonry work at the end of the month. Doheny's force had been increased to 110 men and four carts and was progressing fairly well according to Goldsborough. An explosion was reported to have occurred on September 21, which had injured three men, one possibly fatally, but no explanation of the incident was provided. Goldsborough recommended that a stone arch bridge should be constructed at Big Run and estimated the cost at $16,826. Parsons was notified by Davis that Humbird had contracted to build the arch. By October 17, Humbird was reported to be ready to start work on the structure. Davis noted in his diary on October 4 that the extension was going "very well."

On October 11 a bad wreck occurred on the Cumberland coal wharf when a West Virginia Central train of 20 loaded coal cars came onto the wharf too fast and collided with a line of stationary cars, knocking some off the track and tearing up the trestle. Engine No. 4 was dispatched to assist with the clean up but became derailed in the process. An engine, crane car and crew had to be borrowed from the Georges Creek railroad to help clear up the mess. This accident underscored the West Virginia Central's need for equipment to deal with such incidents.

Early in October, Davis again heard from Bradford, who was still resisting the B. & O's attempted takeover of the G. & G. According to Bradford, the B. & O. had commenced a survey from Buckhannon to the mouth of the Buckhannon River with the sole intention of keeping Davis out of this territory. This encouraged Davis to think in terms of an extension to Belington, but at the same time he wrote to a law firm in Beverly that he was not yet ready to start purchasing land in the area. Parsons was ordered to do a survey of the region between Belington and the Buckhannon River and his report was printed in the West Virginia Central's Sixth Annual Report published on January 24, 1888. This Report also contained a report on the line to Beverly. Parsons was enthusiastic about the coal and lumber resources, particularly along Roaring Creek, noting that one seam, the Upper Freeport, generally referred to as "Thomas coal," was ten feet thick. Parsons also mentioned the connections that could be made with the G. & G. and the proposed Baltimore, Grafton and Charleston Railroad. The report put the B. & O. on notice that Davis was serious about building west from Leadsville.

Davis returned from a trip over the extension on November 4 and again noted that everything was going well. He also wrote that the West Virginia Central was paying and "we all feel good." His enthusiasm was well founded at this time. The stonework at the Tub Run and Flat Rock abutments was being pushed and an additional 130 men had been put to work.

Davis further emphasized his interest in the Belington area by taking a trip with Elkins, starting on November 8, over the G. & G. to Belington. From Belington, the party took a wagon to Beverly, and then by way of Huttonsville to Helvetia. Davis noted that, "the road is very hilly." From Helvetia, Davis and Elkins returned to Buckhannon and then by a special train on Camden's road to Clarksburg.

Following their return, Elkins wrote to Camden, who had been expected to join the expedition, mentioning the B. & O.'s plans to extend to Buckhannon and that such an extension would hurt Camden's railroads. Elkins thought that the B. & O. eventually wanted to take over Camden's lines after it had gained control of the G. & G. He encouraged Camden to consider the purchase of G. & G. stock to get control of the road, and then to extend six miles to a connection with the West Virginia Central.

Back on the West Virginia Central, trouble occurred among the miners in the Upper Potomac region, when Davis attempted to move white miners from the No. 1 mine at Thomas to the No. 4 mine leaving only black miners at No. 1. The miners claimed that the coal at No. 4 was crossed by a layer of slate, which they had to remove at their own expense. This extra work did not allow them to make a living wage. When the miners refused to move, Davis fired 18 and the remainder went on strike on November 10. The striking miners were not supported by their colleagues at Elk Garden or Georges Creek, and the strike eventually fizzled out.

In the middle of November, the decision was made to allow Porter to take charge of all the construction in the Blackwater Canyon including that of Doheny. Goldsborough submitted a report on December 21, when the work had been closed up for the winter, listing the work that had been accomplished during the year. At this time one mile of new track had been laid from the Davis mine, located 1.1/4 miles from Thomas. The roadbed had been excavated as far as Tub Run, where a bridge consisting of two 55-foot girder spans was proposed. The masonry abutments for the bridge had been completed; the central pier remained to be built. Cuts and embankments were almost finished to Big Run where the 20-foot arch had been built up to the springing line. Between Big Run and Flat Rock Run and beyond to the end of the work, the cuts and fills were almost finished except for some additional widening. At Flat Rock Run, where a single 55-foot girder bridge was proposed, one abutment was complete and the foundation finished for the second abutment. The cuts on either side of Flat Rock Run had not been completed to facilitate the work on the abutments. At Spice Lick Run, a masonry box culvert was finished.

At the end of November, Superintendent Harrison was complaining about problems with the journals on the new cars delivered by Carlisle, which were running red-hot even when the car was not fully loaded. Harrison asked that no further cars be delivered until the problem was solved. At this time, Carlisle was building an additional 25 gondolas to be numbered 567-592. On Davis's

orders, these cars were painted green with white lettering.

Davis asked Baldwin to bid on two new freight engines, duplicates of No. 8, for April 1888 delivery. The bid was for $9,775 each; Davis offered $9,600, which was accepted by Baldwin. Davis also asked for bids on an officers' car.

The Buffalo Lumber Company was incorporated in December to build a mill at Bayard. The company also commenced building a narrow gauge railroad some seven miles up Buffalo Creek. This activity started a boom in the town with 20 houses already built by January 1888, and 40 lots sold. The first train over the new line was reported to have run in January 1888.

On December 24, Parsons was instructed to secure the right-of-way to Leadsville and to purchase several hundred acres of land for the junction of the proposed Beverly and Buckhannon lines. Thus by the end of the year, Davis was preparing to challenge the B. & O., both east of Cumberland and in the rich coal and timber lands of central West Virginia.

Davis was very busy during January 1888. He first wrote to Baldwin for a bid on a passenger engine similar to No. 7. Baldwin agreed to build the locomotive for $7,500 and expected to be able to deliver by April 1.

Parsons was ordered on January 7 to survey the Elk Garden and Abram Creek region to see if a railroad could be built directly from the mines to the West Virginia Central, which would avoid the use of the inclined planes. The problem facing Parsons was that Elk Garden lies at about 2,300 feet, while Shaw on Deep Run is at 1,300 feet and the mouth of Abram Creek is at 1,689 feet, both points being approximately 2.1/2 miles, in a straight line, from Elk Garden.

Negotiations also continued with Bretz for the general manager's position, which he was offered on January 11 at a salary of $2,000 per year. Bretz tentatively accepted but told Davis that he would need to agree to a suitable administrative organization for the railroad. Bretz indicated that he would bring his own chief clerk, a train master, and a maintenance-of-way supervisor with him from the Pennsylvania Railroad. He also stressed the need for a tool and derrick car. Davis had already agreed to this and also to moving Harrison from the superintendent's position to traffic agent. It was finally agreed that Bretz would take up his new duties on April 1 at a salary of $2,100 per year.

Davis also hired Charles H. Latrobe, a civil and consulting engineer, to be the consulting engineer on the West Virginia Central at a salary of $25 per day. Latrobe was the son of Benjamin H. Latrobe, who had been chief engineer on the early B. & O. He had begun his career in his father's office and later worked on the B. & O. After the Civil War he was engineer on several projects around Baltimore and in South America. Latrobe accepted the position on January 21, and was to remain associated with Davis and his railroads until his death in 1902. It is not clear why Davis did not continue to use Crawford as his consulting engineer. Crawford wrote to Davis in April that he was available, but by then Davis had hired Latrobe.

The need for a derrick car was again emphasized when Engine No. 4 and eight cars went into the Potomac River on January 13, after hitting a snow slide near Seymour. The wreck injured the fireman, Philip Combs, and a brakeman, Joseph Frost. The engineer, Edward Lippencott, escaped serious injury, but Davis was highly critical as Lippencott had been involved in several previous accidents. The snow slide took a day to clear; passengers were transferred round the obstruction until trains could pass. A week later, Engine No. 5 was sent up to assist in the rescue of No. 4, but was derailed in the process. Engine No. 7 was then sent to the rescue, which delayed a passenger train for over two hours. No 4 was finally fished out of the river and taken to West Virginia Central Junction for repairs.

Seymour seemed to attract an unusual amount of snow as another slide on February 11 delayed a passenger train for three and a half hours. A few days later it was a large rock falling onto the tracks that delayed trains.

At the annual meeting of the stockholders on January 24, it was ordered that the railroad should be extended to Leadsville. Davis was ready, and ordered Parsons to get bids for the cut at the Haddix summit which threatened to be the most difficult part of the new work. Parsons was instructed by Davis that Doheny was to be allowed to bid on the new work. With so much construction planned for the new season, Davis hired a new engineer, J. B. Rohrer, to start in March. His predecessor, Goldsborough, appears to have finished his work at the end of December.

At the same meeting, Davis reported that the P. & C. was being operated by the West Virginia Central on a temporary basis for 60 percent of the gross earnings until a permanent arrangement could be made. This temporary arrangement was to continue for two years.

On February 1, it was reported that the Empire Car Works of York, Pennsylvania was building 100 hopper cars, 60,000 lb. capacity for $470 each. Continued overheating problems with the Carlisle cars had finally convinced Davis to find another supplier. An order was also placed with Jackson and Sharp for a passenger car at a cost of $3,750 for April delivery. Again this car was to be paid for in coal, and became No. 8 when it was delivered. Davis also ordered the three 55 foot girder spans for the Tub Run and Flat Rock Run bridges from the Edge Moor Iron Company in February for delivery in May. Again he hoped to pay for the new bridges with coal.

Davis wrote to Parsons on February 18, instructing him to allow Doheny to bid on the work at Haddix summit. The dimensions for the cut at Haddix summit were noted as being 700 feet long and 40 feet deep at the deepest point. The material to be excavated would be mostly rock. Doheny bid 75 cents per cubic yard for the rock work and 22 cents per cubic yard for the removal of dirt, but Davis thought these figures were too high. Agreement was finally reached and Doheny was awarded the contract for the cut and half a mile of grading on either side on April 5.

Work on the extension resumed at the beginning of March when it was reported that laborers were being shipped from Cumberland to Thomas and labor contractors in Cumberland were trying to recruit more workers. Porter was instructed to pay the laborers $1.20 per day although the same class of worker had received $1.25 the previous year. Initially the reduction did not deter men; the Cumberland Evening Times

reported 200 blacks and Italians had left Cumberland on March 19 for the extension. However, by April the rate had been restored to $1.25 and a charge of $15 per month was made for room and board.

Rohrer was instructed to report to Porter on March 15, and was given charge of construction commencing about two miles below Thomas. Davis also hired two young men to assist Rohrer. The first was Janon Fisher, "who has taken a course in engineering at Princeton College." The second was the son of President Hood of the W. Md., who "has also had some collegiate training and some field experience."

It was reported on March 10 that the J. L. Rumbarger Lumber Company had sold the mill at Davis to the Blackwater Boom and Lumber Company. One of the stockholders of the new company, A. Thompson, became general manager at Davis. The mill at Dobbin belonging to Rumbarger was not included in the sale.

Hood of the W. Md. finally presented a bill in March to the Maryland legislature to allow that company to lease the upper section of the C. & O. Canal between Cumberland and Williamsport, and to use it to build a railroad. He was supported in this effort by President Gambrill of the canal company and by Davis. Hood offered to pay an annual rent of $40,000 for the use of the canal bed, and pointed out that the new railroad would connect with the West Virginia Central (Fig. 47), to eventually give a new line from Baltimore to the southwest. The move was opposed by Cumberland and other interests and did not pass the legislature.

Davis was able to come to an agreement with the B. & O. in March to take traffic destined for that road at Cumberland instead of Piedmont, which was more profitable for the West Virginia Central. A suitable connection would need to be established in

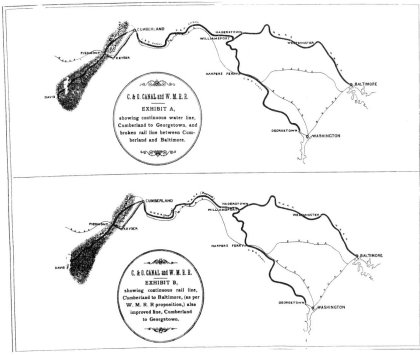

Fig. 47. Western Maryland Rail Road and the Chesapeake and Ohio Canal
West Virginia and Regional History Collection,
West Virginia University Library

Cumberland for the transfer.

Bretz arrived on April 1 to take up his new duties bringing with him from the Pennsylvania J. W. Galbreath as supervisor, and F. P. Naughton as train master. One of the first tasks for Galbreath was to recommend where a connection in Cumberland with the B. & O. should be made. It was eventually decided to make the connection near the B. & O.'s Cumberland viaduct.

Parsons submitted his report on the proposed Elk Garden branch on April 5, which showed two possibilities, the first a five mile route using Deep Run and costing $65,000, and the second a six mile long route using Abram Creek and costing $75,000. The Abram Creek route had less severe grades and fewer switchbacks and also would serve mines at Hartmansville and was therefore recommended to Davis.

It was not long before Bretz was exposed to the problems of the West Virginia Central. At 10:40 A.M. on April 8, Engine No. 7 and a combination car derailed and went down a bank at Dobbin Run near Child on the Davis branch. Bretz reported that there were no wreck tools, derrick or extra power to assist in the rescue, and it was 6:00 P.M. before a wreck train could be assembled, with tools borrowed from the B. & O. The engine was returned to the track by the evening of April 9, and the tender and passenger car the following day. The wreck was reported to be due to bad track and worn wheels. Bretz immediately ordered three hydraulic jacks and inquired about purchasing a derrick car.

Bretz was now short of power until the two new freight engines, Nos. 9 and 10, were shipped by Baldwin on April 23 arriving two days later (Fig. 48). To help keep things moving until the new engines arrived, Bretz was forced to borrow No. 934 from the Pennsylvania at a rent of $37.28 per month. Two cabooses were purchased from the Pennsylvania at the same time for $325 each.

Bretz was in need of the Pennsylvania locomotive when on April 23, Engine No. 3 heading north with 15 loaded cars, hit a stump two miles north of Blaine and was derailed. The engineer, Isaiah Riley, reported that he was traveling at about 12 mph at the time of the accident. Five cars were over the bank; three boxcars were badly smashed, but two gondolas were not so severely damaged. The engine was retracked on the 24th ; the freight cars remained until the following Sunday before they were picked up.

On April 16, Bretz sent Davis a list of all the freight equipment owned by the West Virginia Central on that date (Table 1).

Table 1
Freight Equipment owned by the
West Virginia Central, April 16, 1888

Kind	Capacity	From	To	Total
Iron coal hoppers	30,000	1	200	200
Flat cars	40,000	300	303	4
Gondola, flat bottom	40,000	500	502	3
" , " "	30,000	503	506	4
" , " "	50,000	507	566	60
" , " "	60,000	567	606	40
Box	50,000	700	703	4
"	50,000	704	709	6
Gondola hopper bottom	60,000	800	949	150
" " "	60,000	950	1049	100

Numbers 951 to 1049 were being built by Schall and King with the first 50 to be delivered by the end of April. Fifty additional boxcars were being built by the South Baltimore Car and Foundry Company and these were numbered 710-759 when delivered.

The next concern addressed by Bretz was the lack of suitable passing places for freight trains, which was causing a disruption in service. Such disruptions would only get worse as traffic increased. It was reported for example, that Fayerweather and Ladew would ship 35 cars of bark per day during the summer, twice the business of the previous year.

Work was moving ahead steadily on the extension, although persistent rains in the spring caused some delay. Humbird reported on April 10 that the masonry for the Tub Run and Flat Rock bridges should be finished by June 1, and the arch at Big Run about one month later. The Flat Rock Run bridge masonry was finished on April 29. Humbird was awarded the contract for the masonry on the Blackwater and Shavers Fork bridges where they joined to form the Cheat River. By the middle of May, Porter was urging Humbird to have the stone ready for the bridges as Davis wanted to be in Leadsville before winter. Davis visited the work on May 10, and was in a highly optimistic mood a few days later when he noted in his diary, "We are pushing the extension of the West Virginia Central, expect to get to Leadsville by fall," and also noting that the, "coal trade is good." Davis notified Parsons on May 14, that Rohrer would be transferred from work in the Canyon to supervise the construction of the Elk Garden branch. H. T. Douglas became assistant engineer for the Canyon work but resigned at the end of June apparently unable to understand his role in the construction team. He was replaced by Janon Fisher who had been his assistant.

Latrobe, who had designed the bridges at the crossing of Shavers

Fig. 48. West Virginia Central No. 10
Western Maryland Railway Historical Society

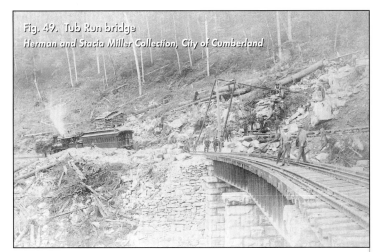

and Blackwater, awarded the contract for the steelwork to A. P. Roberts of the Pencoyd Works in Philadelphia for $30,450. The bridges were to be ready for erection by August 10. The girders for the Tub Run and Flat Rock Run bridges were shipped on June 6. The bridge at Tub Run was completed on July 23, and is shown in Fig. 49 shortly after completion.

Davis received surprising news from Bretz on June 4 when Bretz submitted his resignation. No reason was given by Bretz, but it seemed that Davis managed to convince his general manager to remain and Bretz's service to the West Virginia Central continued.

Bretz's first problem in June, having withdrawn his resignation was to recommend the purchase of additional, more powerful, locomotives, which would be required on the Blackwater grade and the Elk Garden branch. One new engine, slightly larger than Nos. 9 and 10 was ordered in July from Baldwin. Meanwhile, Engine No. 11 (Fig. 50) was received from Baldwin on June 29, which allowed the leased Pennsylvania Railroad No. 934 to be returned.

At the end of June with work in the Canyon well advanced, Parsons was instructed to survey a route from Leadsville to Belington. Porter wrote to Davis on June 30, noting that the stonework at the Big Run bridge was finished (Fig. 51), and that track laying would commence south of Tub Run.

On June 30, Davis wrote to Latrobe noting that the track was expected to be laid to the Cheat River by August 10. Latrobe was instructed to order an engine and pump for the foundation work on the two bridges at this point. Davis also discussed the establishment of a Post Office at the junction of the Blackwater and Shavers Fork, to be known as "Parsons." It was Davis's expectation that Parsons would become the county seat of Tucker County replacing St. George, six miles down the Cheat. Davis also recommended naming the area at the mouth of Abram Creek on the North Fork "Harrison."

Davis paid a visit to the extension in early July going as far as Leadsville and returning by way of Grafton. He noted that 1,000 men were at work. Davis decided to go again but had to cancel when heavy rain, starting on July 8, prevented Porter getting horses to meet Davis. The rains continued through July 9, causing severe flooding throughout the upper Potomac basin and causing extensive damage to the West Virginia Central and the P. & C. Porter reported that the Blackwater was higher than ever recorded, but the bridges in

the canyon were all safe, although the new bridges on the Cheat would have to be five feet higher than planned. A landslide, the largest ever seen by Porter, occurred in a cut south of Big Run. Bretz reported several major washouts, including one at Schell that would need a trestle to get across. Other washouts were 20 feet deep and would also require trestles to allow the trains to proceed as soon as possible. All of the bridges were safe, although considerable trestling in the vicinity of Westernport was washed away. This prompted a letter from Meyer, who thought the C. & P. bridge at Piedmont was in danger from debris, should a wooden bridge, belonging to H. G. Davis and Brother, be washed out. Traffic on the West Virginia Central had to be suspended for ten days until repairs could be made.

The slide south of Big Run was so immense that Porter reported there was no hope of digging out the original line, and was forced to grade a new route around it. Parsons reported at the end of July, that Porter had moved some of his men to work on the route up Haddix Run, and expected soon to have 300 men at work between Doheny's work and Shavers Fork. Latrobe visited the work at the end of July and ordered the proposed bridge across the Blackwater River to be raised nearly five feet to ensure its safety in future floods. The track also was raised at other points where it was judged susceptible to flooding.

Bretz still was wrestling with problems caused by poor track, overworked locomotives and poorly motivated employees. The latter problem was emphasized when Engine No. 4 ran into some stationary cars damaging the cab and tender of the engine. The engineer was immediately suspended. Bretz thought that by instituting a bonus scheme for workers and providing such benefits as reading rooms, a better class of employee would be attracted to the company. Such benevolence would not have helped a day or two later, when on August 3, Engine No. 7 struck a cow between West Virginia Central Junction and Shaw. The engine rolled down the bank and would have ended up in the river, if it had not been stopped by a large rock. The tender and a passenger car were also derailed. No passengers were injured and the only injury among the crew was to the fireman, Patrick Niland, who sprained his ankles when he attempted to jump clear. The track was blocked for a day, but No. 7 could not be rescued until August 12. Again, Bretz was forced to borrow a Pennsylvania Railroad locomotive to keep things moving. A couple of days later Engine No. 2 was derailed by an act of vandalism, and three cars derailed when a brakeman

Fig. 50. West Virginia Central No. 11 (undated)
Collection of William Metheny

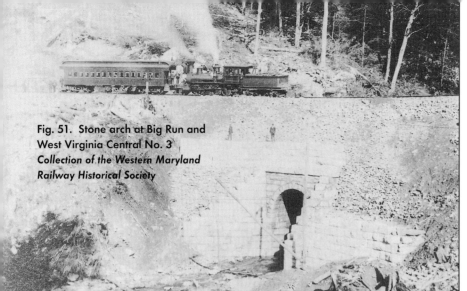

Fig. 51. Stone arch at Big Run and West Virginia Central No. 3
Collection of the Western Maryland Railway Historical Society

threw a switch incorrectly.

Latrobe noted on August 12 that he had contracted with the Edge Moor company to supply the girders for the bridges at Falling Spring Run and Roaring Run and also at Abrams Creek on the Elk Garden branch. Latrobe again wrote to Davis on August 15, reporting that the steelwork for the Blackwater and Shavers Fork bridges was about ready to be shipped, but shipment was delayed until September 1 as track laying had not yet reached the site of the Blackwater bridge . Davis ordered Porter to install a siding at Hendricks to hold the cars on which the girders would be shipped until the steel was needed.

More trouble occurred on August 21 when further flooding was expected but fortunately the damage was restricted to one washout near Schell. Bretz reported that they were shipping ties for the Cheat extension, but that he needed some on the existing trackage, particularly between Shaw and West Virginia Central Junction, "which is not safe to run our heavy coal trains over," according to Bretz.

On August 25, the new connection with the B. & O. at Cumberland was finished and the first train ran over it. It was also reported that a four stall roundhouse was being erected and that a Keystone turntable would be installed.

A wreck occurred on August 25 at the grade crossing in Westernport when a couple of cars loaded with mine props derailed and blocked the C. & P. line. A C. & P. excursion was just leaving Piedmont at the time and reached the middle of the Potomac River bridge before it was stopped. The C. & P. track was not cleared until 11.00 P.M. allowing the excursion to pass. This incident must have confirmed Mayer's worst fears but he was strangely quiet, possibly because C. & P. crews were busy fishing one of their engines out of Georges Creek after a wreck that had killed an engineer.

Bretz did receive a little relief for his problems early in September, when Engine No. 12 was delivered by Baldwin. No. 12 had been ordered originally by the Pennsylvania Railroad, but because of the urgent need of the West Virginia Central, General Manager Pugh had allowed it to be shipped to Bretz. No. 12 cost $11,535, which was nearly $2,000 more than Nos. 9 and 10. A new crane car, with a capacity of 15 tons, was delivered from Bay City,

Michigan at about the same time. During August, Bretz had also complained about a coal car shortage, and Davis had ordered fifty, 60,000 pound hopper gondolas from the Empire Car Works for $450 each. At the end of the month, 50 hoppers and 50 flat cars were ordered from the Ensign Manufacturing Company of Huntington, West Virginia.

Davis finally took Bretz's advice on September 1, when he instituted a two-tier salary schedule for freight train crews. After satisfactory service for one year, an employee would receive a pay increase; for example, an engineer in his first year of employment received $3.00 per day, but in his second year it increased to $3.25 per day. Other ranks received similar increases.

On September 3, Davis took a trip over the extension to Leadsville and then on to Beverly and Roaring Creek. He noted that the track was now within one mile of the Blackwater bridge, which should be reached by September 10. Davis thought the Blackwater and Shavers Fork bridges should be finished in 40 days, and still thought it possible to get to Leadsville by December 15. However, this was beginning to look rather doubtful. Doheny had failed in the Haddix summit work, and Humbird was slow with the masonry work at the new bridge sites. Porter reported on September 20 that one channel pier at Blackwater was up ten feet, and that work had just started on a channel pier at Shavers Fork. The foundations for both bridges were finished on October 7 according to Porter. High water on October 9 slowed the work but two days later, Latrobe reported to Davis that on the Blackwater bridge, only one channel pier had been finished, and three piers partly finished. This left three piers and the abutments, which had not even been started. Because of the delay Latrobe was compelled to postpone the arrival of the steel erectors until October 20. Porter reported that the bridge men had arrived on October 21, but again heavy rains caused delays. It was to be November 5 before the erectors could place the first span from the shore to the first pier on the Blackwater bridge. At the Shavers bridge at this time, two piers were finished and the abutments had been commenced. No work had been done on a smaller bridge across a millrace. Latrobe was doubtful if Parsons would be reached by Christmas.

Other developments in the fall, which were to have an impact on the West Virginia Central, were the purchase of the sawmill at West Piedmont belonging to H. G. Davis and Brother by the Luke brothers who wished to build a pulp mill at that point. The brothers incorporated the Piedmont Pulp and Paper Company in October 1888 but did not commence construction of the plant until May 1889. The first pulp from the new facility was shipped in the fall of the same year. Six more coke ovens were reported to be under construction at Thomas, which would bring the number of ovens in the Upper Potomac region to 30 by the end of the year.

Bretz reported on October 21, that depots were commenced at Thomas and Harrison to facilitate the increased business at these points. Six waiting sheds had recently been completed on the P. & C., including the one at Pinto shown in Fig. 52. The new four-stall roundhouse and turntable at Cumberland were finished at the beginning of October (Fig. 53), and the Y that had been used to turn engines was removed.

Fig. 52. Waiting shed at Pinto

Parsons, during the fall, spent time surveying in the Buckhannon and Middle Fork area, which prompted A. H. Kunst, general superintendent of the Weston and Buckhannon Railroad, to ask Camden if Davis intended to invade their territory. Kunst recommended that if Davis did intend to build to Buckhannon, Camden should extend his road up the Buckhannon River, which was a rich timber country. A few days later, G. A. Newlon, superintendent of the Buckhannon River Lumber Company, wrote to Davis asking what his intentions were, but Davis was noncommittal in his reply. The lumber company owned a narrow gauge railroad up the Buckhannon River, which would be valuable to either Davis or Camden if the two became rivals in the area. That such rivalry would occur became likely when Camden approached Mayer, the new president of the B. & O., to sign a contract allying the Camden roads with the B. & O. Camden had had talks with Spencer about expanding to Fairmont from Clarksburg and also to Sutton. Camden wanted the B. & O. to guarantee the interest on $600,000 of bonds, which would allow Camden to make the necessary investments in mines and coke ovens. Camden estimated that the extensions would generate $1,000,000 extra revenue for the B. & O. and "the B. & O. thoroughly fortified in West Virginia."

What Davis's plans were at this time are not entirely clear. An extension to Buckhannon would have allowed him to connect with Camden's road and given him a route to Clarksburg and perhaps ultimately to Pittsburgh. Elkins was in Pittsburgh at this time meeting with some major industrialists including H. C. Frick. After the meeting, Elkins told a reporter for the Pittsburgh Commercial Gazette that the group had discussed a plan to extend the West Virginia Central down the Monongahela River to a junction with the Pennsylvania Railroad. This would give "an elegant short line from the headwaters of the Ohio to the Tygart Valley River." It would be two years before anything further occurred on this plan.

Bretz returned to the question of locomotives at the end of November. The West Virginia Central was using a Pennsylvania locomotive, No. 814 and offered to buy it, but the Pennsylvania offered to fix up another engine, No. 540, which was delivered on January 5, 1889, at a cost of $2,500. This engine was later renumbered as No. 16. Bretz was also faced with overhauling some of the older engines and finding an engine to work on the Elk Garden branch, which was due to open in December. Bretz recommended fitting all the engines and passenger cars with Westinghouse air brakes; at the time only one engine, No. 11, and one passenger car had these brakes. Bretz recommended the change be made as soon

Fig. 53. Roundhouse and yards at Cumberland, circa 1891. A West Virginia Central three-pot iron hopper car can be seen to the right of center. Several similar B. & O. cars are to the left of the roundhouse
Herman and Stacia Miller Collection, City of Cumberland

as possible. Davis instructed Bretz to order a fourth freight engine from Baldwin, and to get bids on a passenger engine similar to No. 11 for delivery in May 1889. The freight engine was ordered in December for April 1889 delivery.

Davis ran a special train from Cumberland to the still incomplete Blackwater bridges on November 16. The train consisted of two private cars belonging to the B. & O. and was pulled by Engine No. 11. The party consisted of a number of "prominent gentlemen" in addition to Davis and Camden. The party examined the tannery and mill at Davis before descending the Blackwater Canyon. On returning to Cumberland, the inspection was pronounced "most satisfactory."

Latrobe reported on the bridgework on November 30; at the Blackwater bridge at Parsons three spans were in place and the final abutment would be ready in time for the steelwork. Latrobe gave orders for wooden abutments to be built at the millrace so that stone could be placed later. The Shavers Fork masonry was finished and the steel was arriving. Latrobe also examined the millrace at the island at West Piedmont and recommended that the trestle there be replaced with a 60-foot girder bridge.

At the beginning of December, the depot at Thomas was finished; the depot at Harrison was finished by January 21, 1889 (Fig. 54). However, the big news was the completion of the Elk Garden branch, and the passage of the first train of two loaded coal cars from No. 4 mine on December 1. Mine No. 1 commenced shipping on December 11. The cost of the branch, according to Davis, was nearly $100,000.

Elk Garden was now an established town with four working mines and a fifth being established. Four hundred and eighty miners were employed; additional men were being used as laborers and drivers. An Odd Fellows Hall was being built which would seat 500; 20 new houses were also under construction. Sixteen businesses had been established including an oyster saloon, and there were three churches (Fig. 55). Narrow gauge Engine No. 2 was still in service on the tramroad; how long it remained after the completion of the new branch is not known.

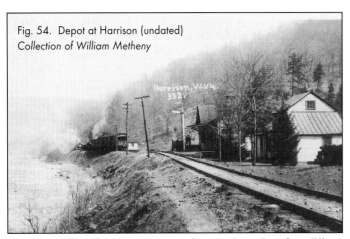

Fig. 54. Depot at Harrison (undated)
Collection of William Metheny

An additional mine was operated across Deep Run from Elk Garden by the Atlantic and Georges Creek Consolidated Coal Corporation. A 1,680 foot plane was used to take the coal down to the Mineville branch.

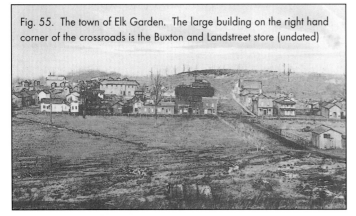

Fig. 55. The town of Elk Garden. The large building on the right hand corner of the crossroads is the Buxton and Landstreet store (undated)

On December 19, Davis wrote to Parsons and told him not use the name "Leadsville" in future, as henceforth it would be known as "Elkins." The village that had been known as Elkins would become "Gorman." This in turn required a new name for the village that had previously been known as Gorman and this became Steyer. Davis contacted the assistant postmaster general in Washington D. C., and asked that the name of the post office be changed to Elkins. Bretz recommended that "Davis Mine" just below Thomas be renamed and in July 1890, it became "Coketon." On January 21, 1889, Bretz reported that a switch had been installed in readiness for a new pulp mill in West Piedmont, and requested a name for the site. Davis recommended the name "Luke," which was the family name of the owners.

Work on the extension was closed up in the middle of December and most of the men paid off. Porter recommended that work start on the cut near Leadsville which threatened to be heavy, as early as February to keep out of the way of the tracklayers. On December 13, Porter reported that the steelwork on the Blackwater bridge was finished, the temporary wooden abutments at the mill race were ready for the girders, and the falsework was being erected at the Shavers Fork bridge. On December 15, the girders on the millrace bridge were being placed and the track laying finished to that point. All the men, except the tracklayers and the bridge crews, had now been laid off.

By January 5, 1889, Porter reported that all the bridgework

was complete except for some riveting which was expected to take no more than three days to finish. A gang of 25 men was completing the last fill at the east abutment of the Blackwater bridge, and when this was finished, Porter hoped to be able to lay track to Parsons. Three days later, track was laid across the bridges. Latrobe made a final report on the bridges on January 14 and noted the line would be in Parsons by January 25. The masonry at the Roaring Run bridge would be finished in a week, the steelwork was ready for erection. Latrobe also recommended that the tracks at Thomas be realigned to make the extension the main line; the line to Davis would then become a branch.

Parsons was finally reached and the first engine, Porter's construction engine, No. 3, ran into the village on January 19, 1889. Work continued at Roaring Run, where the stonework was expected to be finished by January 24.

Engine No. 13 was received on January 9, and was immediately placed in service (Fig. 56). The new engine's arrival was timely as Engine No. 2 had its main frame broken in two places and was in need of general overhaul. The engine was sent to Baldwin for a repair that was estimated to take six weeks and cost $3,000. Baldwin was scheduled to deliver the next two locomotives on February 9; these became Nos. 14 and 15 when received. The Pennsylvania engine, No. 814, was finally returned on February 13.

Davis finally agreed to purchase a combination mail, baggage and passenger car and an officers' car from the South Baltimore Car and Foundry Company on January 14. A second similar combination car was ordered from Jackson and Sharp although this company eventually received the order for both combination cars. An order was placed with South Baltimore for 40 boxcars, 50,000 lb. capacity costing $500 each because of the anticipated need in the bark trade. This business was expected to increase dramatically when it was announced that a tannery was to be built at Gorman by J. G. Hoffman and Son. The new tannery was expected to be even larger than the one at Davis.

On January 11, Davis noted in his diary that he was organizing a new company, the Davis Coal and Coke Company, which would take over the operations of the various small coal companies owned by Davis and Elkins. Another company, organized by Davis during 1889, was the Buxton and Landstreet Company. The company, with Harry Buxton as president and Landstreet as secretary and treasurer, was incorporated to provide company stores in the mining towns. By 1892, stores were in operation in Coketon and Thomas.

Davis must have been feeling optimistic at the time of the stockholders' meeting in Baltimore on January 22, but he cannot have been too pleased to see Irvine Cross there holding a proxy to 10,000 votes belonging to Shaw and his allies. Davis no doubt hoped that his hand-picked board of directors would continue to serve, but William Barnum resigned due to ill health allowing Shaw to be elected in his place. Shaw had not served as a director since 1886. Cross attempted to get himself elected as a director by claiming that he could vote his 10,000 shares cumulatively as was permitted under the laws of West Virginia. This was denied by the Davis group, which claimed that the West Virginia Central's charter predated the law permitting cumulative voting. Cross took the matter to the Circuit Court of Mineral County, which, in March ordered

Fig. 56. West Virginia Central No. 13
Collection of the Western Maryland Railway Historical Society

the West Virginia Central to either hold a special election to elect nine directors to serve with Cross, or to show cause why they should refuse. The railroad claimed that Cross was not a stockholder and this view was upheld by the court in early May. This was the beginning of a long effort by Cross, aided by Shaw, to get a seat on the board of the West Virginia Central.

Davis was involved in another legal battle with Cross during the spring of 1889. This had its origins in a contract signed in 1875 by the North Branch Coal Company to supply coal for three years to the B. & O. from a mine near Bloomington. Davis, through one of his companies, had lent William Brydon, president of North Branch, $3,000 to enable the company to mine the coal. When the coal delivered to the B. & O. began to deteriorate in quality, the B. & O. refused to take any more setting off a prolonged legal battle. Brydon and Davis were eventually awarded $75,000 in damages, but Malcolm Sinclair, a stockholder of the North Branch company, got an injunction to prevent them from collecting the money. Cross became involved as counsel for Sinclair when the case was heard in Baltimore on July 14, 1887, two days after the settlement of the Cookerly Farm affair by Elkins and Mayer. The injunction was upheld when the court ruled on September 26, 1888, in favor of Sinclair. Davis professed not to be too concerned as he held a lien on the North Branch property. The claim of Sinclair was upheld by the Maryland Court of Appeals in March 1889.

On January 31, a wreck occurred on the Mineville branch when Engine No. 5 became "unmanageable" and ran away, crashing into cars standing at Shaw. The damage was confined to standing cars and no one was injured. Bretz noted that the rails were frosty and the engine did not have driving wheel brakes. Bretz also examined the Elk Garden branch and complained that it was in very poor condition, the rails already bending from the weight of coal trains. Davis also was concerned about the Elk Garden branch as it was not generating the savings he had expected. He complained to A. C. Rawlings, the superintendent of mines, about the cost of the coal; he returned to the subject later claiming that he had expected savings of five cents per ton of coal but was getting only one cent.

At the end of December 1888, Camden had written to Mayer, the new president of the B. & O., mentioning his plans for his various railroads, and the freight that could accrue to the B. & O. if he

could proceed with an expansion. Camden asked that the B. & O.'s credit be used to sell $600,000 in bonds. Some form of agreement was made between Camden and Mayer and was noted in the newspapers in January. What Davis thought of his colleague's increasingly close ties with the B. & O. is not known, but he did inform Newlon that he doubted if it would have an impact on the Buckhannon area. He also decided to take a closer look at the G. & G.

Porter wrote to Davis on February 7 reporting that track was laid to a point one mile beyond Parsons, but work had ceased because of the bad weather. Davis recommended that the men be laid off until conditions improved.

Galbreath submitted to Bretz on February 15, plans for new bridges at Westernport, the millrace at the pulp mill and at Wilsonia where a 15-foot stone arch was recommended to replace a trestle. This had to allow for the passage of an existing tramroad and was completed one year later (Fig. 57). Humbird was invited to bid on the masonry for these projects.

Fig. 57. Stone arch bridge at Dobbin Run
Collection of the Western Maryland Railway Historical Society

It was reported also at the end of February, that John G. Hoffman of the tanning company J. G. Hoffman and Sons, had purchased land at Gormania, across the river from Gorman, to erect a "really big establishment." The company already owned a tannery at Wheeling but was attracted to Gormania by the readily available hemlock bark. The company hoped to build as soon as the weather permitted and be ready for production by the fall. Hoffman visited the site with Bretz on March 1 and asked that a bridge be built across the North Branch as soon as possible to allow construction material to be moved to the site. Bretz recommended putting in a trestle across the North Branch to serve the new tannery at a cost of $2,945. Although it was recognized that the trestle would be subject to destruction by floods, the cost of a wooden or iron bridge at about $7,500, was too high and it could not be built in time to satisfy the tannery owners. By April 20 material for the new tannery was reported to be arriving by rail, the trestle having been completed. The tannery was expected to be finished by November and employ 150 men. The new trestle was put to the test in June 1890 when heavy rains led to high water on the North Branch. A logjam formed against the trestle but the structure held firm although there were fears that it would lead to flooding in Gormania. An illustration of the tannery in the 1920's is shown in Fig. 289. Coal had been discovered near Gorman in the fall of 1888 by the Spring Garden Coal and Coke Company so the prospects for the twin towns appeared promising. Perhaps because of all the activity promised for the Gorman area, the depot there was remodeled during 1889 and is

Fig. 58. Depot at Gorman, circa 1910
Collection of Jane Barb

shown a few years later in Fig. 58.

An agreement was reached with Westinghouse Air Brake Company to install that company's brakes on all the passenger equipment commencing March 1. The combination cars being built by Jackson and Sharp would have these brakes fitted before delivery. The two cars were scheduled to be delivered in April, becoming Nos. 9 and 10 (Fig. 59).

Contracts were let in March for station buildings at Elk Garden and Parsons, similar to the one completed at Harrison, for $1,312.50 each. The depot at Elk Garden (Fig. 60) was due to be finished by the end of April, the one at Parsons at the end of May (Fig. 61). Bretz hoped to have trains running to Parsons from Thomas by March 28, but due to the unsettled nature of the track it was to be April 1, before the scheduled service started (Fig. 62).

By March 22 work was proceeding on the cut leading to Elkins and track was being laid at a rate of about a quarter of a mile each day. A month later the track had reached Montrose and it was expected that Elkins would be reached by July 1. Latrobe prepared a plan for the new town on April 6, showing the layout of the streets and the location of the depot and roundhouse (Fig. 63). On May 3, Davis went to the end of the extension and then over to Elkins and looked over the site of the new town for a place for the house that Elkins proposed to build.

Bretz was back on the Elk Garden branch in the middle of April and reported that it was still in bad condition, although two gangs of men were constantly employed in improving the track. Two slides came down which delayed trains for several hours, confirming Bretz's earlier comments that the line had been cheaply built. Bretz was able to report that the depot at Elk Garden would open on April 27.

Davis was to show a renewed interest in the G. & G. during May and he received a report from Bradshaw showing the financial stake of the B. & O. in the line. Bradshaw noted that if the G. & G. board issued 2,500 shares to extend the road, it would give the owner absolute control. News of these negotiations leaked to Newlon who still tried to interest Davis in a Buckhannon line. Newlon claimed he would have to sell his tramroad to the B. & O. - Camden system as it would have a stranglehold on the town. Davis was not able to give Newlon any news that would relieve him of his anguish.

Davis and Camden seemed to be on a collision course at this

Fig. 59. West Virginia Central combination car No. 10. Jackson and Sharp Company builder's photograph
Collection of the Delaware State Archives

time as their rival railroads were moving towards building into the same areas. Davis's reaction is not known to an offer by Camden to Alexander Shaw, to take part in a Camden coal enterprise on the Monongahela River. Davis, however, seemed content to continue with his plans, which included asking Latrobe and Parsons to determine the most economical line to Beverly.

Davis also was still interested in the Roaring Creek coal field and in January had asked I. C. White, a geology professor from West Virginia University, to examine the field. Davis had earlier been approached by F. Brandenburg of Pittston, Pennsylvania, to see if he was interested in the field. While waiting for White's report, Davis wrote to Brandenburg to see if he was still interested in selling. When Brandenburg offered to lease the field, Davis responded on March 2, claiming that he was not interested. He noted that a railroad of about ten miles in length would have to be built into the field and that the grade between Roaring Creek and the upper Potomac was "very heavy and expensive."

White's report was submitted on June 14 and showed that there were two veins of coal that were important. South of Belington, the Masontown coal occurred in a four-foot seam some 60 feet above the Tygart Valley River. This was a good coal for domestic purposes giving a hot, lasting fire. Along Roaring Creek, the Upper Freeport or Thomas coal occurred in veins that averaged seven feet of good coal, although the seam was interspersed with some slate. This coal was reported to be a good coking coal as it was low in sulfur and the coke was firm and strong. The availability of this field for coking coal was important as the Connellsville field, which supplied the Pittsburgh ironworks, was expected to be

Fig. 60. Depot at Elk Garden
Collection of the Western Maryland Railway Historical Society

Fig. 61. Parsons depot in its Western Maryland Railway days (undated)

Fig. 62. First train to leave Thomas for Parsons, April 1, 1889

exhausted in another 20 years. White also mentioned that the Davis or Lower Kittanning seam, which occurred below the Thomas coal, had not been explored in the area and that a shaft of 40 feet at the mouth of Beaver Creek, would test the character of this coal. White concluded by estimating the field to contain 50,000,000 tons of marketable coal, excluding the Davis coal.

Davis's response to White's report was that it was not as encouraging as expected. However, at the same time he had an agent out in the field trying to purchase land without it being known that Davis was interested. Davis at this time was faced with a more immediate problem than the Roaring Creek coal.

Rain started to fall during the morning of May 30, and continued until June 1. Initial reports showed Piedmont to be flooded, and trestles on both the B. & O. and the West Virginia Central to have been washed out. The flood was reported to be the highest ever in the region. Davis noted in his diary that there was little damage south of Piedmont, but between Piedmont and Cumberland three bridges were washed out that would cost $25,000 to replace, although this estimate was later increased to $40,000. The bridges were at Potomac, McKenzies and Caudy's Farm. Trestles at Westernport and Keyser were also destroyed. The West Virginia Central was closed for two days, but the P. & C. was closed for ten days and two weeks after the flood, traffic was still being delivered to the B. & O. at West Virginia Central Junction.

The same floods also caused considerable damage to the C. & O. Canal, sufficient to cause a total cessation of traffic. Because the canal company had insufficient funds to repair the damage, it remained in a devastated state. John A. Hambleton and Company, the Baltimore bankers with close ties to Davis, recommended that the next session of the Maryland legislature should consider selling the canal.

Brandenburg, who had been rebuffed by Davis in March about the Roaring Creek coalfield, tried again in June. This time he was joined by William Benedict, who was a partner with Brandenburg in The United States Coal, Iron and Manufacturing Company. The company owned 3,215 acres and held leases on an additional 2,000 acres of land in the Roaring Creek field. Davis still refused to be directly involved but continued to work through a middleman.

At the end of June, Parsons was down on the Williams and Gauley Rivers looking for a possible route. He noted that the Gauley River would be an easy river to build down, and although there was good timber, the coal seams appeared thin. Davis decided to send Riordan down to examine the coal fields in detail.

Engine No. 2 was received back from Baldwin at the end of May. Bretz became concerned about Engine No. 1 a couple of months later when major repairs were required. He reported to Davis that it would require at least $1,000 to repair the engine. Davis thought that if a few hundred dollars would fix up the engine for light duties that the money should be spent, but when this turned out to be impractical, the engine was scrapped. The new officers' car, named "West Virginia," was received at the end of July, and both Davis and Elkins pronounced themselves pleased with the car. On August 6, Davis and Elkins took a trip over the road in their new car.

Latrobe submitted plans for the freight house and roundhouse at Elkins to Davis at the beginning of July. He also sent proposals for a depot and an office building at the same location. Davis thought that a five-stall roundhouse would suffice rather than the nine stall proposed by Latrobe. Latrobe had also contracted with the Pencoyd Iron Works to supply the ironwork to replace the three wrecked bridges on the P. & C. Four spans were ordered, three of 120 feet and one of 124' 6" at a cost of $20,869. The new bridges were to be delivered by October 10. One bridge, at Potomac, was to be raised five feet to secure it from future floods. The other bridges needed a variety of pier and abutment work before they could be replaced. Latrobe also thought that the wrecked bridges should be removed from the river and repaired for possible future use. Pencoyd agreed to provide the men and equipment to pull the damaged spans to the bank.

Latrobe also noted that the new spans ordered before the flood for Westernport were ready to be delivered. Bretz was having problems with the Lukes who wanted to admit water to the millrace before the masonry for the abutments was completed. John Luke telegraphed Davis that the water would be admitted on July 13, but finally agreed to hold off for a couple of days, just enough to allow the abutments to be finished. The bridge itself was expected to be finished in early August. It was obvious that the Lukes were going to be difficult people to work with, and Davis must have been most upset when he heard that they had approached the B. & O. about putting in a siding. Davis informed T. King, second vice president of the B. & O. that he doubted if the return for the B. & O. would justify bridging the river.

Porter reported that they were still at work on the big cut near Elkins and also the foundations for Elkins's new mansion. It was expected that trains would be running through to Elkins by the middle of August.

An important addition to the administration of the railroad was made in July when Davis offered a Keyser attorney, C. Wood Dailey, the position of company attorney. Dailey was to be a confidant and advisor to Davis for 19 years.

Shaw had toured the railroad and examined the accounts of the company in the spring and at a directors' meeting in July, asked for the appointment of a committee to examine the books. Shaw was concerned that the railroad was not making a profit; behind this

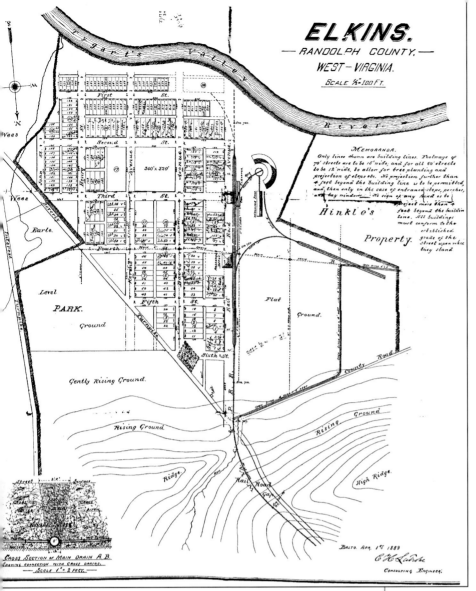

ELKINS.
— RANDOLPH COUNTY. —
WEST-VIRGINIA.
SCALE ½"=100FT.

MEMORANDA.

Only lines shown are building lines. Footways of 70' streets are to be 15' wide, and for all 60' streets to be 12' wide, to allow for tree planting and projection of steps etc. No projection further than 4 feet beyond the building line is to be permitted, and then only in the case of entrance steps, porches, and bay windows. No sign of any kind is to project more than 1 foot beyond the building line. All buildings must conform to the established grade of the street upon which they stand.

Hinkle's Property.

BALTO. APR. 1ST 1889

C. H. Latrobe
CONSULTING ENGINEER.

Fig. 63. Plan of Elkins, April 1, 1889
West Virginia and Regional History Collection,
West Virginia University Library

concern was the fear that the West Virginia Central was subsidizing the P. & C. in which Shaw had no interest. A committee was appointed consisting of Gorman, Elkins and Shaw and an accountant, H. D. Bulkley, was engaged to produce a report.

Bids for the five-stall engine house and a freight house at Elkins were received on July 26. For the engine house, which would include two pits, the bid was for $6,332 complete; the freight house bid was for $3,497. The contractor was then asked to supply new bids for a six-stall engine house and the freight house, if the railroad company did the excavating and masonry work. The new bid for the engine house was for $7,038; the bid for the freight house was reduced by $270. The plans were later sent to Porter who thought the freight house was too small. The dimensions were changed from 30 x 65 feet to 30 x100 feet.

Davis was upset to hear of an unusual incident on July 27, when a foreman was transporting passengers at night on a handcar near Gorman. One of the passengers thought that a light on a nearby mine was the headlight of an approaching locomotive. Two

ladies jumped off; one was slightly hurt, the second was killed. The doctor's report showed that the lady had suffocated because of her "underwear being too tight." Bretz indicated that handcars were to be used only for going to and from work and that the foreman would be disciplined.

On August 5, Camden wrote a lengthy letter to Mayer and Cowan of the B. & O. reporting that contracts had been let for the extension of his railroads to Braxton Court House and along the Buckhannon River. Camden warned the B. & O. that it should take hold of the area around the Gauley River, as Davis, the C. & O. and various other parties were seeking to build into the region. Camden noted that Davis was 35 miles from the Gauley and faced rough country and steep grades. The Camden extension, when completed, would only be 25 miles away with much lighter grades. Camden claimed that he could build to the Gauley, "before Davis could get started by keeping it quiet." These were hardly the words of a colleague. Camden left on a ten day trip to the area shortly after.

The first passenger train to reach the north end of the still unfinished cut at Elkins was an excursion run on Sunday August 11. The train, hauled by No. 18, consisted of four passenger cars with about 300 passengers. The excursion left Cumberland at 7:00 A.M. and returned at 8:30 P.M., about ten minutes late but without incident. The engineer for the first trip was Deffinbaugh with Charles Wenrick as fireman, Baggagemaster Watson and Brakeman Porter.

Encouraged by this news, Davis asked Latrobe to report on the various survey lines that had been run between Elkins and Beverly. Latrobe examined the area between August 20 and August 23 and submitted a report to Davis on August 29. Two possibilities were selected, costing $122,000 and $152,000; both involved one bridge across the Tygart Valley River.

With the road to Elkins almost finished Bretz asked Baldwin for a quote on new freight engines. Baldwin submitted a bid for $9,500 each for two freight engines similar to No. 17, which had cost $10,610 when delivered earlier in the year (Fig. 64). Davis offered $9,250, which was accepted by Baldwin. The locomotives were to be delivered in November. Bretz also was instructed to order two cabin cars from South Baltimore at $450 each. South Baltimore had also received orders for 200 freight cars and an order for a further 100 was placed in November.

Bedrock was finally reached for the new pier at McKenzies at the end of August. Latrobe noted that the original pier did not reach bedrock, which is why it had collapsed. Bretz reported on September 16 that the masonry for all three bridges was almost finished and wrote to Latrobe to hurry the ironwork forward for erection.

On September 9, Davis, Elkins and Kerens started on a trip to Webster County reaching Addison the next day. The party exam-

Fig. 64. West Virginia Central No. 17
E. L. DeGolyer Jr. Collection, DeGolyer Library,
Southern Methodist University, Dallas, Texas. Ag82.232

ined coal veins in the area on September 11, finding one that was 10 feet thick, containing six feet of good coal. A second opening revealed a vein with 6.1/2 feet of good coal, which Davis noted was, "the best vein we saw and appears to be under a large part of the county." The next day was spent examining coal veins along the Gauley and Williams rivers. On Friday, September 13, the party traveled to Helvetia and returned to Elkins the next day. Davis was sufficiently impressed by his trip to buy 9,000 acres of land in the region.

Camden wrote to Davis on September 27, noting that he proposed to extend his railroads to Webster Court House, which would put him only a few miles from the Gauley. Camden wanted to get the Caperton land deal closed and asked if Elkins could attend the hearing at the Monroe Circuit Court on October 7. Davis informed Camden that Riordan had been nearly two months looking for coal on the Caperton and other land in the area, and that I. C. White was also going to examine the region. Davis was also in a hurry to get the matter settled and promised the money as soon as the court confirmed the sale.

Porter reported on September 29, that the cut at Elkins would be finished the next day. He expected to "dispense with all forces," except for those on a ballast train, by October 1. Porter also was able to report that work on the freight house was progressing well.

Even before the cut leading to Elkins was finished, the town had developed considerably. The newly published newspaper, "The Tygarts Valley News," reported in September that there were now two millinery shops, two planing mills, one shoe shop, two jewelry stores, two blacksmith shops, one saddle shop, two barber shops and a meat market. The paper also noted that, "There was not a dude or loafer in town."

Davis also asked E. J. Fredlock to bid on new station buildings for the extension to be similar to the one erected at Bayard. Fredlock's bid of $1,100 was accepted and new buildings were completed at Montrose and Kerens (the new name for the village of New Interest after July 1889), by the end of the year (Fig. 65 and Fig. 66).

Bretz wrote to Davis at the end of October reporting an encouraging increase in trade but not enough cars to move everything. Bretz also stressed the need for additional passing tracks and recommended the purchase of six more engines in 1890. Elkins had also urged Davis to purchase additional power and to purchase

at least 500 more freight cars. Elkins also wanted to build an additional 400-500 coke ovens. Elkins claimed the company was losing business by not being able to ship coal in quantity, particularly to the New York area. Davis did agree to order three new freight engines from Baldwin at the end of the year, one for delivery in April, and two to be delivered in August 1890.

Riordan's report was submitted on October 15, and showed encouraging coal prospects based on 40 openings made throughout the region. Riordan also mentioned that the timber on the Caperton land was the best encountered. Davis and Elkins finally paid for their half of the Caperton lands on October 21 with an outstanding $2,089 being paid by Elkins on November 4. Elkins expressed concern that Camden had proceeded without consulting Davis or Elkins and complained about Camden "seizing our territory and occupying our land." Camden had doubts that he could raise the money for the extension and offered to sell his railroads south of Clarksburg to Davis and Elkins for $1,000,000. Elkins thought that $500,000 was a more realistic figure. During November, Camden negotiated with the B. & O. to try to obtain financial backing for

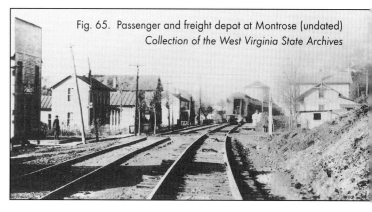

Fig. 65. Passenger and freight depot at Montrose (undated)
Collection of the West Virginia State Archives

Fig. 66. Depot at Kerens, November 1917
Collection of the Western Maryland Railway Historical Society

his expansion but was not too hopeful of success. On December 3, Camden, Davis and Elkins met to discuss their differences, and Camden reported that Davis and Elkins " expressed themselves as acquiescing in the fact that we had anticipated them in securing the right to build a railroad to Gauley, and intimating their intention to confine themselves to the present line of the West Virginia Central, and not to try and interfere with our plans." Davis offered to exchange his one fourth interest in the Caperton lands for Camden's interest in the West Virginia Central. With some minor additions, this was agreed to by the two erstwhile partners, and the separation of the Davis and Camden interests was completed by the end of the year. Elkins held on to his interest until February 1890, but he also finally agreed to sell out to Camden. The final transfer of the lands was made to Camden's newly chartered West Virginia and Pittsburgh Railroad in February 1890.

Bretz reported on November 1, that one span of the McKenzie bridge had been placed on October 27 and the second would be placed within a week. The span at Potomac was ready for erection, and all three bridges destroyed in the May flood should be finished during November.

The freight house at Elkins was finished by early November. At the same time the masonry for the roundhouse was reported to be half finished. By November 24, the stonework was finished and the brick walls were about three feet high. The building was due to be finished by January 1890.

On November 22, Davis asked Jackson and Sharp to bid on two new passenger cars. Jackson and Sharp offered to build the cars for $3,700 each, but also offered an improved car for $4,500, two of which were available. Davis accepted this offer in December, although the cars were to be paid for in coal. The new cars were delivered in April 1890, becoming Nos. 11 and 12. At the suggestion of Bretz, the cars were painted Tuscan red.

Fig. 67. The second West Virginia Central No. 1 near Thomas
Collection of William Metheny

The new freight engines were delivered at the end of November, with No. 19 being placed in service on the Elk Garden branch. The second engine, No. 20, was later renumbered No. 16 replacing the ex-Pennsylvania Railroad engine, which became No. 1 (Fig. 67).

Davis began to take a greater interest in the G. & G. in November as he looked for possible routes to expand. He suggested to Mayer, president of the B. & O. that the two lines should connect in Belington and that this would permit coal moving west to be transferred to the B. & O. at that point. This would require the G. & G. to be converted to standard gauge (Fig. 68). Davis also met with John Bradshaw, president of the G. & G. who was enthusiastic for the West Virginia Central to build to Belington and who noted that business on the G. & G. had declined since the West Virginia Central had reached Elkins. Development of these plans had to wait for the new year.

Cumberland City Council met with Davis on December 27, as it was concerned about the unauthorized use of Creek and Canal streets by the tracks of the P. & C. The council hoped to use this issue to pressure Davis to extend the flood walls along Wills Creek and the Potomac River north and south of the depot. A committee of the council had met with Bretz on November 22 to urge the company to build up the canal bank south of Cumberland station. Bretz supported this as he thought they had been very lucky to avoid severe damage in the floods of May 1889. He also thought a siding could be laid along the top, which would benefit the railroad. This work was started about December 20, when stone for a wall below the station was brought to the site. The work appears to be in progress in Fig. 78, beyond the Cumberland yards. Davis was not willing to do work on Wills Creek up stream of the depot, and offered to pay only one third of the costs, and the matter bogged down.

In December, Davis began to think seriously about a railroad along the C. & O. Canal from Cumberland to Washington. His first step was to send Latrobe to explore the area between the Great Falls of the Potomac River above Washington and Laurel on the B. & O. between Washington and Baltimore. Latrobe's report, which was very encouraging, was submitted to Davis on December 20, but Davis waited for the new year before taking his next step.

Fig. 68. Narrow gauge locomotive of the Grafton and Greenbrier Railroad
West Virginia and Regional History Collection,
West Virginia University Library

Fig. 69. West Virginia Central and Pittsburg Railway timetable, November 13, 1889

		WEST VIRGINIA CENTRAL R. R. Time table, taking effect Sunday Nov. 18th, 1889.		
Southward.		**Stations.**	**Northward.**	
Leave			**Arrive.**	
No. 3.	No. 1.		No. 2.	No. 4.
p. m.	a. m.		a. m.	p. m.
1 30	7 00	Cumb'l'd	11 30	7 15
2 02	7 32	Rawlings	10 56	6 41
2 30	7 59	Keyser	10 29	6 15
2 44	8 12	Westernp't	10 11	5 55
2 47	8 15	W Va C J.	10 08	5 52
3 15	8 47	Shaw	9 40	5 24
3 36	9 10	Blaine	9 20	5 03
3 41	9 15	Harrison	9 15	4 58
4 20	9 52	Gorman	8 39	4 20
4 50	10 22	Wilsonia	8 09	3 48
5 15	10 46	Thomas	7 46	3 25
5 46	11 17	Hendricks	7 15	2 55
5 56	11 27	Parsons	7 05	2 44
6 45	12 16	Kerens	6 21	2 01
7 10	12 40	Elkins	6 00	1 40
p. m.	p. m.		a. m.	p. m.
	Arrive		Leave.	

Additional trains leave Elk Garden at 8 15 a m. and 3 00 and 4 25 p m, arriving at Harrison at 9 00 a m and 3 40 and 4 55 p m. Leave Davis at 7 05 and 10 10 a. m. and 2 45 p. m., arriving at Thomas at 7 30 and 10 35 a. m. and 3 10 p. m.

All trains daily except Sunday. Connection is made with the B. & O. at Cumberland, Keyser, Westernport and W. Va. C. Junction; with the Pennsylvania at Cumberland; with the George's Creek and Cumberland at Cumberland, and with the Cumberland and Pennsylvania at Cumberland and Westernport.

C. L. BRETZ, General Manager

G. W. HARRISON, General Traffic Agent.

Grand Plans and a Fishhook

The report of the accountant, H. D. Bulkley, engaged to review the books of the West Virginia Central, was submitted on January 4, 1890. Although Bulkley was very critical of the accounting procedures of the West Virginia Central and the P. & C., he did not produce the evidence that the West Virginia Central was being drained of funds to support the P. & C. This must have disappointed Shaw but did not stop his pursuit of Davis.

The Annual Meeting of the stockholders of the West Virginia Central was held in Baltimore on January 28, 1890, and was a boisterous affair, again catching the attention of the New York Times. Alexander Shaw attended the meeting accompanied by Irving Cross and a deputy sheriff. The sheriff opened the meeting by presenting an injunction to prevent Davis and Elkins voting 5,000 shares held by the company and which they had voted a year earlier. Elkins presented a resolution that reduced the number of directors from ten to seven, which effectively eliminated Cross from the board, except by using cumulative voting which was not allowed by the by-laws of the company. William H. Gorman made a motion that the P. & C. be leased for a period of 21 years and six months by the West Virginia Central, which would pay all operating costs in return for 60 percent of the gross revenues of the P. & C. The remaining 40 percent would be used to pay taxes and other assessments. This was opposed by Shaw and the minority stockholders so a committee was appointed consisting of Elkins, William Keyser and William Pinkney Whyte to look into the proposed lease and report back to a meeting on March 15. This move upset Elkins who thought the proposed lease should have come to a vote and that it would have been approved. Elkins suggested Davis contact Roberts of the Pennsylvania Railroad to see if he could spare an experienced auditor to go over the books of the two companies and make recommendations to Davis and the committee.

Keyser prepared the committee's report for the March 15 meeting of the stockholders. He explained that he was a minority stockholder, interested only in the West Virginia Central and was sympathetic to the B. & O. by virtue of his interests in that company. He thought that there had been no recourse for the West Virginia Central other than to build the P. & C. to avoid being "bottled up." Keyser noted that there were some minor problems with the lease but these could easily be rectified. However, Shaw had obtained an injunction preventing a new lease, so the March meeting was adjourned with nothing accomplished and the P. & C. continued to be operated as before.

Davis did not allow the obstructionism of Shaw to delay his plans. The C. & O. Canal, which had remained a total wreck since the floods of spring 1889, was to feature in Davis's plans and also in the meeting of the Maryland legislature, which opened on January 1, 1890. The meeting was addressed by the governor, who pointed out that the canal was in default because it had not met its obligations under an 1878 mortgage. The largest holder of these bonds was none other than the B. & O. The governor did not want

the canal to fall into the hands of the B. & O., but claimed that the state could neither provide the money to fix the canal nor could it authorize a sale. The governor did think a lease was feasible and that several companies had expressed an interest in leasing the canal. This was confirmed when the Cumberland Times reported that Latrobe set off to survey the waterway on January 23. No indication was given as to who Latrobe was working for.

On February 3, the Washington and Cumberland Railroad Company filed for incorporation. The object of the company was to build a railroad from Washington to Cumberland and to accomplish this, the company proposed to lease the canal. Listed among the incorporators of the new company were John A. Hambleton and Enoch Pratt of Baltimore. The new company offered to lease the canal for 99 years and to pay off the 1878 repair bonds and other indebtedness. The total cash value of the offer was estimated to be $1,250,000. The New York Times recognized that the W. & C. was "a new name under which the West Virginia Central Road is masquerading."

Although well disguised, Davis's hand was behind the W. & C. but other interests were also involved including certain unnamed Philadelphia parties. Elkins was concerned that unless the Davis and Elkins interests held a majority of the new company, the West Virginia Central would not secure any benefit.

It was reported in early February by the Baltimore Sun, that Latrobe's January survey had been in the interest of the W. & C. and included a possible route to Baltimore. It was claimed that this extension would only be built if suitable rates could not be obtained over the W. Md. However, the W. Md. and the B. & O. had an agreement whereby the W. Md. would not try to get the canal in return for advantageous freight rates from Cherry Run. Having eliminated the W. Md. from contending for the canal, the B. & O. supported a group that aimed to repair the canal and return it to an operating waterway. When this failed, the B. & O. asked for receivers, which were appointed on March 3.

On March 14, the Maryland senate approved a bill to lease the canal to the W. & C. At the end of March the legislature also passed a bill permitting the W. Md. to build to Cherry Run to connect with the B. & O. This extension, along with others proposed by the W. Md. at this time, are shown in Fig. 70.

Davis noted that up to the end of March $9,194.23 had been spent on the W. & C. This included $574.75 for Latrobe's surveys and $7,500 to Senator A. P. Gorman who had worked behind the scenes to ensure passage of the W. & C. bill.

Although the proposed W. & C. was an ambitious undertaking, it was not the only project engaging Davis's attention. On March 1, Davis wrote to Roberts of the Pennsylvania expressing an interest in building from Elkins to the Pennsylvania state line, if the Pennsylvania would build south to a junction. Davis pointed out that such a route would pass through a "large and fine coal region a good portion of the way." Davis estimated the cost of the road at

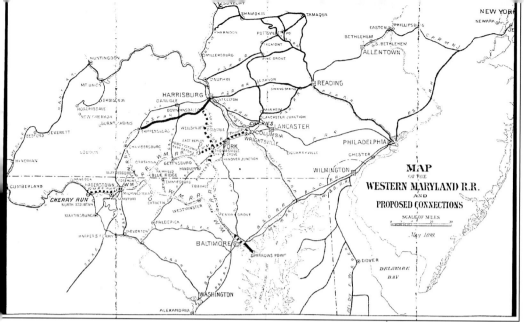

Fig. 70. Proposed extensions of the Western Maryland Rail Road, May 1890
West Virginia and Regional History Collection,
West Virginia University Library

$3,000,000 for 114 miles. Davis wrote again a few days later suggesting an arrangement similar to that between the P. & C. and the Pennsylvania whereby the latter road would set aside five percent of the gross earnings to cover any deficits incurred by the new road. Davis also mentioned that the B. & O. had arranged to control the Camden system south of Clarksburg, and also the road between Fairmont and Clarksburg along the Monongahela River. Davis expected, however, to build on the west side of the river which contained the best coal, and along which a road known as the West Virginia and Pennsylvania Railroad, usually known as the "Lowndes" road after its president, R. T. Lowndes, had established a prior right. Davis planned to absorb the Lowndes road and also to take up considerable coal acreage. Roberts replied to Davis on April 9, expressing an interest on behalf of the Pennsylvania and arranging a meeting for April 21 at which he encouraged Davis to believe that the Pennsylvania would build to the state line. However, the Pennsylvania was not the only railroad interested in such a route. The Pittsburgh and Lake Erie Railroad, a subsidiary of the New York Central, was also reported to be surveying a route up the Monongahela and a corps of engineers was in the vicinity of Morgantown. Elkins met Hamilton McK. Twombley of the N. Y. C. who indicated a willingness to cooperate with Davis if the Pennsylvania did not wish to build. The N. Y. C. did not wish to antagonize the Pennsylvania and would wait to see what was the outcome of the negotiations.

The winter of 1890 seemed hard on the West Virginia Central, particularly around Chaffee. On January 17, seven cars came off the track north of Chaffee, causing passengers on two trains the next morning to be transferred round the wreck. On March 14, a gang of men were at work removing a slide north of Chaffee and had attached a chain to a large rock lying on the track. As they were pulling it clear, another rock came down killing a foreman, James Lambert, and two Italians, Numbers 970 and 976. A second foreman, Van Reed, died shortly afterwards, and two other Italians, Numbers 978 and 981 were severely injured. Italian laborers were

generally referred to by number rather than name, a practice that was to continue for a few more years. Bretz reported that the banks were very soft and considerable trouble was being caused by slides. Another derailment occurred near Chaffee on March 29 when six cars derailed and rolled down a bank. Heavy rains may have been responsible as it was also reported that a trestle near Westernport had been damaged by high water.

The most serious wreck occurred on April 3 on the Mineville branch, when Engine No. 12 and 12 loaded coal cars ran away and derailed near Shaw station. The engineer, Edward Lippencott, jumped off the train and received only minor injuries. The fireman, McAbee, was buried under the engine and was killed instantly. The conductor, John Dunlap, was severely injured and not expected to live. Two brakemen suffered assorted broken bones. Bretz noted that No. 12 had lost its cab and the tender was a wreck, but otherwise the locomotive was not badly damaged. Twelve coal cars, ten belonging to the B. & O., were destroyed. Bretz reminded all trainmen of correct braking proceedures for descending steep grades, and insisted that six miles per hour was the maximum speed. Dunlap later exonerated Lippencott of responsibility for the accident, although Davis was inclined to think that Lippencott had been negligent.

Davis was not the only one to suspect Lippencott of negligence. Dailey wrote to Davis in August noting that he had been contacted by the attorney for Mrs. McAbee, the indefatigable Robert Gordon, saying that they would sue if Mrs. McAbee was offered anything less that $2,500 for the death of her husband. Dailey explained that the company would be liable if they knowingly retained an incompetent engineer, but if McAbee had also known of the engineer's incompetence, but still continued to work with him, his wife would have no claim. The case was finally compromised in January 1892 for $800, which included $400 from the relief fund.

Elkins wrote to Davis on April 4, noting that he had visited the Davis Coal and Coke Company's mine at Coketon and that everything there seemed to be going well. He reported that 78 coke ovens were under construction and recommended that an additional 50 be built to give a total of 200 by the end of the year (Fig. 71 and Fig. 72). In spite of Davis's intention to consolidate the coal holdings under one company, the mines at Thomas continued to be operated by H. G. Davis and Brother until May 1 when the H. G. Davis Coal Company took over. The new company noted that it was selling coal from three seams, the Big Vein, the Davis and the Thomas seams. The Big Vein coal was coming from yet another Davis company, the Davis and Elkins Coal and Coke Company, which had opened the Old Virginia mine at Windom in 1889. The new company noted that the Big Vein was an excellent steam, smithing and domestic coal. The Davis coal was specially suited for blacksmithing purposes; the Thomas coal was suitable for both steam and domestic purposes. The Big Vein coal was also mined at

Fig. 71. General view of Coketon (undated)

Elk Garden by the coal department of the West Virginia Central, but was not sold through H. G. Davis Coal Company but rather through various agencies. One other "Davis" company, the Davis Brothers and Elkins Coal Company, had operated a mine using the

Fig. 72. Coke ovens at Coketon (undated)
Collection of the Western Maryland Railway Historical Society

Hampshire plane near West Virginia Central Junction, but this was reported abandoned in October 1889.

The mines along the West Virginia Central were spared any major strikes during the spring of 1890. A miners' convention held in Clarksburg on April 26 demanded an advance of rates, but apart from a strike of about 40 miners at Thomas on May 5, there seemed to be no other stoppages. The strike at Thomas was due to a demand by the miners to be paid for the actual weight of coal mined, but this was refused and the strike fizzled.

In April, the first of the new 2-8-0 locomotives ordered at the end of 1889 arrived and became No. 20. This seemed to have prompted a flurry of orders for new freight cars, which by June had reached 300. This included 100 hopper bottom gondolas from Schall and King (Numbers 1,400 to 1,499) at $450 each, and 100 from South Baltimore (Numbers 1,500 to 1,599) at the same price. In addition, South Baltimore provided 75 flat bottom gondolas (Numbers 2,007 to 2,081) at $415 each, and 25 coke gondolas (Numbers 2,082 to 2,106) at $481 each. Five maintenance-of-way cars were also ordered from South Baltimore and Bretz also received approval to order a couple of cabooses.

The two new passenger cars ordered from Jackson and Sharp in November 1889, were delivered in April becoming Nos. 11 and 12. Bretz had inspected the cars in March and pronounced them "substantially built," although not as fine as the first class cars of the Pennsylvania. Passenger car No. 11 can be seen in Fig. 45, along with combination car No. 14 and engine No. 8.

On the West Virginia Central, Bretz had been urging Davis since the beginning of the year to expand the office space available in Cumberland by putting a second story on the freight depot. Davis was not pleased with the idea but eventually agreed to allow the construction of a new building. A contract for this was let on April 10 to Groves and Weber for $3,500.

Latrobe had submitted a plan and estimate for a new station building at Elkins to Davis on February 14. The new building would have cost $25,000 and would have allowed Davis to transfer some of the offices from Cumberland. Elkins was aghast at this figure and thought that a temporary building costing $1,500-2,000 would suffice. Porter noted on April 10, that stone was being quarried at both Haddix and Blackwater Canyon for the depot and turntable and also for Elkins's new mansion. At the end of April it was reported that the machine shop at Elkins had been laid off. Porter also recommended that the proposed blacksmith shop be increased in size to 35'x60' from 25'x40'. This recommendation was accepted by Davis.

By the beginning of May, Davis was becoming concerned about the B. & O. and ambitions it might have to extend the G. & G. south from Belington. Parsons was ordered out to survey the route between Belington and Elkins with a view to filing the location in the secretary of state's office, which would prevent the B. & O. from building on the same line. Davis also became concerned about the possibility of the B. & O. purchasing the C. & O. Canal outright, but he was assured by his attorneys that the W. & C. could condemn a route along the canal, and that a purchaser could not defeat that right. Davis's hopes were raised when the receivers reported on June 9 against repairing the canal, and he received more encouragement when Latrobe submitted a report dealing with the extension of the line across Rock Creek to a depot at B. and 17th Streets in Washington.

Attempts by Davis to secure a line into Pittsburgh also received some encouragement in June when he was contacted by J. E. Sands, secretary of the Lowndes railroad, offering to sell the road. Davis efforts to gain control of the route had been conducted by a third party, although it is probable that Sands knew Davis and Elkins were behind these efforts. Sands claimed $50,000 had been spent on the route, some grading had been completed, and subscriptions raised from Harrison and Marion counties.

Davis however had some new ideas. He had met with Thomas King, second vice president of the B. & O., to discuss a connection with the G. & G. at Belington, if the B. & O. would undertake to widen the gauge. Davis wrote to King again on July 29 pushing this proposal, and suggesting a similar agreement to that being negotiated with the Pennsylvania Railroad, whereby the bonds of the new extension would be guaranteed by the revenues derived by the B. & O.

Davis also informed President Roberts of the Pennsylvania of these talks. He pointed out that if the freight went over the G. & G. to Grafton, and then from there to Fairmont over the B. & O., it would leave only 45 miles of new road to be built from Fairmont to the state line to connect with the Pennsylvania. He also noted that the distance using this route would be approximately the same as the Clarksburg route. Roberts was supportive of the new proposal, but expressed some concerns about the cost to the Pennsylvania of building from Fairchance to the state line.

Davis did not receive good news on the third leg of his grand design - the route to the C. & O. Parsons returned from a trip over the proposed route on August 21 and reported that the first 36 miles through Beverly to Mingo Church would be light but the next 23 miles to the Greenbrier River would be "stupendous work." Three tunnels would be needed, all of which would have to be lined. At least 13 trestles would be required, some of which would be over 100 feet high. Parsons summarized his report by saying "it is questionable whether it would be prudent for your road to undertake so expensive a work." Davis agreed and noted on September 2 that the road could not be built at reasonable cost.

Although the extension beyond Beverly appeared to be out of the question, it was announced on August 1 that the line to Beverly would be built. This, along with the proposed line to Belington would ensure that Elkins would become an important railroad center, a role originally envisaged for the town of Davis. Davis incorporated the Valley Improvement Company in May to be responsible for the sale of lots in the town and to make the necessary civic improvements such as an adequate water supply. Davis also contracted with the architectural firm of Baldwin and Pennington to draw up plans for a hotel and noted that he and Kerens would shortly start work on their houses. Elkins's new mansion was scheduled to be finished in June (Fig. 73), and was named

Fig. 73. The Elkins mansion, "Halliehurst"

Hallihurst when it was completed. The depot, blacksmith shop and the machine shops were reported to be coming along well. Porter was ordered on July 9 to get stone ready for a bank building in Elkins. On the same day Davis notified Kerens that a hill had been leveled ready for Kerens to build his house. C. F. Graves and Company were notified on August 16 that they had received the contract to build the Elkins Hotel for $11,500, excluding foundations and plumbing, the building to be finished by January 1, 1891. Davis applied for a charter for the Elkins Hotel Company on August 11.

The end of July saw another runaway train on the Mineville branch, although on this occasion there were no fatalities. Damage to the locomotive was reported to be slight, but Bretz estimated the damage to the coal cars to be $1,000.

The second new locomotive arrived in August and became No. 21. Baldwin had promised delivery of this engine and its sister No. 22 in July, but No. 22 was not received until November.

Davis still had hopes of acquiring the C. & O. Canal and noted in his diary on August 21 that the subscription books were opened for stock in the W. & C., and "I think this is an extension that will be of great good value." Steps also were being taken to seek approval from Congress for the W. & C. to enter Washington from the terminus of the canal in Georgetown. A bill to allow this was approved by a Senate committee on September 1, and placed on the Senate calendar. It was later passed over "without prejudice" and waited for a later session. On September 1, Judge Alvey ordered that the canal be sold as there was no chance that it could ever be returned to a profitable condition. The Baltimore banking house of John A. Hambleton was delighted with the judge's decision and looked forward to a connection between the W. & C. and the W. Md. at Williamsport and an increase in business for Baltimore. The circular published by the bank concluded, "It is to be hoped there will be no further useless opposition and that we shall see another rail route to the bituminous coal fields."

On September 3, Davis received the news that the court had sustained Shaw in his suit to have cumulative voting allowed for directors of the West Virginia Central but no action appears to have been taken at this time. Shaw also obtained a court order allowing him to examine the books of the P. & C., which he did on October 1 in the company of an accountant.

Porter reported on September 16, that the Y had been removed at Elkins and that the main line was being extended to the Tygart Valley River. South of the river, a crew of sixteen was busy cutting the right-of-way and stone was being cut in readiness for a bridge across the river. Latrobe was asked to prepare plans for this bridge.

Latrobe also was asked to look at the Wills Creek bridge in Cumberland, which had proved to be an obstruction during times of high water and was also subject to scour, so much so that the timber grillage beneath one pier was exposed at low water. Latrobe recommended that the pier should be removed and a lattice girder span of 45 feet substituted for the two deck girder spans. Latrobe estimated the cost of the work at $11,500 including the masonry but the four girders could be used on the extension to Beverly, giving a net cost of $6,700. Bretz thought that the work should be commenced immediately to avoid having trestlework in the creek during the spring floods. Davis gave approval for the work to start at the end of October.

During September, Davis and Elkins visited the coalfield between Morgantown and Fairmont. They were accompanied by Lowndes and Sands and also by Professors White and Jackson of West Virginia University. Jackson was a professor of civil engineering at the University and had done some survey work around Fairmont for the West Virginia and Pennsylvania Railroad. Davis thought that the coal below Fairmont was better than that above the town but also noted that the coalfield between Clarksburg and the state line "is the greatest and best coalfield in the world." He was later reported to have purchased 7,000 acres for $195,000, and in December, the Empire Coal and Coke Company was chartered to "take up coal above and below Fairmont."

The opposition to the sale of the C. & O. Canal that the Hambleton bank hoped would not materialize, soon did so, particularly from the various groups of canal bondholders, one of which was the B. & O. The opposition was led by John K. Cowan, counsel for the B. & O., who claimed on September 20 in circuit court in Hagerstown, that the canal should be turned over to the bondholders. On October 2, Judge Alvey passed a decree ordering the sale of the canal, but suspended the implementation of the sale for four years starting May 1, 1891. The decree gave the trustees until May 1, 1891 to repair the canal and then four years in which to show the canal could be operated profitably. To ensure compliance, the trustees were required to post a bond of $600,000. The B. & O. paid the bond to the court on November 28, putting the canal into the hands of the railroad. What Davis and the other stockholders of the W. & C. thought of this move is not recorded. The state of Maryland was not too pleased and filed to have the decision of the judge overturned.

Davis wrote to Lowndes on October 13 enclosing a draft of an agreement to cover the purchase of the West Virginia and Pennsylvania Railroad, but Davis appeared to think that Lowndes was making some impossible demands. Lowndes wrote back on October 16 claiming he could not agree to the proposal. Davis tried again on November 13, but was unsuccessful.

Possibly because of the difficulties encountered with his northern and canal extensions, Davis took another look at extending to the C. & O. Riordan had spent three months examining coal prospects in Randolph, Webster, Nicholas and Upshur counties and submitted a report to Davis on October 15. This showed extensive coal deposits throughout the region with some seams up to 16 feet thick. On November 11, Davis wrote to M. E. Ingalls, president of the C. & O. proposing a meeting to discuss a connection between the two roads. Ingalls noted that the C. & O. was going to build two branches, one into the Warm Springs valley and the second to Huntersville from White Sulphur Springs, and suggested that Davis build to meet one of these branches.

Davis met with President Ingalls and Vice President Decatur Axtell of the C. & O. and their financial advisor, C. H. Caster, at the end of November. He later reported to Elkins that the C. & O. expected to start work on a branch to Warm Springs at once, and would connect with Davis's proposed extension somewhere between the branch and Huntersville.

Parsons returned from a trip over the proposed route to Covington and Clifton Forge on November 26 and recommended a route to Covington beginning at Hendricks and going up Dry Fork and Glady Fork and then over to the Greenbrier River. From the Greenbrier the route led by way of Knapps Creek to Mountain Grove; Back Creek and Jackson River could then be followed to Covington for a total distance of 122 miles. Parsons mentioned the iron ore deposits alone would make it worthwhile to build the extension.

Elkins met with Parsons on his return and became enthusiastic about the route particularly as it would be possible to connect with

the Richmond and Alleghany and the Norfolk and Western with short extensions.

The possibility of the West Virginia Central being extended to the Virginia iron ore fields interested Andrew Carnegie. Davis had sold his Connellsville coal lands to Carnegie a year earlier, although whether this was Davis's first contact with the steel magnate is not clear. Certainly after this date the two capitalists were frequent correspondents, and Carnegie was to encourage Davis in his expansion south. Davis invited Carnegie to tour the West Virginia Central on October 31, the tour taking place on November 6 and 7. The party stayed overnight at Halliehurst before returning to Cumberland.

Another individual interested in encouraging Davis to build into Virginia was A. B. Fleming, governor of West Virginia, who had interests in the Goshen Land and Improvement Company. Fleming promised $100,000 cash or more in land if Davis would build to Goshen, which was some 20 miles northwest of Lexington.

Engine No. 22 was finally received from Baldwin at the end of November. The arrival coincided with a request from Bretz to purchase a 0-6-0 switching engine. Bids were obtained from Baldwin ($8,480) and from Pittsburgh ($8,600). Bretz recommended that an order be placed with Baldwin immediately. Davis suggested offering Baldwin $8,000 for a spring 1891 delivery. Earlier, Davis had given Bretz permission to purchase a second crane car for $1,800.

On December 8, Davis was offered $100,000 to build down the Elk River to Charleston, but he declined pointing out that Camden's road would possibly go that way.

That idea was furthest from Camden's mind at the time. He wrote to Davis on December 15 saying that he was purchasing 50,000 acres of iron ore lands along Potts Creek near Covington. This was to assure business for the W. Va. & P. when it extended to a connection with the C. & O. at Covington. Camden's route took him from the Williams River over to Marlins Bottom (now called Marlinton). From Marlins Bottom, the route followed that projected by Parsons. Camden suggested that if Davis also built to Huntersville, it would be an added inducement for the C. & O. to build to meet them. If the C. & O. did not build, then he and Davis could build a joint road of 15 miles to meet the C. & O.'s Warm Springs branch.

This prompted Davis to order Parsons to prepare the maps and report of the route from Hendricks to the C. & O. as soon as possible. Davis asked also about the possibility of a route to Goshen using the Jackson and Cowpasture rivers. Parsons submitted his maps on December 24 with a copy to Elkins. Parsons showed three possible routes, one from Hendricks and two from Elkins one of which was the route from Beverly, which had earlier been judged impractical. The second Elkins route left the town via Goddin Run, crossed over to Shavers Fork and then to Glady Fork, which was followed to the West Fork of the Greenbrier. This route was nine miles shorter than the Hendricks route and for traffic going to Pittsburgh, there was a saving of 40 miles. Elkins also noted that the line would be 60 miles shorter for traffic going to Pittsburgh than Camden's proposed route. Elkins was most enthusiastic and recommended a more careful survey. Davis was not so sure and indicated a preference for the Hendricks route.

On December 8, Davis met with Mayer of the B. & O. and

where the possibility of the B. & O. widening the G. & G. to standard gauge was discussed. Another possibility was for the B. & O. to sell the road to Davis. In a memorandum written after the meeting, Davis noted that, "Mr. Mayer talked right, and said he would take it up any time with us and make fair arrangements." In a letter to Elkins on the same day he mentioned the meeting and that Mayer was also receptive to the B. & O. building from Morgantown to Uniontown to a junction with the Pennsylvania. Perhaps in case nothing should come of the contact with Mayer, Davis asked Jackson to survey possible routes around Fairmont. Davis also informed Lowndes in the middle of December that the negotiations were suspended, citing the talks with Mayer as the reason.

In spite of the bad weather during December, Bretz was able to report good progress initially on the Wills Creek bridge. On December 8, Bretz reported that the new pier was nearly at the low water mark and that the new foundation was four feet below the level of the old grillage. By December 19 Bretz noted that the pier only needed another three courses of stone to be finished and that the cofferdam was being removed. At the same time Latrobe reported receiving bids for the iron work on the Wills Creek and the Tygart Valley River bridge at Elkins. The Youngstown Bridge Company submitted the low bid for the Wills Creek structure at $10,100; the contract for the Tygart Valley River bridge was given to the Edge Moor company for $7,300.

Heavy snows on December 18 caused the cancellation of all freight trains on the West Virginia Central except local trains and these were reported to be running 10 to 12 hours late. One train was reported to have required three engines to get from Thomas to Fairfax and even then was nine hours late. Cars were derailed at numerous points, and Engine No. 5 was off the track at Gorman for eight hours, all because of the weather. The Davis branch was completely closed and seven feet of snow were reported at Elk Garden. Bretz hoped to have everything back to normal by December 20 if there was no more snow.

A second storm occurred on December 27 with heavy snows again around Elk Garden. One engine was snowbound on the Elk Garden branch all night. On December 28, Bretz reported that he had two engines and 80 men at work on the branch trying to shovel it out. A second gang was at work at Black Oak bottom where a second train was stuck. Bretz hoped to have the Elk Garden branch reopened on the afternoon of the 28th and to bring down 20 cars of coal. The quarry supplying stone for the bridge at Wills Creek was forced to close by the snow and this prevented further work on the pier. Bretz also reported that there had been a delay in obtaining tools for the machine shop at Elkins and hence it would not be ready before the middle of January 1891.

Caster wrote to Davis on December 29 agreeing to recommend a contract between the two companies to the C. & O. board. At the insistence of the Pennsylvania Railroad, the contract with the C. & O. included clauses similar to those in the Pennsylvania contracts, setting aside a percentage of the gross earnings to cover payment of bonds if necessary.

By the end of 1890, Davis became concerned about a looming financial crisis in the country, which had influenced his decision

not to continue negotiating with Lowndes, and also caused the Pennsylvania Railroad to rethink its proposed contract with the West Virginia Central. The Ninth Annual Report, published in January 1891, contained a map of all the extensions being considered by Davis at this time, but only the Belington and Beverly extensions were actually under construction (Fig. 74).

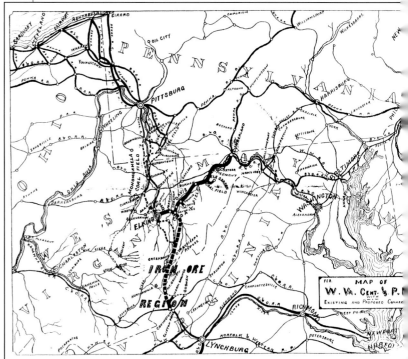

Fig. 74. Proposed extensions of the West Virginia Central, February 1891
West Virginia and Regional History Collection,
West Virginia University Library

Davis returned to the Wills Creek bridge problem in January 1891, ordering Bretz to remove the abutment as soon as the weather permitted. He reminded Bretz that the bridge was to be completed by April 10. The old girders were to be taken to Elkins for use on the Tygart Valley River bridge, which was to be finished by April 25.

On January 9, John McGraw wrote to Camden mentioning the problem that the Piedmont Pulp and Paper Company was having getting an adequate supply of pulpwood for the mills at Piedmont and Harpers Ferry from suppliers along the West Virginia Central. A year earlier, McGraw had tried to set up a contract between the G. & G. and its proposed extension to Charleston, and the Lukes but was not successful. Now McGraw hoped to interest Camden in supplying the Lukes from his lands along the Williams River. McGraw also mentioned that there was some friction between the Lukes and Davis as to whether Davis had overstated the amount of pulpwood that was available when he had persuaded the Lukes to locate at Piedmont. The Lukes now noted that the price of pulpwood had increased and that had encouraged other companies to get into the business.

McGraw, as an associate of both Camden and Davis, frequently tried to use this position to further his own interests. He had purchased a considerable acreage of land on the Greenbrier River and was always trying to encourage Davis or Camden to build to these lands, which had virtually no value without a railroad. In November 1890, he had asked a surveyor to report on the possibility of a railroad from Mingo Flats to either the Greenbrier or Williams rivers. The report was much more encouraging than the report of Parsons that had led Davis to abandon a route beyond Beverly. McGraw sent a copy of the report to Camden but Camden does not appear to have been too interested. In spite of his maneuverings, McGraw never became a leading player in the political or commercial development of West Virginia.

The annual meeting of the stockholders of the West Virginia Central was held on January 27 at Piedmont. As in the past Cross attempted to vote the Shaw holdings cumulatively, which would have given him a seat on the seven man board of directors but again this was denied. After the reading of the annual report, Cross submitted a minority report, which claimed that the coal holdings of the company were being rapidly depleted, and that the new extensions proposed were of doubtful value. He also claimed the company's property was being used by the officers to the advantage of other companies in which they had an interest. After Cross had finished, Elkins offered a resolution saying "That the protest read by Mr. Cross, being slanderous, malicious and false in every particular, the same be laid on the table without discussion." The resolution passed. On February 9, the Supreme Court of Appeals of West Virginia supported the position of the directors of the West Virginia Central in the cumulative voting matter, and reversed the decision of the Circuit Court of Mineral County. Shaw however, thought that the Supreme Court had acted only on a technicality and vowed to continue the fight.

Davis ordered two new freight engines from Baldwin on February 14, to be similar to No. 22. Baldwin initially quoted $9,950 but because demand was low, agreed to accept $9,640. Davis as usual had to try for an even lower price and offered $9,600. The order was placed for the two engines to be delivered in July and August. The order for the engines was followed by a request to Jackson and Sharp for prices on passenger and combination cars, and 50 coke cars and five maintenance-of-way cars from the South Baltimore Car Works. After the usual haggling, Jackson and Sharp agreed to build the passenger car for $4,250 and the combination car for $3,250, half the purchase price to be paid in coal. The passenger car became No. 13, and the combination car No. 14 when they were delivered a few weeks later. The combination car can be seen in Fig. 45.

Davis was still interested in pursuing a line to Pittsburgh and received a report from Jackson in January of possible routes around Fairmont that would avoid the B. & O. Parsons had received orders on January 7 to explore the country between Elkins and Fairmont by way of Simpson Creek and Bridgeport. He reported to Davis on February 18 that a route via Flemington would be eight or ten miles shorter than the route by the G. & G. through Grafton to Fairmont but would involve some heavy work.

On February 20, the Maryland Court of Appeals sustained the position of Judge Alvey giving the C. & O. Canal to the bondholders, which meant that the B. & O. were now firmly in control. Although there was talk of the W. & C. condemning a route along the canal, this seemed to be the end of the battle.

J. M. Hood, president and general manager of the W. Md.,

wrote to Davis on February 21, referring to discussions that he had had with the B. & O., which would have allowed the West Virginia Central favorable rates between Cumberland and Cherry Run. Davis had agreed to drop his fight for the canal if he could be assured of such rates. Now that the B. & O. had a tight hold on the canal, they did not feel obliged to deal with Davis in this matter.

With the battle for the canal decided in the B. & O.'s favor, Davis returned to his original idea of building across country from Cumberland to Hagerstown and again Parsons was sent to examine the country. Parsons's report of February 25, noted that the work would be "heavy and difficult" but that the best line seemed to be that developed by the W. Md. a few years earlier. This would give a route of between 65 and 66 miles to Hagerstown. The route would require two tunnels and some high trestles. On March 3, Parsons was instructed to look for a line along the Potomac River avoiding both the B. & O. and the canal.

The New York Times reported on February 26, that the N. & W. had a bill before Congress to allow it to build into Washington along the line of the C. & O. Canal. When Senator Gorman added an amendment to allow the W. & C. the same privilege, this killed the bill and upset President Kimball of the N. & W. He wrote to Davis, saying that because of the unfriendly actions of Gorman, he was no longer interested in a traffic agreement should the West Virginia Central be built into Virginia. Davis responded that such a position would make Gorman even more unfriendly, and this might be fatal for any future legislation sought by the N. & W.

Davis outlined his plans for the coming construction season to Parsons on March 9. Porter was to build the Beverly extension and the bridge across the Tygart Valley River. The Belington extension would be put under contract and Parsons was ordered to locate the line and to prepare the necessary data for the contractors. Parsons was asked to ensure that the line went through the best coalfields as Davis anticipated purchasing between 3,000 and 4,000 acres in the area. When this work was completed, Parsons was then to resume work on the Shavers Fork route. At the time of Davis's orders, Parsons was at work on Glady Fork, but assured Davis he would be ready to start the Belington work on March 16. It was also noted that Latrobe would take charge of the survey between Cumberland and Hagerstown.

McGraw wrote to Davis on March 6, mentioning his lands along the Greenbrier and at Marlins Bottom and asking about the prospects of a connection between the Camden road and the West Virginia Central at that point. Davis replied that there were no plans as yet for the southern extension but did meet with McGraw to discuss taking an interest in the lands. He also asked Parsons his opinion of a junction at Marlins Bottom but Parsons was not enthusiastic about the idea.

It was reported on March 13, that the iron and lumber for the first bridge south of Elkins had arrived at the site. The stonework was expected to be completed on April 1, and one half mile of grading had also been finished. Porter was in charge of the work and had a gang of 90 men; a full team was expected by April 1. Parsons wrote to Davis on March 19 that the Belington work would be ready to advertise by the end of March and that the work could commence on May 1. It also was announced at this time that the West Virginia Central would build a car repair shop at Elkins.

Although the repair of cars was the immediate goal, it was hoped eventually to build new cars there.

At the end of March it was found that a mistake had been made in the measurement of the main span of the Tygart Valley River bridge. It had originally been designed by Latrobe to be 147 feet long. A mistake in locating the piers was discovered in November 1890, and the span increased by eight inches to compensate. When the span was delivered it was found that a second mistake had been made in measuring the piers and the span was now 16 inches too long. Latrobe noted that it would fit the piers, but would give an "ugly and ill constructed looking job." Latrobe complained to Davis that "I never knew a worse case of carelessness," but no heads seemed to have rolled as a result.

The New York Times announced on March 18, that negotiations were proceeding between the City of Baltimore and the W. Md. looking for a possible sale of the road. The same article noted that the West Virginia Central was not interested as it could build its own line to Baltimore at a cost of only a little more than the bonded indebtedness of the W. Md. This was not quite accurate, as Davis did meet with Mayor Davidson of Baltimore towards the end of March, noting in his diary that he was thinking of purchasing or leasing the W. Md. Again on April 10, Davis wrote in his diary, "For several months I have been looking into the condition of the Western Maryland with a view to leasing or buying it to get a tidewater connection for the West Virginia Central and Pittsburg by way of Hagerstown." He also noted that he was to meet with Senator Gorman and Roberts and Thompson of the Pennsylvania and that they would take a one third interest.

Davis still was negotiating with Roberts about the route to Pittsburgh, but by March 30 Roberts seemed a little less enthusiastic. He pointed out that the latest version of an agreement between Davis and the B. & O. seemed to benefit the B. & O. more than the Pennsylvania. He suggested that Davis secure running rights for West Virginia Central trains over the B. & O. tracks. Davis replied that the B. & O. had adamantly refused to allow such rights, but the B. & O. would build the necessary track to connect with the Pennsylvania at Fairchance, thus saving the West Virginia Central and the Pennsylvania a considerable sum. Davis met with Mayer on April 10 and noted that an agreement between the two railroads would provide for; a. the West Virginia Central to build to Belington, b. the B. & O. to change the gauge of the G. & G. to standard gauge by April 1, 1892, and c. the B. & O. to build from Morgantown to Uniontown and connect with the Pennsylvania by October 1, 1892. A formal agreement incorporating these provisions and also setting up a framework to set freight rates was approved on May 16, 1891.

Major N. S. Hill was appointed on March 26 to be the superintendent of construction between Elkins and Pittsburgh, but when he subsequently withdrew, the duties were given to Porter on April 20. Both extensions were to be built by the company's forces under the supervision of Porter, the only outside contractors to be used were the bridge erectors.

At the end of March, the Supreme Court of Appeals of West Virginia handed Shaw the victory that he had long sought, when it issued a writ commanding the West Virginia Central to accept Cross as a director based on the cumulative vote. Thomas B.

Davis, who had received the smallest number of votes, notified Cross that he would surrender his seat in accordance with the court ruling. Although Cross was now a director, Davis fought throughout the summer to keep him from having access to all the company's records, but because of the broad nature of the Appeals Court decision, he eventually complied.

Spring was late arriving on the West Virginia Central in 1891. On April 4, 14 inches of snow were reported at Thomas and again service on the Elk Garden branch had to be suspended. The bad weather set off numerous landslides causing delays in schedules. On May 1, the Italian workers on the work train struck for higher wages, and Bretz gave them $1.20 per day. When he requested the same advance for the trackmen, pointing out that the sawmills were paying more and that they were losing the best men, Davis only granted a raise to $1.15. This was the same rate that the B. & O. paid its trackmen after raising the rate from $1.10 on April 24.

Davis did agree to get bids on two Pennsylvania style cabooses at the end of April. Bids of $495 each were received from South Baltimore and the Schell Company, although the order went to South Baltimore for $460. Davis noted that the interior cushions were to be filled with "sea moss."

It was reported that work on the new shaft at Thomas commenced in April. The shaft cost $60,624.50 to construct and the first coal was shipped in November 1891.

During April, Davis decided to build ten new double houses in Elkins, five on Davis Avenue and five on Kerens Avenue at a cost of $600 each. The new hotel, named the Randolph, opened at this time, at a reported cost of $45,885 (Fig. 75). A reporter from the

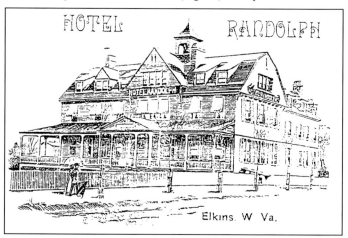

Fig. 75. The Randolph Hotel, Elkins
West Virginia and Regional History Collection, West Virginia University Library

Cumberland Daily Times, touring the railroad during April, noted that there were now 100 houses in Elkins and a population of approximately 800, remarkable growth in two years.

Following through on his interest in purchasing the W. Md., Davis asked Latrobe to organize a survey party to determine a line to Hagerstown. The survey party set out from Cumberland on April 18 with George D. Coryell as engineer in charge.

Davis wrote to Thompson on April 28, mentioning the possibility of leasing the W. Md. from the City of Baltimore and noting that the B. & O. opposed such a move. A request to purchase the W. Md. was received by the city on April 29 for $1,500,000.

However, the indebtedness of the W. Md. to the city amounted to about $8,000,000 so the city took no action. Davis told the New York Times that he had not made the offer. President Hood of the W. Md. was adamantly opposed to the sale of the railroad, and pointed out that the prospects for the W. Md. had never been better.

The bridge south of Elkins, which had been of such concern to Latrobe, was reported finished on May 2, and that the cofferdam for the second bridge on the Beverly extension was under construction. The ironwork for this structure was to come from the bridges at Potomac, McKenzie and Caudys, which had been wrecked during the floods of 1889. Replacement pins and eye bars were to be provided by the Edge Moor company and Latrobe expected a saving of $1,250 over the price of a new bridge.

It was noted on May 4, that C. M. Hendley had been appointed as assistant to the President Davis. Hendley was to remain in Davis's employ in various capacities for the next 25 years.

Late spring saw two items that at the time seemed insignificant but were to be of considerable importance to Davis in a few years. On May 22, George Price, a Charleston attorney, wrote to Davis noting that a group of Charleston businessmen were hoping to raise $2,000,000 to build a railroad up the Elk River to Braxton Court House (now called Sutton). Price asked Davis for help and also asked if he would build over from the West Virginia Central to connect with the new road. Davis indicated that Senator Camden would be the appropriate person to involve, and took no further interest. Although other schemes had been advanced to build up the Elk, this one actually succeeded, at least in part, when the Charleston, Clendennin and Sutton Railroad was built.

A few days later a similar announcement appeared in the Parkersburg newspapers mentioning that a group of businessmen hoped to build up the Little Kanawha River. Although some preliminary grading was done at this time, the company that was to actually build up the river, the Little Kanawha Railroad, was not incorporated until 1896. Part of the reason for the delay was the threat of competition from river borne traffic. The Little Kanawha River had been improved for navigation by the Little Kanawha Navigation Company, which had built four locks between 1867 and 1874. A fifth lock was built by the federal government in 1891 below Burning Spring, which made the river navigable as far as Glenville during periods of high water.

Davis at this time was more concerned about the fires that were sweeping through the forests served by the West Virginia Central, many of which had been started by the locomotives. The first report, on May 6, noted that fires were raging around Davis. On May 18, a fire was reported near Dobbin, which threatened to destroy the village. A day later, a fire near Pendleton destroyed 500 acres including hemlock bark and logs that had been skidded during the winter causing an estimated $2,000 damage. Two tramroads were also destroyed for an additional loss of $4,000. Fires also threatened Coketon, and did damage the trestles there.

On May 20, Davis wrote to Fairfax S. Landstreet, secretary of the H. G. Davis Coal Company and also a relative, concerning rumors that the Blackwater Boom and Lumber Company at Davis was having financial difficulties. Landstreet thought that the company was in good shape as they had 8,000,000 feet of logs in the river and in the woods valued at $40,000, and $20,000 of manufactured lumber in the yard ready to be shipped.

Parsons submitted his report of his explorations towards the Greenbrier on June 1. He mentioned meeting survey parties from the C. & O. heading towards Huntersville, and reported that Camden's party was at work on the Williams River. Yet another party was at work on the Cowpasture River in Virginia. Parsons thought that a good route could be found from the Greenbrier to the state line with light grades. Parsons later wrote that a route along the Greenbrier from the Forks to Marlins Bottom would be "out of the question." McGraw wrote to Davis on June 29 asking if Davis was going to take up his option on the Marlins Bottom lands. Encouraged by Parsons's report that Marlins Bottom would not lie on his line Davis finally declined McGraw's offer. Parsons closed up his survey work in the area on July 3, confirming that a route from the head of the Tygart Valley River was out of the question, and that a route from Elkins would be "too heavy." He favored the route from Hendricks that " would be light and cheaper of construction."

Engine No. 24 made its first trip over the West Virginia Central on June 11. Engine No. 25 was at the shops at West Virginia Central Junction ready to be set up for service.

It was noted on June 2 that George Cadle had contracted to remove the girders from the old Wills Creek bridge and to repair the ironwork of the wrecked bridges ready for erection on the Beverly branch. It also had been decided in May to realign the tracks below Thomas to better serve the mine at Douglas, which meant that a new bridge would have to be constructed across the Blackwater. Latrobe was advised on June 20, that the masonry for this bridge would be finished by August 1 and was given permission to obtain bids on new girders.

By the end of June, one pier of the Beverly bridge was under construction and all of the stonework was expected to be finished by August 1. The stonework for the bridge on the Belington line was to be finished by August 15. Considerable delay was experienced on the Wills Creek bridge although the ironwork was expected to arrive by the end of July. The Edge Moor company expected to ship the replacement eye bars and pins for the Beverly bridge by August 1. On July 24, Latrobe reported that he had awarded the contract for the Thomas bridge ironwork to the Phoenix Bridge Company at a cost of $3,497.

Latrobe also kept Davis informed as to the progress on the Hagerstown survey by Coryell. After two month's work, Coryell was reported to be 37.3/4 miles from Cumberland and 11 miles from Hancock. Latrobe reported that up to June 1, the survey had cost $1,800. He later recommended that it was not a good idea to go beyond Hagerstown to Baltimore as such a line would never pay for itself, but recommended a junction with the W. Md. By July 7 the survey team was three miles east of Hancock. A week later the party made contact with the W. Md.'s Cherry Run extension some 60 miles from Cumberland. The party finally reached Hagerstown on August 5 making a connection with the Cumberland Valley Railroad a mile north of Hagerstown and with the W. Md. in the town.

With the railroad now reaching towards Belington, Riordan was ordered on July 19 to explore for coal along the Tygart Valley River in the Roaring Creek field. Davis had purchased some land at the mouth of Roaring Creek at a commissioner's sale in October 1890. Riordan's first report on July 27 was not very encouraging and his final report on August 10 indicated finding veins only two or three feet thick. Other individuals in the area seem to have been more fortunate. O. C. Womelsdorf, who had been involved with the field from its early days, was reported to have negotiated the sale of 5,500 acres of land on July 23. In February, Womelsdorf had written to Davis requesting an annual pass over the West Virginia Central as he thought that his work was beneficial to the company. As neither Davis nor Bretz had heard of him at that time, the request was denied.

It was noted in the Cumberland Times on July 9 that the first canal boat to leave Cumberland since the flood of 1889 left for Williamsport. The canal opened along its full length on October 9, when a boat arrived in Georgetown. The captain reported that the trip took 13 days and that there were still some shallow sections.

Davis received an important letter on July 9 from Major John Hutton of Huttonsville asking if Davis would extend to that place from Beverly if he were provided a free right-of-way and ground for a depot. Because business was dull at this time, Davis did not pursue the matter. In fact he was short of money and had to ask Hendley to secure a $20,000 loan for four months to tide him over.

A stockholders' meeting was held at Piedmont at the end of July where, as usual, the proceedings were enlivened by the presence of Cross. The contract between the West Virginia Central and the B. & O. for the connection at Belington was approved. Cross then proposed a resolution calling for all future meetings to be held in Baltimore. The resolution was tabled. Cross then criticized the building of the extension to Elkins, which he claimed led to the railroad being ridiculed in public as a "long siding of the Baltimore and Ohio Railroad in the shape of a fishhook" and asked for a committee to look into the extension. This resolution was also tabled.

Davis received a letter, dated July 29, from John G. Luke, the general manager for the pulp mill at Piedmont, complaining about the rate charged on pulpwood delivered to the mill. He noted that the original rate on pulpwood had been 90 cents per cord but it was now $1.40 per cord. The mill was receiving 175 tons of pulpwood per day, which was nearly twice the amount that had originally been envisaged. This confirmed that an expansion of supply had taken place since McGraw's letter to Camden in January. Luke also noted that the average monthly payment for freight on wood and other materials used by the mill, to the West Virginia Central, was $2,303. This figure must have been gratifying to Davis, who turned a deaf ear to the request. Luke noted that the company proposed to build a paper mill at Piedmont to give an outlet for the company's pulp. Work on the mill commenced in the fall, and was to be finished by December.

On August 4 an accident occurred at Switchback on the Elk Garden branch when an individual was killed when an engine hit a fallen tree. Early reports indicated that the accident had occurred on the West Virginia Central, but it turned out to be on a lumber tramroad belonging to the Whitmer Lumber Company. An engine was leaving to go into the woods and, as was usual at the time, was carrying 17 woodsmen and two women, who were going to pick berries. When the engine hit the tree, it overturned crushing one man, and scalding several others including one of the women.

The West Virginia Central was not immune to such accidents. The Mineville branch was once again the site of a wreck on August 11, when an engine jumped the track and severely injured the engineer.

A few days later, it was reported that the bridge on the Beverly extension was finished except for one stringer that would not fit into the stonework. Latrobe accepted responsibility for the mistake as he had assumed that all of the stringers on the wrecked bridges were the same length, which was not the case. By substituting another stringer, the bridge was finished on August 27 and declared ready for trains (Fig. 76).

Fig. 76. Bridge No. 3 on the Beverly extension
Collection of the Western Maryland Railway Historical Society

Because of the delay in getting the ironwork for the Belington bridge, it was decided to build a temporary trestle across the river to allow work to proceed. The trestle was finished on September 9.

The ironwork for the Wills Creek bridge finally arrived on September 10; erection of the bridge started on September 14 under the supervision of Cadle. After only a few hours work, an ironworker fell off the bridge while trying to catch an errant hat. At the time he was holding a roller (reported to weigh 1,000 pounds), which pinned him to the bed of Wills Creek. He was rescued with only a broken arm.

The ever hopeful McGraw wrote to Davis on September 14, mentioning that Camden and the C. & O. had reached an agreement to connect at Marlins Bottom, and that a company was being set up to transact business in land at that point. McGraw asked if Davis would care to be involved in the new company, but he declined. Davis did write to Camden for information on the contract with the C. & O. The new company proposed by McGraw, the Pocahontas Development Company, was chartered at the end of September to build the new town at Marlinton. In what was to become a familiar ritual with towns brought to prominence by the railroads, there was an immediate effort to move the county seat from Huntersville to Marlinton.

On September 19, Bretz submitted a proposal from the Marion Steam Shovel Company, to supply a shovel for $5,200. Davis suggested $5,000, which was accepted, and the shovel was to be delivered at the end of the month.

The end of September saw a series of wrecks on the B. & O. and the West Virginia Central that almost isolated Cumberland by rail from the rest of the country. The trouble started at 6:15 A.M. on September 27 when two B. & O. trains collided at Cedar Cliff.

The B. & O. track being blocked, trains were rerouted over the P. & C. between West Virginia Central Junction and Cumberland. The first eastbound B. & O. express to enter Cumberland was due in at 7:15 A.M. but did not cross the Potomac River over the P. & C. bridge until 1:15 P.M. When it reached the trestle leading from the bridge to the depot, it derailed but fortunately stayed on the trestle. A second eastbound express was now stalled behind the first when it also suffered a derailment. Men from all the railroads in Cumberland were rushed to the scene to get things moving. The second express finally made its way into the B. & O. depot nearly eight hours late. A third B. & O. train suffered three derailments, supposedly because of sharp curves, when it attempted to use a siding at Keyser. Even before the wrecks, Bretz had been complaining that the B. & O. was blocked with freight because of difficulties in unloading trains at Locust Point in Baltimore, and that freight was going by way of the Pennsylvania.

Two companies were incorporated in October, which were important for Davis in the Roaring Creek area. The first was the Cassidy Fork Boom and Lumber Company, which proposed to build a boom on the Middle Fork River, but which was to have its office on Roaring Creek. Listed as an incorporator was William Diller of Lancaster, Pennsylvania. Diller later wrote to Davis asking for an annual pass and also asking for any information that Davis might have on a route for a railroad up Roaring Creek. The second new company was the Randolph Coal Company, incorporated by Davis to develop a mine on the Belington extension. It was to be managed by Davis's elder son, Henry Jr., who was a troubled young man, and it was Davis's hope that the job would help his son to settle down.

At the beginning of November, it was reported that the floor beams were being installed on the Wills Creek bridge and by the middle of the month, the Edge Moor company had started to fabricate the ironwork for the Belington bridge.

It was reported on November 13, that Davis and a party in the car "West Virginia," had gone over the entire line as far as Beverly. As this was the first passenger train to arrive in the town, it seemed that the total population of 400 or 500 people turned out to welcome the guests.

In anticipation of expanded business, Davis decided to order 50 coke cars from the South Baltimore Car Works on November 20 for $462.50 each. These were to be numbered 2157-2206. South Baltimore also provided Davis with an experimental coal car for trial, although no details of the car were given. During its sojourn on the West Virginia Central it was numbered 1600. Davis also thought that a second switching engine and two road engines should be ordered. The order was placed by Bretz, with the Baldwin Locomotive Works, on December 8, for one switch engine at $8,700 and for one road engine for $9,820. Delivery of the new engines was to be February 1892. The new freight engines were to be slightly larger than previous locomotives and to have a larger tender. Bretz also ordered a combined mail, baggage and express car from Jackson and Sharp for $2,800 to be paid in coal.

On November 16, track laying on the Belington extension had reached Beaver Creek but because the bridge girders had not arrived, the construction crew was put on ballasting the track. The girders finally arrived on November 23 and were installed in a cou-

ple of days. Porter expected to reach the Randolph mine with track in a week or less. Porter also reported that the depot at Beverly would be ready for freight in two weeks and that he expected to turn the branch over to the operating department at the same time.

The Wills Creek bridge was reported to have been completed on November 30 and the old girders removed and taken to Elkins for use on Bridge No. 1 south of the town.

Bretz gave Davis on December 15, a list of the machinery for the new car shop that had been purchased and was being set up. He hoped that the new shop would be ready for use by January 1, 1892. The car shop, with a later extension, is shown in Fig. 109.

Bretz went over the new line as far as the Randolph mine on December 15 with Thomas Davis. He recommended that as much ballasting as possible be finished before regular service commenced, as the track had already been damaged by excessive use. He also examined the Beverly branch and reported that the depot should be ready for use by January 1, although considerable grading was still required. Grading was also required at the Randolph mine for a siding. Bretz also reported that the new alignment near Thomas was almost complete and should enable a locomotive that normally pulled eight cars at this point to manage 12.

Track laying was completed to Belington on December 17 (Fig. 77). Davis wrote to the B. & O. reporting that the connection had been made and hoping it would push the change of gauge on

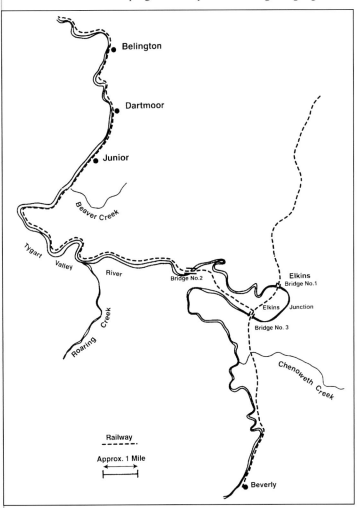

Fig. 77. Map of the Beverly and Belington extensions

the G. & G. Bretz reported that only three miles of the G. & G. had been re-gauged at that time. Vice President Smith of the B. & O. told Davis that his company hoped to have the G. & G. converted to standard gauge by March 1. He also noted that work on the road between Fairmont and Morgantown had been delayed by the sickness of the chief engineer. With the track now at Belington,

Bretz reported that 18 bosses and 140 laborers had been discharged.

It was decided to wait until spring 1892 before either branch would open for regular service, although a couple of freight trains were run each week to Beverly and a train was run to the Randolph mine to deliver and collect coal cars.

Fig. 78. Cumberland yards, circa 1890. Work on the stone retaining wall below the Central Station can be seen in the distance
Herman and Stacia Miller Collection, City of Cumberland

The new year, 1892, started on a sour note when Davis received a letter from President Hood of the W. Md. warning Davis against seeking control of the W. Md. Hood claimed the general public "will (not) stand much more of this unfair treatment of this important city interest." Davis was not intimidated by Hood's letter, and wrote to Kerens on January 18 that the W. Md. project was moving well. However, Davis did not give up on his idea of an independent route to Baltimore; the Baltimore and Cumberland Railroad was reported to have taken out a charter in the middle of January. The route of the proposed new railroad is shown on a map, published in January 1892, and reproduced in Fig. 79.

Pennsylvania Railroad was converting to 100 pound rail but that the West Virginia Central still had some sections of un-ballasted 56 pound rail. The engine quoted by Baldwin also could be obtained in compound form, and this did interest Bretz.

The problem with the lightweight bridges was underscored on January 15 when a car loaded with pulpwood derailed in the middle of one span of the bridge at Schell, damaging the bridge. Bretz thought the span would have to be removed for repairs, and in the interim, ordered that a trestle be built to allow trains to pass. Service over the trestle commenced on January 17. Bretz estimated that a girder span would cost $3,949 and a truss bridge $4,717. He urged an immediate decision, as he doubted the trestle would withstand the inevitable spring freshets. Davis, surprisingly, was not too disturbed at news of the calamity, noting that trade was poor at the time. Latrobe was given the job of arranging for a new bridge and received a bid from the Youngstown Bridge Company. Youngstown agreed to build a new lattice girder span for $4,523, remove the old span, and be finished in 60 days.

The Tenth Annual Report of the West Virginia Central published in January 1892, noted that a new shaft mine had been completed at Thomas by the H. G. Davis Coal Company. The shaft had been started in the spring of 1891 and had reached a depth of 30 feet by May 19 when it reached rock and progress slowed.

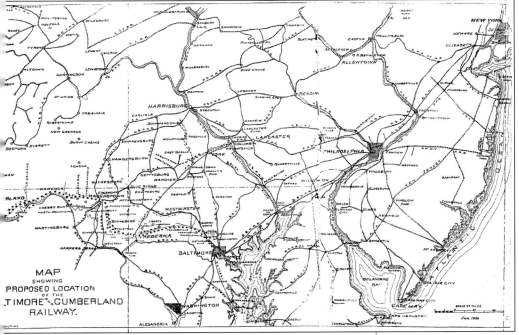

Fig. 79. Proposed location of the Baltimore and Cumberland Railway, January 1892
West Virginia and Regional History Collection,
West Virginia University Library

Davis became interested in the possibility of providing much larger locomotives for the West Virginia Central similar to the Northern Pacific's No. 500. The No. 500 was a 2-10-0 and weighed 145,000 pounds; some 18 tons heavier than Nos. 24 and 25 delivered in 1891. Bretz was against the idea as such engines would require the use of 85 pound rail and ballast throughout. The Potomac River bridges at Harrison, Schell and Bayard would need also to be replaced. Bretz recommended that another freight engine, similar to the one presently being built by Baldwin, be ordered for June delivery. Baldwin also quoted on a 2-10-0 engine similar to those built for the Erie at $14,000 plus $810 for Westinghouse brakes. Bretz again thought the engine was too heavy for the West Virginia Central tracks noting that the

New coal companies continued to spring up along the Belington extension. At the beginning of January, the Junior Coal Company was chartered with Davis and son Henry, Jr. listed among the incorporators. At the end of the month, a group from Philippi incorporated the Belington Coal and Coke Company. Like other towns on the West Virginia Central, Belington was poised to become an important railroad and mining center. The population was estimated to be about 500, and a hotel and bank were scheduled for construction during the year. A report on the mine at Junior was made on February 5 by A. C. Finley, assistant to Thomas Davis, which noted that ten miners were employed and 453 tons of coal had been mined in January. The report also noted that the opening had been driven in 264 feet and rail had been laid from the opening to the tipple. The siding on the West Virginia Central also had been completed.

The Piedmont Herald reported on January 22, that the new paper mill of the West Virginia Paper Company had produced its first paper a few days earlier. The new mill initially had two

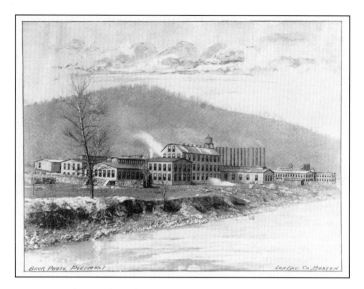

Fig. 80. Piedmont Pulp and Paper Company mills at Piedmont, circa 1893
Collection of Westernport Heritage Society

paper making machines and produced various grades of paper for printing and packaging. The two mills occupied about 50 acres on Davis Island (Fig. 80), and employed about 300 men and women.

Davis received a letter from R. P. Chew of Charlestown, West Virginia, mentioning that a route to Baltimore could be built through Winchester, Harpers Ferry and Frederick with the possibility of connecting with the Loudoun and Hampshire Railroad. Davis mentioned the route to Parsons who thought the line feasible and offered to survey the route when the weather improved. Parsons later summarized the route as being 145 miles long and having light grades. Davis decided to abandon this project on February 26 in favor of the Cumberland to Hagerstown line.

Parsons later presented Davis with a summary of his work on possible routes to Covington. All three routes met at a common point on Cochrans Creek referred to as "88 mile." The line from Hendricks to this point was 88 miles in length and estimated to cost $1,274,000. The route from Elkins would be 83 miles long, involve some rugged work and would cost $1,732,000. The final route from Beverly would be the shortest at 70 miles, but would require four tunnels, and cost $2,015,000. Parsons described this route as requiring "stupendous work" and it had already been eliminated as a possibility. This did not stop Davis asking Parsons to take one more look at the route in September.

The annual meeting of the West Virginia Central stockholders was held at Piedmont on January 26. Just before the ballot was taken to elect directors for the coming year, Elkins introduced a resolution that disallowed anyone from being a director of the company who held less than 200 shares of stock (Cross held 100) and who was an attorney in a lawsuit against the company. The resolution passed. Although Cross received enough votes, counted cumulatively, to be on the board, he was barred by the new rule. Cross wrote a fiery letter to Davis after the meeting complaining of fraud, and demanding to be included on the directorate. Not satisfied with the response, he filed suit with the West Virginia Supreme Court of Appeals on February 3.

This was followed by a complaint filed in the Circuit Court

of Baltimore by Shaw on February 18 against Davis, Elkins, Thomas Davis, the West Virginia Central, the P. & C., the Pennsylvania and others. Shaw asked for an injunction to prevent the leasing of the P. & C. by the West Virginia Central. The judge gave the defendants until April 2 to show cause why an injunction should not be issued.

Bretz reported on February 9, that the depot and freight shed at Beverly were finished although the siding still needed to be laid (Fig. 81). It was also recommended by Bretz that toolhouses, similar to those on the Pennsylvania, be built along the West Virginia Central. By June 1894, 27 of these structures were dotted along the road, one of which, at Montrose, is shown in Fig. 82. A few days later, it was reported that crossties were being laid on bridge No. 2 on the Belington extension (Fig. 83).

Fig. 81. Depot and freight shed at Beverly (undated)
Collection of Pocahontas County Historical Society

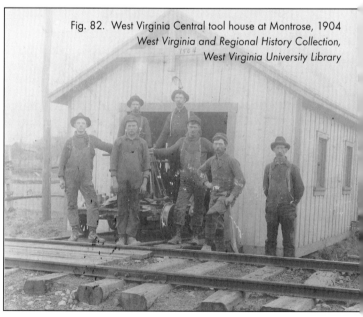

Fig. 82. West Virginia Central tool house at Montrose, 1904
West Virginia and Regional History Collection,
West Virginia University Library

Engines Nos. 26 and 27 arrived from Baldwin on February 18. Bretz discussed the engine situation with Davis a few days later, pointing out that another engine would be required if and when trade picked up. Again he claimed that the existing engines were heavy enough for the track, but thought that a compound 2-

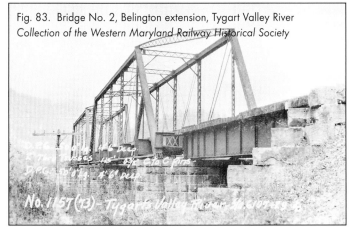

Fig. 83. Bridge No. 2, Belington extension, Tygart Valley River
Collection of the Western Maryland Railway Historical Society

8-0 could be used to advantage on the Elk Garden branch. Compound engines used steam twice, once in a small high pressure cylinder and then in a large low pressure cylinder. Bretz noted that such an engine would weigh eight tons more than No. 27, which in turn weighed 9,000 pounds more than any other engine.

Bretz also reported that the combination baggage, mail and express car had arrived from Jackson and Sharp on March 8 and would become No. 2 to replace a combination car that had been destroyed on the Elk Garden branch on October 26, 1891.

For some time Bretz had been trying to persuade Davis to allow the appointment of an assistant general manager. With the new extensions due to come into service in April, Davis finally allowed Bretz to proceed. Bretz recommended W. H. Bower of the Pennsylvania Railroad, and Davis accepted this nomination. Bower had 18 years of practical railroad experience and also was a good telegraph operator. According to Bretz, Bower "has never taken a drink of liquor, neither smokes nor chews; his family consists of wife and one child." Bower began his service on the West Virginia Central on March 15.

Davis thought that no additional locomotives would be required until the fall but then on March 26 he changed his mind and allowed Bretz to try one of the Baldwin compounds. At the time Nos. 26 and 27 were ordered, Baldwin had agreed to build three locomotives and take the price in coal. As only two engines had been ordered the offer for the third still stood and this had convinced Davis to permit the trial.

Davis decided on March 24 that the Belington and Beverly branches would open on April 20, although Bretz was still concerned about the state of the track. Bretz also asked that names be given to points along the route where sidings and mines had been established. It was agreed that the area formerly known as Rowton would become Junior. Another point on the line was later named Custer after General George Custer of Little Bighorn fame. By the end of March the B. & O. still had not decided when work would be finished on the G. & G. to allow the interchange of traffic.

Bretz also asked Davis to consider the effect that the large number of coal companies, all essentially owned by the same people, was having on the revenue of the West Virginia Central. The problem was that coal of one company might be held up and the West Virginia Central was thus denied the use of the cars. He

recommended consolidation of all the companies but Davis was not yet receptive to this idea.

Davis noted in his diary on March 28 that he had submitted a bid to the mayor and city council of Baltimore for the lease of the W. Md. A couple of days earlier, Hood had reported to the finance committee of the council that the prospects for the company were improving and that the monthly earnings were increasing even though trade was dull. Hood criticized certain city officials as being too ready to denigrate the W. Md. in the hope of achieving a quick sale. It was reported after Davis made his offer, that public opinion was against the proposal as it was not enough for a road that had cost $10,000,000 to build. Whether he was successful in his bid for the W. Md. or not, Davis intended to pursue the line to Hagerstown and ordered that surveying between Cumberland and Hancock be started again on April 15.

Davis recorded in his diary on April 10, " business only fair," but this did not prevent him from ordering 20 boxcars from South Baltimore Car Works at $593 each.

Davis heard again from the Diller clan on April 26, this time it was Samuel Diller, who indicated that he was interested in building a line from Roaring Creek and asked to meet with Davis. Davis later declined to take a financial interest in Diller's railroad and nothing further was heard from the Dillers until the end of August.

Latrobe submitted a report to Davis on May 5 revising the cost of the Cumberland to Hagerstown extension. The most difficult section was between Cumberland and Hancock, a distance of 50 miles and costing $2,223,197. This section included five tunnels and heavy grades. Between Hancock and Hagerstown, a distance of 27.2 miles, there were no tunnels and the grades were easier, and the cost was estimated at $909,699. The total cost was estimated to be $3,132,896. Davis met with President Kennedy of the Cumberland Valley Railroad and it was agreed to continue the survey work with Davis being responsible for the Cumberland to Hancock section, and Kennedy the Hancock to Hagerstown section. Davis was also encouraged to continue the survey work by Roberts of the Pennsylvania but both Roberts and Kennedy urged Davis to try to work out an equitable traffic arrangement with the B. & O. to use that company's line between Cumberland and Cherry Run.

A carpenters' car was reported to have been destroyed by fire on May 8 at Chaffee. This car had originally been combination car No. 3 but Bretz noted that it was worn out and only suitable for a carpenters' car.

Bretz reported on May 14 that the G. & G. expected to complete the conversion of its track to standard gauge in two days, although he doubted they would be ready to ship freight immediately. The first standard gauge train, consisting of two passenger cars and three freight cars, left Grafton for Belington on May 28.

On May 19, Bretz informed Davis the bridge at Schell had been finished within the specified time and was in use. It also had been decided to replace the wooden trestle in Cumberland, leading from the Potomac River bridge to the depot, with an iron structure. A contract was awarded to the Pencoyd Bridge Company for this work.

Davis cannot have been too pleased with Latrobe's revised estimate for the Cumberland to Hagerstown extension. He ordered Parsons to examine a possible route along the Potomac River between Cumberland and Hancock that avoided both the B. & O. and the canal. Parsons's initial report of May 22 showed that some heavy work would be required as cliffs came right down to the canal or the B. & O., and that several long river crossings would be required.

Davis wrote to Kerens on May 18 reporting that he doubted if much would happen in regard to the W. Md. before summer. However it was announced on May 28 that the W. Md. would resume interest payments to the city on its various obligations. The company had been informed that if such payments were made, the city would refrain from trying to lease or sell the road. This would seem to have foiled the Davis scheme, but he still had other ideas to enable the West Virginia Central to obtain the W. Md.

Latrobe submitted two reports to Davis on June 28, the first dealing with the condition of the Belington and Beverly extensions and the second with the bridges on the extensions. Latrobe was well pleased with the state of the extensions and noted, "both branches are in good working order and rapidly improving everyday." He noted that the bridge across the Tygart Valley River on the Belington extension, 330 feet long, was built to the highest modern standards. The bridge on the Beverly extension, 200 feet in length, was designed also for the heaviest traffic.

Two days later, Latrobe submitted another revision to the cost of the proposed Cumberland to Hagerstown railroad. This showed some savings could be achieved on the excavation work, and the total cost of the extension was now put at $3,129,919.55.

Davis wrote to Orland Smith, vice president of the B. & O., to see if that company would allow connections with the P. & C. at Keyser and Rawlings. Smith recommended that the connections be installed, the two companies sharing the expense. Davis and Elkins met with Smith on July 18, to see if a trackage arrangement could be worked out between the two companies between Cumberland and Cherry Run. Davis was encouraged by the meeting and thought that an arrangement could be made. Kennedy was pleased to hear that the talks were progressing well and recommended that any arrangement also include Martinsburg to allow for an interchange of traffic with the C. V. Kennedy also submitted a report from Chauncey Ives, chief engineer of the C. V. showing that a road could be built from Hancock to a connection with the C. V. for slightly less than $1,000,000.

Bretz met with an official of the B. & O. on July 19 and agreed that the connection between the G. & G. and the West Virginia Central would be made at 11:15 A.M. on August 1. It was also agreed that both companies would provide one combined car and one passenger car for the two passenger trains that would provide a through service. Bretz requested that two additional passenger cars be purchased, as it was necessary on occasion to borrow cars from the B. & O.

or the G. C. & C. The roster of cars owned by the West Virginia Central at this time was five combination cars, one full baggage and express and seven passenger cars. Bretz obtained a quote from Jackson and Sharp for $4,550 for a passenger car, a price Davis thought was too high. Eventually a price was agreed on for the new car, which became West Virginia Central No. 15.

The 11th Annual Report of the West Virginia Central dated June 30, 1892, contained a recommendation from Bretz that a three-stall engine house should be erected at Thomas. Bretz returned to the subject in July when he suggested to Davis that a two-stall engine house, built with corrugated iron, be constructed. He requested that it be built before winter set in as it was expensive to have locomotives standing in the open in such a cold place. It is not known exactly when the engine house was built, but the 12th Annual Report in 1893 noted that a two-stall engine house, measuring 44 feet by 65 feet, had been completed during the year. During the W. Md. years, this engine house became a car repair shop and can be seen in the center of Fig. . Bretz also recommended in the 1892 Annual Report that a paint shop be built at Elkins, and this also was completed by the following June.

The first compound engine, No. 28, arrived from Baldwin on July 25. A few days later Bretz reported that it pulled a 50-car train through Shaw and that he expected No. 28 to pull 45 loads north when it was "limbered up." A month later Baldwin wrote to Davis noting that because business was slack, they had built a second engine, similar to No. 28, and would be willing to sell it for the same price as No. 28, i.e. $10,650, and would be willing to take coal or coke in exchange. Davis was agreeable to the proposal and gave Bretz permission to purchase the engine on August 26. Bretz was impressed by No. 28, claiming it used one-fourth less coal than a conventional engine. The new engine, No. 29, was delivered during the first week of September (Fig. 84).

On August 4, John G. Luke met with Thomas Davis and mentioned the possibility of the Piedmont Pulp and Paper

Fig. 84. West Virginia Central compound engine No. 29
Maryland State Archives, Miller Collection

Company building a pulp mill at Davis. The proposed mill would make a lower grade of pulp than the Piedmont facility, and would use waste slabs and culls from the mills. Of critical importance to the new enterprise was the question of freight rates. Luke pointed out that the company's mill at Harpers Ferry was receiving its lumber from sources along the Camden road at a rate less than was being charged by the West Virginia Central even though the distance was greater. Luke mentioned that the spruce along the West Virginia Central was dying, and it was to the railroad's advantage to move it as quickly as possible while it still had value. A meeting between Davis and John G. Luke was held on August 5 leading to an agreement on most points governing freight rates to and from the new mill. Davis also agreed to sell the Lukes five acres of land in Davis for the mill. The railroad agreed to install the necessary sidings and to build a bridge across Beaver Creek, with half the expense being borne by the Lukes.

Samuel Diller wrote to Davis on August 31, asking about freight rates and rebates on coal and lumber shipped to Pittsburgh, New York, Philadelphia and Baltimore. He also asked whether more favorable rates could be obtained if his projected road connected with the West Virginia Central at Belington rather than the mouth of Roaring Creek.

McGraw wrote to Davis on the same day mentioning that "New York parties" had purchased 15,000 acres of land on the Greenbrier and Cheat rivers, and were considering the possibility of building a narrow gauge line into the area from Hendricks. He again asked Davis what his plans were for a southern extension. McGraw wrote again on October 21 noting that the parties had now increased their holdings to 27,000 acres and were contemplating the construction of a sawmill, pulp mill and a tannery at the Forks of the Greenbrier or at Marlinton, if a railroad could be built to either point. In the absence of a railroad, they proposed to float logs down the Greenbrier to Ronceverte. Davis responded that the Greenbrier was not a good river to float logs, but that he had no idea when he would build a railroad into the area.

The question of the W. Md. came up again in early September, when Davis was advised by Frank Thomson, first vice president of the Pennsylvania, that the Reading Railroad was after the W. Md. At this time the Reading was aggressively expanding in various directions, so a move towards acquiring the W. Md. was not entirely unexpected. This prompted Davis to think about trying to capture control of the W. Md.'s board of directors, although Davis and his allies did not own a majority of the stock. Hood, in a letter published in the New York Times, pointed out that of the 13 directors, eight were appointed by the City of Baltimore, and five elected by the stockholders; the city also participated in the stockholders' election. If Davis could get the city's proxy in this election, he could elect his own directors and then possibly influence the city's directors sufficiently to gain a majority. A lease of the W. Md. would then soon follow. Hood was adamantly opposed to control by the West Virginia Central, and claimed that the shares held by the company and its allies had cost less than $50,000 whereas Baltimore's interest had cost $7,500,000. He thought that the West Virginia Central could hardly claim a seat on the board when its interest was less than one half of one percent of that of the city. Hood concluded with a parting shot at Davis and Elkins by saying that, "the designs of selfish parties who, in connection with these Western Maryland crusades, are seeking individual profit at the public expense." The election was not due to be held until October and in the meanwhile the politicking continued. In the middle of October, the city council decided to appoint a commission to investigate the financial health of the W. Md. thus postponing for at least three months the election of directors.

On September 14, it was reported that a train of 40 cars near Seymour split in two, the rear section then colliding with the front section wrecking 11 cars. Bretz estimated the damage at $1,000, and blamed the engineer for the wreck. During the fall, the lack of freight cars became a major concern for Davis and shippers along the road, and wrecks such as this could not have come at a worse time.

Davis gave Bretz permission on September 19 to order 100 hopper coal cars from South Baltimore Car Works at $500 each. Davis also ordered that all freight cars be painted red with large letters on the side. The new coal cars, when delivered, received numbers 1601 through 1700. A couple of months later, South Baltimore received an order for 50 coke racks at $462.50 each and 50 gondolas at $430 each. The coke racks were numbered 2207-2256 and the gondolas were numbered starting with 3001.

President B. Gilpin Smith of the Beaver Creek Lumber Company at Davis wrote on September 28 complaining that there were no cars to shift lumber already cut and sold. He also noted that he had 75 car loads of pulpwood ready to ship and that salesmen were refusing orders because they could not guarantee delivery. This letter was followed a few weeks later by a similar appeal from the York Haven Paper Company in Maryland, which received all their pulpwood from the West Virginia Central, claiming they would have to close their mills unless they could get at least a couple of cars a day. Davis wrote to the B. & O. and the Pennsylvania to try to get a better supply of cars but the situation did not improve.

The suit brought by Alexander Shaw against Davis, Elkins, Thomas Davis and others began in Circuit Court in Baltimore on October 17. Shaw, who was represented by W. Irvine Cross, sought an injunction to prevent the West Virginia Central leasing the P. & C. until an accounting of all monies spent by the West Virginia Central could be made. The West Virginia Central was defended by William Pinkney Whyte, and as might be expected, the trial proved to be lively. During his defense, Whyte became annoyed at the frequent interruptions by Cross and asked the judge to defend him from this "miserable wretch." Davis must have been delighted at this description of his nemesis. Presentation of evidence in the trial concluded on October 26.

By the beginning of November, two months after No. 29 had been delivered, Bretz reported problems with the boiler leaking. Baldwin agreed to put in new flues, the West Virginia Central paying the cost of the labor. Bretz thought that the problem was more extensive than the flues, but Baldwin pointed out that the water provided for the engines at Ridgeley was responsible for similar problems in all the engines. Tests had shown that the water was highly corrosive towards iron and steel and it was suggested that because of the prevailing drought, the quality of water had deteriorated. Bretz recommended that city water from Cumberland be used at Ridgeley to alleviate the problem.

At the end of November, Axtell of the C. & O. reported on the progress of that company's surveys towards Marlinton. Three routes were being examined, the route preferred by Axtell leaving the C. & O. at White Sulphur Springs. McGraw was getting a little concerned at the lack of progress in getting a railroad to Marlinton and the possibility that a railroad might not be built at all. He thought that Camden had given up the idea of building in that direction and his hopes now rested with Davis and the C. & O.

Davis wrote to Parsons at the end of November about putting a survey party to work during the winter on the route east of Cumberland. Surprisingly, Parsons told him that such additional work was not needed until a decision was made to build the road. Parsons thought that once the decision had been made to proceed, the work could be finished and ready for letting by June 1893.

December was a busy time for the incorporators of new railroads in West Virginia. The first to be incorporated was the Dry Fork Railroad on December 14, planned to go from the West Virginia Central up either Laurel, Glady or Dry forks to the Greenbrier and the C. & O. Included among the incorporators were R. F. Whitmer, Martin Lane and Levi Condon. The same group also incorporated the Dry Fork Boom and Lumber Company on December 23. Thomas Davis and James Parsons were listed among the incorporators of the Cumberland Railway Company designed to run from Cumberland to Moorefield, and finally the grandly named Point Pleasant, Buckhannon and Tygarts Valley Railroad Company was incorporated to run from Barbour County to the Ohio River.

By December 1, the supply of cars to the West Virginia Central was still insufficient and Davis wrote to Thomson of the Pennsylvania seeking help. Davis reported that the West Virginia Central now had 1,600 cars, 1,500 of which were available for the coal trade. During the period September 1 to November 23 only 641 cars had been received from the Pennsylvania while in the same time 2,853 loads had been delivered. During the same time, the B. & O., not exactly a friendly road, delivered 1,220 empty cars and received 2,165 in return. In addition, movement of cars on the Pennsylvania was slower than on the B. & O. However, in a letter to Mayer on the same day, Davis was much more indignant about the problems the West Virginia Central had with the B. & O. Not only was the West Virginia Central being shortchanged in the supply of coal cars, it also was being seriously disadvantaged in freight rates on coal and coke going both east and west compared to competitors in the Fairmont region. Davis claimed that customers were being lost and trade depressed by the policies of the B. & O. He was also upset that it was taking, on average, 20 days for a coal car to make the trip to Baltimore and return rather than ten days.

However, worse was to come near the end of December when the Pennsylvania was unable to move any loads from Cumberland, the West Virginia Central having 185 loaded cars at that point. On December 28, it was reported that the

Pennsylvania was moving again and only 80 loads remained in Cumberland. By December 31, the situation on the Pennsylvania again deteriorated as Davis was informed that the Bedford Division could not accept any cars. Davis complained to Roberts but to no avail.

Another problem for Bretz occurred on December 26 when the freight depot at Elkins was destroyed by fire causing minor damage to the passenger building. Bretz recommended replacing it with a smaller building costing about $2,200. The new building, measuring 64'X30' was completed by the spring of 1893. Davis was most concerned about the number of fires that had occurred during the past year on the railroad, and asked Bretz to examine very carefully all buildings and cars where it was necessary to have fires.

The suspension of traffic by the Pennsylvania's Bedford Division continued into January 1983, with Davis noting that 268 cars still waited to be moved on January 4. By January 13, the backlog of loads for the Pennsylvania had increased to 304 and even the B. & O. was affected with 189 loads stuck on various sidings along the line to Cumberland. Davis complained again to the Pennsylvania on January 20 that there were still 292 loads waiting at Cumberland. To help matters, the B. & O. requested the loan of a couple of West Virginia Central engines. By January 28, the Pennsylvania had moved the accumulated loads at Cumberland, but the B. & O. still had 110 loaded cars waiting at Belington. Davis later reported that the Pennsylvania blockade had caused a loss of $8,000 compared to the same time last year.

The problems with the Pennsylvania and the B. & O. in December and January intensified Davis's wish to have an independent outlet to the east. Davis, Elkins and Kerens met with Roberts and Kennedy on February 5, and it was agreed that the Pennsylvania and the C. V. would assist with the project. Davis noted in his diary, "We have lately been in a bad way as to transportation of coal, coke and lumber. Only half as much done in December and January as ought to have been. Neither the Pennsylvania nor the B. & O. would haul our freight. We see no way but to build out from Cumberland."

Davis prepared a memorandum on January 20 outlining the cost of the road to Hagerstown and the estimated profit. The road was estimated to cost $2,786,000 including the right-of-way and buildings. This was less than the estimate submitted by Latrobe on May 5, 1892, which totaled $3,132,896. The source of Davis's new figures was not given in the memorandum. Based on the traffic on the P. & C. road, the gross revenue for the B. & C. was estimated at $640,000. After subtracting working expenses estimated at 70 percent of gross, and payment of interest on bonds, a net revenue of $42,000 could be expected.

This figure was sufficient to convince Davis to push ahead with the project, although the coal business at this time was very depressed. On January 22, Landstreet, now the general manager of the Davis Coal and Coke Company, reported that the miners at Coketon were still working although their wages had been reduced to 47.1/2 cents per loaded mine car, each car estimated to hold 1.1/2 tons. Landstreet also noted that orders were in short supply, and the mines were working reduced hours.

Davis, who usually regarded himself as a friend of labor, became concerned about new legislation that was being considered in the West Virginia legislature and which "might prove troublesome." The proposed legislation would make it illegal for an employer to fire an employee for belonging to a labor organization. A second item would eliminate the "doctrine of fellow servants" and make employers responsible for injuries to their employees even if such injuries resulted from the negligence of a fellow employee. A final bill sought to force employers to pay their men monthly for all work up to ten days before payday. Davis was so concerned about the possible effects of these bills that he wrote to the presidents of the B. & O., C. & O. and the N. & W. seeking their help in getting them defeated.

On January 29, Davis received a telegram reporting the death of James Parsons. No reason for the death was given. Davis appointed Galbreath as engineer for the West Virginia Central and gave him Parson's duties.

There was more trouble at the end of January with bridges, this time on the P. & C. On January 30, Bretz reported that ice on the Potomac River had caused a shift in the river's flow, and sent water against one of the piers of the bridge at Caudy, which normally saw little if any flow. The pier was undermined and tilted over. Bretz rushed men and material to the scene to get a trestle in place but was hampered by the ice that was a foot thick for some two miles above Cumberland. Attempts were made to dynamite the ice, but Bretz was concerned that ice further up the river would demolish the trestle. He reported on February 3 that trains, which had been using the B. & O., were now using the trestle.

There was some good news at the end of January when it was reported that the new pulp mill at Davis had commenced to produce pulp (Fig. 85). By the end of the year, the new mill was reported to be producing 15 tons per day of unbleached sulfite fiber and employing 75 men. This was the last major industry to be established in Davis. The mill is shown on a map published by the H. G. Davis Coal Company in March 1893 (Fig. 86). Davis also noted that engineers were at work on locating the Dry Fork Railroad. Samuel Diller reported that he was ready to start work on his railroad to either the mouth of Roaring Creek or to Belington depending on receiving satisfactory freight rates.

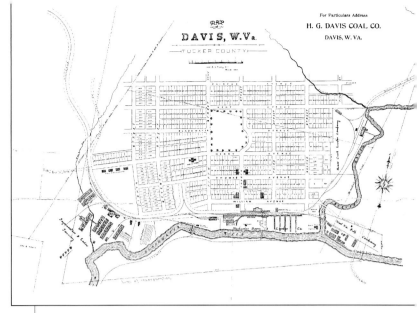

Fig. 86. Map of Davis, March 1893
West Virginia and Regional History Collection,
West Virginia University Library

Chauncey Ives was appointed chief engineer of the B. & C. on February 15 and immediately sent out three engineering parties to complete the survey work. The B. & O. was reported also to have an engineering party at work near Cumberland in an effort to block the new road. Davis's immediate problem was to find a route east of Cumberland where the B. & O. and the C. & O. Canal already occupied the best line. Davis asked Dailey to see if the B. & C. could condemn the land required or if the charter of the Washington and Cumberland could be used to condemn land along the canal.

Davis's problems with the B. & O. were not limited to its obstructing work on the B. & C. The Beaver Creek Lumber Company still was having a problem trying to obtain sufficient cars for its needs, and asked Davis if it could lease 100 cars for its exclusive use. Davis complained to the general manager of the B. & O. who was not at all helpful, claiming that there had been "hardly an empty car out of Baltimore in two weeks."

The middle of February found Davis finally heeding Bretz's advice from the previous year, and giving some thought to the consolidation of the various coal companies. He wrote to Kerens and mentioned a consolidation of companies, but did not feel a need to rush as the companies were doing well.

Bretz reported to Davis on March 10 on the condition of the various trestles along the road and whether they should be replaced. The bridge across the canal at Cumberland was rotting faster than anticipated although Bretz thought it would last through the present year. Bretz recommended immediate replacement of several trestles with the old bridge girders that were stored at Elkins. Davis gave approval for the trestles at Rawlings, Shaw and Green Spring to be replaced and this work was finished by June.

W. G. L. Totten, secretary to the newly chartered Point Pleasant, Buckhannon and Tygarts Valley Railroad, wrote to Davis on March 10 noting, "Our name is long but we don't mean all of it." Apparently the purpose of the company was to build

Fig. 85. Pulp mill at Davis (undated)

from Buckhannon to a connection with the West Virginia Central in the vicinity of Belington either by building directly across country or by way of the rivers.

Davis also heard from E. C. Vincent of the equally impressively named Atlantic, Staunton and West Virginia Railway. This railroad had been incorporated in Virginia in February 1892 and now planned to build from tidewater through Staunton and Elkins and then to Clarksburg and Morgantown. Vincent hoped to get a letter from Davis stating that the West Virginia Central would have friendly relations with the new road, which could then be used by Vincent to induce capitalists to invest in his enterprise. Although the company renewed its charter in December 1895, it was to remain a "paper railroad."

Davis reported in his diary on March 13, that he had walked from Cumberland to Old Town with Ives and the right-of-way agent to look over the proposed route, and noted, "I think it will have to go back from canal." He later met with his Cumberland attorney who doubted that the charter of the W. & C. could be used to condemn land belonging to the canal, which would interfere with navigation on the canal. The attorney thought there would be no problem in condemning land needed for a bridge if no such interference occurred. This seemed to satisfy Davis who reported that land was being purchased for the right-of-way.

The case brought by Shaw against the West Virginia Central, Davis and Elkins in October 1892 in the Circuit Court in Baltimore, was decided by Judge Dennis on March 21 in favor of the defendants. The judge also dissolved the injunction preventing the West Virginia Central from leasing the P. & C. The result did not please Shaw who determined to carry the case forward to the Maryland Court of Appeals.

It was reported on March 24, that Landstreet had been appointed receiver for the Blackwater Boom and Lumber Company, although the report noted that the company had not failed. The Beaver Creek Lumber Company was still clamoring for more cars at this time, and reported that workers in one of its mills had gone on strike in an effort to ensure steady work.

Meanwhile Condon and Lane were moving ahead with the Dry Fork Railroad, of which 9.1/2 miles had been surveyed by J. W. Moore. Davis asked A. C. Finley to review the work and make an estimate for a bridge across the Blackwater River at Hendricks. Finley reported that the grades and alignment were good and estimated the cost of grading at $17,190. The bridge at Hendricks could be built for $4,500. Davis later wrote to Thomas Davis and mentioned that he would be willing to build the bridge and lay the rails if Condon and Lane would do the grading. No agreement on these lines was reached and the lumbermen built their own road.

Bretz decided at the end of March that after five years as general manager, it was time for a pay raise. Pointing out that the road had increased in length, and now possessed 29 engines and "we have not had a collision on the road," he felt justified in asking for an increase. Davis awarded an increase to $4,200 without a murmur.

Bretz also thought that a new combination car would soon be needed and asked for a quote from Jackson and Sharp. Jackson

and Sharp made a bid of $3,375 but after the usual haggling, agreed to take $3,325. The car was to be delivered in July and would become No. 16. It is not clear whether the new car was a combination baggage and mail or whether it included a passenger compartment. It was listed in the August 1894 Annual Report as a baggage/mail car although Bretz referred to it as a passenger, baggage and mail car. By 1895, No. 16 appears to have been reclassified as combination passenger car.

The Railway Age noted on April 21 that the Roaring Creek and Charleston Railroad had been incorporated with a capital stock of $300,000. The stockholders included Samuel Diller, William Diller and O. C. Womelsdorf.

Davis wrote to Kerens on April 22, noting that the Pennsylvania Steel Company and the Maryland Steel Company had both failed and that this would have an impact on new ventures. These two failures were the latest in a series of business failures that had started with the collapse of the Reading in February. The failures did not seem to have an immediate impact on the West Virginia Central. Davis, Thomas Davis, and Elkins toured the railroad and mines at the end of April; Davis noted in his diary on April 29 that "road and mines in good working order and improving." On May 1, Davis complained of a tight money market. May 1 actually was the first day of a turbulent week on the New York Stock Exchange, which the New York Times would label at the end of the week as the worst panic since 1873. The paper confidently expected things to return to normal after the market had had time to adjust. Unfortunately, these events were to be the start of a severe recession that was to last three years.

In May, Davis returned to the problem of consolidating all of the small coal companies into one large company. A state law at the time prohibited a company from owning more than 10,000 acres of land and Davis wrote to Camden to see if there was a way around the law. Camden noted that several of his companies owned more than 10,000 acres but the excess was held by trustees. The law also allowed a railroad company to own more than the limit if it was required to build the road. Davis decided to go ahead and merge the Fairfax Coal Company, the H. G. Davis Coal Company, the Davis and Elkins Coal and Coke Company, the Henry Coal and Coke Company, and the West Virginia Coal and Coke Company into the Davis Coal and Coke Company. Elkins was elected president, Thomas Davis vice president and Landstreet became general manager.

It was reported on May 5, that an election was held in Tucker County to change the site of the county seat from St. George to Parsons, and that the proposal had received more than the required three fifths of the vote. Parsons became an incorporated town on June 12, 1893, and officially became the county seat on August 7, 1893 (Fig. 87). The new town was given a boost in July when Thomas Gould of Milton, Pennsylvania indicated an interest in building a tannery to tan 150 hides per day.

A second tannery was erected during 1893 at Bayard. Two sawmills were reported to be operating in the area as early as 1885, one by McCulloh Brown and the second by Sol Clark. Both were small operations employing between eight and ten men. In 1892 one of the companies was reported to be operating

Fig. 87. The town of Parsons, 1894 (damaged negative)
Mrs. Robert Hebb Collection, West Virginia State Archives

a mine, probably to supply coal for its own needs. Bayard was incorporated as a town in 1893. The population of the town was 540 in 1900.

Davis reported in his diary that ground was broken for the B. & C. on May 13 at the foot of Knobley Mountain in Ridgeley. The ceremony was performed by Mayor Hopewell Hebb of Cumberland, who also happened to be the cashier of the West Virginia Central. Davis noted that a large force of men were at work and expected the number to rise to 500 in two weeks.

About the same time it was noted that the office of general traffic agent, occupied by Captain Harrison, had been abolished and Harrison was appointed general passenger agent with an office at Westernport. William T. Hunter was appointed general freight agent at the same time with an office in Cumberland. Although Hunter was the general freight agent, he seems to have been active in promoting excursions over the West Virginia Central (Fig. 88).

The mill of the Blackwater Boom and Lumber Company was destroyed by fire on May 25 although the box factory was saved. The company was still in the hands of the receiver at this time.

Surveys were progressing on the B. & C. route to find a shorter line with easier grades using Evitts Creek but it was found a tunnel of 5,000-6,000 feet would be required. The route was examined by Kerens, who reported to Davis on June 20 that east of Hancock it was an easy line. The first 12 miles west of Hancock were also quite favorable, but a long cut would be needed when the line reached the Potomac River at North Mountain. Beyond, at Sideling Creek, a viaduct 600 feet long and 125 feet

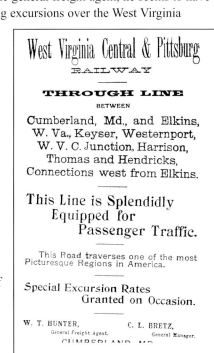

Fig. 88. West Virginia Central poster (undated)
Collection of John King

high would be needed, but overall Kerens was encouraged by what he saw. He also mentioned that Ives was talking about setting up a syndicate of contractors to build the line and take one third of the cost in bonds and the rest in cash. Kerens concluded by noting that "money is tighter than ever," but he had no doubt that it would be possible to arrange financing for the road.

Davis was well aware of the tight money situation as Hendley had been trying to obtain a $15,000 loan from banks in Baltimore to pay obligations due on July 1. Although the company had sufficient money on hand to meet the payrolls, Hendley noted that Ives had three corps of engineers in the field, the salaries of which amounted to $1,835 in June, and which Hendley thought was excessive. Hendley recommended cutting back to one corps noting that, "there is no special reason for hurry now."

Kerens wrote to Davis on July 1 noting again that the money situation was getting worse and that it was expected to be bad for at least a year. Kerens recommended that the offer of the contractors to build the road for one third the cost in bonds not be accepted, but that the bonds be marketed when conditions improved and to do nothing in the meantime.

A new company appeared on the scene in early July, when F. P. Rease, the general manager of the U. S. Coal, Iron and Manufacturing Company, reported that the company was proposing to build 50 coke ovens at Harding on the Belington extension and asking for information on freight rates.

Another company interested in increasing coke production at this time was the Cumberland Coal Company of which William Gorman was the president and Davis was a large stockholder. The company already had 45 ovens in operation at Douglas near Thomas, and wanted to build five more at a cost of $230 each (Fig. 89). By the end of July, Gorman had changed his mind and decided to abandon the idea, citing the financial condition of the country. He noted that, "the coke trade is in the most demoralized condition I have ever known."

Fig. 89. Cumberland Coal Company at Douglas circa 1897
West Virginia and Regional History Collection,
West Virginia University Library

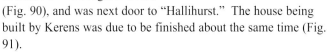

Davis did receive some good news in July when he noted that he was going to move into his new house on July 4. The house was named "Graceland" in honor of his daughter Grace (Fig. 90), and was next door to "Hallihurst." The house being built by Kerens was due to be finished about the same time (Fig. 91).

Elkins still was not convinced that the line chosen for the B. & C. was the best available and wrote to Davis on July 7 recommending that the river route be given another review. However, the financial crisis was beginning to take its toll and Elkins was informed that the work at Knobley Mountain had been reduced.

Elkins was pleased to hear of this and recommended closing the work entirely, mentioning that factories were closing and that the

Fig. 90. "Graceland," the home of Henry Gassaway Davis in Elkins

Fig. 91. The house of R. C. Kerens at Elkins

outlook for coke was "especially discouraging." On July 11, Elkins noted that the day had been particularly bad on the New York stock exchange and he did not think times were going to improve. Landstreet confirmed the bad news reporting that orders for coke would keep only 50 ovens working but 160 were in blast.

Davis issued orders to Bretz on July 17 on savings that had to be made and noting those projects, which could continue. Trestles were to be repaired as necessary but the wooden canal bridge at Cumberland was to be replaced by an iron girder, and the Elkins shop extension could proceed. A reduction of ten percent was to be made in section men and in the machinery department. By July 24, Ives had completed his surveys between Hagerstown and Cumberland, and Davis immediately ordered him to discharge all the men.

On August 9 Davis and Kerens went to Hancock and met Rea of the Pennsylvania and Kennedy of the C. V. to go over the route to Cumberland. Accompanied by Ives, they went as far as Sideling Hill Creek on August 10, and from there to Cumberland the following day. Davis thought the route "fair," except between Sideling Hill and Fifteen Mile Creek, which would be very expensive.

The visit by Rea produced some new thinking on the route between Sideling Hill and Fifteen Mile Creek, which included a plan to cross the Potomac River into West Virginia to avoid the

difficult terrain. Davis again visited the area at the end of August and was pleased to note that such a route would eliminate the need for two tunnels and two high viaducts.

On September 1 newspaper reports indicated that the mill of the Blackwater Boom and Lumber Company would be rebuilt by its new owners. The mill had been sold to Frank Thompson, acting for W. H. Osterhout, at the beginning of August for $110,000. Also interested in acquiring the mill was Robert Eastham, and when he was not successful in his bid, he became very antagonistic to the company and its officers with deadly results.

At about the same time it was reported that the grading had commenced on the Roaring Creek and Charleston Railroad. The work was being carried out under contract by George Potts, who had 75 men at work early in September.

Bretz reported to Davis on September 2 that work on the tannery at Parsons would start on September 4. Bretz arranged for a switch to be installed for the new company's use so that materials could be brought to the site. This was followed by a report on September 10 that the Edge Moor Bridge Works, which had been the low bidder on the canal bridge, agreed to build the bridge for $2,000, remove the existing wooden Howe truss, and be completed in 90 days.

The question of annual passes arose again when Dailey asked Davis to consider giving passes to sheriffs and other county officials. Dailey thought that issuing passes to such officials would do much "towards creating a friendly feeling among the people for the company and could often discourage litigation." Dailey continued that the passes would not be an "improper influence," but would leave the officials impartial in their tasks. He was supported in this opinion by Elkins, who suggested that such passes be issued on Dailey's recommendation. The question of a pass for O. C. Womelsdorf also came up again in September, when Samuel Diller asked for a pass for him as he was now general manager of the R. C. & C.

Ives was still at work on the B. & C. in September and was able to report that the improvements in alignment suggested earlier had eliminated the need for two viaducts and by using four crossings of the Potomac River, he could eliminate the need for two tunnels. Ives was due to meet with Rea on September 22 to go over the plans for the improved route before they were presented to Davis and Roberts. Hendley, who was secretary and treasurer of the B. & C., was present when Ives and Rea met, and later reported to Davis that Rea was in favor of the new route. Although the new route increased the length by half a mile, it gave considerably better grades.

At the end of September, Bretz was complaining that the Pennsylvania was not moving West Virginia Central cars but was sending Pennsylvania cars in their place. At least 270 West Virginia Central cars had been held on the Philadelphia Division for at least a month, but when Bretz threatened to send Pennsylvania cars over the B. & O. to Locust Point, the cars were freed.

An accident near William in early October caused by a Buckeye automatic coupler breaking while in use on a double-headed freight train, prompted Davis to question the wisdom of such long trains. Bretz pointed out that all railroads were having trouble with automatic couplers, both Buckeye and Janey, and that the devices had not yet reached an acceptable level of reliability. With regard to double-heading, Bretz pointed out that one engine could move 45 loaded cars from Harrison to Cumberland, but that two engines were required to move 48 empties from Cumberland to Thomas, although a double-header could also move 80 or 90 cars as far as Harrison. Bretz further noted that during September, he had achieved a saving of $232.54 using double-heading when possible.

Bretz was also having trouble with Diller and Potts of the R. C. & C., who insisted that the West Virginia Central grade and lay track as far as the bridge across the Tygart Valley River. If this was not done, they would extend their line to Belington and connect directly to the B. & O. Bretz thought that this was unlikely noting, "they have about as much on their hands as they can get through with."

Bretz had to report to Davis on October 20, another accident involving a handcar in which two men were killed. According to Bretz, the handcar was being used in violation of company rules when it ran headfirst into an engine near Lime Rock. The two men killed were on the front of the handcar and had no chance to jump when they saw the engine.

More trouble for Bretz occurred on October 23, when someone put dynamite under a tool house near Barnum in which four Italian track laborers were sleeping. The explosion destroyed the corner of the tool house, but the Italians survived with a bad shaking. Bretz noted that because of a lack of suitable housing, it had "been impossible to keep this section gang filled up except with Italians." Davis was most upset and ordered Bretz to offer a reward "for the detection of the perpetrators of so gross and inhuman an act." Housing for laborers on the railroad, particularly during construction, was generally rudimentary (Fig. 92). Italian laborers were generally housed in the simplest of quarters, referred to as "Italian Shanties." This term was still in use as late as 1917 when the W. Md. Valuation survey noted several such structures along its line.

As if these were not enough problems for the general manager, he was also beset with problems concerning coal cars loaded with coal and nowhere to go because of a lack of orders. He wrote to Davis noting that there were 35 loaded cars at Thomas and 46 at Coketon for which there were no orders. In addition the B. & O. refused to accept any more cars because of a backlog at Locust Point and Brunswick.

A lack of orders for coal was only one of Davis's problems at this time. Early in October, A. C. Finley submitted a report on the condition of the mines at Elk Garden. Finley reported that Mine No. 1 would last from 14 to 16 months, Numbers 3 and 4 would last until spring 1894 and No. 5 would be exhausted by the end of the present month. Mine No. 6 was producing 1,200-1,500 tons daily, but this was below the level expected. Mine No. 2 had been reported closed in July 1890.

Towards the end of October, Davis gave some thought to raising the money to pay for the B. & C. John Gill, president of the Mercantile Trust and Deposit Company of Baltimore, who had originally been interested in the proposal, claimed that the present stringency in money matters precluded his company's involvement. Elkins was also at work on the problem in New York but without success because "so many railroads are defaulting and so many making no money that investors are discouraged."

Another conference was held in Philadelphia on October 26, to go over the proposed route of the B. & C. In attendance were Davis, Kerens, Hendley, Ives and Rea. Again some suggestions for improvements were made and Ives was ordered to prepare the necessary revisions.

Bretz reported on November 10, that he had met with Whitmer of the Dry Fork Railroad, which now had 12 miles of the route graded. Whitmer was trying to determine whether to bring his road to a connection with the West Virginia Central at Hendricks, which would mean moving his mill from Bretz, or to extend along the existing tracks belonging to the Welch Brothers to Hulings. Bretz preferred a junction at Hendricks and suggested that a freight contract be offered similar to that given the R. C. & C., which would involve prorating on lumber, pulpwood and bark.

Fig. 92. Laborers' shanties on the Blackwater grade
Collection of the Western Maryland Railway Historical Society

Relations with the R. & C. did not proceed so easily, as it was reported that surveyors were out on the west side of the Tygart Valley River looking for a route to Belington. Bretz noted on November 21 that the "Rease people" were clearing the right-of-way on the west bank of the river and that there seemed to be a "warm fight" between the companies of Diller and Rease. This intensified when Diller incorporated the Roaring Creek and Belington Railroad on November 11, 1893 and the Rease interests incorporated the

Belington and Little Laurel Railroad a couple of weeks later. Both companies hoped to get a right-of-way through the lands of the Belington Improvement Company and by December 8, both companies had parties at work on the west bank. The president of the U. S. Coal, Iron and Manufacturing Company wrote to Davis at the end of November complaining about a lack of cars at the mines at Harding, but expressing a desire for "the most harmonious relations with your company." He did not mention the work on the west side of the river.

On November 28, Hendley again met with Ives to discuss the B. & C. Hendley was most upset to find a corps of engineers still at work. Ives claimed that the changes suggested by Rea would take a corps a month to work out on the ground, in addition to new lines that Ives wanted to develop. Hendley thought Ives was merely trying to safeguard his salary in difficult times. Hendley recommended to Davis that Ives be given specific instructions to disband the corps. Davis did indeed instruct Ives to disband the corps and this was accomplished by December 1. This left Ives, Howard Sutherland the right-of-way agent and a draftsman still on the payroll.

Ives was still working with Elkins to try to form a syndicate of contractors to take $3,000,000 of bonds and build the B. & C. but progress was slow. Davis mentioned to Elkins that $20-30,000 had already been spent on grading near Cumberland and also tried to get Kennedy of the C. V. to submit his portion of the expenses.

In December, the worsening financial situation continued to take a toll. Miners at the Hampshire Mine of the Davis Coal and Coke Company went on strike when the rate for mining coal was decreased from 50 cents to 40 cents per ton. On December 18, Bretz was ordered to look for ways to save money, but Bretz thought that any further reductions would jeopardize service. He noted that reduction in the maintenance-of-way payroll had already produced a saving of 37 percent compared to November. He suggested that if this was not enough, that a ten percent reduction in all salaries greater than $40 per week be instituted. Bretz did try to persuade the B. & O. to reduce the rate charged for the shifting engine at Cumberland from one third of the daily cost to one quarter, but was unsuccessful.

The Piedmont Pulp and Paper Company was also feeling the effects of the recession and claimed to be running their mills at only one third of capacity and asked for a reduction in rates for pulpwood and coal. The company was also concerned that proposed changes in tariffs would allow increased competition from imported pulp. Bretz was not sympathetic to the request, thinking that the Lukes were merely trying to strengthen their position in the industry and that the rates were as low as they could be. Davis, however, was more sympathetic, and allowed the Lukes a five percent reduction on pulpwood to Piedmont and on coal to Davis. The Lukes do not seem to have been too appreciative of Davis's help, as early in the new year they started discussions

with the B. & O. to try to get that company to build across the Potomac to their mill at Piedmont.

The year ended as it had begun with the news that yet another great railroad system had passed into the hands of the receivers, in this case the Atchison, Topeka and Santa Fe. Locally, bad news of a different sort was reported by Bretz to Davis, when it was learned that Homer Huston and three other workers had been killed in a dynamite explosion on the Dry Fork Railroad. Huston had been a construction foreman for the Dry Fork, and was well known to both Bretz and Davis. The Charleston Evening Mail, in reporting the accident, had a large headline, shouting "Blown to Atoms." Attention to such graphic detail was characteristic of newspaper reports of the time when dealing with some calamity.

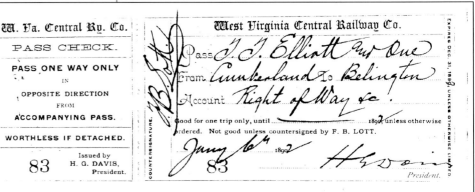

Fig. 93a. West Virginia Central pass, January 6, 1892
West Virginia and Regional History Collection,
West Virginia University Library

Fig. 93b. Conductor's cash fare receipt
Collection of Rob Whetsell

8

More Plans

There was no improvement in the financial health of the country at the start of the new year, 1894. Davis was able to take advantage of the depressed conditions to purchase the Franklin Consolidation Coal Company's mine near Piedmont for $59,000. Included in the sale were 1,798 acres of coal lands and the nearby Phoenix mine. The purchase was made at a receiver's sale by the company of H. G. Davis and Brother. He also received a report on the number of coke ovens along the West Virginia Central that showed a total of 406 distributed as follows:

Thomas	22
Coketon	328
Douglas	44
Custer	12

Davis did not mention how many were in use given the depressed state of the coke industry. Davis asked Bretz to consider a five to ten percent reduction in wages for all employees earning more than $30 per month, including trainmen. Bretz was against including the trainmen but Davis claimed if they were not included, the savings would be negligible. A five percent reduction was introduced for miners and laborers of the Davis Coal and Coke Company later in January.

Bretz reported on January 7 that the earnings for December were down because of a large decrease in passenger and miscellaneous freight earnings and a large decrease in coal shipped from Windom and Hampshire mines. The only good news was the percentage of operating expenses to income was a very respectable 53.4 percent. This ratio had long been used to demonstrate how efficiently a railroad was run. Bretz also reported that the depot at Junior would be finished on January 15, although it was to be the end of February before it was placed into service (Fig. 94). This building had been contracted for in October 1893 at a cost of $1,100.

Fig. 94. Depot at Junior

Bretz also reported that the "Rease people" were shipping three cars of coal per day via the B. & O. to Philadelphia. The West Virginia Central was earning 59.5 cents per ton when the coal moved from Harding to Cumberland. Bretz thought that if a cheap rate could be obtained from the Pennsylvania Railroad, it would prevent Rease and Diller combining their interests in building a road to Belington.

The appeal of Major Shaw to the Court of Appeals of Maryland in his suit against Davis, Elkins and the West Virginia Central, was denied by the court on January 11. Shaw maintained that the lease of the P. & C. was disadvantageous to the West

Virginia Central and that the line had been poorly constructed to throw the costs onto the latter company. The judge, in denying the appeal, could find no reason or evidence to support such a claim. The case was followed a few days later by a hearing of the libel case brought against Shaw by Davis in the circuit court of Mineral County. Before the case could be heard, an order was received from the U. S. Circuit Court transferring the case to that court. Davis noted in his diary on February 11 that he had agreed to a settlement with Shaw. The Cumberland Evening Times reported that after the dismissal of Shaw's appeal on January 11, negotiations between the two parties with John Gill as an arbitrator had commenced. This led to an agreement that both parties would drop all pending lawsuits and Shaw would sell his 9,900 shares of West Virginia Central stock to Davis. Elkins was surprised at the settlement and thought Davis had acted too quickly as the proposed settlement was not fair to Davis or the West Virginia Central. He also thought that the board of the West Virginia Central should have been consulted as the board had, by a resolution, ordered the suit against Shaw. Elkins wondered also what was behind Shaw's haste in agreeing to a settlement.

A disastrous fire occurred at Davis on January 12, in which the Opera House and three other buildings were destroyed. No railroad property was damaged and Bretz estimated the damage at $30,000.

Davis had decided late in 1893 to build a new office building in Elkins to house the offices of the West Virginia Central. Galbreath was given the job of producing plans for the new building and he submitted two versions on January 18 to Davis. Both plans called for a three-story brick building, one plan costing $13,500 and the second $18,000. Davis seemed rather keen that the new building should have a tower and this was included in the second design.

President Kennedy seemed to be getting a little impatient about progress on the B. & C. when he wrote to Davis on January 18 asking what steps had been taken towards contracting the work. Elkins had been in discussions with the contractors who were proposing to take bonds for the work, and reported that they were asking $40,000 per mile to build the road, which Elkins thought was too high. He suggested, given the current recession, that $33,000 was more reasonable, and he later revised this figure to $30,000. A proposition was made to the contractor, Collins, Rickerts and Company, but it does not seem to have been accepted. A second contractor, Drake and Stratton, also expressed an interest in February, but again no agreement was reached. The engineer corps, which had been disbanded on December 1, 1893, was called back to service under the supervision of Ives. Bretz prepared a plan for a Y connection with the new road at Ridgeley, so everything was ready for construction to start.

Bretz was engaged in negotiations with R. F. Whitmer, president of the Dry Fork Railroad, concerning freight rates from Hendricks. Whitmer wanted the same rate as shippers from Davis, but Bretz thought this unreasonable given the extra distance involved. Davis also heard from the president of the Point Pleasant, Buckhannon and Tygarts Valley Railroad, J. W. Heavner, who mentioned that there was a proposition before the voters of Upshur County to approve an issue of $30,000 in bonds for the new road. Heavner later wrote to Davis to see if the West Virginia Central would lay the track and operate the line if the P. P., B. & T. V. would do the grading and provide the cross ties. Davis declined the offer.

At the beginning of February, Davis was informed by H. G. Buxton, who had replaced Thomas Davis as vice president of the Davis Coal and Coke Company, that there was no improvement in the coal trade. Landstreet also reported that the mines were working "very short time." This led Davis and Elkins to propose, effective February 1, that the rent on company houses would be reduced by $1 per month. Physician fees would also be reduced, no charge at all being made for those employees earning less than $15 per month. Davis also wanted to close the Windom mine but this was opposed by Landstreet who thought they would be unable to fill orders for Big Vein coal. Landstreet doubted that the Windom miners would be likely to agree to a reduction to 40 cents in the price paid for coal. Landstreet also recommended that the Franklin mine be sold to the Davis Coal and Coke Company since as it was in Maryland, it would not be covered by the 10,000 acre per company rule. Davis agreed with the suggestion and the transfer was completed in April 1894.

Whitmer wrote to Davis at the beginning of February reporting that the Dry Fork Railroad had now graded 25 miles and had purchased 60 pound rail ready to commence track laying on March 1. He asked that the connection be installed at Hendricks so that the company could start shipping rails and crossties. Bretz noted that the D. F. had the piers in for the bridge across the Dry Fork and that the company proposed to erect a wooden Howe truss bridge across the river.

Bretz also advised Davis that the R. C. & C. was not having much luck with its bridge across the Tygart Valley River as the approach trestles had washed out on February 5 leaving the two iron girders across the main channel of the river. The company had been ready to lay rail across the bridge.

Although the Lukes had not been able to persuade the B. & O. to build a bridge across the Potomac River to the mill at Piedmont, they had arranged with the B. & O. to accept their shipments to New York and New England from Piedmont at the same rate that the Pennsylvania charged from Cumberland. This eliminated the West Virginia Central from hauling cars from Luke to Cumberland that was earning the company about $7.20 per car. The Lukes still had to pay $2.00 to get the car to Piedmont so they were still saving $5.20 per car. The West Virginia Central on the other hand was losing $500 per month. Bretz wanted to charge the Lukes $5 per car for the Luke to Piedmont movement. Davis was not in favor of the idea as it may have forced the Lukes to try for a direct connection with the B. & O. Bretz asked the Pennsylvania to lower their rate so they could stay competitive with the B. & O., but did not think a bridge to the B. & O. would be built, as the Lukes could not afford to antagonize the West Virginia Central and the Pennsylvania. There were some destinations reached by the Pennsylvania that

could not be reached by the B. & O., and the mill at Davis gave the West Virginia Central an advantage.

Bretz also was most upset to find a coal car destined for the Lukes in the siding at Merrill which when weighed was found to be 14,300 pounds overweight. The Lukes had had a history of shipping cars of pulpwood that were overweight and not only was this damaging to the cars, it also resulted in a loss of revenue for the West Virginia Central. The practice ceased when the railroad put in a set of scales. The South Baltimore Car Works had proposed to build a gondola specially designed for the transport of pulpwood, but the Lukes did not want to use an open car as they claimed dirt and cinders got imbedded in the wood and resulted in a lower quality of paper. Bretz recommended that an order be placed with the South Baltimore Car Works for 50 new 60,000 pound boxcars for this trade, which also could be used to transport bark.

The Lukes were indeed difficult people with which to deal; Bretz complained frequently about their sharp practices and hoped that they would deal fairly with the West Virginia Central.

Some important personnel changes occurred on the railroad and in the supervision of the mines starting in February. Bretz was unhappy with the performance of E. W. Lippencott as master of machinery and recommended that he be relieved of his post and offered the position of foreman at West Virginia Central Junction. Bretz recommended that the master of machinery position be offered to John S. Turner who had worked in the Pennsylvania's Altoona shops. Turner was highly recommended by General Manager S. M. Prevost and other officials of the Pennsylvania. He accepted the position and was due to start on April 1; Lippencott chose to resign rather than accept the foreman's position. A. C. Finley became superintendent of the Elk Garden mines in place of A. C. Rawlings who became manager of the Franklin mine. Also starting in a new position on April 1 was Charles Robb who became stenographer and secretary to Davis. Robb was to remain in Davis's employ in one capacity or another for 15 years.

Davis wrote to Kerens on March 2 mentioning that he had been advised by Rea to set April 1 as the date to open bids on the B. & C. work. Davis spent some time in Cuba early in March leaving Kerens in charge of the B. & C. Kerens noted on March 22 that Rea and Ives estimated the cost of the road, ready for operation, at approximately $4,250,000. The figure alarmed Kerens who wanted the road built for no more than $3,250,000. Davis reported to Elkins on April 3 that the bids were higher than expected, and that two contractors, Drake and Stratton and Ryan and McDonald, had bid on the whole work. By April 9, Thomas Davis was also becoming concerned at the prospect of building the B. & C. and recommended that negotiations be reopened with the B. & O. looking towards a traffic arrangement to Cherry Run. Davis did not share the concerns and noted in his diary on April 10 that he was still working on the B. & C. and "hope to be able to build." In spite of Thomas Davis's concerns, it was reported that he was elected president of the B. & C. at a meeting of directors on April 14. On April 18, Kerens wrote that the financial outlook for the country was getting worse and recommended against "expending any money in railway construction." Kerens was also concerned that both he and Davis were getting on in years and did not think that such an adventure was wise at their age. He also pointed out that they still had to provide between $200,000 and $300,000 to finish buying the Shaw stock.

A day later, on April 19, Hambleton wrote to Davis about a meeting he had had a few days earlier with an unnamed director of the B. & O. and the banker, John Gill. The discussion centered on improving the relations between the B. & O. and the West Virginia Central so that it would be unnecessary to build the B. & C. Hambleton was encouraged by the meeting, and thought that the B. & O. did not want to repeat the mistake that was made when the P. & C. was built. He encouraged Davis to open negotiations with the B. & O. immediately.

By April 26, Davis was having doubts about building the B. & C. and wrote to Elkins suggesting they build only between Cherry Run and Hagerstown to connect with the C. V.

No decision was made on the future of the B. & C. Contractors interested in bidding on the work examined the ground in early May, and it was announced that bids would be opened on May 21 by Ives and Hendley. Davis met with Kennedy on May 3 and examined the proposed junction with the C. V. Davis also examined the line between Hagerstown and Hancock and noted that, "The line is a good one." However, Davis had more pressing concerns during the spring that required his attention.

The year 1894 was to be marked as a year of considerable labor unrest as wage reductions, prompted by the economic downturn, led to strikes in a number of industries. Trouble had occurred in the southern West Virginia coalfields early in the year and a strike in the Connellsville coke region was threatened for the beginning of April. Talk of a national miners' strike filled the newspapers in April but it was generally thought that the mines along the West Virginia Central would not be affected because of the rent reductions offered by Davis.

Davis felt sufficiently confident to give Bretz permission to replace the bridge at Potomac, which required three 50-foot deck girders, two new piers and an abutment. Bretz received bids on the girders on April 11, which showed a low bid from the Pennsylvania Steel Company of $1,945 for steel girders. Up to this time, all the bridges on the West Virginia Central had been built of iron, and Bretz was a little uncomfortable with the new material. Bretz wrote to the Pennsylvania for advice, but Richards, the maintenance-of-way engineer, wrote to say that the Pennsylvania had not used steel to this time but recommended a two percent increase in weight over the same girder in iron. The contract was eventually given for the steel girders. A bid for the masonry for $2,740 was accepted at the same time.

Bretz received a request from Diller on April 7 requesting the loan of an engine. Bretz agreed to loan him No. 2 for $12.50 including the cost of an engineer and fireman.

The anticipated national coal strike was called for April 21 by President McBride of the United Mineworkers of America. A meeting of the Georges Creek miners a day earlier had expressed no support for a strike although wages had been reduced at the beginning of the month. Landstreet reported that notices had been posted at the Davis Coal and Coke Company mines for a meeting on April 22, but that things were generally quiet. However, on April 23, miners at Douglas and Coketon went on strike and a day later the miners at Thomas joined the strike. A meeting of the miners was held with Landstreet who told them that those who wished to work could do so; everyone else would be discharged. Bretz reported on April 24 that apart from Coketon and Thomas all other mines were working and 116 cars were loaded. Buxton told Davis that there was trouble in the Connellsville coke field but expected this to help shipments of coke from the Davis Coal and Coke Company. Elk Garden was still working and had increased production to 1,400 tons per day. To encourage the miners to stay at work, the same reduction in rents and physician fees as had earlier been given to the Davis Coal and Coke Company employees, was put into effect at Elk Garden on April 25.

By May 5, production at Elk Garden had reached 1,900 tons per day and the price of coal had increased dramatically, but by May 7 it was rumored that Elk Garden miners would join the strike. Landstreet, who was totally out of sympathy with the miners, ordered one of their leaders arrested on grounds of threatening the life of a miner who wished to work. Landstreet also commenced proceedings to evict the strikers from their houses, but noted that it would take six days before the evictions would start. Davis was not in favor of the evictions thinking that it would make the men more desperate. Landstreet thought that the evictions would help the men who did want to work and also allow the company to bring in new men.

Elk Garden miners joined the strike on May 7 and by May 8, the strike had spread to Georges Creek. Buxton reported on May 9 that all the mines along the West Virginia Central were idle except for the Franklin and Junior mines.

Bretz, concerned about the reduction in coal traffic, asked Davis for permission to reduce shopmen to eight hours. Bretz also received a telegram from Landstreet advising him that 20 black replacement miners would arrive in Cumberland on the afternoon of May 10 and to provide a special to take them to Coketon "as quietly as possible."

The strike was also having an effect on the coastal shipping trade in coal. On May 11, it was reported that shipping piers of the Pennsylvania and the Reading had closed. The B. & O. embargoed all coal destined for Baltimore and was using some coal in transit for its own engines. The pulp mill at Piedmont was forced to close on May 11 for lack of coal.

Layoffs began on the West Virginia Central on May 12 when Bretz released one engine cleaner, three car repairmen and one laborer all of whom were paid at a rate of $1.50 per day. Bretz was optimistic that the strike would end in a few days as the miners at the Consolidation Coal Company mines on Georges Creek were still at work and had refused all efforts to get them to strike. An attempt was made to close these mines on May 12, but the presence of a sheriff, 30 deputies and the wives of the workingmen was too much for the 800 strikers and the mines remained open.

The Cumberland Evening Times editorialized on May 17 that the strike along Georges Creek could last only a few more days but also noted that the men at the Franklin mine had been paid off. Thomas Davis was also optimistic that the Elk Garden miners would return in a few days. Finley reported that some men at Elk Garden had applied to work and he also thought that work would resume on May 22. The strikers were determined that this would not happen and posted notices requesting that the miners stay out

(Fig. 95). Twenty-eight miners did report for work and mined 125 tons. The next day only about six miners reported for work. Dailey, who was at Elk Garden, reported that the workers were jeered at by the wives of the strikers. Thomas Davis realized that it was futile to try to keep the mine open and ordered it closed.

Although Elk Garden closed, some progress was made in the Upper Potomac region when it was noted on May 23 that one car was loaded at Thomas, ten at Coketon and eight at Douglas. With the strike showing no sign of ending, Bretz issued an order on May 22 reducing all officers and employees, except trainmen, to three fourths time.

On May 23, Bretz reported that another 150 blacks would be transported to Coketon arriving about midnight. The men were put to work immediately and Landstreet reported that 220 men were now at work and that 400 tons could be loaded; this would rise to 600 tons when another 40 blacks arrived in a few days (Figs. 96 and 97). Landstreet also thought that this would help get the Thomas mine and shaft back in production but if not, then blacks would be used at these mines also. Kerens, in a letter to Davis on May 28, included a handwritten note,

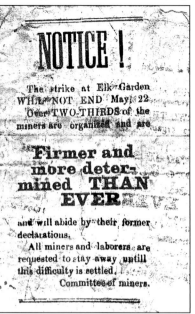

Fig. 95. Strike notice at Elk Garden
West Virginia and Regional History Collection,
West Virginia University Library

Fig. 96. Striking miners at Coketon, May 26, 1894
Collection of the Western Maryland Railway Historical Society

"Glad to hear Landstreet is succeeding so well at Coketon and Thomas. Colored miners are the best. It is so in the west." On May 28 it was rumored that strikers from Elk Garden, Windom and Atlantic were going to go to Coketon and close the mine. About 100 strikers did go, but were outnumbered by the black miners and no trouble occurred.

Landstreet reported at the end of May that the situation was improving. He noted the striking miners were voluntarily vacating their houses and that there would be need for few, if any, evictions. It was later reported that three evictions occurred.

The mine at Thomas started up on June 5; on the same day 38 cars of coal were shipped from Coketon and Douglas. Thomas

Fig. 97. New miners, protected by deputies, arriving at Coketon, May 26, 1894
Collection of the Western Maryland Railway Historical Society

Davis reported 20 men were at work at Thomas and an additional 25 blacks were on the way along with 10 men from Elk Garden. Along Georges Creek, the strike was growing more threatening and the governor sent 600 troops to keep the peace. A couple of days later, Landstreet reported that everything was quiet at Thomas and Coketon, production was increasing, and although rumors persisted that the strikers would try to close the mines, nothing serious happened. By June 7, Landstreet was feeling a little less certain of the situation and telegraphed the New York office to ask them to send 20 rifles and ammunition. Hendley, who was in New York at the time, could only manage to locate 17 Winchester rifles that he dispatched to Bretz with the wish that a show of force was all that would be required. It was reported on June 15 that 14 deputies had been sworn in and provided with Winchester rifles to guard the workers and the mines.

Trouble did arise the following week when attempts were made to sabotage the West Virginia Central, prompting Bretz to post a $500 reward for information (Fig. 98).

A riot occurred at Thomas on June 12, which led to 30 people, including the local justice of the peace and his daughter, being indicted for inciting a riot by the Tucker County Grand Jury. To prevent a similar occurrence at Elk Garden on June 18 when it was hoped to reopen the mine, Dailey had a restraining order issued by the Mineral County Circuit Court. This order forbade the assembly of persons in Elk Garden before daylight, and from parading in the streets and blowing horns, and from the use of opprobrious epithets such as "scab" or "blackleg." Landstreet again thought that by taking full advantage of the law, the miners at Windom and Hampshire could be induced to return to work.

The move appears to have been successful as it was reported that between 200 and 250 miners returned to work at Elk Garden on June 18 for the same 40 cent rate they were

REWARD!

Certain Persons having interfered with Switches and obstructed the Track of the Company at certain places for the evident purpose of throwing Trains from the Track and destroying Life and Property, and threats having been made to interfere with Running of Trains on the Road, a Reward of $500 is hereby offered for information that will lead to the Arrest and Conviction of any Person for misplacing Switches, obstructing Tracks, or preventing by Force the Running of Trains on the Road.

C. L. BRETZ, Genl. Manager,
W. Va. Central & Pittsburg Ry. Co.

Fig. 98. Reward advertisement
Cumberland Evening Times,
June 13, 1894

receiving before the strike began. By June 19, work resumed at some of the Georges Creek mines and some of the troops were withdrawn. Bretz telegraphed on June 19 that the strike had been declared officially over and that 300 men were now at work at Elk Garden.

Some pockets of resistance remained. On June 21, strikers attempted to block a crossing in Elk Garden, but when the sheriff and his deputies arrived and arrested the leader, the demonstration quickly collapsed. Dailey reported on June 23 that everything was now quiet and that 109 men were at work in No. 6 mine, which was 35 more than the previous day. He mentioned an incident the previous evening when "two pretty rough customers" were arrested. One was knocked down when he refused to submit to the officers. This started a rumor that a striker had been killed and caused a great deal of excitement but no trouble occurred. The final act in the strike occurred on June 26 when a group of armed strikers started a parade at a time when the working miners were setting out for the mines. The appearance of the deputies caused the strikers to break ranks and head towards Shaw and they were last seen crossing the river at Chaffee. The mines at Windom and Hampshire were still closed at the end of the month but were expected to reopen on July 2.

Although the mine strike had been the focus since April, other matters demanded Davis's attention particularly the B. & C., and the new connecting roads. Bretz reported on May 10 that he had received a request from Diller to purchase ties for the R. C. & C., but was a little concerned about Diller's financial standing and thought the West Virginia Central should be careful in its dealings with the R. C. & C.

President Roberts of the Pennsylvania Railroad wrote to Davis on May 16 agreeing with the idea of building only between Cherry Run and Hagerstown initially and encouraging Davis to seek a trackage agreement with the B. & O. between Cumberland and Cherry Run. Roberts concluded by saying, "The present is so unpropitious a time that it would be quite unadvisable to make any large expenditures now." Obtaining an equitable trackage arrangement with the B. & O. was not to be easy. Hendley reported on a conversation with Keyser, who said that although officers of the B. & O. were agreeable, President Mayer would never agree to such an arrangement.

The bids for the shortened B. & C. were opened on May 21 and ranged from $311,870 to $410,959. Elkins wrote to Davis on May 23 but was not much help noting, "I hardly know what to say about building the new road." Davis and Kennedy discussed the matter and agreed to postpone any new construction for the immediate future. On May 25, Ives issued an announcement to the bidders informing them of the postponement. Kennedy also suggested to Davis that Ives and Sutherland be kept on the payroll to continue work on right-of-way matters, but Hendley informed Ives that everything was to be closed up on June 1, and his services would not be required after that time.

Kerens was relieved to hear of the postponement pointing out that 55,000 miles of railroads were at present in bankruptcy and concluding, "the future is most gloomy."

With the decision made on the B. & C., Davis turned his attention to the West Virginia Central. Bretz had received bids to build a new depot at Hendricks, and Davis approved accepting the low bid

of $1,795 on June 3. The 50 boxcars ordered from South Baltimore Car Works in March for $450 each arrived in June, but were found to be poorly constructed. Davis made some deal with the builder and Bretz was told to keep them.

The Elkins Inter-Mountain reported that the first trainload of coal came off the R. C. & C. on June 17. The train, hauled by No. 2, went as far as Elkins where it collided with No. 6, which was pulling into a siding. The damage to both engines was slight, but it was not an auspicious beginning.

News of two railroad projects reached Davis in early July, the first involving McGraw. McGraw, now an officer of the Rochester Boom and Lumber Company, reported that the company was interested in building from its lands at the Forks of the Greenbrier over to the Dry Fork Railroad. McGraw wanted to determine if Davis would give fair treatment to freight coming off the new road. Davis replied that the Dry Fork Railroad would be willing to make a traffic arrangement and that the West Virginia Central "would welcome your company and treat them fairly." Hendley informed Davis that a syndicate, including the contractor Drake and Stratton, had been formed to extend the railroad presently being built up the Elk River from Charleston. The road, the Charleston, Clendennin and Sutton Railroad, was now 25 miles above Charleston, and the new syndicate proposed to build another 30 miles. Hendley thought the syndicate also might build through to Beverly and a connection with the West Virginia Central.

Bretz reported that the Pennsylvania Steel Company expected to erect the steelwork at Potomac on July 15 and that he had lent them a crane car to assist with the unloading. However, misfortune struck and the hoisting rope either broke or slipped and the car and girders fell off the trestle. One man was injured in the mishap and passengers had to be transferred around the accident site.

On July 18, the first head-on collision ever to occur on the West Virginia Central happened near McKenzies Bridge between a work train and a freight train, due to the engineer on the work train misunderstanding his orders. The work train, in charge of Engine No. 4, was pushing some flat cars loaded with Italian track laborers returning to camp when the whistle of the oncoming freight was heard. Most of the laborers managed to jump clear before the work train was hit by the freight. Fortunately the freight, hauled by Engine No. 25, was only traveling at about four miles per hour but this was sufficient to cause the engine to ride up and over the flat cars. Engine No. 4 was only slightly damaged but Engine No. 25 broke its frame and had to be removed to the shops for a general overhaul. Six or seven cars were badly smashed; Bretz estimated the damage would amount to about $2,000. No injuries were reported among the laborers although a water boy was severely cut on the head.

Davis received an interesting letter from President Ingalls of the C. & O. on July 26, in which he proposed an agency be created to control all coal produced in Pennsylvania and West Virginia, agree on the percentage allowed each road and avoid selling coal at ridiculously low prices. Ingalls suggested that the presidents of the coal carrying roads meet, "to manage the business .....and keep it out of the newspapers." So much for competition!

Bretz reported on August 1, that the coal tonnage the previous day was as follows:

Franklin	550
Hampshire	189
Windom	432
Elk Garden	1575
Thomas	964
Coketon	764
	4,474

Number of cars required was 248

Bretz reported a sufficient supply of cars to move all the coal at present, but was pressed for engines and men. Thus he was pleased to note that the R. C. & C. had received its first engine and could return No. 2. The engine had been purchased from the Pennsylvania and was similar to West Virginia Central's No. 1. Bretz had earlier notified Davis that Diller had paid the rental on No. 2, and paid also for the ties he had purchased. However, Bretz's suspicions of Diller's financial stability were not unfounded.

Although Bretz reported a sufficiency of cars in early August, by the end of the month the situation had deteriorated. On August 25, Elk Garden was able to load only 575 tons. The problem seemed to be with the Pennsylvania Railroad, which, now that the mines along its road were getting back to normal production, had reduced the supply of cars to the connecting roads. Bretz complained to Prevost that the Pennsylvania was supplying as many cars to the C. & P., a road owned by the B. & O., as it was supplying to the West Virginia Central. Bretz was not able to report any improvement in the situation.

Bretz was able to report that the new depot at Hendricks was finished on August 10 (Fig. 99). Two weeks later the first freight

Fig. 99. Depot at Hendricks (undated)
Collection of the Tucker County Historical Society

train on the Dry Fork Railroad arrived at the depot. The train consisted of four cars of bark destined for the tannery at Parsons.

Bids were received on August 27 for new 48-foot girders for the bridge at Dawson. The low bidder was the Pennsylvania Steel Company, which again bid on a steel girder. Bretz hoped the company would do better this time as it had had to pay the injured worker at Potomac over $100 and the West Virginia Central $325 for damage to the crane car.

Towards the end of August, the R. C. & C. was reported to be complete as far as the new town of Womelsdorf. By early September Bretz received a complaint that only eight or ten empty cars were being received daily by the R. C. & C. and this was only half the number required. It was claimed that 600 to 800 tons of coal could be shipped daily from Roaring Creek. However, Bretz's suspicions of Diller's financial stability were confirmed on September 3, when the cashier at the Elkins National Bank reported to Davis that Diller was kiting checks.

Davis noted in his diary on September 10, "Our railroad is doing fairly well. Coal trade, considering the country, is fair."

Later in September, Bretz met with officials of the B. & O. to try to get more cars from that road. However, a decision to change the proportion of cars sent to the various connecting roads would have to be made by President Mayer, and Bretz got the impression that this would not occur until the B. & C. idea was finally abandoned. Davis did ask for bids for up to 100 new coal cars, but no purchase was made, and in fact, no new equipment of any kind was purchased during the fiscal year ending June 30, 1895.

Davis was not yet ready to abandon the B. & C. He received a letter from Kerens, dated September 16, in which Kerens expressed optimism in the future and thought that the bonds of the B. & C. could now be sold. Davis wrote to Rea asking for his opinion on the advisability of building, and whether he thought that contractors would accept payment half in bonds and half in cash.

Davis's optimism was not shared by Landstreet, who recommended that a 25 percent reduction in salaries for all monthly employees of the Davis Coal and Coke Company commence on October 1. The reason given was the continuing depressed condition of the coal market and the low prices being obtained for coal. This action was criticized a few weeks later as being politically inspired as Davis was accused of trying to influence his employees to vote against the Democratic Party's nominee for Congress who was opposed to tariffs.

Bretz received bids for a station to be built at Roaring Creek Junction and on September 10, he recommended that the contract be given to the low bidder, W. C. Russell at a price of $2,251. The building was expected to be finished by January 1, 1895.

On September 19, Davis and his family, accompanied by Whitmer and Lane, took a trip over the Dry Fork Railroad. He noted that the track was laid 21 miles to a mill on Gandy Creek and noted, "This road bids fair to be a good feeder to the West Virginia Central."

The New York Times noted on September 25, that J. W. Reinhart had returned to his home at Hot Springs, Virginia. Reinhart had been president of the A. T. & S. F. at the time of its collapse, and then served as receiver of the railroad until his resignation on August 8. There was some suggestion of financial impropriety at the time, but nothing was proved. Reinhart's arrival in Virginia was to have an impact on Davis and his railroad in a few years.

John G. Luke, vice president of the Piedmont Pulp and Paper Company, wrote to Davis on October 5, again complaining of poor business conditions and asking for a reduction in freight rates. Bretz doubted that the company was as bad off as it claimed, and reported that net revenue on the West Virginia Central was decreasing. He claimed that any further reduction in rates would mean the railroad would be subsidizing the transportation of supplies to the mill and recommended against any further reductions. This time Davis agreed, and no reduction was granted.

Early in October, Davis decided to try to build the B. & C. and looked around for an engineer to take Ives's place. He also wrote to Drake and Stratton and to Charles McFadden and Sons of Philadelphia asking for bids on construction. Hendley, who seemed to be in charge of the B. & C. at this time, hired Andrew H. Onderdonk on October 15, as chief engineer at a salary of $125 per month. Onderdonk had been chief engineer of the Roanoke

Southern and came highly recommended by Latrobe. Hendley and Onderdonk went over the proposed line together and reviewed some of the changes suggested by Ives. The prospects for building the new road lessened on October 18, when John Gill wrote to say that the Mercantile Trust and Deposit Company would not provide a loan to build the road. Hendley was not surprised as he thought the company was heavily influenced by the B. & O.

Davis was not discouraged by this news as at the time of the meeting, he had taken his family to stay at the clubhouse of the Sportsman's Association of Cheat Mountain at Cheat Bridge. While there he examined a route between Shavers Fork and the Greenbrier River and pronounced it suitable for a railroad and decided to have it surveyed. Davis asked F. A. Parsons, son of James Parsons, to conduct the survey.

There was a bad passenger train wreck on October 26, when the front truck of combination car No. 3 climbed over a switch north of Dawson bridge. The car derailed and rolled down a bank and the following passenger car tipped over onto its side. Although the wreck was serious, only eight people were slightly injured, including the mail clerk, James Woodward, who was badly bruised. The company willingly agreed to settle claims, the most significant being from a passenger, John Shay, who had a badly bruised back, for $69. However, it was later found that one of passengers, an attorney by the name of J. W. S. Cochrane, who had injured a finger, was threatening to sue, but agreed to accept $300 compensation.

The poor financial conditions of the country were also taking a toll on the lumber industry along the West Virginia Central. J. J. Rumbarger, secretary of the J. L. Rumbarger Lumber Company, which had been operating at Dobbin since 1883, wrote to the Elkins Inter-Mountain on October 19, that in 1892 the company employed over 350 men but this had now dropped to 55. Business was only 25 percent of what it had been two years earlier and prices had declined 40 percent. The letter was in response to an attack that had been made earlier that Davis had tried to persuade the Rumbarger company to close its mills to influence the upcoming election, a charge that J. J. Rumbarger emphatically denied.

At the beginning of November, the newspapers reported some trouble among the Italian laborers at Womelsdorf on the R. C. & C. By the middle of the month, the reports became more ominous. It was stated that between 400 and 500 Italians had not been paid for nearly three months and were in a state of revolt. Switches on the railroad were torn out and the company's engine and several West Virginia Central cars were trapped at Womelsdorf. On November 13, Randolph County Circuit Court appointed J. Bennett Phillips as receiver, and arrangements were made to settle the debts. Bretz wrote to Phillips to get settlement of the West Virginia Central's outstanding accounts but could get no information as to when this might happen.

Davis received a report on November 23 on the state of the West Virginia Central's mines at Elk Garden from the new superintendent, W. T. Blackiston, who had replaced A. C. Finley on November 15. He reported that No. 6 mine still contained a large quantity of good "red" coal, which was coal that had been stained by water percolating through from above. Mines Nos. 1, 4, and 5 still had some coal that could be worked, but Mines Nos. 2 and 3

were worked out and Mine No. 7 was not being worked at the time. Problems occurred in selling the red coal and it spoilt the appearance of ordinary coal when the two were mixed. Blackiston later reported that the U. M. W. A. was making a determined effort to get all the men at Elk Garden to join the union. Blackiston knew the names of the leaders and recommended to Davis that they "get rid of them." At this time Landstreet was busy surveying at the Franklin mine with a view to building an incline to load coal directly into West Virginia Central cars rather than into C. & P. cars.

Kerens wrote to Davis at the end of November encouraging him to build the B. & C. and noting that the sale of the bonds was being considered.

Early in December, Bretz received bids on supplying steam heating equipment for 13 passenger and combination cars, the private car and five engines. The use of such systems had been mandated in Maryland. A low bid was received from the Safety Car Heating and Lighting Company for $1,807.50 plus $400 for labor. Elkins preferred this company and it received the contract.

Davis received reports on December 1 on the two proposed extensions, the first from Hendley on the B. & C. Hendley had been with Onderdonk over the two major variations still remaining on the route, referred to as the tunnel route and the river route. Sutherland was still at work getting options on the right-of-way. Expenses for the project during November amounted to $715.32.

The second report from Parsons showed that a route from Elkins via Cravens Run to Shavers Fork was feasible although a short tunnel would be required. Shavers Fork would then be followed to Cheat Bridge, a distance of about 40 miles. The route then crossed over to the Greenbrier along the route examined earlier by Davis. The total distance would be 65 miles and was estimated to cost $658,000.

Bretz received an offer to buy an engine from the contractor working on the Pennsylvania Midland Railroad and recommended that No. 1 be sold for $1,500. According to Bretz, No. 1 was worn out and it would cost $4,000 for repairs. Because it was an "odd" engine, requiring different parts, Bretz thought it would be cheaper to buy a new engine. Davis's response is not known although No. 1 remained with the West Virginia Central for nearly five more years.

On December 22, Elkins met with Vice-President Odell of the New York and New England Railroad, and discussed the proposed B. & C. Elkins mentioned that he had just about concluded negotiations for the sale of the B. & C. bonds. Odell, who had been the general manager of the B. & O., thought it would be disastrous to build such a road paralleling the B. & O. Odell wrote to J. K. Cowan, general counsel of the B. & O. reporting that Davis and Elkins were seeking an agreement to allow them to run their trains over the B. & O. tracks from Cumberland to Cherry Run. He recommended that Cowan investigate the additional costs that would be incurred by the B. & O. if such an agreement were approved. Odell offered also to be an arbitrator in the negotiations. Odell submitted a report to Davis comparing the cost of the B. & C. and the returns, with the profit that could be expected from a traffic arrangement. Bretz, when he reviewed the proposal at the end of December, was strongly opposed to the proposed arrangement. He noted that the B. & O. could only just manage to move its own traffic over the line, and that Odell's figures were suspect as more men and engines would be needed than was reported. Bretz thought that the B. & C. could turn a profit based only on the anticipated coal traffic; when other freight and passenger service was considered it would generate a net income of $107,054 per year.

Davis received favorable news from Onderdonk at the end of the year when he reported that a better line in the vicinity of The Narrows had been found. The Narrows, was where the B. & O., the canal and the Potomac River were forced very close together. The route was examined by Latrobe, who noted that while it was one third of a mile longer, it would cost less and have easier curvature.

The financial condition of the country at the end of the year was still unsettled but showing some signs of improvement. The number of railroads placed into the hands of receivers during 1894 was only half that of 1893, which was an encouraging sign. Bretz noted that the W. Md. was now doing quite well but that the stock of the B. & O. was down. The B. & O. did seem to be doing well enough that it was reported by the New York Times to have purchased both the Monongahela River Railroad and the West Virginia and Pittsburgh from Camden. The report, however, was incorrect.

Bretz was more concerned with the weather at the end of the year and reported that there was two feet of snow at Elk Garden and Thomas, but that the trains were getting through on time.

Davis seemed determined at the start of 1895 to build the B. & C. The first step was to have the bonds of the B. & C. endorsed by the West Virginia Central, which was approved at the stockholders' meeting on January 5. The amount of bonds endorsed was $3,600,00. Along with Kerens and Elkins, Davis met with Roberts and Green of the Pennsylvania on January 7 to discuss the situation. The conversation must have been encouraging to Davis as he wrote to Bretz the next day saying that work would start soon on the B. & C. By the middle of the month, Davis noted in his diary that he was negotiating with both the Mercantile Trust and Deposit Company of Baltimore and Hambleton and Company for the sale of $1,500,000 worth of bonds, "with a fair prospect of closing." However, the Pennsylvania was not as enthusiastic as Davis thought. Rea sent a report to President Roberts on January 15, indicating that although Davis estimated the cost of the new road at $3,000,000, he thought the figure would be at least $4,051,800 excluding equipment. Davis's figures were based in part on digging cuts that were two feet narrower than those of the Pennsylvania. Roberts wrote to both Davis and Elkins on January 16, suggesting to Elkins "the uncertainty of the future, both commercially and financially, it would be manifestly unwise to go forward at the present time." To Davis he wrote, "it would seem to me of very doubtful expediency to launch so large an enterprise at this time." Davis mentioned the matter to Bretz who thought the Pennsylvania wanted a delay, as the completed B. & C. would pull traffic away from their road. Davis wrote on January 22, to ex-President Benjamin Harrison, who was interested in the road, that it would be built in the spring. Davis was due to leave on a trip to Mexico and California in early February and so the matter waited for his return.

The R. C. & C. was still in trouble when it was announced on January 3 that the U. S. Circuit Court for West Virginia, on an application of a trustee of the railroad, appointed a second receiver. The receiver appointed by the state court, Bennett Phillips, refused to relinquish the property to the U. S. receiver, setting up an interesting confrontation. Bretz reported that Diller was in Belington on January 15 and expected soon to have the affairs of the railroad in order. However, the R. C. & C. received another setback when floods destroyed a section of trestle on the Tygart Valley River bridge and damaged one of the stone piers.

Bretz reported on January 16, that the new office building in Elkins was coming along; the windows were now in and the plasterer expected to be finished in 30 days. The steam heating equipment had been installed in a passenger car and a baggage car and work started on installing it in the private car. Bretz also thought that Sunday passenger trains should be discontinued for the winter as traffic was very light, and they were taken off starting January 27.

The Lukes were after Bretz again in January to lower freight rates, but Bretz was adamantly opposed, claiming the Lukes were playing the B. & O. off against the West Virginia Central. He told Davis that the switching service provided the mill at Luke cost the West Virginia Central $239 but generated an income of only $110 per month. Bretz still doubted that the Lukes would attempt to connect their plant to the B. & O. by a bridge across the Potomac. Bretz was able to find out from one of the Lukes' competitors, that the mills had more orders for pulp than they could fill and that the paper mills used to make a 50 percent profit, but this was no longer the case. Bretz thought this was what was upsetting the Lukes.

Landstreet, on January 24, submitted to Davis an estimate of costs to deliver coal from the Franklin mine directly to the West Virginia Central. This showed that $11,216 would be needed if a wooden bridge was used. Such a bridge could be expected to last seven years, which was about the time that the "Big Vein" coal in the mine was expected to last, although there was some small vein coal that could be mined. Davis approved the project and advertisements appeared in the local newspapers requesting a supply of ties for the incline and tramway.

A snowstorm at the beginning of February played havoc with the train schedules on the Pennsylvania, B. & O. and the West Virginia Central and caused the cancellation of all freight trains. Bretz noted that it had taken him two days to get back to Cumberland from Philadelphia. He reported that five engines, which had gone to the rescue of a stranded passenger train near Black Oak, had also got stuck, and that three more engines were stuck on the Elk Garden branch. By February 11, things were beginning to return to normal and trains were making good time; the Elk Garden branch was expected to be clear by February 12.

While in Philadelphia, Bretz met with Diller and Phillips and was told that "someone" was putting money into the R. C. & C., and that the West Virginia Central's bill of $940 would soon be settled. Bretz thought that the Berwind White Coal Company, a major Pennsylvania company, was putting up the money.

Hendley reported that Onderdonk had finished his work on the B. & C. on February 18 and had been dismissed. Onderdonk's revised calculations showed considerably more excavation would be needed than Ives had estimated, and that the final cost of the new road would be at least $150,000 over Ives's estimate. This confirmed Rea's opinion that the road was going to cost more than Davis expected. A new engineer, S. E. Weir, who had been with the C. & O., had been hired to start on March 1, but his arrival was delayed until final approval was given for construction to start.

Weir was later placed on the payroll of the West Virginia Central.

On March 11, with the onset of warmer weather, several small slides occurred including one near Chaffee that derailed several cars of a freight train. Bretz recommended that 700 feet of the track at this point be realigned as he thought a major slide could occur at any time and block the track for several days.

In the middle of March there was some talk of a strike by coal miners starting on April 2, but it was not taken seriously on the West Virginia Central or in the Georges Creek region. Blackiston reported that there were some dissatisfied miners at Elk Garden agitating for a strike, but they were not making much progress. A strike of miners at the Manor Big Vein Coal Company at Shaw also increased the pressure on the Elk Garden miners, but no strike occurred.

Hendley reported that the improvements at the Franklin mine should be finished by June 1, and the mine reopened at that time. He also recommended that a company store, operated by the Buxton and Landstreet Company, be opened at West Virginia Central Junction near the mine, and this was approved by Davis. Landstreet later asked permission to open a store at Elk Garden, and although Davis appeared reluctant, he finally gave permission.

On March 23, Davis wrote to President Mayer of the B. & O. complaining about the B. & O. charging the West Virginia Central a wheelage charge for their cars on the West Virginia Central tracks but not those of the C. & P. or the G. C. & C. Davis noted that it was "very much in the nature of discrimination against us."

Davis wrote to Kerens on March 25 noting that the B. & O. and the Board of Public Works in Maryland were holding discussions on the future of the C. & O. Canal. This raised Davis's hopes once more that he might be able to get hold of the canal for a railroad. Until the canal question was settled he proposed to postpone all work on the B. & C. Davis also wrote that the new office building at Elkins was almost complete and that the office force would move in on May 1 (Fig. 100).

Fig. 100. West Virginia Central office building, Elkins
Collection of the Western Maryland Railway Historical Society

Kerens was enthusiastic for a canal route and agreed with postponing work on the B. & C. Kerens also noted that he had traveled down from Chicago in his new private car, which he had named the "Katharyne" after his daughter. The car had been built by Pullman, and although it was lettered for the West Virginia Central, it was not listed as belonging to the company (Fig. 101). Some repair work was, however, charged to the West Virginia Central. In November 1900, for example, Bretz was told by Davis to charge the railroad for the cost of installing new steel platforms on the "Katharyne."

Davis informed Bretz on March 29 that the West Virginia Central had a balance of $2,000 at Jackson and Sharp and to pur-

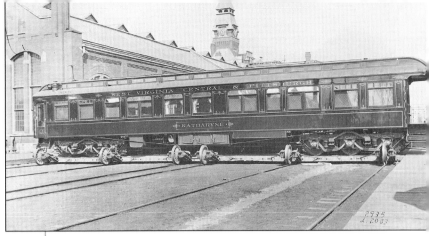

Fig. 101. R. C. Kerens's private car "Katharyne" at the Pullman works
E. L. DeGolyer Jr. Collection, MSS 61
DeGolyer Library, Southern Methodist University

chase either a passenger or a combination car. Bretz ordered a passenger car and this became No. 17 when it was delivered on July 20. It was also reported that car No. 14, which had been involved in the wreck at Dawson, had been repaired at the Elkins shops and returned to service.

At the end of March, Bretz was able to report that business was improving and recommended that the ten percent reduction in wages that had occurred earlier be canceled and wages restored on April 1. It is not stated if the ten percent was returned, but Davis noted on April 1, "Our trade in railway and coal only fair (a little increase) sign of times slightly improving." Signs that business was indeed improving could be found in the spring. Significant for Davis was the announcement that the Pennsylvania coke workers had received a 15 percent wage increase and this had led to an increase in the price of Pennsylvania coke by nearly 50 percent.

The realigned track at Chaffee had been put into service on March 24 and this prompted Bretz to ask Davis to consider other improvements. An improvement in the alignment near the 21st bridge was already under construction and Bretz asked that a realignment near Rosedale, costing $19,800, be considered. This figure would also enable a grade improvement to be completed at the same time that would enable trains of 50 or 60 cars to be used at that point. Bretz thought that if this and other similar improvements elsewhere were implemented, it should be possible to haul 50 car trains from Fairfax to Cumberland. Bretz calculated that with the present level of business, the savings that could be expected by adding five cars per train would be $2,358 per year and if ten cars could be added the savings would increase to $4,287. Davis gave permission for the work and it was reported to have started by June.

On March 23, Davis received $20,000 for the B. & C. from ex-President Benjamin Harrison, who was informed that a decision would be made in a month or two as to when the work would start. By April 22, Harrison was informed that the decision had been made not to start on the B. & C. during 1895.

During May, Davis again heard from McGraw asking about plans for a railroad to the Greenbrier. Davis informed McGraw of his plans to go from Elkins to Shavers Fork but now thought that the route would cross over to Glady Fork rather than continue up Shavers Fork. McGraw was thinking of extending the Dry Fork Railroad to the Greenbrier and Davis could see no problem with

McGraw's proposal.

Davis wrote to Ingalls of the C. & O. on June 11, telling him that the time was now right to build the lines to the Greenbrier. Davis expected to build 70 miles at a cost not to exceed $20,000 per mile, leaving the C. & O. to build 40 miles. A meeting was held on June 15 at Elkins with Davis, Elkins and Kerens present at which, according to Davis, "we agree to favor building railway from here south to connect with the C. & O. road." The group also decided to take a horseback trip over the proposed route in July.

Davis must have been encouraged by the improving financial conditions and allowed Bretz, on June 19, to order a 70 ton consolidated freight engine from Baldwin for $10,000; half the purchase price in cash, the remainder in coal. The contract with Baldwin called for the engine to be delivered by the middle of August, and it became No. 30 when it was received. He also met with Galbreath and agreed to allow the reconstruction of several sharp curves at an estimated cost of $18,000.

William Gorman of the Cumberland Coal Company noted that demand for coke had picked up and requested permission to build several more coke ovens. Bretz had earlier reported an increase in the demand for coke and had begun replacing the racks on coke cars from which they had earlier been removed to allow them to be used in the coal trade (Fig. 102). The Davis Coal and Coke Company had also become involved in the export of coke to Mexico where it was used in the production of silver. In January, the com-

Fig. 102. Coke cars at the coke ovens, Coketon
Collection of the Western Maryland Railway Historical Society

pany had secured a contract to supply 1,200 tons of coke per month to the Compania Metalurgica Mexicana. The coke was shipped from Baltimore to Tampico and gave the coal company a profit of $1.125 per ton. The contract expired in June and it was expected that the Mexican company would increase its demand to at least 2,000 tons per month.

A new factor entered into Davis's plans for extending to the C. & O. when it was announced on May 14 that the Chesapeake and Western Railroad had been incorporated. This was the latest in a long line of railroads planned to run from tidewater to the West Virginia coalfields. The president of the new company was J. W. Reinhart, ex-president of the A. T. & S. F. Reinhart was acquainted with both Elkins and Kerens and the three met in late June to discuss the proposed route of the C. & W. Reinhart had asked Kerens to join him in the scheme and Kerens thought that it would be a good idea for him to become involved "just to control it as an outlet for our West Virginia interests." Kerens did not want Ingalls informed of these plans, although Kerens and Elkins had met with Ingalls to discuss the Greenbrier scheme before meeting with

Reinhart. Davis was interested in these talks, but thought that the route to the C. & O. should be the immediate task; a route to tidewater could be left for the future. Davis did ask the secretary of state for West Virginia if the "Coal and Iron Railway" could still be used, although it would be a few years before it was needed.

During this time, Bretz was enjoying a well deserved trip to England to attend the International Railway Congress. Bretz was most impressed that the Congress had been opened by the Prince of Wales on June 26, and that the delegates were to attend a tea party at Windsor Castle with Queen Victoria. More to the point were his observations to Davis concerning English railroads, specifically the coal docks in South Wales, which had attracted his attention. He reported that coal cars were picked up and the coal dumped directly into a waiting vessel without using trestles as was common in the U. S. Bretz thought the railroad tracks, "almost perfect," but that the facilities for handling passengers and baggage, "seem rather crude."

With Bretz away in England, Elkins asked Bower, the assistant general manager to prepare a rough estimate of the earnings and expenses of the Dry Fork Railroad for June 1895. Bower's estimate, reported on July 13, indicated that the Dry Fork was covering its expenses and was turning in a minuscule profit. The interest of Davis and Elkins in the Dry Fork was to be short lived.

Coincidentally, the Baldwin Locomotive Works contacted Davis on July 22, to ask about the credit worthiness of R. F. Whitmer and the Dry Fork as they had recently ordered a new engine costing about $7,500. Davis's report must have been favorable as the engine, No. 3 (Fig. 103), was delivered soon after.

Fig. 103. Dry Fork Railroad No. 3
Collection of the West Virginia State Archives

Davis, Elkins, Thomas Davis and Weir left Elkins on July 18 for their trip over the proposed route to the C. & O. The first night the party stayed at Flint on Glady Fork. From there they crossed over to the West Fork of the Greenbrier and followed this down to the East Fork and then to Travelers Repose. After a night at Travelers Repose, the party followed the Greenbrier to Huntersville and then to Monterey. From Monterey, the group headed back west to Cheat Bridge and returned to Elkins on July 23. Davis noted that the route was practical and "reasonably cheap" at $20,000 per mile.

The increased demand for coke, which had been noted earlier, led to a car shortage in July. Landstreet complained that the shortage was leading to an accumulation of coke in the yards and in the ovens. The Davis Coal and Coke Company had 328 ovens in blast and the Cumberland Coal Company had a further 45. Both companies were building additional ovens that would bring the total to 439. If all these ovens were in blast, 33 cars a day would be required to move the coke and to provide these cars, a pool of at least 347 coke racks would be needed. The West Virginia Central possessed only 175 racks and no major purchases were made during the year, although the shops at Elkins turned out 76 new racks between July 1, 1895 and June 30, 1896.

A new coal company, Watson and Company, leased 1041 acres of Big Vein coal lands along the line of the West Virginia Central between West Virginia Central Junction and Warnocks, and requested on July 24 that a siding be installed. Bower agreed to install the siding but could not give the new company a guarantee that it would always have a sufficiency of cars. This satisfied the company, which hoped to start shipping coal by October 1. During 1896 and 1897, nearly 16,000 tons of coal were shipped from Warnocks.

Elkins met with the officers of the Pennsylvania on July 30, and reported that Roberts seemed in favor of building the B. & C., but that Thomson was very reluctant to give his approval. President Kennedy of the C. V. was very much in support of the new road but still no action was taken.

The Piedmont Herald reported on August 16 that contracts had been let for the construction of the Roaring Creek and Belington Railroad, and a few days later it was noted that a new passenger car had been delivered to the R. C. & C. On August 29, Davis gave J. O. Black, chief engineer of the R. C. & B., permission to cross the West Virginia Central with an overhead bridge. Bretz was still in the dark as to who was behind all this activity, but strongly suspected that it was the Berwind-White company as they were taking the Roaring Creek coal. Bretz also thought that the B. & O. could be involved, but this was denied by the B. & O.

Bretz had also talked to Whitmer of the Dry Fork Railroad, and was told that The United States Leather Company had offered to furnish the money needed to extend the D. F. to ensure an adequate supply of bark. The U. S. Leather Company, which had been formed by a combination of a number of smaller companies including Fayerweather and Ladew, already had $100,000 of bonds of the D. F. for money advanced for the construction of the line to Horton. Whitmer did not appear to favor this proposal. McGraw also seemed to be working with the leather company as he met with Elkins on September 24 to encourage the West Virginia Central to extend to the Greenbrier. McGraw's interest was still to get a railroad to his lands to exploit the lumber, and selling the bark to the leather company was an added incentive. September 24 was a busy day for Elkins as he met with McGraw, Reinhart and E. R. Ladew of U. S. Leather at different times. Elkins thought the leather company was about ready to sign a contract with the D. F. to extend the road, or that they would be willing to assist the West Virginia Central to extend the D. F. if Davis took it over. Elkins again met with the U. S. Leather representatives on September 25 and was asked for an immediate decision on whether the West Virginia Central would extend to the Greenbrier. Elkins reported to Davis that he doubted that the leather company would build their own road but that McGraw had agreed to sell them his bark if and when a railroad was built. Although Elkins was pushed for a response, he refused to give a definite answer until he had consulted with Davis and had estimates prepared for the cost of acquiring and upgrading the D. F.

Elkins wrote to Whitmer indicating that the West Virginia Central would not build from Horton, at the end of the D. F., without having a running agreement over the D. F. rails. As an alternative, Elkins offered to take an interest in the D. F. but Whitmer was not interested in having additional partners. Whitmer suggested that if the West Virginia Central wanted to build it should be from Elkins, but that if the D. F. extended, he wanted to have control. Whitmer pointed out that the D. F. had been cheaply constructed with no ballast and wooden bridges throughout as it was intended only for the passage of lumber.

Meanwhile, Davis had met with Ingalls of the C. & O., who was confident that a connection between the C. & O. and Pittsburgh would be "a paying road." Ingalls was also aware of the explorations of Carnegie's people in the iron ore fields in the region, although Davis and Carnegie had tried to keep the matter quiet.

By October 11, The U. S. Leather Company was pushing Elkins for a response on building. Elkins wrote back on the same day noting that the West Virginia Central was not in a position to decide, and recommending that the leather company proceed with whatever other plans it might have.

Davis did ask Weir to review the two routes and he submitted his report on October 14 showing that the route from Elkins to the Forks of the Greenbrier would cost $700,000 and from Horton, $500,000. However, to use the Horton route the D. F. would have to be upgraded at a cost of $200,000.

One reason that Davis and Elkins did not pursue an extension to the Greenbrier at this time was their renewed interest in the C. & O. Canal.

When Judge Alvey awarded the canal to its trustees, principally the B. & O., in 1890, he gave them until May 1895 to show whether it could be operated advantageously. The Board of Public Works of Maryland was against this, and advertisements appeared on August 3, 1895 inviting proposals to purchase the state's interest in the canal, which was estimated to be worth nearly $3,000,000. Davis, Elkins and Kerens spent the first week in October preparing bids for the canal, which were opened by the governor on October 10. Three bids were received. The first was from John Cowan, trustee but on behalf of the B. & O., for $310,000. The second bid, on behalf of the Washington and Cumberland Railroad, was made by Hendley. The railroad offered to accept the lease of the canal, as authorized by the Maryland Assembly in 1890, and would make certain payments for bonds and claims. Since this was not, strictly speaking, a cash offer, a third bid was made by Kerens in the amount of $526,000. Consideration of the bids was deferred until the whole board could review them. At the end of November, the Board of Public Works rejected all three bids and requested the attorney general to press the pending appeal of the state against the bondholders.

The fall of 1895 was exceptionally dry in the Upper Potomac area, and this had two consequences for the West Virginia Central. The first was from the forest fires, which were particularly bad that year. The first damage occurred at Elk Garden on September 4 when 11 houses and one storeroom were burnt, but there was no damage to the railroad or its mines. Fire broke out at Coketon on October 22, which destroyed five double houses, and a single house had to be demolished in an effort to contain the fire. A few days later, forest fires were reported to have surrounded the town of Davis, which was only spared when the wind shifted. Several miles of tramroads were destroyed.

The second effect of the drought was to decrease the quality of water available for the locomotives, which in turn caused problems with the boilers. Bretz first complained about the problem on October 15 when he noted an increase in the number of engines failing on the road because of a lack of steam. On October 21, two engines, Nos. 21 and 28, had to be towed to Elkins, and Bretz ordered the shops to work overtime to keep the engines running. At one point, 13 engines were out of service. Most of the trouble occurred between Cumberland and Gerstell where the water came from the Potomac River and was heavily polluted by the pulp mill. To avoid problems at Gerstell, Bretz ordered a well to be drilled to provide a source of clean water. This was finished at the end of December at a total cost of $605.87 and gave an adequate supply of clean water. Bretz's problems, although compounded by the drought, did indicate a need for additional locomotives. As early as August, Bretz had reported that No. 1 was still in use although only capable of carrying 90 lb. steam pressure. He recommended that the engine be scrapped and a new passenger engine purchased. No. 1 was still in use in September, when Bretz received bids from Baldwin for a freight engine, similar to No. 30, for $10,400, and a passenger engine, similar to No. 18, for $8,000. Orders for a new freight engine and a new passenger engine were placed with Baldwin on October 15, but Bretz was forced to try to borrow engines to keep the West Virginia Central in operation. Baldwin offered to loan an engine on November 7 while the two new engines were under construction. At some point the order for the passenger engine was changed to an additional freight engine, and the two new locomotives, Nos. 31 and 32, were at work by the middle of December. Engine No. 1 continued to work for a few more years in spite of Bretz's concern that it was unsafe.

Although Elkins appeared to have terminated all discussions with the leather company about the southeast extension, Davis was not quite ready to quit. Davis wrote to McGraw on October 14 to try to find out what the leather company would do towards aiding a new road. A day later he wrote to E. R. Ladew mentioning that Elkins was the logical starting point for the extension and also stating that Elkins was not as impressed by the scheme as was Davis. During the next few weeks, Davis and McGraw continued to hold discussions on the topic.

These discussions led to a memorandum of understanding between Davis and McGraw dated November 27 whereby The United States Leather Company agreed to erect a tannery at the Forks of the Greenbrier, and the Rochester Boom and Lumber and a group from Ronceverte would also erect sawmills. In return, a railroad would be built from Elkins in which the Davis group would hold 60 percent of the stock, and McGraw, the leather company and their associates, 40 percent. The West Virginia Central would operate the new road at 68 percent of gross earnings.

Davis's interest in the line was not due solely to the timber and bark in the region. He had a healthy skepticism of railroads built just to exploit timber resources, since when the timber was gone, there was usually nothing to take its place as freight. Davis, however, was convinced of the value of the iron ore deposits in the region and in this he was supported by Andrew Carnegie, who had engineers out testing the deposits. At the end of December, Davis wrote to B. M. Yeager, a land surveyor from Marlinton, to see if he could obtain a free right-of-way from the people of Pocahontas County. However, when he wrote to McGraw on December 30, he reiterated that his colleagues were not as interested in the new road as he was, and asked if the November 27 agreement could be modified.

While Davis was looking to the southeast, the railroad connecting Roaring Creek and Belington, known locally as the Link Railroad, was making steady progress. The grading was expected to be finished by November 1 and iron for the bridge across the Tygart Valley River was delivered in the middle of October (Fig. 104). The road was finished by early December and it was reported that a passenger train was now running between Womelsdorf and Belington.

Fig. 104. Roaring Creek and Belington Railroad train on the Tygart Valley River bridge. The tracks of the West Virginia Central are between the stone piers. *Collection of the Western Maryland Railway Historical Society*

Davis had heard that Diller was negotiating to sell his railroad interests when he wrote to Thomson on November 6, but he did not know who was the purchaser. The next day he received a letter from W. J. B. Patterson offering to sell 2,000 acres of coal lands stretching from Roaring Creek to Belington and owned by the Roaring Creek Consolidated Coal Company. Davis did not seem interested but did arrange to buy some coal lands between Little Laurel Run and Zebs Creek on the west side of the Tygart Valley River.

Bretz reported on December 31, that the railroad was finishing the year in good shape with plenty of cars and that Elk Garden had loaded 2,050 tons the previous day. Davis was concerned about the earnings and expenses of the road south of Coketon. Bower pointed out that during September 1895, there had been 320 freight train movements over this portion of the road, which consisted of steep grades and sharp curves and hence much effort was required to keep the track in good condition. In addition work was still required in ballasting the track and improving the cuts and fills, which should have been charged to construction rather than to an operating account. Additional expenses were incurred taking coal and supplies to Elkins. Galbreath noted that the engines frequently ran backwards over the heavy grades and this led to an increase in the tendency for the track to spread.

Bretz returned to the problem of expenses in the new year, 1896, when he complained to Davis about the facilities at West Virginia Central Junction and Cumberland. At West Virginia Central Junction, light repairs were done on freight cars but Bretz thought that the facility was inadequate. Similarly at Cumberland, where 14 engines laid over, there were facilities for only four.

Trains were frequently delayed when cars requiring repairs at the Junction had to be switched out from freight trains. Bretz's solution was to expand the facilities at Ridgeley, but Davis was not yet ready for this idea.

Discussions between Davis and McGraw on the proposed new railroad continued into 1896. McGraw indicated on January 6, that he was expecting a proposition from the leather company, which could form the basis of an understanding between the parties. Davis, meanwhile, had had conversations with Carnegie about the movement of iron ore over the new road. Carnegie told Davis that he could guarantee that 1,000 tons of ore would be moved daily to the Pittsburgh area, and that he would help also in the raising of money for bonds. McGraw submitted a proposal to Davis on January 29, in which he offered to take $100,000 of stock. Although Davis thought the proposition "not in business shape," he did think it could provide the basis for future discussions.

Davis reported to Kerens on January 17, that he had purchased an additional 200 acres of Big Vein coal at Elk Garden, known as the Vandiver lands, for $20,000. Kerens offered to take an interest in the new land, but it was decided to allow the West Virginia Central to take possession with the money being paid from earnings of the coal department. Kerens also mentioned that several individuals, including the vice president of the A. T. & S. F., had been considered as possible candidates for the presidency of the B. & O. Kerens doubted that any man of "experience and reputation will undertake the management of it with the financial difficulties that now beset it, unsettled." Thus it was perhaps no surprise that an insider, John K. Cowan, became president of the B. & O. on January 24.

Davis wrote to Ingalls on January 30, to tell him that construction of the new railroad could start in the spring. Davis did hear from Jed Hotchkiss on February 4, who reported that he had examined the ores in the Anthonys Creek region and found them to be of a very high quality. Hotchkiss also mentioned that the C. & O. had a surveying party examining a route from Huntersville to White Sulphur Springs.

Bretz reported on February 2 that work on filling in the trestle at Craven Run, north of Elkins, was complete. A 14 foot stone arch was built over the Run and was completed by the time the 15th Annual Report was published in August 1896 (Fig. 1).

Davis noted in his diary on February 7, "All goes well with our business." However, on the same day he wrote to Elkins complaining about discrimination in the distribution of cars by the B. & O.

Davis had another problem in February, when Elkins wrote on February 22 that he wanted to resign as president of the Davis Coal and Coke Company, claiming that he could not give proper attention to the business. He noted, "I never felt I was more than nominally president and feel now less so than ever." Davis mentioned that he had hoped Buxton, the vice president, would have been up to the task of running the company, but apparently this was not the case. On February 29, Landstreet was appointed general sales manager of the Davis Coal and Coke Company.

Davis and McGraw signed an agreement, dated February 20, which had resulted from their meetings over the past weeks. McGraw was to provide $75,000 and a free right-of-way and in return, Davis was to build a railroad from Elkins to Huntersville.

By now, Davis was a little concerned about the financial outlook for the country, and included in the agreement a clause that road would be built, "as early as practical, consistent with the condition of the money market."

A bad wreck occurred on February 22 near the Empire mine when one freight train ran into the back of another, fortunately without causing any injuries. One train, pulled by Engine No. 22, had stopped to set off a car. A flagman was supposed to go back to warn any approaching trains of the danger ahead, but unfortunately in this instance he did not go back far enough to allow the second train time to stop. The engine, No. 5, was derailed and went down a bank but was not seriously damaged, although the tender was wrecked. A caboose and two cars were smashed. Bretz estimated the cost of the accident at $1,200 and dismissed the flagman. No. 5 was hauled back onto the tracks on February 24.

In an effort to speed up the start on the new road, McGraw sent Davis the charter for the West Virginia Central and Midland Railroad Company. McGraw, Hotchkiss and others had incorporated the railroad, which was planned to run from Rowlesburg, via the Cheat and Greenbrier rivers, to White Sulphur Springs. Whether McGraw ever hoped to build the road is not clear, but now he tried to interest Davis in taking over the charter to save time should Davis decide to build. McGraw thought that Davis could save six weeks by building under the charter, but Davis was not going to be rushed. Davis informed McGraw that Ingalls was not yet ready to build. Also, he expected the B. & O. to be forced into receivership, which would be a great financial disadvantage "to us all."

The B. & O. went into receivership on March 1; the new president, Cowan, and Vice President Oscar G. Murray, becoming the receivers. At the end of February, Davis had met with Cowan to discuss car discrimination and other problems existing between the two companies, and reported to Bretz that the meeting had been satisfactory. A day or two later, he met with Receiver Murray and listed the complaints he had against the B. & O.

An agreement was signed at the end of February for the sale of the Blackwater Hotel to F. and A. Thompson of the Blackwater Lumber Company for $7,500. The Thompsons thought that if the hotel were improved, it would help the image of the town. During the years since it had been carved out of the forest, Davis had enjoyed a boom. Its population had risen to 918 by 1890, according to official census figures. In 1892, the population of Davis and the surrounding area was estimated at approximately 2,000 rising to about 3,000 in 1897. There were six churches, about 20 stores and a public school employing eight teachers. The town was supported by two lumber mills, a tannery and the Luke brothers' pulp mill, as can be seen in the "aerial" view in Fig. 105. Davis had completed a stone bank building in 1892, but his interest in the town waned as he became associated with the development of Elkins. The depot at Davis, which had been constructed during 1885, is shown in Fig. 106.

The Lukes wrote to Bretz again at the end of February requesting reductions in freight rates to the mills at Luke and Davis. Earlier it had been noted that the Lukes were going to build a new paper mill and the company had requested the West Virginia Central install additional sidings. The cost to the railroad was estimated at $1,206.

It was announced on March 23 that the Georges Creek miners would receive an increase of five cents per ton in the price paid for coal. Landstreet proposed a similar increase for the miners of the Davis Coal and Coke Company to take effect on April 1. Notices appeared around the mines demanding a further increase of five cents or there would be a strike. Superintendent Blackiston was sure the miners would stay on the job unless the Georges Creek men interfered. April 1, the day called for the strike, passed peacefully.

Davis was informed by McGraw on April 17, that the Roaring Creek railroad and coalfield had passed into the control of Edward Berwind, president of the Berwind-White Coal Mining Company. Bretz had earlier been contacted by the B. & O. about improving the facilities at Belington, and erecting a depot for all three railroads, but nothing was done on the proposal. It also was noted that a contractor was at work on the bridge at Roaring Creek Junction preparing stone for new piers.

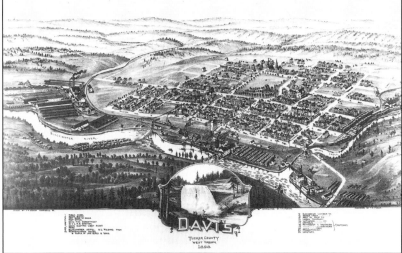

Fig. 105. View of Davis in 1898. The bank building is in the center of the picture. The tannery is off to the left and the Beaver Creek Lumber Company is on the right. The Blackwater Lumber Company is in front of the bank building and the pulp mill is to the right across Beaver Creek. Smoke from the Blackwater mills is blowing over the West Virginia Central depot.
West Virginia and Regional History Collection,
West Virginia University Library

Central including the depots at Junior and Hendricks.

Bretz was contacted by Whitmer in June, asking to purchase ten miles of used 56 pound rails. Coincidently this was the amount of 56 pound rail still remaining in the main line of the West Virginia Central between Bayard and Bradshaw, which was worn and needed replacing with 70 pound rail.

Unfortunately Bretz did not think he could afford to purchase all the new rails that would be needed at this time. Whitmer agreed to accept an initial installment of three miles but haggled over the price. An agreement was reached and 100 tons of rails were sent to the Dry Fork at the end of June. Bower also sent rails from the Mineville branch which was closed when the Atlantic mine was exhausted. The rails were needed by Whitmer to get to spruce lumber in the forests and were not part of any expansion plans. It was later announced that the Condon-Lane Boom and Lumber Company had secured an order to supply 500,000 cords of wood to the Piedmont Pulp and Paper Company.

The C. & O. Canal was back in the news in June. The extension of time granted by Judge Alvey on October 2, 1890, to the

Fig. 107. Map of the proposed Little Kanawha Railroad
West Virginia and Regional History Collection,
West Virginia University Library

Fig. 106. Depot at Davis, circa 1912

After many years of effort, a railroad was incorporated on May 1, to build up the valley of the Little Kanawha River from Parkersburg to Burnsville and a junction with the West Virginia and Pittsburg. The railroad was incorporated by Parkersburg businessmen, and, except for raising money and distributing publicity (Fig. 107), nothing much was done until the following year.

On May 12, it was announced that Davis's elder son, Henry Jr., had been lost at sea when returning from a trip to South Africa. Davis decided to give his younger son, John T. Davis, supervision of the mines at Junior.

Spring saw a reoccurrence of the fires that plagued the West Virginia Central in the previous fall. Bretz reported fires near Pendleton and thought that the trestle there and the mill belonging to Thomas Burger were in danger, and also the mills and houses around Davis. By May 11, the winds dropped and the danger passed. On May 12, it was reported that a planing mill in Elkins, belonging to Thomas Leonard, had burnt to the ground, but this was thought to be an isolated act of arson. The mill had supplied much of the lumber for the buildings along the West Virginia

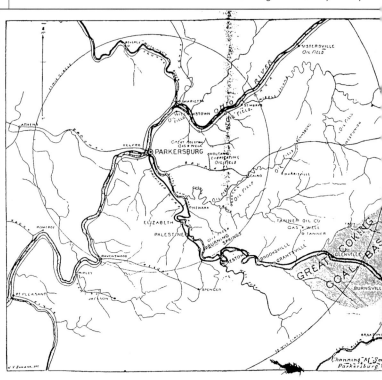

trustees of the bondholders to prove that the canal could be operated profitably, expired on May 1, 1894. The canal was to be sold if a profit could not be realized. The trustees went to court and asked for an extension, claiming that $430,000 had been spent on repairs, but the miners' strikes and a lack of confidence by canal boat operators had made a profit impossible. The court agreed and gave the trustees until May 1, 1901 to show a profit. The decision was immediately appealed to the court of appeals by the state. In June 1896, the court of appeals upheld the lower court's decision. Davis was most upset by the news and instructed his attorney in the matter, B. A. Richmond, to "let these people know that an injustice has been done." He could not believe that the B. & O., the power behind the trustees, had spent $430,000 on repairs, when the highest estimate had been for $250,000. Davis wrote to Kerens on June 27, informing him the court's decision and noting that it delayed all possibility for the purchase of the canal for four or five years. Davis was not quite ready to abandon the idea of an eastern extension and ordered Weir to review the line of the B. & C. In November, he told Elkins that there was a chance of securing the canal as far as Cherry Run, although it is not clear how this was thought to be possible. He did ask the court of appeals for a re-argument of its decision of June 1896 on the basis that fraud had been committed by the B. & O. The court reported that there was no evidence in the record of such fraud, and denied the request, although admitting, off the record, that Davis was probably right. Davis finally decided not to pursue the matter any further.

It was noted at the end of June that the B. & O. had commenced to construct a bridge across the Potomac to the Piedmont Pulp and Paper Company's mill at Luke. Landstreet met with John Luke on July 7 and was told that a contract for the bridge had been signed a year earlier as the company wanted to reduce switching charges. Luke also claimed that the B. & O. could ship to New York in two days less than was required by the Pennsylvania. Landstreet was assured that this was not a hostile act but was merely to give the mill a competitive advantage. Davis was still not pleased and complained to Oscar Murray claiming that this was indeed a hostile act and an unnecessary expense for the B. & O. Murray replied on August 1, pointing out that the material for the bridge had been ordered and the contract could not now be canceled. Elkins had made a similar complaint to Cowan and was also told that the contract had been signed but that the mill was paying for the bridge. This activity did have one effect that was desired by the Lukes; Bretz canceled the switching charge on July 13. David Luke noted that the new paper mill would increase business by 100 percent. The new bridge was built downstream of the existing West

West Va. Junction.

Virginia Central bridge (Fig 108), and both bridges still remain to serve the mill to this day.

Davis noted on June 23 that he had examined the coal along Laurel Run and Zebs Creek on the

Fig. 108. B. & O. and West Virginia Central bridges at West Virginia Central Junction. The new B. & O. bridge is on the left

west side of the Tygart Valley River and reported that he had purchased 250 acres, which gave him a total of 500 acres in the Roaring Creek field.

The forest fires of spring were followed in July by severe floods. The rain started on July 22 and by July 23 reports were coming in of river levels being the highest ever recorded. One of the first casualties was the R. C. & C. bridge across the Tygart Valley River at Roaring Creek Junction. Bridges on the D. F. and on the B. & O. between Belington and Grafton were also destroyed bringing all train service in the region to a halt. It also was reported that the B. & O.'s 21st bridge was damaged and could not be used. Davis tried to get through from Cumberland to Elkins on July 23, but only got as far as Polands before the tracks disappeared under water. He tried again on July 24 with the same result and it was to be July 25 before he reported that the waters were receding and the road was open. On July 26 he was able to report that, "all trains are running as usual." Bretz reported on July 30 that crews were at work at Rosedale and Hampshire where some damage had occurred, and that an immense amount of riprap would be needed along the banks to make them secure against future washouts.

Whether it was because of the flood, or whether it was Davis's dislike of wooden trestles, he ordered Bretz on July 29 to get rid of all such trestles and to replace them with masonry and iron. The first projects were the trestles at Glade Run and Rawlings, and on July 31, Weir was ordered to replace the trestle at Corricks Ford near Parsons.

The Fifteenth Annual Report of the West Virginia Central for the fiscal year ending June 30, 1896 included a note from Bretz that an extension to the Elkins car shop was expected to be finished by October 1 (Fig. 109). The West Virginia Central was saving money by building its own cars at Elkins; Bretz had reported that in November 1895 ten new coke racks had been built and during December, eight racks were finished. Compared to the price of similar cars from the South Baltimore Car Works ($430.00), a savings of $25.77 was being realized.

During July, signs of an economic slowdown were becoming evident. The Pennsylvania Railroad was reported to have canceled all work that was not absolutely necessary. Because of this, Davis wrote to Ingalls on July 17, informing him that he was putting off all consideration of building the connecting line until conditions improved.

By September, Davis was encouraging Bretz to try to reduce expenses including those for maintenance-of-way. Bretz listed all the employees in the maintenance-of-way department as follows:

North End	South End
1 engineer	1 engineer
1 assistant engineer	1 assistant engineer
1 supervisor	2 supervisors
2 painters	22 track foremen
No carpenters	111 laborers
17 track foremen	1 foreman and 30 men on work train
85 laborers	1 foreman carpenter
1 watchman	4 carpenters
1 foreman and 30 men on work train	2 laborers
1 foreman and 33 men at Copperas Rock	12 carpenters (new buildings)
6 men riprapping	

Fig. 109. Car shops at Elkins. The new car shop is on the right
Collection of the Western Maryland Railway Historical Society

Bretz was reluctant to reduce the trackmen as he thought they were only just beginning to get the track back in shape after the July floods. He recommended the work train on the north end be continued until the winter, as there was still a need to continue with the riprap work. The work train on the south end could be dropped at the end of September. If additional reductions needed to be made, then Bretz recommended that the shop force be reduced to nine hours. Davis approved the recommendation on October 12.

The advisability of continuing the riprapping and other work to protect against floods was demonstrated at the beginning of October when high waters again damaged the B. & O.'s 21st bridge and led to all of that company's trains being run over the West Virginia Central's track. Transfer of the trains back to the B. & O. at Cumberland was a tedious process and led to discussions between the two companies on ways to improve the connection at the canal wharf. By the end of October an agreement was reached whereby the B. & O. would build a double track connection across the wharf, and the West Virginia Central would pay one third of the cost. The West Virginia Central would also pay one third of the $5,000 compensation required by the canal company for taking its land. The connection allowed trains from the West Virginia Central to move directly onto the B. & O.'s westbound tracks without any switching (Fig. 110). Both companies would have preferred an eastbound connection, but the canal company refused to provide the land for this connection. The new connection was completed at the beginning of April 1897.

Bretz returned in November to the question of improving the facilities at Ridgeley, which he had raised with Davis in January. Bretz thought that this matter was now more urgent because of the proposed new connection with the B. & O. across the canal basin, which would effectively bypass the old Cumberland yards, except for traffic bound for the Pennsylvania. Bretz recommended the construction of a 12-stall roundhouse and a small blacksmith shop at a cost of about $15,000. He thought the savings produced would pay for these improvements in three years.

At the beginning of December, Bretz was complaining about the performance of the two compound engines, Nos. 28 and 29. He recommended that both engines be converted to simple locomotives and that this would cost $1,225 for new cylinder castings for each engine. Bretz thought that Baldwin should pay a portion of the cost since it had recommended the engines to the West Virginia Central. Davis, who was by now becoming very concerned about future business prospects, told Bretz not to hurry the conversion.

The year ended with two bad wrecks, the first at Warnocks on December 8. It was not established what caused this wreck, but it was thought that something, possibly a brake bar, had dropped onto the rails causing the ninth car in a 39 car train to derail. An addi-

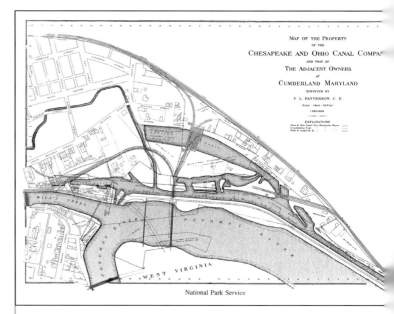

Fig. 110. Westbound connection between the West Virginia Central and the B. & O., December 1896
Collection of the National Park Service

tional 16 cars piled up on top, totally destroying seven coal cars. Fortunately, the wreck happened in the passing siding at Warnocks so that traffic was not unduly delayed, although the wreck was expensive. Bretz estimated the cost at nearly $3,000.

The second wreck occurred on December 30 and appeared to be due to an act of sabotage. A passenger train passed through Westernport at 6:30 P.M. without a problem, but a following freight train, hauled by No. 15, was diverted into a siding by someone opening a switch. The engine left the tracks and turned over, the tender and at least five coal cars piling up on top. The engineer and fireman had jumped clear when they saw the danger, and were uninjured. The only injuries recorded were to a couple of laborers, who were at work clearing the wreck, when the roof of a boxcar fell on them. Damage to the engine was not as bad as had first been thought.

Davis informed Bretz on December 15 that the outlook did not appear promising, and asked if the shopmen could be reduced to eight hours and salaries could be cut by ten percent. As an economy measure, Bretz wondered if something could be done with Weir, who had been carried on the engineering payroll since the end of the work on the B. & C. Weir was later appointed general superintendent of the Davis Coal and Coke Company with an office in Thomas.

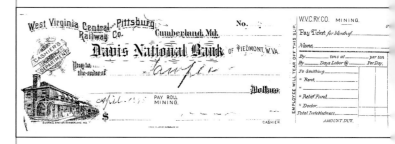

Fig. 111. Sample of checks for the West Virginia Central, April 1895
West Virginia and Regional History Collection,
West Virginia University Library

Fires, Floods, Wrecks, Shootings and an Extension

9

The first months of the new year, 1897, seemed like a rerun of the last months of the old year, with floods and wrecks and a bleak financial outlook. Davis noted in his diary on January 15 that, "Business on road and in coal and coke only tolerable."

Davis first wanted to know if all the lumber companies that were cutting on lands belonging to the West Virginia Central were up-to-date in monies owed the company. Howard Sutherland, who had left the B. & C. to become land agent for the West Virginia Central, reported that three companies were at work on the railroad company's lands. At Coketon, the Coketon Lumber Company had paid $15,000 for all the timber on a tract; it was paying this off at $200 per month and was up-to-date. Thomas Burger and Sons Company had operations at Douglas and Pendleton Run and was also up-to-date in its payments. At William and Hambleton, R. Chaffey paid royalty on bark, timber and pulpwood.

Davis informed Bretz on January 15, that he had met with John Luke, and although the B. & O. bridge had been finished to the mill at Luke, he thought the long term advantages in supplying wood and coal to the mill outweighed any immediate loss. He had agreed to allow the B. & O. to use the sidings belonging to the West Virginia Central at the mill.

The first wreck of the year occurred on January 15 when a wheel burst under a freight car at Maple Run near Schell derailing seven cars. The wheel showed no sign of excessive heating due to hard braking, but Bretz suspended the conductor and the brakeman "to make others more cautious in the use of brakes."

It was announced on January 22, that the Otter Creek Boom and Lumber Company had received its articles of incorporation and had taken over the mill and timber rights of the Welch Brothers at Hulings. The new company was building a bridge across the Black Fork (Fig.112), and had constructed an additional six miles of railroad into the forest.

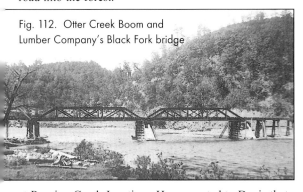

Fig. 112. Otter Creek Boom and Lumber Company's Black Fork bridge

Bretz was becoming impatient at the lack of progress by the R. C. & C. in repairing the bridge at Roaring Creek Junction. He suggested to Davis that perhaps Dailey could write to the company reminding it of its obligations under the agreement to interchange traffic. Bretz also mentioned that he had heard from the McClure-Mabie Lumber Company, located on the R. C. & C., and which proposed to ship 1,000 cars per year over the West Virginia Central, but was unable to do so with the bridge still out. Bretz also was upset that the R. C. & C. refused to pay its portion of the cost of the depot at Roaring Creek Junction.

A second accident occurred on January 26, when Engine No. 13 jumped the track near Stony River. Because the accident happened in a cut, it caused considerable delay to traffic until the engine could be removed. Damage to the engine was slight; Bretz thought the engine had been going too fast and he proposed to discipline the crew.

Bretz complained that the B. & O. was still charging the West Virginia Central mileage for the use of their cars. Bretz thought the B. & O. was going to make other companies, such as the C. & P., pay the same charge, but was not sure if this had been implemented. The Pennsylvania Railroad did not make the West Virginia Central pay a mileage charge, but Bretz thought that the B. & O. should not be informed of this. The mileage charge issue was to surface again in a few years and cause additional problems.

Davis noted on January 30 that business was still dull and the "expected boom after McKinley election has not come." A couple of days later, Davis commented on the death of President Roberts of the Pennsylvania Railroad, which had occurred on January 30, noting, "He was a great and noble man. He was my friend and also to our railroad and coal interest." He also thought that Roberts had died of overwork. Frank Thomson was elected president of the Pennsylvania to succeed Roberts.

Early in February, Bretz was pleased to hear that Davis had signed a contract with the Reading in which that company agreed to open up its territory to shipments from the West Virginia Central. In return, the West Virginia Central agreed to send some of its coal shipments to tidewater over the Reading.

Bretz reported on February 11, that there were 36 cars waiting to be repaired at Cumberland. These would have to be taken to Elkins to be repaired, which was an expensive proposition. Bretz again asked Davis to consider improving the facilities at Ridgeley to handle these tasks and to let the Elkins shops handle the construction of new cars.

The series of wrecks that had plagued the West Virginia Central during the winter continued on February 12, when a wheel burst under a passenger car near Barnum. The car left the rails and landed on its side three feet from the track. Injuries to the passengers and crew were minor.

On February 22, Bretz reported that heavy rains had brought the river level in Cumberland up to within 20 inches of where it had been in 1889. Bretz was concerned that if the rain continued there would be trouble. The rain did continue and four feet of water covered the tracks at Cedar Cliff and 15 inches covered the yard in Cumberland. Bretz reported some damage but the track was reopened to Elkins by the evening of February 23. The damage along the Belington and Beverly branches was more severe and service was not restored until February 24. Damage from the flood was estimated by Bretz at $3,000. Bretz warned all the engineers to proceed slowly as the banks were still very soft. However, on

February 25, Engine No. 19 hit a rockslide near Pine Swamp and was derailed. It then rolled over and over before coming to rest upside down about 20 feet from the track. The engineer did not see the slide as it was now snowing and the slide was covered in snow. The engineer and fireman jumped to safety before the engine left the track and were uninjured. Bretz estimated the damage to the engine at $1,200.

The West Virginia Central was lucky to escape the flood with so little damage. The B. & O. was badly flooded and the trestle leading to the new bridge at Luke was destroyed. Thirteen trestles along the C. & P. were also reported to have been washed out. Considerable damage was reported along the Dry Fork Railroad, and one span and some trestles on the new bridge at Hulings built by the Otter Creek Boom and Lumber Company were destroyed.

No sooner was traffic restored to normal when another wreck occurred on February 27. A freight train heading north with 35 loaded cars and running at no more than six or seven miles per hour derailed a box car near Dobbin. Six other box cars, all loaded with coke, plowed into the derailed car totally destroying two cars. The track at this point was in good condition and Bretz could only surmise that the wreck had in some way been connected to the automatic couplers and the slow speed. Bretz did report that he was getting "greatly discouraged over the situation all round."

More trouble occurred when efforts were made to get No. 19 back on the track. Attempts were made to pull the engine up the bank using a crane car but this ended when the crane car and its engineer also rolled down the bank. According to Bretz, there was no supervisor at the accident site because the supervisor had, "missed the train." The supervisor was dismissed. Bretz also reported that a foreman and some of the track crew were drunk when they were picked up by the wreck train. They were also dismissed.

A final wreck occurred on March 5 when an empty gondola on a southbound train derailed near Westernport. The car dragged along the ground until it reached the C. & P. grade crossing when the following gondola also left the tracks and ended up crashing through the wall into a neighboring house. Fortunately, no one was injured.

McGraw finally realized that Davis was not going to build to the Greenbrier in the near future, when he wrote on March 12 asking that the February 20, 1896, agreement be canceled. McGraw claimed to have some negotiations in progress that he would be more comfortable in pursuing if he was not bound by the agreement. McGraw assured Davis that the negotiations would not be detrimental to Davis's interests. Davis agreed to the cancellation on April 3.

Although Elkins, like all the new towns along the West Virginia Central, had had its share of fires, the one that started on March 16 at about 7:15 A.M. was by far the most destructive. At one time it was feared that the whole of the business district would be destroyed but a shift in the wind saved the town. By the time the fire brigade from Davis arrived on the noon train, the fire was under control. Both the Randolph Hotel and the railroad office building were slightly damaged; Bretz estimated the damage to both at $250.

Bretz was quite optimistic about the fire claiming it would improve the appearance of Elkins.

Since the railroad had reached the new town in 1889, Elkins had grown to become an important center, with a population of about 2,000 in 1896 (Fig. 113). Two sawmills were in operation in the town as well as a small foundry company. A brick works, the Elkins Brick and Tile Company, had been chartered in March 1896, but had not yet started operations.

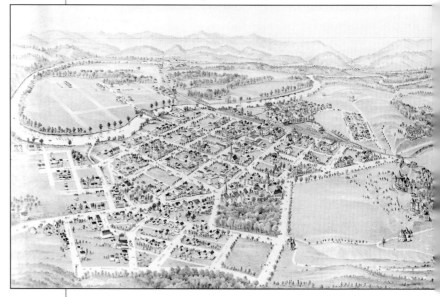

Fig. 113. Bird's-eye view of Elkins in 1897. The West Virginia Central office building is just to the right of center, the depot is between this building and the railroad yards. The mansions of Davis, Elkins and Kerens are on the right of the picture
West Virginia and Regional History Collection, West Virginia University Library

No sooner had the excitement over the fire died down when a shooting was reported on March 18, in a West Virginia Central passenger car at Parsons. The shooting involved two of the most prominent citizens of Davis and became a cause célèbre in the area.

The case started when a young man from Davis was found guilty of fathering a child outside of marriage and was ordered to pay maintenance. A petition was drawn up asking for a new trial and was signed by 65 citizens of Davis. The judge, however, decided that this was intimidation and ordered the 65 to appear before him in Parsons. Included in the group was Colonel Robert Eastham who had worked with Davis in clearing the site of the new town of Davis in 1884. After the hearing the group boarded the special train that was to take them back to Davis. Frank E. Thompson, manager of the Blackwater Lumber Company, who was not a member of the group, also attempted to board the train. He got into an argument with Eastham, blows were exchanged, and Thompson fired his pistol at Eastham causing superficial wounds. Eastham returned the fire and fatally wounded Thompson. Bretz prepared a special train to take Thompson to the hospital in Cumberland where he died a couple of days later. There had been ill feeling between Eastham and the Thompson family for some time stemming from disputes over timber and river rights in the Canaan Valley. After the death of Thompson, Eastham was indicted for involuntary manslaughter by a grand jury in June after two other grand juries failed to turn in a verdict to the judge's liking. C. W. Dailey was part of the Eastham defense team and he reported to Davis that public sentiment was in favor of Eastham. This sentiment did not find favor with Bretz who thought that Eastham should have gone to his grave at the time of the shooting. The verdict was appealed to the Supreme Court of Appeals of West Virginia in September, but the court split, and the indictment was allowed to stand.

During March, Davis and his family took a trip to Bermuda. On his return he seemed to be in a more optimistic mood, noting in his diary on April 5 that the coal and coke trade was good. Orders had been given to build a new plane and tramway at the Franklin mine to tap into the Seven Foot Seam. He also told Weir to construct another 60 coke ovens at Coketon.

Davis also received estimates for the cost of the improvements at Ridgeley, which came to nearly $28,000. The estimate included a 12-stall engine house (later changed to 14), blacksmith's shop, sand house, oil house and a 65 foot turntable. A contract for the roundhouse was announced on May 14.

Davis noted in his diary on April 21, that he had met with officers of the B. & O., W. Md. and the Reading in connection with traffic destined for the Reading from Cherry Run. He was pleased to note that a highly favorable traffic agreement had been signed involving all four railroads.

Although Davis seemed highly optimistic about the future, his optimism was not shared by Kerens or Elkins. Kerens, after meetings in New York, was reported on April 7, as saying, "The railroad condition is alarming and distressing ...... all the roads would be forced into bankruptcy." The reason for Kerens's concern may have been a recent action by the U. S. government to appeal to the Supreme Court a decision of a circuit court that had found in favor of the Trans-Missouri Association. This association had been formed by railroads in the southwest to set freight rates; this action was claimed by the government to be a violation of the anti-trust law and the interstate commerce act. The Supreme Court upheld the government's position later in 1897 in a decision that was to later impact the eastern railroads and ultimately the West Virginia Central.

A month later, Elkins was interviewed about the coal trade and the interview was widely disseminated by the local papers in West Virginia. Elkins claimed a coal war had developed in the east due to overproduction. He also claimed that wages must go down and that, "Wages in America stand against any revival of business."

At the beginning of May, Bretz reported that maintenance-of-equipment expenses during April had been higher than expected as both Engines Nos. 28 and 29 had been "simpled," and the repairs to No. 19 had been expensive. No. 29 is shown in its "simpled" version as W. Md. No. 348 in Fig. 310. Work also continued fitting automatic couplers and air brakes to the freight equipment; during April, 17 cars had been fitted with brakes and 43 with couplers.

At the end of May, newspaper reports were indicating a revival in the lumber business. It was noted that the two large mills at Womelsdorf had been finished, and that McGraw had purchased a mill on the Holly River at a sheriff's sale. It was also noted that the ground breaking for the Little Kanawha Railroad had occurred in Parkersburg on June 5.

Of more immediate interest to Davis was the news that the Randolph County Courthouse at Beverly had burnt to the ground on May 20. Although it was obviously to the advantage of the Davis interests to have the courthouse moved to Elkins, Davis wrote to Elkins on May 24 mentioning that "our people" should have no part in the decision to relocate the courthouse. Davis was contacted by Martin Lane, of the William Whitmer and Sons Company, asking if he wanted the lumber company to use its influence in the Dry Fork region to create a "sentiment" for the removal of the courthouse. Lane thought, "that when the time comes for voting or otherwise, people will be thoroughly educated up to that idea." A vote on the matter was scheduled for October 5. Although Davis did not want to appear to be involved, he wrote to Lane mentioning that he would furnish rooms and a hall rent-free for five years for the courthouse and also would provide room for a jail.

The U. M. W. A. called for a strike of mineworkers on July 5 in the coalfields of Illinois, Indiana, Pennsylvania and Ohio where the union was strong, but to be effective, the strike needed the support of miners in West Virginia. Davis was concerned about the strike spreading to the mines along the West Virginia Central and asked Weir and Blackiston to use "spies" to keep him informed of the situation and if any outside agitators appeared. On July 20, Blackiston reported that the majority of the men opposed the strike and he doubted there would be any trouble. On the same day, striking miners in the Fairmont area returned to work and Eugene Debbs, an organizer for the union, reported that the strike in West Virginia was a failure. Although there were no problems for the Davis mines, the strike continued around Wheeling, Pittsburgh and elsewhere, and there was considerable agitation in the Fairmont area. The strike finally ended on September 11.

During August, Bretz asked Baldwin to bid on a new freight locomotive similar to No. 32. The Baldwin bid was for $11,090 although No. 32 had cost only $10,460. Baldwin refused to lower the price, pointing out that wages had been exceptionally low when No. 32 had been built but this was no longer the case. Bretz obtained bids from the Pittsburgh and Richmond locomotive works but they were slightly more expensive. Baldwin was also willing to take coal for the engine and Bretz recommended that the order be placed with Baldwin immediately for delivery before the end of the year.

On August 23, Davis met with a delegation from Huttonsville to discuss extending the line from Beverly up the Tygart Valley River. At the end of the month he reported that he would send an engineering party south as conditions looked favorable.

There was considerable excitement in the newspapers in early September about a major land sale by McGraw of some 300,000 acres along the headwaters of the Cheat River. The Vanderbilts were supposedly part of the syndicate making the purchase. As early as July, Robert Whitmer had been negotiating with McGraw for the purchase of the lands, but then McGraw had suddenly broken off the talks and offered to purchase the Dry Fork Railroad. Whitmer had declined to sell as Davis had the first option to purchase the D. F. McGraw later denied to Davis that he had attempted to purchase the D. F. and implied that Whitmer had his own ulterior motives for the claim. The reports that the Vanderbilts were involved attracted the attention of the Pennsylvania when S. M. Prevost, the third vice president, wrote to Davis to ask him if there were any truth to the reports. Davis replied on December 3, that the stories of the involvement of the Vanderbilts in West Virginia were totally untrue. He claimed that it was a group of New York investors associated with McGraw that had purchased the lands.

Bretz reported on September 16, that Watson and Company was preparing to build a tipple, and grade a siding at Barnum, and had requested that the West Virginia Central put in a switch and lay the tracks. Watson and Company had shipped coal from Warnocks during 1896 and 1897; it is not known why the company wished to move to Barnum. Bretz reported the company was anxious to start work and estimated the cost of the improvements to the West Virginia Central at $800. Watson and Company was reported to have sent five cars of coal to the Maryland Steel Company for trial on January 15, 1898.

At the beginning of October, Davis noted that, "business generally appears to improve. Our trade fairly good." He also noted that the election to approve moving the courthouse to Elkins would be held on October 5 and that "it looks well for Elkins." The proposal needed a three-fifths majority but fell short of this by 62 votes. In spite of Davis's early claim of non-interference, he asked Dailey if it were possible to have the county seat moved by act of the legislature, but was assured that this could not be done.

Davis noted on October 4, that Weir was examining a route from the Tygart Valley River over to Shavers Fork and then to the Greenbrier. This was the route that had been examined before and discounted as being too expensive.

By the end of October, Davis noted that additional coke ovens were being fired up in the Connellsville region and that coke had advanced 25 cents per ton. Encouraged by this news, Davis ordered bricks to build a further ten ovens at Junior. He also noted that the 14-stall engine house at Ridgeley was nearly finished and that the tracks were being laid to enlarge the yard. Davis also invited President Harris, Vice-President Henderson and George F. Baer, "a V. I. P. of the Reading," to tour the West Virginia Central. Davis noted that, "I expect to do a large coal and coke trade with the Reading road." The party arrived in Cumberland on October 27 for its tour.

Prodded by Bretz, Davis wrote to Edwin J. Berwind, president of the Berwind-White Coal Mining Company, on November 24, threatening to withdraw the privilege of the R. C. & B. to cross the tracks of the West Virginia Central if the bridge at Roaring Creek Junction was not repaired. Berwind refused to be drawn into the argument and suggested that it be left to the general managers to come up with a solution. This was precisely what Bretz had been unable to achieve.

The trial of Robert Eastham commenced in Parsons on November 23 and lasted until December 16. Dailey and McGraw were both part of a large defense team, but Eastham was found guilty of manslaughter and was sentenced to two years in jail. However, he was not to serve his full sentence as he escaped on May 8, 1898 and settled in Virginia.

At the beginning of December, it was announced that William Whitmer and Sons had purchased the property of the J. L. Rumbarger Lumber Company at Dobbin. The Rumbarger company had been in the hands of a receiver, Thomas B. Davis, since October 1896, but with the sale completed, the receiver was discharged in

February 1898.

Bretz noted on December 29, that an additional locomotive might be needed in 1898 if traffic increased substantially, which he suspected would be the case. The West Virginia Central had already taken an option on a new engine from Baldwin, similar to No. 33. The option was extended until April 1, 1898. Bretz also recommended scrapping No. 1, which was being used for work train service but was unreliable. Bretz reported that the Elkins shops were now turning out seven new coal or coke cars each week. The shops had also recently finished a new horse and carriage car, which had cost $1655.05 to construct and entered service as No. 3.

The end of the year saw Hendley trying to close the books on the B. & C. railway project. The accounts showed that almost $101,000 had been expended on the project for surveys, right-of-way and also the purchase of 140 shares of W. Md. stock. At year's end, $5,500 was still owed and Davis, Elkins and Kerens were each billed for their portion of the debt. With this final act, the B. & C. disappeared from view.

On December 31, Davis met with Axtell of the C. & O. who reported that all the necessary surveys had been completed for the Greenbrier railroad, and the survey crew discharged. No decision had been made on whether to build, although a new company, The Greenbrier Railroad, had been incorporated by Ingalls and Axtell and held its organizing meeting on December 16.

Further west, the Little Kanawha Railroad was reported to be ready to run trains between Parkersburg and Elizabeth by January 1, 1898 although this was later changed to late February.

Davis was in a highly optimistic mood at the beginning of the new year, 1898. On January 20 he wrote, "Business generally in the country looks better. Our coal and coke trade shows signs of improvement and we expect to market in 1898 1,300,000 tons of coal and 20,000 tons of coke." Davis's relations with the Lukes had also improved as a result of both Davis and Elkins helping the company secure a contract to supply the government with printing paper. In return, the Lukes agreed to ship all the paper made for the contract by the West Virginia Central to Cumberland. The company had earlier secured a contract to manufacture postal cards for the government, which had set the B. & O., the Pennsylvania and the West Virginia Central scrambling to secure the transport of the cards. The fight was finally settled in January when the Post Office Department divided the transportation contract equally between the three companies.

The Lukes reorganized their three separate companies in January into a single new company, the West Virginia Pulp and Paper Company. The company at Luke, the Piedmont Pulp and Paper Company, had become involved in a protracted legal battle with the City of Cumberland over the pollution of the Potomac River. Cumberland derived its water supply from the river but the company not only denied any pollution, but threatened to close the plant and move it to a more hospitable location.

Bretz returned to the question of new engines in January, mentioning that Rease wished to purchase a second hand engine and recommended that No. 1 be sold for $1,000. He received a revised bid from Baldwin reducing the price of an engine by $150 to $10,885. Baldwin offered to build two engines for this price and agreed to take cash for one and coal for the other. An order for the two engines on these terms was placed on February 20.

Hendley, writing for Davis on February 8, noted that the Post Office at Ridgeley was now called "Barncord." He pointed out that the West Virginia Central owned between 25 and 30 acres of land at Ridgeley, and that the improvements there had cost between $40,000 and $50,000. Because the West Virginia Central had been using Ridgeley in all its documents, he was also quite emphatic that the Post Office there was to be called "Ridgeley" after a pioneer family in the area.

By March 1 the need for the new engines had become pressing and Bretz was forced to increase the hours of the shopmen to ten per day to try to keep up with the repairs. Bretz also recommended that money be set aside to replace No. 1, which was still unsold.

Davis met with another deputation of citizens from Huttonsville on March 11, who were enthusiastic for Davis to extend to their town. Davis sent Weir to survey a route but would not commit to building unless he received a free right-of-way. He also expressed concern about the possibility of war following the sinking of the battleship "Maine" in Havana on February 15, 1898.

Dailey reported to Davis that a petition with over 1,500 signatures had been submitted to the county court on March 28, asking that the courthouse question be placed on the ballot at the general election in November. The citizens of Beverly objected to some of the signatures and succeeded in delaying any action until June. In the meantime a committee recommended a plan for a new courthouse to be built at Beverly. Dailey asked Davis if he wished to get involved in the fight at this time. Davis declined to get involved, and somewhat surprisingly, claimed that the matter was not that important to Elkins.

News reports at the beginning of April indicated that business at the Blackwater Lumber Company at Davis was booming and both the mill (Fig. 114) and the box factory (Fig. 115) were working day and night.

Fig. 114. Blackwater Lumber Company at Davis, circa 1899
From "West Virginia Central and Pittsburg Railway" by S. Griffin

The Otter Creek Boom and Lumber Company at Hulings (Fig. 116), was also experiencing an increased demand for its products and tried to get Davis to give the company the same rates from Hulings as from Davis, claiming the distance was only some three miles further.

The Annual Report of the Davis Coal and Coke Company for 1897 noted that, "The most serious problem confronting the management is to keep down the cost of production of coal and the making of coke." To see how this could be achieved, Elkins hired C. E.

Fig. 115. The box factory at Davis, circa 1910

F. Burnley to examine all the mines and coke plants of the company and make recommendations for improvement. Burnley submitted his report on April 19 giving first a detailed account of the mines and coke works as he found them.

Burnley, noted that the Franklin and Hampshire mines, both working the Big Vein and the Tyson vein, were worked out and that the present workings were restricted to removing pillars and narrow strips of coal left by earlier miners. At Elk Garden, the Big Vein and the Tyson vein were also mined but flooding in the winter restricted working in the latter vein to the summer months. The Big Vein was mined at No. 6 drift, which Burnley

Fig. 116. Otter Creek Boom and Lumber Company at Hulings (later Hambleton) in 1910

found to be in excellent condition and a tribute to the manager, Blackiston. Burnley was not so pleased with the Thomas Shaft, sunk 180 feet to the Davis vein. Water was a constant problem and a pump was necessary to keep it under control. Even with the pump in action, the haulage roads were knee deep in water and mud. Forced ventilation was non-existent and smoke remained in the working areas long after blasting "so that it is with difficulty that the miners can see to pick out bone and slate." No mention was made in the report of difficulties in breathing; certainly conditions were far from pleasant. The report suggested the mine should produce 1,000 tons per day but was at present producing only half that amount. The Thomas drift, which was mining the Thomas coal, was found to be in excellent condition although the presence of clay veins hindered production. Thomas No. 2, a drift mine one mile south of the Thomas drift and located on the Davis branch, also flooded during the winter and could only be worked during the summer. At Coketon, the No. 1 mine was worked out, and at the No. 2 mine, only the lower part of the Davis vein, some 3' 6" in thickness, was being worked as the upper bench was high in sulfur. The No. 3 mine, on the opposite side of the ravine from Nos. 1 and 2, supplied the coke ovens with coal, but the area of coal available was restricted. Other problems found in this mine were poor roofs and excessive water, but the mine was producing about 600 tons of coal per day. Burnley noted that there were 482 coke ovens in use, of which 22 were at Thomas and the remainder at Coketon. At Thomas, the

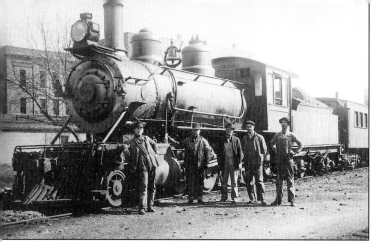

Fig. 117. Western Maryland No. 355, ex-West Virginia Central No. 34
Collection of William Metheny

coke produced was not of good quality because of high levels of ash. At Coketon, the ovens using coal from No. 3 mine were producing an excellent grade of coke, comparable to the best from the Connellsville region.

In his recommendations for improvement, Burnley noted that the coke crusher lost ten cents on every ton of coke crushed and its use should be discontinued. Burnley also claimed that the cost of coal production was high as the wages paid to the miners were too high in comparison to the wages paid in competing fields. He also thought that there were too many salaried supervisors. The cost of mining coal in the Pocahontas field was given as 50 cents per ton, but Burnley thought only the Elk Garden mine could achieve this figure because of favorable physical conditions. He estimated that at Thomas and Coketon it should by possible to produce coal for 52 cents and at the Hampshire mine the cost should be 62 cents per ton.

What Davis thought of the report and what steps, if any, were taken to implement its recommendations, are not known.

Davis wrote to Kerens on May 7 reporting that the Huttonsville extension would cost about $100,000 or $9,000 per mile. Four bids were received to build the road including one from W. E. Porter. The lowest bid, for $30,358, was from the Columbus Construction Company, and acceptance of the bid was recommended by Weir. On May 16, Davis signed an agreement with W. F. Patterson of the Columbus company to build the road. The company was to be paid 16.1/2 cents per cubic yard for excavation, trestles would be $22.50 per foot and masonry would be paid at a rate of $7.50 per cubic yard. The first two miles to the Tygart Valley River were to be finished ready for the tracklayers by July 1, and all the grading was to be finished by October 1.

Bretz reported that the two new engines, Nos. 34 and 35, were received on May 9, but would not be placed in service until business picked up (Fig. 117).

Davis finally decided to eliminate the confusion surrounding the name of the town of "Hulings," and requested on May 20 that it be changed to Hambleton. A depot was erected here sometime during the first half of 1898 (Fig. 118). At the same time he requested that the present Post Office named Hambleton be renamed Henry. Davis had high hopes that Henry

Fig. 118. Depot at Hambleton, circa 1906

would become an important mining center and had instructed that trial borings be made prior to a shaft being sunk (Fig. 119).

The work was supervised by the new general superintendent of mines, W. R. Davis, who had taken over from Weir, who was now in charge of the Huttonsville extension. W. R. Davis did not last long in his position and resigned on July 16. Davis appointed Bower as acting general superintendent of mines.

Work started on the Huttonsville extension on June 6, with Davis expecting that work to be completed by November 1, 1898. Galbreath requested that the track on the Mineville branch, which was to be used on the new work, be pulled up and shipped to Elkins to be ready for relaying.

Galbreath also looked at the bridge at Roaring Creek Junction and gave Davis two estimates for its repair. The first estimate replaced the washed out trestles with girder spans and amounted to $4,500. Renewing the trestles would reduce the cost to $2,950. Davis tried to get the Pennsylvania Railroad to pressure Berwind to replace the bridge by pointing out it was losing traffic to the B. & O. W. H. Mabie of the McClure-Mabie Lumber Company claimed his contract with the R. C. & C. was for delivery of loads to Roaring Creek Junction and that he wished the bulk of his shipments to go over the Pennsylvania. Bretz met Berwind on July 20, but was

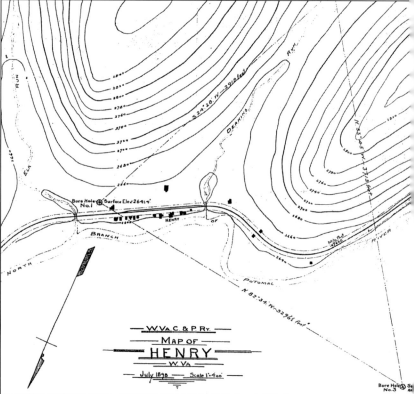

Fig. 119. Trial borings in the vicinity of Henry, July 1898
West Virginia and Regional History Collection,
West Virginia University Library

unable to get a commitment to replace the bridge. Bretz again requested that Dailey initiate proceedings against the R. C. & C., but Dailey thought it would be necessary to go to the U. S. court and ask that the receiver be instructed to rebuild the bridge. This was likely to be a time consuming process as the railroad was mired in a legal battle between its various owners.

Galbreath proposed a plan for a Y and additional sidings to hold 100 cars at Fairfax on August 11, to cost $7,750. It was proposed to use the steam shovel to do the work and the project was approved by Davis

Landstreet reported to Davis on August 22, about a meeting he had had with Colonel James M. Schoonmaker, vice-president of the Pittsburgh and Lake Erie Railroad, a subsidiary of the New York Central. Schoonmaker was interested in determining if the West Virginia Central was tied up in any way with the B. & O. or the Pennsylvania as his company was interested in building down the Monongahela and Cheat rivers and would connect with the Davis road. Whether Davis had met Schoonmaker prior to the meeting with Landstreet is not known, but certainly after this time they did establish close personal and business relations.

On August 23, Davis noted that the Huttonsville extension was well behind schedule. Five miles were to have been finished by August 1 but only two miles had been completed to this time. Progress on the line was slowed further when Weir died of typhoid fever in early October. His duties were taken over by Galbreath with George Mason as assistant engineer. Part of the delay occurred at the Tygart Valley River bridge, where a trestle leading to the bridge was reduced from 300 feet to 200 feet, which necessitated extra fill (Fig. 120 and Fig. 121). This extra work took 50 days instead of the expected ten days originally estimated.

Fig. 120. Trestle at the Tygart Valley River bridge, Huttonsville extension, December 5, 1917
Collection of the Western Maryland Railway Historical Society

Fig. 121. Tygart Valley River bridge, Huttonsville extension, December 5, 1917
Collection of the Western Maryland Railway Historical Society

On November 12, Bretz reported that he had awarded a contract to S. B. Opdyke for $1,400 to remove the bridge at Bayard and re-erect it at Mill Creek. This included erecting two new girder spans at Bayard; the girders were to be fabricated by the Carnegie company and a temporary trestle was erected to allow the trains to pass.

Mason reported on November 12, that the depot at Huttonsville was nearly finished. By November 16, Galbreath reported six miles of track were laid and the tracklayers had nearly caught up with the graders. He thought that the track laying would reach Mill Creek by the end of the month. By November 18, the Columbus Construction Company claimed that grading would be finished in 15 working days although heavy rains on November 18 and 19 stopped all work. Removal of the bridge at Bayard was expected to start on November 23, the new girders being on hand. By November 26, Galbreath was complaining that the construction company was not moving fast enough and that the railroad company might have to do some grading. Galbreath reported that the Bayard bridge would be dismantled on November 28 and the crew would erect the new girders before moving south to install the old bridge at Mill Creek by December 6.

A new election to determine the site of the Randolph County courthouse was held in November but again the result went against Elkins. An appeal was made to the County Court for a recount, but Davis was convinced the decision would be in Elkins favor and ordered Galbreath to clear space in the West Virginia Central office building for the county officials. Davis wrote to Bretz on November 19, noting, "Some of Elkins people seem determined to do by force what should be done by law, and we should be careful and not mix with it." Bretz was ordered not to run any special trains unless ordered by Daily. Daily was instructed at the same time to "let officials have time before resorting to force."

On December 7, Galbreath wrote that the work was proceeding slowly on account of the weather and a shortage of laborers and regular West Virginia Central trackmen were being used to lay track. He still hoped to have the track finished to the Mill Creek bridge by December 10. By now, 8.1/5 miles of track had been laid and 1.2/5 remained to reach Mill Creek. Patterson was reported to be trying to get additional laborers from Thomas, Davis and Womelsdorf by offering the princely wage of $1.25 per day but could only find two takers. Galbreath thought that the ground between Mill Creek and Huttonsville was too marshy to allow the use of teams, and men with shovels would have to do all the work making the need for additional men even more critical.

Bretz reported on December 7 that the graders should reach Mill Creek by December 8 and that the tracklayers would be there two days later. The depot at Huttonsville was finished except for the platforms, which would be installed by the railroad company. Bretz thought that this depot was one of the best that had been constructed (Fig. 122). He expected the track to be laid to Huttonsville by the first of the year.

By December 11, Bretz was able to report that the track was within 2,000 feet of Mill Creek, but as the grading to that point was not yet completed, it was December 12 before

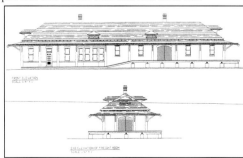

Fig. 122. Blueprint of the Huttonsville depot (redrawn for clarity)
West Virginia and Regional History Collection, West Virginia University Library

Mill Creek was reached. The Columbus Construction Company finally finished their work on December 21 and by December 26, the Mill Creek bridge was almost finished requiring only the removal of the falsework.

Delays completing the Huttonsville extension were not the only problems for Davis during the second half of 1898. Davis, Elkins, and Thomas Davis met on August 29 to plan the future course of their coal holdings. It was agreed that a shaft would be sunk at Henry, the Simpson tract near Clarksburg would be developed and an additional opening made at the Franklin mine. It also was decided to build additional houses for miners at Thomas and Coketon.

Concern was expressed in September by Elkins and Kerens about the safety of the track at Canyon Point on the Blackwater grade. A washout had occurred there during the flood of February 1897, and Bretz, who examined the location on October 10, reported that, "it is certainly anything but an inviting looking place," and should have attention. Galbreath was asked to prepare estimates for improvement and these included a tunnel costing $35,000 and a cut costing $22,000. The stream could be bridged with girders for $4,220 or a masonry arch at a cost of $4,700. An iron bridge would be susceptible to damage from rocks rolling down the hillside and consequently Galbreath preferred a stone bridge as this would be very nearly immune to such damage. Galbreath submitted a rough plan of the present track at Canyon Point and the effect of changing the curvature would have in avoiding the gulch that was the cause of the problem (Figs. 123 and 124).

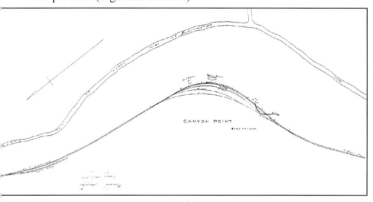

Fig. 123. Plan of Canyon Point in the Blackwater Canyon
West Virginia and Regional History Collection,
West Virginia University Library

On October 24, Davis, Elkins and Thomas Davis again met to discuss the coal company. Davis noted that, "Elkins is president of the company but has not been active in management." It was agreed that Elkins should have full control and be able to organize the company as he wished.

On the same day, the U. S. Supreme Court ruled against the railroads in a second traffic association case. This time it was the Joint Traffic Association of the eastern railroads that was declared to be in violation of the law. The association had been set up "to establish and maintain reasonable and just rates, fares, rules and regulations on State and inter-State traffic." Again, the demise of this association would have an impact on Davis in a couple of years.

With the Huttonsville extension nearing completion, interest by the lumber companies in the area increased. Hench and Dromgold, a company of farm machinery manufacturers in York, Pennsylvania,

Fig. 124. The scene at Canyon Point
From "The Life and Times of Henry Gassaway Davis" by
C. M. Pepper

purchased a couple of tracts near Huttonsville and was interested in procuring lands owned by Davis in the area. Also interested was B. Gilpin Smith, president of the Otter Creek and Beaver Creek lumber companies, who offered to purchase lands in the vicinity of Mill Creek. Davis also discussed with John Luke the possibility of building a pulp mill at Huttonsville to use the timber on between 20,000 and 30,000 acres nearby. The Lukes had expressed an interest in a new pulp mill and inspected various sites on the West Virginia Central at the end of the year. At this time they favored either Hendricks or Parsons. Davis increased his holdings in the Mill Creek area by exchanging with Camden, 3,311 acres of coal lands along the Monongahela River for 6,446 acres of spruce lands.

The Board of Public Works of Maryland decided on November 18 to sell the state's interest in the C. & O. Canal and set February 7, 1899 as the day to open bids. One of Davis's attorneys in Cumberland thought the whole scheme was a device for the B. & O. to retain control of the canal. Davis, although suspicious of the B. & O., was still interested in gaining control of the waterway.

Davis reported to Rea on December 22, that the New York Central was purchasing a right-of-way along the Monongahela and Cheat rivers. He stated that this action was not in the interest of the West Virginia Central and should be stopped.

Elkins, now that he was in charge of the Davis Coal and Coke Company, reorganized the company at the end of the year, leading to the resignation of Vice-president Buxton. Landstreet assumed all of the sales duties that had been Buxton's responsibility starting on January 1, 1899. The variety of coal and coke offered for sale by the company at this time is shown in Fig. 125. Bower, who was still acting as general superintendent of mines, recommended the construction of an additional 30 double houses at Thomas and six at Coketon. This would attract 40 additional miners needed in the shaft mine at Thomas and 50 in the drift mine. Kerens was informed by Davis of the reorganization, and also that while the canal question was still open, the W. & C. and the B. & C. companies would be kept alive.

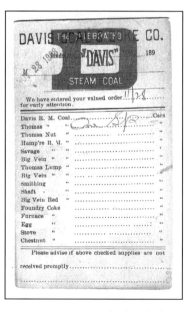

Fig. 125. Post card acknowledging receipt of an order for coal from J. G. Hoffman and Sons tannery at Gormania, November 28, 1898

Galbreath reported to Davis on January 14, 1899, that 4,000 feet of track still needed to be laid in order to reach Huttonsville. Heavy rains had slowed progress, but Galbreath thought they could be there in two days. This seems to have been the case as the first construction train ran into the Huttonsville depot on January 17. The first scheduled passenger train reached the town on February 6 at 9:02 A.M. The train, hauled by No. 18, was greeted by a large crowd. The first timetable for the extension showed one train each way daily, except Sunday. The service was increased to two trains each way daily, except Sunday, on May 14.

First order of business in 1899 for Bretz was to obtain bids on a new passenger engine. Baldwin bid $10,500, and the Rogers Locomotive Works of Paterson, New Jersey, $8,700 for essentially the same engine. In a departure from past passenger engine purchases, Rogers was also asked to bid on a 2-6-0 and a 4-6-0 engine. At Davis's suggestion, the 4-4-0 was ordered from Rogers on January 18 at a final price of $7,350.

Bretz also had a new superintendent of motive power, J. Chambers, who proposed to institute a piece work plan in the Elkins shops to improve productivity. He claimed this would produce savings of 20 percent in the cost of repairs. The idea was supported by Bretz who recommended that it be given a trial.

Hench and Dromgold were still after Davis to sell additional timber lands near Mill Creek, to its lumber subsidiary, Hench, Dromgold and Shull. The company wished to move its mill to the new site within three months and to double its current output. R. F. Whitmer was also still interested in these lands.

Davis continued to negotiate with the Lukes to locate their new plant along the West Virginia Central, and at the end of January, the Lukes asked Davis what freight rates could be expected by the new mill. At this time, the plant at Luke had been indicted for water pollution and there was some talk that the plant there would be closed. John Luke sought Davis's help in the case by requesting that Hopewell Hebb, the ex-mayor of Cumberland, and Galbreath be kept from the trial, which was scheduled for early March, so that they could not testify against the paper company. Davis was happy to go along with the suggestion and also to allow Thomas Davis to testify on behalf of the Lukes. Davis's helpfulness was not repaid by the Lukes, who complained that the freight rates proposed for the new mill were not to their liking.

On January 31, Bretz asked Davis to consider the purchase of an additional shifting engine to be used around Coketon and Thomas. Davis suggested that Bretz wait until the next semi-annual meeting of the board. Bretz prepared the following table (Table 2), comparing the cost of the new passenger engine and the proposed new shifting engine, with the existing locomotives. Davis finally approved of the order from Rogers of a 2-6-0 for delivery in July.

Table 2
Comparison of recent locomotive purchases

No. of Engines	Weight	Size of Cylinders	Cost
Pass. Eng. #11	80,000	17 x 24	$ 8,091.05
New Pass.	100,000	17 x 26	7,350.00
Shiftg. Engs. 23 & 26	109,000	20 x 24	8,774.00
New Shifting Eng.	147,000	20 x 26	9,400.00
Engine #35	140,000	21 x 26	10,885.00

On the same day, Bretz informed Davis that Chambers had submitted his resignation as superintendent of motive power, effective February 10. Davis left the hiring of a replacement to Bretz, advising him to pay the new man what he was worth but, "not exceeding what you paid Chambers." Bretz interviewed R. O. Cumback and offered him the position after receiving a recommendation from Chambers who thought Cumback " will likely remain with us."

Dailey reported to Davis that the case involving Womelsdorf, the R. C. & C. and various other parties, would be heard in Parkersburg on February 20. Dailey had filed a petition asking for an order to rebuild the bridge at Roaring Creek Junction. He also asked Davis to confirm the possibility of the West Virginia Central rebuilding the bridge and being reimbursed from the freight carried forward from Roaring Creek Junction. The plan did not find favor and the bridge remained unusable.

Davis noted in his diary on February 1, that he was preparing a bid for the February 7 auction of the state's interest in the C. & O. Canal. However, sometime prior to the opening of the bids on the 7th, he came to an agreement with the B. & O. and the Pennsylvania to withdraw his bid in return for a favorable traffic agreement and $190,000 as compensation. There was only one bid on the table at the opening, that from the B. & O., in the amount of $300,000 and this was rejected by the board. Davis finalized his withdrawal from the battle for the canal when he ordered the Washington and Cumberland Railway be closed up on February 10. Davis also noted a little later that he had been approached on several occasions to purchase the City of Baltimore's interest in the W. Md. but had refused.

Problems had arisen with the Columbus Construction Company, which claimed that additional payments were due as the West Virginia Central engineers had changed the plans for the Huttonsville extension, making it more expensive. President Casparis of the construction company claimed that it had cost $35,343.85 to build the road, which was nearly $5,000 more than the bid price. Galbreath claimed that the West Virginia Central was due damages as the road had not been finished in the time specified and traffic had been lost because of the delay. Davis agreed that the West Virginia Central was owed $4,375.59 due to lost revenue. Casparis again claimed that the delay was due to Weir changing the plans and calling for more excavation. The disposition of the controversy is not recorded.

Davis met with J. W. Reinhart, ex-president of the Atchison, Topeka and Santa Fe and now president of the Chesapeake and

Western Railroad, on February 13. At this time the C. & W. extended 27 miles from Elkton on the N. & W., through Harrisonburg on the Southern Railway and the B. & O., to Bridgewater. The C. & W. had surveyed an additional 83 miles to Osceola in West Virginia where it would connect with the West Virginia Central's southeast extension. Reinhart pointed out that the two roads would not be in competition as the freight generated by each road was quite different, and the C. & W. also would be a valuable outlet for the West Virginia Central. Reinhart hoped that Davis could assure his company a minimum amount of freight as he then could use this information to secure financial backing to complete the 83 miles.

Davis was noncommittal in his response beyond welcoming the new road. Reinhart was not deterred and wrote to Davis on February 14 asking that the West Virginia Central traffic department provide him with the information on the minimum tonnage that the C. & W. could expect. Again he pointed out the considerable advantages the C. & W. could offer the West Virginia Central in opening up a route to the southeast. Davis again refused to give a firm tonnage figure that would satisfy Reinhart.

John Luke wrote to Davis on March 2 informing him that the Lukes had recently purchased 60,000 acres of timberlands known as the Dewing property at the head of the Greenbrier River. These lands could be reached by the Dry Fork Railroad or by the proposed extension of the C. & O. up the Greenbrier. Because the Lukes had not been impressed by the freight rates offered by the West Virginia Central, they were now considering a site for a pulp mill somewhere along the C. & O.

Davis wrote to John Luke pointing out that the Dewing lands were mainly along Shavers Fork and the headwaters of the Elk and Gauley rivers, and therefore could not be reached from the C. & O.'s extension. The property could be reached by an extension from Huttonsville through the Mingo country or from the Dry Fork Railroad.

However, the Lukes had already eliminated the D. F. from consideration, which had upset Robert Whitmer. Whitmer had been involved with the Lukes in the negiotiations for the Dewing lands, but when the Lukes could not get freight rates that were to their liking, they continued on their own. Whitmer complained to Davis that he had been cut out of the deal because of unfavorable freight rates and this he blamed on Bretz and the West Virginia Central. He thought that unless Davis took some drastic action, the whole of this trade would be lost to the C. & O.

Bower added a few more details when he wrote to Davis on March 13. He noted that the Lukes now had purchased additional timberlands bringing their total holdings in the area to 140,000 acres. Ingalls of the C. & O. had offered the Lukes the same rate from their new mill to New York as they now received from Piedmont. Bower thought that if a lumber company would build a railroad up Shavers Fork that the business still could be captured by the West Virginia Central.

However, on March 17, John Luke wrote to Davis noting that they had decided to build the new pulp mill on the C. & O. as the freight rates and cheap coal they had been offered eliminated Parsons and Hendricks from consideration. In a swipe at Whitmer, John Luke claimed that the "wood people on the West Virginia Central have an exaggerated idea of the value of their spruce timber."

The loss of the Luke business prompted Whitmer to write to Davis asking for cheaper rates. He claimed that he had received an offer to buy his lands for pulp timber, but would decline if he could be assured of low enough rates for the Condon-Lane Boom and Lumber Company to turn a profit. Davis was less than sympathetic, pointing out that he had been very generous in encouraging Whitmer's company. Whitmer also had asked for an extension of time to pay a note due to the West Virginia Central, but Elkins recommended against extending the deadline.

Cumback does not seem to have fared too well as superintendent of motive power and was reported to have contacted typhoid. He was expected to be out for an extended sick leave during March. Bretz hired D. C. Courtney, who had been a master mechanic at the B. & O's Connellsville shops, as acting superintendent on March 25. This seems to have prompted R. G. Kenley, who had been hired as an assistant engineer for maintenance-of-way, to tender his resignation. Bretz complained that it was difficult to find suitable men for these positions noting, "The kind of men the B. & O. have been sending here in the Engineering Department are scarcely worth their board, and the new men on the P. R. R. are not much better." Cumback was never to return to his position, and Courtney was made superintendent of motive power in the middle of June.

Not only was Bretz having trouble retaining his engineering staff, but the trainmen demanded also an increase in wages on March 27. The request was part of a coordinated demand by trainmen of all the railroads entering Cumberland. Bretz agreed to meet with the men on April 9, but would not meet with any representatives "of any Order." The men were reported to have been pleased with the meeting, although no wage increase was promised.

At the end of March, it was agreed that Galbreath would join the Davis Coal and Coke Company as superintendent. One of Galbreath's last tasks as chief engineer was to recommend the construction of a depot at Belington to be similar to the one built at Huttonsville. He estimated a building in brick at $4,000 and a frame structure at $3,100. The necessary sidings would cost an additional $450. Galbreath was replaced by Edwin Mitchell as engineer of maintenance-of-way at a salary of $125 per month.

Elkins, who had asked for Galbreath to join the Davis Coal and Coke Company, had some ambitious plans to expand coal production, which included making additional openings at the Franklin and Hampshire mines. Buxton was concerned that they did not have sufficient miners at work at Coketon and Thomas and that another 200 men could be used immediately. To fill this need, black miners were recruited in Virginia, and a car full was reported to have passed through Cumberland at the end of April. The mines at Harding also reopened when ownership passed to the Junior Coal Company.

During early April, Davis received a proposition to purchase the West Virginia Central and the P. & C. from DeWitt Smith, president of the Richmond, Petersburg and Carolina Rail Road. Smith also was associated with Reinhart in the C. & W. The offer amounted to $5,500,000 for the two companies. The offer was refused by Davis on April 14, which apparently "surprised and disappointed," Smith. The offer led Davis and Elkins to confer with President Thomson of the Pennsylvania with a view to consolidating the West Virginia Central and the P. & C. under one charter. Davis also proposed a traffic agreement between the West Virginia Central and the C. & W. but Smith was not yet ready to give up on buying the railroad. One of Davis's objections to the sale involved the Davis Coal and Coke Company and Smith was reported to be ready to acquire both properties. Davis also recommended that Smith consider the purchase of a narrow gauge railroad running from Orange in Virginia through Fredericksburg to the Potomac River rather than build to York Point. The road, the Potomac, Fredericksburg and Piedmont, was owned by L. Richards of Philadelphia, and Davis wrote to see if it was for sale, but later declined to take an interest.

Bretz reported that the new engine from Rogers, No. 36, arrived on April 17 and took out its first train on April 20. Bretz thought that the engine was better than No. 18, the last passenger engine built by Baldwin, and had cost $1,400 less. Bretz, noting that passenger traffic was increasing, recommended the purchase of a new passenger car from Jackson and Sharp, but Davis disapproved of the purchase.

Davis still had hopes of obtaining the pulp wood trade to the Lukes new mill, and suggested to Whitmer on April 27, that the West Virginia Central "control" the Dry Fork Railroad, and extend it to the Forks of the Greenbrier. He offered to trade timberlands along Laurel Fork for the railroad and also offered to sell the timberlands around Huttonsville for $7.00 per acre. Whitmer was interested and asked Davis to make a firm proposal. It appeared that the Lukes were running into some opposition to their plan to build on the Greenbrier, particularly from a fishing club that feared the Greenbrier would become as polluted as the Potomac. Davis again suggested that the Lukes locate at either Parsons or Hendricks, but the Lukes had decided by May 1 to build the new mill at Covington, as they had been assured there would be no problems there. Davis tried one last time to convince the Lukes to locate on the West Virginia Central by offering to match the rates granted by the C. & O. He had met earlier with Cowan and the B. & O. had agreed to work with the West Virginia Central to match the C. & O.'s rates. John Luke replied on May 8 that his company was now firmly committed to build at Covington.

Whitmer thought Davis's price for the oak lands around Huttonsille was too high, and his company also was looking to purchase lands along the C. & O. He claimed that an offer for the D. F. of $10,000 per mile had already been received. Whitmer hoped to be able to interest Davis in the purchase of coal lands around Bayard, but Davis was not convinced of the value of the coal. With Whitmer not interested in the Huttonsville land, Davis then tried to interest Hench, Dromgold and Shull.

Davis and Smith finally agreed on a traffic agreement between the West Virginia Central and the C. & W. on May 10. Davis informed Smith that he might not be able to purchase the D. F. but that he would consider building from Elkins to a connection with the C. & W. at the Forks of the Greenbrier. This would be a preferable route as Davis expected considerable tonnage for the new road would come from the Roaring Creek coalfield. Davis mentioned the proposal to Elkins and claimed that it would be better than the D. F. route, which would have required a heavy grade. Smith also favored the new proposal.

Newspaper reports began to circulate in early May of plans by the New York Central, the B. & O. and the Pennsylvania to purchase all the minor roads between Boston and Chicago. This was denied by Chauncey M. Depew of the N. Y. C. However, Elkins reported that there was some truth in the reports, particularly as regards the closer relations between the Pennsylvania and the B. & O. This move confirmed for Elkins the desirability of selling the West Virginia Central. Cowan, in a meeting with Davis on May 9, claimed there was nothing to the reports.

The battle for the Randolph County courthouse erupted again in May. Although the Elkins supporters had gained a majority in the November 1898 election, there had been a court challenge to the results. This was decided on May 7, 1899 when Elkins was declared the winner but the order was delayed for 40 days to give Beverly time to appeal. This upset the citizens of Elkins who asked Bretz to provide a special train to go to Beverly and fetch the records. This was opposed by Dailey because of the court order, so the citizens decided to organize a wagon train to go to Beverly. Again Dailey intervened and the effort was postponed until 5:00 A.M. on May 8. However, when it was learned that the courthouse was guarded by armed men, the effort was abandoned. The case was not settled until February 1900, when the West Virginia Supreme Court ordered that the records be removed from Beverly to Elkins.

Davis finally reported on May 13, that he had sold the timber on the lands around Huttonsville to Whitmer for $6.50 per acre.

Bretz reported on May 13, that the work at Canyon Point and on a track realignment south of Hendricks was progressing well. He also thought that a new freight engine should be purchased similar to No. 35. Rogers bid $11,000 but Baldwin's bid was lower at $10,885 and the company agreed to be paid in coal and coke. Both companies agreed to an October delivery. Davis was reluctant to approve the purchase, noting that Bretz was ordering engines faster than the earnings were increasing and it was to be early July before he gave his approval.

At the end of May, the C. & O. announced it would build up the Greenbrier River and agreed with Davis to a junction at the Forks of the Greenbrier.

On June 5, it was announced that President Thomson of the Pennsylvania had died, which immediately gave rise to speculation on his successor. Davis favored Charles E. Pugh, the second vice-president, but on June 10, A. J. Cassatt was elected president. Cassatt had served as first vice-president a few years earlier but had retired so his election was somewhat of a surprise.

Although Davis was getting impatient for the sale of the railroad, Elkins, who had met with Smith and Reinhart on June 7, noted that it would be at least June 22 before they would make a formal offer. Landstreet also mentioned that Smith and Reinhart could be expected to offer at least $10,000,000 for the railroad and the coal company so Davis agreed to an extension. Elkins met with Smith on June 21, and recommended that a further ten day extension be granted. Elkins also noted that if Smith purchased the two companies, that he might be interested in buying back the coal companies from Smith if an equitable agreement could be made. On June 23, Landstreet reported a second bid for $10,000,000 had been received; the party agreeing to pay for the stock with four percent first mortgage gold bonds running for 50 years. Landstreet preferred the second offer, as they were "a better crowd." At the end of the month Smith and Reinhart, accompanied by Bretz, toured the West Virginia

Central and Bretz reported that they were very pleased with everything they had seen.

Bretz received a report from William Pratt, the Pennsylvania's engineer of bridges, who recommended that the old bridges at Schell and Harrison be replaced within five months. One span of the Schell bridge had been replaced after the January 1892 accident, leaving one span in need of replacing. Bretz ordered Bower to obtain bids on steel girders and hoped to be able to interest the county in using the old structures as road bridges. At the same time bids were obtained to build additional houses at Thomas for more miners.

Bretz reported that he had visited the Blackwater Lumber Company on June 30 and found the mill working day and night, cutting 175,000 feet per day. To meet a rush order the mill had cut 238,000 feet in a ten hour period during the previous week. The other major lumber companies operating along the West Virginia Central and the Dry Fork were also reported to be working at capacity. Even Whitmer's Condon-Lane Company at Horton, seemed to be doing well, as Whitmer asked Davis for preference in the distribution of scarce lumber cars so he could pay his debts to Davis.

Fig. 126. Depot at Fairfax
Collection of William Metheny

Bretz submitted his report for the fiscal year ending June 30, 1899, for the 18th Annual Report, noting that double track at Fairfax had been extended, a Y built for turning locomotives and a depot and an agent's house constructed at that point (Fig. 126). The report also noted that repairs to the Tub Run bridge had been completed, by the addition of a 40 foot girder span made necessary by the collapse of an abutment earlier in the year (Fig. 127).

The 18th Annual Report was also the last (the first had been 1896) to include a map showing the proposed B. & C. railroad (Fig. 128), although Davis did refer to it occasionally after this time, and it continued to be shown in timetables.

On July 1, the B. & O. emerged from receivership with Cowan as president and Murray as vice-president. Davis had been assured that when the company was removed from the hands of the receivers,

Fig. 127. West Virginia Central No. 7 and the rebuilt Tub Run bridge
Collection of the Western Maryland Railway Historical Society

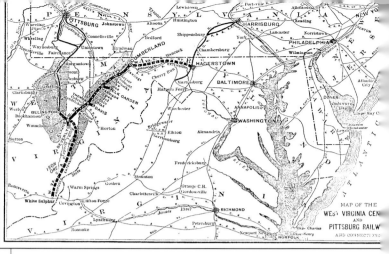

Fig. 128. Map of the West Virginia Central and proposed extensions West Virginia and Pittsburg Railway Company, 18th Annual Report, August 8, 1899

he would receive the $190,000 due as part of the canal settlement. For his part, Davis instructed Pinkney White to prepare to transfer the stock and charter of the W. & C. to the B. & O.

No sooner had the B. & O. emerged from receivership, than reports appeared in the New York Times that the N. Y. C. and the Pennsylvania had entered into an agreement, which became known as the community of interest. The two railroads recognized that the recent Supreme Court decisions on the traffic association cases had effectively eliminated this as a way of fixing rates. To avoid competition, control rates and recognize each others' territories, the N. Y. C., led by William K. Vanderbilt and Hamilton McK. Twombly, and the Pennsylvania under its new president, Cassatt, conceived of a major plan where they would buy controlling interests in competing eastern railroads. Purchases of stock for this program would start in November 1899.

On July 10, Davis sent Landstreet a memo outlining the conditions of the sale to Smith. Davis noted that he would deliver two thirds of the stock of the P. & C. and four fifths of the stock of the West Virginia Central and the Davis Coal and Coke Company. He then would deliver the remainder within six months. He also wanted the Junior and Douglas coal companies, which were not part of the sale, to receive favorable treatment. Also excluded from the sale were the Buxton and Landstreet stores and the B. & C. railway. The new owners would build to the Forks of the Greenbrier. Landstreet was to meet with Smith on July 14 and would have a copy of the contract ready, as he was convinced that Smith had the money for the purchase. On July 24, there was to be a final meeting with the attorneys to go over the contract.

It was announced on July 22 that the contracts had been awarded for the first 50 miles of the Greenbrier River railroad. Axtell wrote to Davis on August 2, sending him maps of the Forks of the Greenbrier area and asking him to consider where the two railroads should connect.

Final copies of the agreements were turned over to Reinhart on August 2, with the expectation that they would be signed by August 8. On August 3, Davis noted that negotiations were continuing with the price now set at $10,300,000 to include the Buxton and Landstreet stores. Davis wrote to Reinhart on August 7 noting that "I trust the matter will be disposed of one way or the other soon, as the delay of final action is troublesome and wearing to all parties." A couple of days later, Davis was almost out of patience and wrote to Landstreet to either close the deal or call it off. By August 15, even Landstreet was becoming pessimistic and tried to determine if the delay was due to Smith's inability to come up with the money, but he was assured that the money was there. Davis set another deadline, August 22, for the deal to be closed, but again Smith asked for more time. Smith requested that the deadline for the first payment be made September 15, but both Davis and Elkins found this to be unacceptable and set September 8 as the deadline for the first payment. The initial payment was to be $250,000 and by September 15, Smith was to pay one third of the total due. When the initial payment was not made on September 8, Davis informed Smith that the deal was off.

While the attention of Davis had been directed towards the sale of the road, Bretz did not neglect the business of the railroad. The new shifting engine, initially numbered No. 37, was received from Rogers on August 4 (Fig. 129).

Fig. 129. W. Md. No. 1000, ex-West Virginia Central No. 37. No. 37 was later renumbered West Virginia Central No. 1 Collection of Harold K. Vollrath

Bretz reported that work on the stone arch at Canyon Point was proceeding satisfactorily, and had cost $2551.97 so far. The work at Hendricks was proceeding also and had cost $1,718.40.

Davis contracted with Sam Griffith in August to produce a prospectus of the West Virginia Central, which would describe the resources of the country and the opportunities for investment. Griffith was to print 5,000 copies of the booklet and was to receive a payment of $50 plus $20 for each page of paid advertising. The prospectus, of about 100 pages, gives an interesting picture of the businesses, buildings and people along the railroad, and even today, it is still being reprinted.

With the deal with Smith off, Davis gave his attention to obtaining an adequate supply of cars from the B. & O. He complained to F. D. Underwood, second vice-president and general manager of the B. & O., about the lack of cars, and also the number of cars going to the R. C. & C. Bretz and Landstreet later met with Underwood who agreed to help in every way possible with the distribution of cars. Davis also ordered Bretz to take up with Underwood the provision of a depot at Belington.

Davis suggested that the new engine being built by Baldwin become No. 1, replacing the second No. 1 (ex-Pennsylvania No. 540), which was finally sold at the end of October for $1,800. It was later suggested by Courtney that No. 37 become the new No. 1, and

the new Baldwin engine, now expected in January 1900, would then receive the number 37. This had the advantage of keeping similar engines numbered together. Bretz recommended to Davis on October 19, that two freight engines be ordered from Baldwin for delivery in the spring of 1900. At Davis's suggestion, the two engines were to be heavier than the one that Baldwin was currently building to perform better on the Blackwater grade.

On October 11 the Buxton and Landstreet store at Thomas caught fire supposedly from a faulty furnace. Blasting powder that was stored in the building exploded and the building was totally destroyed. The building also housed the offices of the Davis Coal and Coke Company and an employee who was in the building at the time was killed. A temporary store was opened in Thomas with the expectation that a new store and an office building for the Davis Coal and Coke Company would be started in the spring.

Davis noted in his diary on October 20, that Elkins had resigned as president of the Davis Coal and Coke Company and that Davis had been elected to replace him. A month later, Davis, Elkins and Kerens agreed to combine the West Virginia Central and the Davis Coal and Coke Company, giving one and a half shares of West Virginia Central stock for each share of coal company stock. Stockholders of both companies met on December 11 and approved plans for the merger. The planned consolidation was scheduled for January 1, 1900, although each company would retain its own organization.

At the same stockholders' meeting on December 11, approval was given to build to the Forks of the Greenbrier to meet the C. & O. In anticipation of this approval, Davis had confirmed that the new railroad would be named the "Coal and Iron Railway." A charter for the new company was issued on December 14, 1899. Even before the formal approval of the stockholders, Davis had been working on plans for the new railroad. On November 13, a draft agreement was drawn up between the C. & I., the C. & O. and the West Virginia Central in which the C. & I. and the C. & O.'s extension were to be completed to the Forks within one year. Davis also included in the draft a section that gave the West Virginia Central and the C. & I., the same freight rates on coal, coke and timber shipped to New York as that shipped from the Kanawha region. Davis sent a copy of the draft to Ingalls for approval and noted that he hoped to start work on the two tunnels this year. Ingalls objected to some of the provisions in the draft including the New York freight rates. Davis also wrote to Andrew Carnegie mentioning the discussions of previous years to build from Pittsburgh to the West Virginia iron ore fields and indicating that he was ready to resume the talks. He later asked Carnegie for a letter indicating the tonnage that could be expected for the new road as an aid to selling its bonds. Carnegie replied that he was waiting for a report on the iron ore lands before making any commitment.

Latrobe was hired as consulting engineer for the new road and John W. Moore, Jr., became chief engineer. By November 21 Moore was at work locating the line up Goddins Run and locating a loop at Isners Run. By November 28, the location on the west side of Cheat Mountain was completed and the three miles on the east side to Shavers Fork was expected to be completed by the end of the month. Moore then proposed to move to Flint and locate the second tunnel. Latrobe was ordered to prepare specifications for the tunnels so that they could be sent out for bids. Davis hoped that construction could start on the tunnels by February 1 and grading by May 1. Track laying would be done by the company's own forces. Latrobe recommended that two resident engineers be hired to take charge of the tunnel work under Moore's overall supervision. Moore recommended C. H. Scott who had been chief engineer on the Seaboard Air Line for one of the positions.

A new timetable went into effect on November 19, 1899, which made some changes to the service between Cumberland and Elkins, but some major changes between Elkins and Huttonsville (Fig. 130). The citizens of Beverly were not to pleased with the changes as it meant they could not travel beyond Elkins and return the same day.

Fig. 130. West Virginia Central timetable (branches only,) November 19, 1899 Collection of Robert Shives

By the end of November, Landstreet became aware of the efforts of the Pennsylvania, as part of the community of interest, to secure control of the B. & O. He reported this to Davis and noted, "It appears to me it does not put us in as near good position as formerly."

The Pennsylvania initially spent $8,400,000 to acquire 100,000 shares of the B. & O.'s preferred stock, but by 1902, the investment was to increase to 40 percent of the stock for a total expenditure of $65,000,000. At the same time, the N. Y. C. began to purchase stock of the C. & O., in which the Vanderbilts already had an interest. President Ingalls of the C. & O. was also president of the Cleveland, Cincinnati, Chicago and St. Louis Railway, usually known as the "Big Four," which was also controlled by the Vanderbilts. The N. Y. C. and the Pennsylvania eventually owned 40 percent of the stock of the C. & O., enough to give them control.

The complicated court battle involving Womelsdorf, Edwin Berwind and the Roaring Creek and Charleston Railroad ended in early December. It appeared that Womelsdorf won the case prompting the Berwind-White Coal Mining Company to leave the Roaring Creek area. Berwind contacted Davis to see if he were interested in taking over the Berwind-White interests in the region. However, by December 10, Diller seems to have straightened matters out, and was

again in control of the R. C. & C., the R. C. & B. and the various coal lands. Apparently he still had the backing of the Berwind-White Coal Mining Company, as Berwind informed Davis on December 16, that he was no longer interested in selling his properties along Roaring Creek.

Landstreet reported to Davis on December 20, that President Newman of the Lake Shore and Michigan Southern Railroad, another N. Y. C. subsidiary, had been instructed to build from Brownsville up the Monongahela and Cheat rivers. Construction would be carried out by the Pittsburgh and Lake Erie, as had been forecast earlier by Schoonmaker to Landstreet.

At the same time a group of New York capitalists was attempting to buy the Western Maryland by purchasing the City of Baltimore's interest. This effort was independent of the community of interest and for once, Davis took no part in the battle. He also assured Cowan that he had nothing to do with a recent bid for the C. & O. Canal.

By December 13, Latrobe reported that specifications had been sent to 23 companies that had expressed an interest in the tunnel work. He also recommended that Edward McConnell be hired as engineer for the second residency at a salary of $125 per month. The Coal and Iron Railway Company was incorporated in Charleston on December 14 by Davis, Elkins, Kerens, Hendley and T. B. Davis.

Latrobe was acting also as consulting engineer for the Davis Coal and Coke Company and the planned mine at Henry. Specifications for bids for this project were sent out at this time. The Davis Coal and Coke Company had a number of other construction projects at this time, including building additional coke ovens at Thomas and Coketon. A test bore was completed at William, which, although going down to a depth of 701 feet, found only disappointing traces of coal.

On December 13, the Cumberland Times reported that trouble was brewing in the shops at Elkins, as the men were reported to have demanded an advance in wages. This was the first Bretz had heard of the problem but conceded that common laborers in the mines and mills along the West Virginia Central were earning more than the shopmen. He mentioned to Davis that John T. Davis was paying his laborers $1.40 per day. Bower and Courtney met with a committee of the shopmen on December 27 and presented a new schedule of wages. The committee agreed to take the new proposal to a meeting of the men on December 28 to see if it were acceptable. Later reports indicated that the trackmen had received a ten cent increase and that the shopmen would get an increase commencing January 1, 1900.

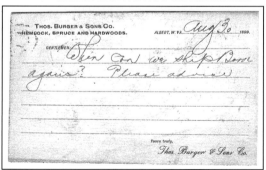

Fig. 131. "When can we ship bark again? Please advise." Post card from Thomas Burger and Sons to J. G. Hoffman and Sons tannery, August 30, 1899

11

The Coal and Iron Railway

Several news items during January 1900 may have attracted Davis's attention although he did not make any comments. The first, reported in Parkersburg on January 1, concerned a coal-field in Braxton and Gilmer counties, in which G. A. Newlon, W. Van Winkle and Col. George Gillmor were taking up options. A later report indicated that entrepreneurs controlling the Zanesville and Ohio River Railroad were interested in obtaining control of the Little Kanawha Railroad and extending it to the coalfield to give a direct outlet to the Lakes. The third news item concerned the chartering, on January 2, of the Belington and Northern Railroad, by N. T. Arnold. This road was proposed to run from Belington to Morgantown.

The first order of business for Elkins in 1900 was to recommend that the P. & C. be merged with the West Virginia Central in a similar manner to the Davis Coal and Coke Company. Both Davis and Elkins had become aware that if the West Virginia Central was sold without the P. & C., then the P. & C. would be rendered valueless. Elkins recommended that 1.1/2 shares of West Virginia Central stock be given for each share of P. & C. stock.

The bids for the tunnel work showed that the firm of Rosser, Coleman and Hoge was the low bidder, but required 15 months to complete the work, whereas Walton and Company would be finished in nine months. Davis was inclined to give Walton the contract unless Rosser, Coleman and Hoge could complete the work any quicker. By January 5, it was decided to give the contract to Rosser, Coleman and Hoge.

Bretz recommended to Davis on January 6, that no further wooden cars be built, and that all future cars be of steel. He noted that the Pennsylvania and the B. & O. were purchasing 100,000 lb. capacity steel cars. Bretz noted that the use of such cars would mean that wooden cars would have to be hauled at the end of trains, as they were too light to be mixed with steel cars. Davis was not impressed and noted that the N. & W. was building 100,000 pound capacity wooden cars and that a change to steel would create unemployment in the Elkins shops. Bretz pointed out that the B. & O. claimed to be able to haul 46 percent more freight in steel cars with the same engine than in wooden cars but Davis still was not convinced. Davis was to remain attached to wooden cars throughout his life.

Bretz also presented Davis with a list of improvements needed during the coming year amounting to $67,340. The projects included new turntables at Elkins and Thomas, a new roundhouse and freight depot at Thomas, new depots at Rawlings, Dobbin, Belington and Thomas and new water towers at Ridgeley, Shaw and Steyer. Bretz was somewhat dubious concerning the improvements at Thomas, as he thought the space was limited, and preferred to move to Fairfax where more space was available.

Davis wrote to Kerens on January 8, mentioning that the Pennsylvania and the B. & O. were now closely allied and arranging to control other railroads. It was Davis's custom to host a dinner for railroad executives each year, and this year's dinner, in Davis's words, was a "celebration of the partial pooling of the interests of the B. & O., C. & O. and the Pennsylvania Railroad." The guests included Chauncey M. Depew, president of the N. Y. C.; M. E. Ingalls, president of the C. & O. and the Big Four; J. K. Cowan and Oscar Murray of the B. & O.; Samuel Spencer of the Southern Railway; J. S. Harris and George F. Baer, president and vice-president respectively of the Reading; and A. J. Cassatt, president and John P. Green, financial vice-president of the Pennsylvania. Rounding out the guest list were Elkins, Kerens, Senator Arthur P. Gorman, and W. L. Elkins of the Widner-Elkins Syndicate. W. L. Elkins was Elkins's brother; the Widner-Elkins Syndicate was heavily involved in streetcar lines.

Andrew Carnegie wrote to Davis a few days after the dinner and was pleased that the new railroad combinations would result in stable rates. However, both Davis and Carnegie were to misjudge the impact of the community of interest on their businesses. For Davis it would mean the end of the cozy relations he had enjoyed with the Pennsylvania. The relationship actually came to an end a few days before his dinner, when M. Trump, the general superintendent of transportation for the Pennsylvania, wrote to Bretz and demanded that the West Virginia Central start paying mileage on Pennsylvania cars. Davis was quite upset, as this would cost the West Virginia Central a "couple of thousand extra per month." Bretz complained to Trump that the proposal was discriminatory as the C. & P. and the Georges Creek railroads were not paying mileage but was not able to get any relief. Davis indicated that he would see either Cassatt or Prevost on the question.

Although the mileage question was to be an irritant between the West Virginia Central and the community of interest partners, Bretz reported that the B. & O. wanted to install an eastbound connection at Cumberland and run trains directly into the yard at Ridgeley. The B. & O.'s assistant general manager, Daniel Willard, asked Bretz if the Potomac River bridge at Cumberland were strong enough to take the B. & O.'s heaviest engines, which weighed 171,000 pounds. Bretz assured Davis that the bridge was strong enough to take the new engines that the West Virginia Central had on order from Baldwin, which would weigh 185,000 pounds.

Bretz reported on January 21, that the increase of traffic from Thomas and points south was taxing the engines to their limits. He expected the shifting engine, No. 37, to be delivered by Rogers on February 1 although it had been promised the previous November. Bretz also urged Baldwin to hurry the delivery of the two new freight engines. Thus the last thing Bretz needed was a wreck that would deprive him of the use of another engine.

On January 26, Engine No. 27 with 42 loaded cars ran into the back of a train hauled by No. 28 at Cedar Cliff, some 3.1/2 miles south of Cumberland. No 28 had failed for want of steam, and although a flagman was sent back to warn the following train, he was not seen by the engineer of No. 27 due to heavy snow. Early reports indicated that the injuries to the crew were not serious, and that the caboose and one coal car were over the bank. No. 27 was off the track but could be rerailed readily. Unfortunately, the fireman had received a severe scalding and died the next day. Engine No. 27 also was badly damaged.

At the end of January, Bower was instructed to get bids on 40 miles of 85 pound rail for use on the main line. This would then allow the 70 pound rail that it replaced to be used on the C. & I.

Latrobe reported to Davis on February 5 of a visit he had made to the C. & I. a few days earlier. He noted that the line from South Elkins up to tunnel No. 1, including the crossing of the Tygart Valley River, was now located. Outside work at this time must have been miserable as Latrobe reported it was below zero on one day and only 15 degrees the next. Parsons was reported to be locating between tunnel No. 1 and No. 2, and was expected to be finished by February 28. So that the party was not slowed by the poor weather, Latrobe sent Parsons two secondhand tents. Latrobe also mentioned meeting with a C. & O. engineer to discuss the junction of the two lines at the Forks. The engineer thought that the C. & O.'s line would be finished by August 1900.

Moore wrote at the same time and indicated that the tunnel contractor was at work and had erected some shanties for the men. Work was due to commence on February 8 with wheelbarrow gangs, and 50 men were reported to be at work. By the middle of February, Latrobe was reported to be designing the masonry for the Tygart Valley River bridge in South Elkins and a number of stone culverts up towards tunnel No. 1. Moore reported that the right-of-way to the first tunnel was cleared and three gangs were at work on the south end. The north end was not yet opened and at tunnel No. 2, the contractors were erecting shanties.

Davis wrote to Andrew Carnegie on February 6, noting that planning for the C. & I. was going forward and reminding him that the completed road would provide access to Newport News and the iron ore deposits of West Virginia. He concluded by asking Carnegie for a letter of support that could by used in a prospectus for the new road. Davis wrote similar letters, asking for letters of support, to the presidents of the eastern railroads that could benefit from the C. & I., including the N. & W. and the Southern. To Cassatt of the Pennsylvania, he pointed out that the C. & I. would serve as a link in a line stretching from Pittsburgh to Newport News. This would give the Pennsylvania freight from Pittsburgh to Fairchance, Pennsylvania, where it would be transferred to the B. & O. for movement to Belington and the West Virginia Central. Cassatt was impressed and provided Davis with encouragement to build the road. Davis in return thanked Cassatt for his support and continued, "I am glad to see, largely through your influence, that the trunk lines as well as the coal roads appear to be much more in harmony, and that there is likely to be much more uniformity in freight rates in the future." He did not mention the mileage controversy which was still irritating Bretz.

The C. & I. was not the only railroad on Davis's mind as he still was concerned about the P. & C. He wrote to Vice President Green of the Pennsylvania, suggesting that the company turn in its P. & C. stock for West Virginia Central stock on the basis of one share of P. & C. for one and a half shares of West Virginia Central,

and asked for his ideas. He noted that there remained only $629,000 of un-issued stock in the treasury of the West Virginia Central, but that it could be used to assist in the purchase of the P. & C. He suggested that if the Pennsylvania turned in all its P. & C. stock for that of the West Virginia Central, it would give " the Pennsylvania quite a holding in the West Virginia Central."

Bretz received bids on two new 70-foot turntables for Thomas and Elkins on February 16 and Davis agreed to their purchase. It was anticipated that the old turntable from Elkins would be installed at Belington. Bretz recommended a five stall roundhouse at Thomas, as there was insufficient room for a larger structure, but recommended leaving the old engine house for the repair of engines.

On February 17, Davis noted in his diary that the "Coal trade is good, railroad doing fairly well." He further noted that the price of coal was $2.75 per ton "which is about an 80 percent advance from six months ago." Two days later he recommended to Prevost that lumber rates be advanced, a suggestion that was bound to upset the Whitmer and other shippers. Davis also discussed with Bretz the rates the Lukes would be charged for pulpwood on the C. & I.

Davis complained to Bretz that the passenger equipment was getting run down, although Bretz thought it was the cars that were getting a little antiquated. Bretz suggested that two passenger cars and a combination baggage, mail and express car would be needed when the C. & I. opened. He recommended the immediate purchase of a new passenger car for approximately $4,800. However, no new cars were purchased during the year.

Bretz still was trying in early March to persuade Trump of the Pennsylvania not to institute the mileage charge, but admitted defeat and turned the matter over to Davis. Davis complained to Prevost who was also adamant that the West Virginia Central should pay the charge.

Latrobe reported to Davis on his visit to the C. & I. at the end of March, noting that the contractors were waiting for the weather to improve before pushing the work. At tunnel No. 2, where there were eight inches of snow on the ground, 16 shanties had been built and 25 men were at work. The only construction so far was the completion of a drainage ditch to divert a stream from the work. Davis wrote to Axtell on April 9 informing him that the work was progressing on the tunnels and that the bids would be opened for grading on April 16. By the middle of April, the tunnel contractor was hiring black workers from the Newport News area of Virginia and bringing them to the tunnels.

At the end of March, Landstreet submitted to Davis a list of improvements suggested for the coal company. The list included installing electric haulage and a bridge over the Potomac at the Buxton mine (Fig. 132), and making new openings at the Franklin and Hampshire mines. The total cost of the recommendations for the lower Potomac mines was $62,550. At the upper Potomac mines the following were recommended: a new office building at Thomas to replace the one destroyed in October 1899, 40 new coke ovens for Thomas, and a shaft mine for Henry. The total cost of the upper Potomac improvements was put at $139,225, giving a total for both regions of $201,775. Davis approved work to start at once on the shaft mine at Henry and a steam drill was reported to

Fig. 132. The Buxton mine near Piedmont prior to 1909

be in operation on April 11.

At the beginning of April, Bretz reviewed the status of the new work and thought that perhaps construction of the new stations at Dobbin and Thomas could be delayed for a year. The old building at Dobbin is shown in Fig. 133.

Davis was still negotiating with the Pennsylvania about the consolidation of the P. & C. with the West Virginia Central. Green suggested Davis personally buy the

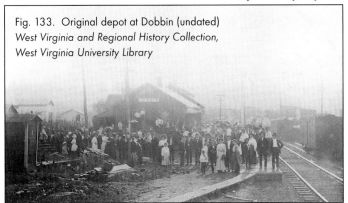

Fig. 133. Original depot at Dobbin (undated)
West Virginia and Regional History Collection, West Virginia University Library

Pennsylvania's P. & C. stock, but Davis could not afford to do this. Green finally agreed to an exchange of stock as had been earlier recommended.

In early April, G. A. Newlon met with Davis and tried to interest him in the Little Kanawha Railroad and the coalfield in Braxton and Gilmer counties. This approach was followed by a letter to Davis from H. C. Jackson, a colleague of Newlon, who noted that the coal field is "quite an inviting one ….. and the railroad is a logical outlet for your road to the west." Newlon wrote a few days later to say that he and Jackson "virtually controlled" the coalfield, having options on 25,000 acres and again recommending control of the Little Kanawha Railroad.

Jackson and Newlon, along with A. B. White and W. W. Jackson, were at this time, the principal stockholders of the Little Kanawha Railroad. During the time they were taking up options in the Gilmer and Braxton coalfield, David A. Nease and his associates also were purchasing options, which had the effect of driving up prices. To avoid this, the two groups agreed to pool their resources with each group having a 50 percent interest. However, the parties do not seem to have cooperated too well, and indeed Nease spent considerable time and money in litigation with his own

associates. The dispute led eventually to a deal being struck on May 5, 1900, whereby it was decided to separate the Nease interests from those of the Jacksons, Newlon and White. The Nease interests were then valued as being equivalent of 20 percent of the prevailing royalties from the coal. The Newlon group would take whatever they could make out of the sale of the lands; Nease and his colleagues also would receive back the money they had advanced, which for Nease, amounted to $11,200. The agreement also stipulated that the Newlon interests would arrange for the financing to complete the Little Kanawha Railroad to the coalfield and to pay for the coal lands before December 1, 1900. If this was not done by December 1, Nease and his partners would receive 49 percent of the coal. The approach to Davis in April was in anticipation of the signing of this contract.

Bretz reported on April 6, that the B. & O. was at work on an eastbound connection at the canal wharf in Cumberland. The work was expected to be finished in about a month (Fig. 134). The cost was estimated to be $6,500, one third of which would be paid by the West Virginia Central, the balance by the B. & O.

However, rumblings of discontent were beginning to be heard from the miners in early April. Davis noted in his diary on April 10 that the coal and coke trade was good, but there was agitation in all the coalfields. Galbreath reported to Davis on April 11 that the miners' union had called for a strike if its demand for 60 cents per ton was not met. Galbreath claimed there was no support for a strike in the upper and lower Potomac fields. By April 17, the

Fig. 134. B. & O. connections at the canal wharf, Cumberland, 1900
Collection of the National Archives

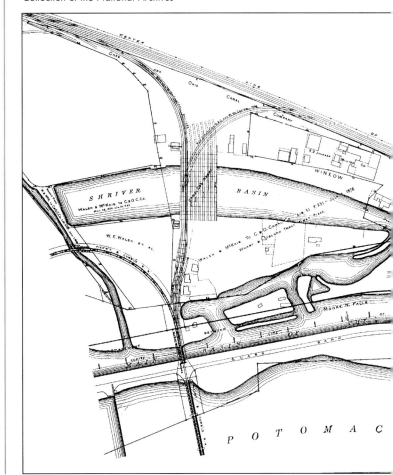

lower Potomac mines were on strike but both Elk Garden and the upper Potomac mines were still working. The mines of the Junior Coal Company were also not affected.

By April 21, Galbreath noted the mines around Piedmont and on Georges Creek were still closed, although noting that some reports indicated the strike was almost over. This proved to be the case with the lower Potomac miners who began returning to work on April 24 and by April 27, all the mines around Piedmont were working normally. The strike along Georges Creek continued until August 1.

April 16 was the last day for bids to be received for grading along the C. & I., and a few days later Latrobe was asked to review the bids. The contract for the work was given to the Walter, Purcell and Moorman Company, which commenced work at Elkins in early May.

Bretz reported to Davis on April 17 that the citizens who used the depot at Custer on the Belington branch, were rather unhappy with the name. The Post Office in the area was known as Dartmoor and Davis approved changing the name of the depot to Dartmoor.

Davis finally wrote to Cassatt on April 19 complaining about the imposition of the mileage charge. Cassatt responded immediately claiming that the free use of cars had been to encourage the West Virginia Central during its infancy, but this was no longer the case. Davis was thus made aware that the community of interest partners intended to have a tight hold on all rates even on the feeder roads that they did not control. Bretz was told of Davis's failure to obtain the concession and agreed to start paying mileage on April 22. The B. & O. had not yet made a similar demand, but did so in July.

Davis did receive some good news at this time when Whitmer decided to build a pulp mill at Parsons at an estimated cost of $200,000. Davis was informed on April 23 that land had been purchased for the new company, to be called the Parsons Pulp and Paper Company. Davis had earlier corresponded with Robert Roe, who was to be the superintendent of the new company, and agreed on freight arrangements and the sale of timber off 20,000 acres of land for $10 per acre. It also was reported that R. Chaffey, who operated a large mill at William, was to build a new sawmill at Henry.

Davis decided on May 1, to visit Thomas and look over the ground where the new developments were planned. He had approved the construction of a new station at the junction of the Davis branch and the main line, and also a new freight depot. Bretz had urged Davis to build a larger roundhouse to avoid keeping engines in the open, and a new building was approved.

Early in May, fires again were a problem. The pulpwood sawmill at Horton, along with several boxcars, was burnt to the ground around May 1. On May 9, Bretz reported that forest fires threatened Thomas, Coketon and Henry and that shanties and the waiting shed at Pendleton Run had already been destroyed. The situation was saved when heavy rains doused the fires. At the end of the month, fire destroyed the mill and lumberyard of the Burger Brothers at Douglas, along with four houses belonging to the Cumberland Coal Company.

Latrobe visited the C. & I. during the first week of May and reported that no work had been done on the north end of tunnel No. 1 as the contractor was waiting for a steam shovel. Latrobe complained that the contractor was paying $1.50 per day for common laborers. This was too much as it gave the workers the opportunity "to spend too much idle time."

Bower reported on May 1 that there was trouble again with the shopmen at Elkins, who were demanding an increase in pay. Some of the men quit when their demand was refused but later asked for their jobs back. Bretz was firmly instructed by Davis not to take back any of the strikers (Fig. 135).

Fig. 135. Boilermakers at the Elkins shops, May 1900
Collection of Rob Whetsell

It was noted in the Charleston Daily Gazette, that charters had been issued on May 8, to the West Virginia Spruce Lumber Company and the Pocahontas Supply Company. The lumber company had been set up by the Lukes to operate a large sawmill at Cass on the C. & O.'s new Greenbrier extension; the supply company was to operate the company store.

The Lukes also owned land that was on the route of the C. & I. and on which Davis needed the right-of-way. On May 14, John Luke wrote to Davis claiming that he was willing to grant the right-of-way in exchange for fair treatment on freight rates. He also mentioned that the Lukes had purchased the Merrill coal property near Westernport and expected Davis to give his company a right-of-way should they ever decide to mine their own coal.

Davis was not at all pleased at this news and ordered Bretz to increase the rates on pulpwood ten or 15 percent. As was to be expected, the Lukes were not pleased and complained to Bretz. Bretz claimed the new rates were still lower than the new rates on the B. & O., which were due to go into effect on June 1. The new rates on the West Virginia Central went into effect on June 18, again causing complaint from the Lukes. For once, Davis stood his ground with the Lukes, and told them on July 3 that the rates were as low as they possibly could be.

Davis ordered Bretz to start work on the new station at Rawlings on May 17. Possibly because the building was to be erected on land purchased from Governor Lowndes of Maryland, or because Rawlings was the summer home of Alexander Shaw, Davis insisted on a "creditable" building. The new building was completed by the end of July; the original waiting shed was then moved to McKenzie. The new building cost $1,000, which was $100 over estimate.

Fig. 136. Builder's photograph of West Virginia Central No. 39
Collection of the Pennsylvania Railroad Museum

Davis was not too pleased, during a visit to Thomas on May 25, to find the steam shovel standing idle and only one man at work clearing the land for the new engine house. Bretz complained that the laborers were only being paid $1.20 per day and that men could not be obtained at these rates. Davis gave reluctant approval to increase the rate to $1.25. A few days later, Bretz reported that the masons would start work on the roundhouse, but that there was still a shortage of labor.

The two engines from Baldwin, Nos. 38 and 39, were shipped on May 16, with No. 39 (Fig. 136) arriving at Elkins on May 24. Bretz recommended that additional engines be ordered for delivery in March or April 1901.

In June, Davis took a renewed interest in an independent route to tidewater. Whether this was due to the activities of the community of interest partners or whether it was due to his brush with DeWitt Smith and Reinhart is not clear. He asked Latrobe to review the possibility of a line leaving the West Virginia Central west of Cumberland, possibly at Keyser, and heading east via Patterson Creek. Latrobe thought the work might be rather severe with a climb out of Keyser and then rough work beyond. Davis does not appear to have followed up on this route, although he would return to a route to tidewater later.

J. C. Watson, of the Watson-Loy Coal Company at Barnum, contacted Bretz on June 7 suggesting that the "railroad station" at Barnum be moved. At this time, the "railroad station" consisted only of a platform with the coal company being in charge of railroad business. Watson wanted to build a new storeroom and office south of the present location and requested that the West Virginia Central build the platform. Davis was agreeable to the change, noting that it was only a "short mile" from the present location. The new building was erected during August and contained a ticket office and a room for freight (Fig. 137). The Watson-Loy Coal Company sold out to the Monroe

Fig. 137. Monroe Coal Mining Company building at Barnum, circa 1910
Collection of Don Henderson

Coal Mining Company in July 1902.

Bretz hired a new maintenance-of-way engineer to replace Mitchell who was to retire on July 15 because of ill health. The new engineer, H. T. Douglas Jr., reported for work on July 5.

Latrobe was back over the C. & I. in the middle of July and reported work on the tunnels was not as advanced as it should be. The grading was being pushed by the main contractor and a number of subcontractors. Latrobe also examined the ground at the Forks of the Greenbrier and pronounced it suitable for a junction. He noted that it would resemble Elkins in many ways.

Bretz was negotiating with the contractor W. A. Liller of Keyser to build the new depot at Thomas for $3,500, to be finished in 90 days. The railway company was to build the foundation and to supply the bricks, and it was expected that the depot would be finished by November 20. Work started on the foundations for the depot on July 30. Bretz was looking also for masons to start work on the new roundhouse at Thomas but was not able to find any. At the same time Liller received the contract to build the new Buxton and Landstreet store at Thomas for $30,000.

In a report to Davis on July 20, Bower noted that three cars of stone and one of sand had been delivered to the site of the Tygart Valley River bridge. The contractor was reported also to have reached a good foundation for one of the abutments. A day later, Latrobe reported to Davis that five companies had bid for the steelwork on the two bridges on the C. & I. at the Tygart Valley River and the Shavers Fork crossings. The Pennsylvania Bridge Company was the low bidder at $10,700. A drop in steel prices caused Latrobe to ask for new bids, which he reported to Davis on August 17. Again the Pennsylvania Bridge Company was the low bidder, this time with a bid of $10,000, and received the contract on August 17.

Landstreet gave Davis an update on July 27 of the affairs of the Atlantic and Pacific Company that had been organized during 1898. The A. & P. had been organized as a brokerage company by the individuals who looked after the sea borne trade in the various sales offices of the Davis Coal and Coke Company, including California. Whether the company had gone beyond brokerage, and had actually purchased some vessels is not clear, but three boats were reported in the 19th Annual Report as belonging to the West Virginia Central. The three were the barges "Elk Garden" and "Hampshire" and the schooner "William L. Walker." The three boats were reported to have cost $70,627.92.

By August 5, Bretz was able to report that the new turntable at Thomas was in place and work had started on replacing the turntable at Elkins. The new water towers at Ridgeley, Shaw and Steyer were expected to be in place in about a month and a new tower at Dobbin was already in use. Work at Thomas was finally progressing well.

Fire struck again on September 1 when the mill and lumberyards of the Otter Creek Lumber Company at Hambleton were destroyed. The fire was so intense that it threatened buildings in Hambleton across the Black Fork. The bridge across the Black Fork was saved when an engine of the Dry Fork Railroad was used to pump a constant stream of water onto the bridge.

Latrobe had a conference with Davis on September 15 at which Davis asked for input on a proposal to reduce the grade in the cut just north of Elkins. Latrobe thought that the work would be a great improvement and agreed with Douglas's estimate that the excavation would cost 80 cents per cubic yard, although no total estimate was provided. Latrobe also thought that the bridge crossing the B. & O. at 21st should be renewed and defective masonry repaired at once.

Davis noted in his diary on September 15, that he was considering buying 20-40,000 acres of coal lands in Barbour County and also iron ore lands in Pendleton County. He again noted an interest in a route to tidewater. On September 26 he asked Latrobe to give some thought to such a route.

Davis decided to take a look for himself at a proposed route and left Elkins on October 15, accompanied by Hendley, Latrobe, and Elkins's son, Davis Elkins. The party traveled to the Forks of the Greenbrier and from there to Travelers Repose where they stayed the night. The next day, Davis and company left Travelers Repose for Franklin by way of the East Fork of the Greenbrier and Hardscrabble Gap. At Franklin, a day was spent examining Iron Ore Mountain, but Davis was only "tolerably impressed." On the 18th, the party left Franklin via Broad Run Gap and then across the Shenandoah Mountain at Big Low Gap and down to Rawley Springs, some ten miles from Harrisonburg. Davis then took a train on the C. & W. ("poorly built") to get to Elkton and from there to the Rapidan River. The party returned home on October 20.

Davis was impressed enough by his trip to have a memorandum drawn up showing the cost of 230 miles of railroad to tidewater would be $10,000,000 including equipment, and coal, timber and ore lands. Davis estimated that 750,000 tons of coal and 75,000 tons of coke moved over the new line, plus the trade in ore and timber, would give a net surplus in the second year of operation of $311,813.

While Davis was on his trip to tidewater, John T. Davis and Landstreet were sent to examine the Barbour County coalfield. Both reported finding good veins of Roaring Creek coal, one four feet and the second nine feet thick. Davis noted in his diary that most of the coal had been purchased but that "we are buying some."

Axtell sent Davis a blueprint of the proposed arrangement of tracks at Durbin. Davis thought that neither road would reach Durbin this fall, but Axtell reported on October 19 that the grading was practically finished to within one mile of the Forks and the bridges were ready. He expected the first 56 miles to Marlinton to be turned over to the operating department by November 10. Davis did not expect the two tunnels on the C. & I. to be finished before the spring of 1901 but still thought the line would reach the Forks by midsummer.

Davis noted on October 25 that the coal and coke trade was improving and asked Bretz to get bids on two new freight engines and a heavier passenger engine. At the beginning of November, Davis also recommended the purchase of a steam crane to be used around Thomas. Bretz, who thought that two such cranes were needed, had refrained from asking earlier because of the high expenditures recently incurred. A bid of $11,500 was received

from the Bay City Industrial Works for a 50-ton crane for April 1901 delivery, and Davis gave approval for the purchase. The crane was delivered at the beginning of May 1901, for a final cost of $11,571.39, and became West Virginia Central No. 3 (Fig. 138). It was noted also that Pullman had delivered a new passenger car to the West Virginia Central sometime during the early fall; payment for the car was made on November 25 although no other information was given. Davis recommended that the Elkins shops continue to build wooden freight cars.

Fig. 138. Steam crane No. 3, circa 1905

On October 29, Davis wrote to Newlon asking if there were any maps available of the Gilmer County coalfield. Newlon gave a description of the field to Davis on November 3, and noted that the options were held by George Gillmor as trustee. Newlon also owned some land near the head of Roaring Creek in which he tried to interest Davis. Davis informed Newlon that John T. Davis, Davis Elkins and I. C. White would leave on November 7 to examine the Gilmer field, but that the Roaring Creek land was too far from Davis's operations in the area. Whether Davis was aware of the deadline faced by Newlon and his associates to sell the coalfield and refinance the Little Kanawha Railroad by December 1, is not known, but certainly Davis was not going to be rushed. The initial reports that Davis received from John T. Davis and White must have been encouraging, as he then asked Perry Thompson, a land agent, to check the options on 10-30,000 acres of coal on Sand Fork above Glenville, but to do so "quietly." Thompson was then instructed on November 21 to secure Pittsburgh vein coal in the Glenville region at a reasonable price. He noted that Newlon's people had "disposed of or tied up in some way their interests, so make no move or inquiries, and say nothing concerning that coal."

Since Davis did not seem likely to act before the December 1 deadline, Newlon and his colleagues had signed a contract with B. E. Cartwright of Ridgeway, Pennsylvania, on November 17 to finance the coal purchase and to extend the Little Kanawha Railroad. This contract was in accordance with the agreement with the Nease group. However, on the same day, a second contract was signed, setting up a company, the Braxton Coal Company, to take over both the railroad and the coal lands, with Cartwright furnishing the money for both. Newlon and his partners would receive 25 percent of the net profit realized from the transaction.

The second contract was not shared with Nease and his group. When Nease found out about the second contract, which he considered prejudiced against his interests, he unleashed a barrage of lawsuits that were to continue for 15 years.

Landstreet mentioned the Little Kanawha Railroad deal to Davis on November 23 and reported that he knew nothing about the matter, but was aware of B. E. Cartwright's reputation for involvement in "shady transactions."

The Gilmer field was not the only coalfield of interest to Davis at this time. Prior to his trip to Gilmer County, I. C. White had examined the country between the Tygart Valley River and the Buckhannon River. He reported that the whole region was underlain with two workable coal veins, one of which was already worked at Junior. He summarized by saying the area contained a "desirable" coalfield and recommended purchasing at $10 to $15 per acre. Davis noted in his diary on November 23 that he was purchasing 13-14,000 acres in the field.

John T. Davis also was trying to expand the coal lands owned by the Junior Coal Company and was negotiating to buy lands owned by the United States Coal, Iron and Manufacturing Company. Davis wrote to Dailey on November 22, reporting that his son was at work on this purchase and asking Dailey "to see that he does not get into trouble." The cause of Davis's concern was a complicated legal battle involving the Dillers, the U. S. C. I. & M. Co., the R. C. & B., the Belington and Little Laurel Railroad and the Berwind-White Coal Company. Dailey was concerned that the litigation would involve the Junior Coal Company if it went ahead with a purchase. Some lands along Roaring Creek were purchased where there was no dispute as to the title. Some of these lands were located on Grassy Run near Roaring Creek and Davis ordered Moore to survey a line through these lands. Moore set out for the survey on December 1, and after a few hours of work, a party led by Rease appeared and began grading. Moore filed his survey with the county clerk's office as was required by law, and which then gave Davis a right to the route. Rease had not filed a survey but nevertheless ordered Moore off the land a day or two later.

I. C. White filed a brief report with Davis on his visit to the Gilmer County coalfield on December 1. White estimated the coal field to be approximately 1,250 square miles and to contain ten feet of exploitable coal, giving eight billion tons of coal, of which about half could be mined above drainage.

Thus in the space of approximately one month Davis had expanded his interests into three new coalfields that were to set the direction of his future railroad and mining endeavors in ways that were not yet foreseen.

Back on the C. & I., Moore submitted to Davis on November 14, an account of the expenditures on the new line up to November 1, 1900. This showed that the contractors had completed $281,073.36 worth of work for which they had received payment of $256,751.90. Moore noted that 60 percent of the work on the approaches to the tunnels was finished and that ten percent of the tunnel work had been completed. He also reported that Division No. 1 was 70 percent completed; the other two Divisions were both 25 percent finished.

Bretz reported to Davis that he had received bids from Baldwin on two new freight engines for $13,375 each and for a 4-

6-0 passenger engine at $12,900. The price of the freight engines was less than had been paid for No. 38 and 39 but Davis was alarmed at the price of the passenger engine. After bids from other companies failed to produce better prices, Davis approved the purchase of the freight engines and the order was placed with Baldwin on December 4, with payment to be made in coal and coke. Bretz asked Baldwin for a better price on the passenger engine and Davis recommended offering $250 less than Baldwin were asking. Eventually an agreement was reached and two passenger locomotives were ordered.

Moore wrote to Davis on November 26 that all work on the C. & I. was suspended on account of a week of heavy rains leading to floods along Shavers Fork. The floods washed away a county highway bridge across Shavers Fork at Alpena, which was good news to Moore as it was in the way of the C. & I. Not such good news was the report that a large slip had occurred at the south end of tunnel No. 1. Latrobe recommended leaving it there until the spring but thought that tunnel work could continue throughout the winter. Some damage was reported on the West Virginia Central but was quickly repaired. Not so fortunate was the Dry Fork Railroad, which was badly damaged and caused Davis to wonder if Whitmer would be able to pay his bills on top of the expenses caused by the flood.

The Elkins Inter-Mountain reported on November 29 that the first baggage and mail car built at the Elkins shops had been completed a few days earlier. The 20th Annual Report for the year ending June 30, 1901 showed two such cars being built at Elkins during the year; it was not reported when the second car was finished.

Latrobe had been ordered by Davis on November 20 to get someone to lead a survey from the C. & I. to Harrisonburg. Latrobe recommended A. A. Chapman for the position and also reported that engineers from the C. & W. were at work on the route. Chapman was working on the Great Eastern Railroad in North Carolina at the time but could start on January 2, 1901, at a salary of $150 per month. Latrobe was later to describe Chapman as a "mere slip of a man physically, but very tough, as he needs to be for a winter survey."

Davis had been in contact with Carnegie about the progress on the C. & I., most recently on November 7, when he mentioned the new relationship among the Pennsylvania, the B. & O. and the C. & O. Davis reported that he was thinking of a line from Pittsburgh to tidewater and asked Carnegie if he was interested. Carnegie was well aware of the new relationships among the eastern railroads when he wrote to Elkins on December 10 complaining that the Pennsylvania had increased the freight rates in the Pittsburgh area, in some cases by up to 100 percent. Carnegie noted, "We may have serious times in Pittsburgh …… but I am in for the fight to the end, and can force this if necessary, as you know."

Carnegie's comment undoubtedly referred to the efforts of George Gould (Fig. 139) and the Wabash Railroad to enter Pittsburgh as part of a planned railroad empire stretching from the Atlantic to the Pacific. George Gould had inherited his father's railroads when Jay Gould died in 1892. The Wabash ran as far east as Toledo, Ohio, and had trackage rights over the Grand Trunk Railroad to Buffalo. This did not concern the community of interest partners unduly, but when Gould acquired the Wheeling and

Fig. 139. George Gould,
February 1915
Collection of the Library of Congress

Lake Erie Railroad in early 1901, putting the Wabash within 60 miles of Pittsburgh, a bitter fight ensued between Gould and Cassatt. The approach of Gould to Pittsburgh was certainly good news for Carnegie, who had long battled the eastern railroads, but Gould was also going to have an impact on the Davis and Elkins properties in West Virginia.

On December 4, Davis prepared another memo outlining the costs of the eastern extension. This memo gave the estimated cost of a line from the Forks of the Greenbrier to Harrisonburg and a connection with the Southern Railway as $2,500,000 for 90 miles. This was followed a couple of days later by a letter to Samuel Spencer, now president of the Southern Railway, suggesting a meeting to discuss a connection between the Southern and the new extension in Harrisonburg. Davis and Elkins later met with Spencer and Davis was sufficiently encouraged to note in his diary "looks like we will build." Spencer was notified at the end of the year, that Chapman was to start surveying eastward from the Forks on January 12, 1901, but that Latrobe, Moore and Chapman would make a preliminary reconnaissance on January 7.

Bretz reported on December 14, that work was continuing on the cut at Elkins but that a serious slip had occurred and the steam shovel had broken down causing delays. The new roundhouse at Thomas would be ready by December 18 (Fig. 140), however the attached boiler house would not be ready for another few days. The boiler house was designed to provide steam for the roundhouse and the new offices of the Davis Coal and Coke Company. The new depot at Thomas was not expected to be ready before January and even this was to prove optimistic. Bretz also noted that the Dry Fork Railroad was back in business after being closed down for three weeks by the floods in November. The first Dry Fork train of 30 cars of lumber to attempt to use the repaired line, had three cars wreck on a trestle, and had to call on the West Virginia Central for a wreck crew to get things moving again.

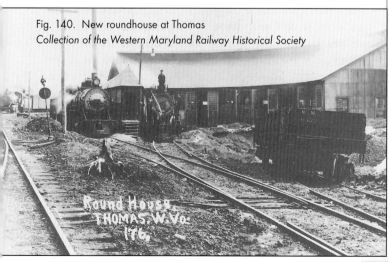

Fig. 140. New roundhouse at Thomas
Collection of the Western Maryland Railway Historical Society

The year ended on a tragic note when at least six Austrians working on the C. & I. were killed when some dynamite was put in a fire to thaw and exploded. At least three others sustained injuries from which they were given little hope of recovery.

The sad news continued into the new year, 1901, when two engineers working for the Davis Coal and Coke Company, were struck by an engine at Thomas and killed. The two men were walking along the tracks by the new depot and did not see an approaching engine because of escaping steam from another engine. This was followed a few days later by the death of a hostler at Thomas who was also struck by an engine.

Davis wrote to Spencer on January 7 recommending that they conclude a traffic agreement between the Southern and the new extension so that it could be used to help sell bonds. Davis sent Spencer a memo showing the cost of the road from the Forks to Harrisonburg, a distance of 90 miles, would be about $2,500,000. Davis estimated the new road would earn $1,227,000 in its first year of operation, which after paying expenses and interest, would leave a profit of $13,547. The earnings were expected to increase at 15 to 20 percent annually for several years. Davis also asked Spencer if the Southern could build from Harrisonburg to the West Virginia state line, but was told that the Southern's charter did not permit such construction. Davis did come to an agreement with Spencer for the Southern to guarantee the bonds of the C. & I.

Landstreet wrote to Davis on January 11, after meeting with Edwin Berwind, who had expressed an interest in selling his Roaring Creek properties. Landstreet was instructed to find out exactly what Berwind did own in the area and how much railroad. Davis noted, "If we could control that road without too much cost, it would be well for us to do so."

Bretz noted on January 11, that the new bridge across the tracks at Market Street in Cumberland was almost ready. The railroad and the Cumberland council had agreed in July 1886 to build a bridge, with the city building the abutments and doing the grading and the West Virginia Central erecting the bridge. In spite of many complaints by the council over the years, it took nearly 15 years for the bridge to be built. The bridge finally opened on February 22, 1901 (Fig. 141).

Bretz recommended on January 12, that two new passenger cars be purchased although Bower thought that four would be needed. After the usual haggling, Jackson and Sharp agreed to build the cars for $4,600 each for delivery in June. Bretz also recommended that all the passenger stock be renumbered as follows:

Baggage, Mail and Express cars 1-15
Combined cars 16-30
Passenger cars 31-100

The recommendation was approved by Davis. The new cars, Nos. 45 and 46, were delivered to Cumberland on April 25. One of the cars, No. 45 is shown in excursion service in Fig. 142.

Latrobe reported to Davis on January 12 on the results of his initial reconnaissance to the Valley of Virginia. Latrobe noted that three possible routes were available east of Harrisonburg through the Shenandoah Mountain, namely a northern route through the "Big Low Place" leading to Franklin, a middle route over the North River Gap and a southern route over Mossy Creek. Latrobe also

Fig. 141. Market Street bridge and the yards of the West Virginia Central in Cumberland. Immediately behind the Market Street bridge is the building of the German Brewing Company, which had purchased the land for the brewery from Davis in early 1901. To the right of the brewery is the "Gashouse" bridge across Wills Creek, which collapsed in 1915.

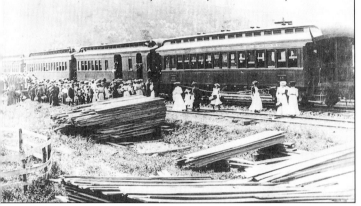

Fig. 142. West Virginia Central passenger car No. 45 (undated) *Collection of the Western Maryland Railway Historical Society*

reported meeting with Peter and William H. Rickard, two influential farmers in the Valley, who would be helpful in obtaining rights-of-way. The Rickards had incorporated the American Trunk Line Railroad a few years earlier to build west to the West Virginia coalfields and Davis hoped to be able to use this charter to build his new extension in Virginia, but it had expired. To avoid any unpleasantness with the community of interest partners, Davis decided to incorporate a new railroad, the Central Railway of Virginia, to build to the West Virginia line, but kept his own interest in the line concealed. The railroad was incorporated in Virginia in February 1901, to build a standard gauge line through Rockingham or adjacent counties to the Virginia/West Virginia line. The act was amended the following year to enable the line to extend to the Chesapeake Bay. The incorporators of the new railroad all lived around Harrisonburg and included W. H. Rickard, P. W. and D. C. Rehard, Herman Wise, J. B. Peale, H. B. Miller and A. A. Chapman.

At the end of January, another slip came down at tunnel No. 1, but Latrobe thought that the present slopes would now be secure. Latrobe reported that the heading of No. 1 was in 500 feet and he expected it to be through by April 1, and the tunnel to be completed by June 1.

At the beginning of February, Davis became interested in expanding his fleet. Landstreet had reported that two more vessels had been purchased, a schooner, the "Belle Holliday," which cost

$7,626 and a bark, the "Obed Baxter," which had cost $31,284.24. The "Obed Baxter" was later converted to a barge. Davis wanted to purchase an ocean going tug for his barges but the cost, $70,000, may have been a deterrent and no further vessels were acquired. Davis later informed Landstreet that he thought the West Virginia Central should take over the Atlantic and Pacific Company giving the railroad total control of its coal operations.

On February 4, Carnegie entered into an agreement with George Gould and the Wabash whereby if the Wabash built a railroad into Pittsburgh, Carnegie would route one fourth of his traffic west from Pittsburgh over the new line. Interestingly, this agreement was signed just a few days before Carnegie sold his steel company to J. P. Morgan to become the U. S. Steel Company. When the Pennsylvania heard of the agreement with Gould, it took all steps possible to prevent the new line from being built. However, Gould was fully determined to fight and not only did he push the line to Pittsburgh (which was eventually reached in June 1904), he also cast a glance to the south with a view to building a new trunk line through West Virginia.

Latrobe wrote on February 18 to say that the Jennings Gap line looked very promising and that he and Davis should meet to look over both the Jennings Gap and Dry River routes and determine where a tunnel should be located (Fig. 143).

Fig. 143. The passes through the Shenandoah Mountain considered by Latrobe

On February 20, Davis met with N. T. Arnold of the Belington and Northern Railroad to consider connecting the two roads. The goal of the B. & N. was to build to Kingwood, but the immediate aim was to reach a coal property north of Belington on the west side of the Tygart Valley River. Davis agreed to allow the B. & N. to move its cars over the West Virginia Central to the B. & O. until such a time as the B. & N. made its own direct connection. In return, the West Virginia Central would get preference on handling the B. & N.'s freight. Arnold needed to have an agreement so the location of a bridge across the Tygart Valley River could be determined.

Another railroad that entered Belington at this time was the Belington and Beaver Creek Railroad using the tracks of the R. C. & B. This line was owned by the Weaver Coal Company, which had earlier developed a mine at Leiter on the R. C. & B. under the name of the Maryland Smokeless Coal Company. The company was now mining a 13-foot vein of coal at Weaver, some six miles from Belington. Relations between the Weaver Coal Company and Rease of the R. C. & B. seem to have deteriorated to the point where the coal company now wished to connect with the West Virginia Central. Bower recommended that the B. & B. C. connect with the West Virginia Central above Belington near the overhead crossing of the R. C. & B. The B. & B. C. eventually wanted a direct connection with the B. & O. but this was expected to take at least another six months. Even when such a connection was made, the B. & B. C. was willing to give the West Virginia Central all its eastern shipments. At this time there were 125 men at work in the Beaver Creek mines producing 30 cars per day, which was expected to increase within a year to 3,000 tons per day. Bretz expected

Fig. 144. Freight depot at Thomas, circa 1917
Collection of the Western Maryland Railway Historical Society

Fig. 145. The Buxton and Landstreet store at Thomas, (undated)
West Virginia and Regional History Collection,
West Virginia University Library

Fig. 146. The new depot at Thomas. The Davis branch is behind the depot, the Thomas mine of the Davis Coal and Coke Company is on the left. The coke ovens do not appear to be working, which must have been a relief to the householders on the hillside above the ovens

the B. & B. C. traffic would earn the West Virginia Central between $50 and $100 per month. The connection between the two roads was installed on March 30.

The first of the new buildings approved by Davis during 1900 for Thomas had opened the previous November. This was the freight depot on the Davis branch adjacent to the new Buxton and Landstreet store (Fig. 144). Buxton reported on March 11 that the new store was almost finished, requiring only installation of shelves and counters (Fig. 145).

The new depot at Thomas was not finished until the beginning of May, nearly five months behind schedule (Fig. 146). The depot, with an unusual rounded end, was unique along the West Virginia Central. The depot was connected to the town by a bridge across the Davis branch.

The date the third major building in Thomas was completed, the offices of the Davis Coal and Coke Company, is not recorded (Fig. 147).

Fig. 147. The offices of the Davis Coal and Coke Company, 1997

The three new buildings put Thomas second only to Elkins among the towns along the West Virginia Central, although the population, according to the 1900 census, was about the same at approximately 2,000. The Davis Coal and Coke operated three mines in the area, the Thomas drift, the Thomas shaft, and mine No. 3 which had recently opened on the west side of the North Fork of the Blackwater River. In

Fig. 148. Davis Coal and Coke Company, Thomas

addition 522 coke ovens were in operation with more being constructed (Fig. 148). Typical company housing along the Coketon

Fig. 149. View of Thomas with the roundhouse on the left and the Davis branch freight house in the upper right corner.
Collection of Paul C. Mullins

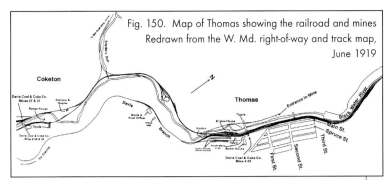

Fig. 150. Map of Thomas showing the railroad and mines Redrawn from the W. Md. right-of-way and track map, June 1919

road is shown in Fig. 149, along with the new roundhouse and the freight depot on the Davis branch. The layout of the railroad and the town as it appeared in a W. Md. 1919 track map is shown in Fig. 150.

The two new freight engines, Nos. 40 and 41, were received in March (Fig. 151). Bretz was advised that the two passenger engines would be delivered shortly afterwards. Because the C. & I.

Fig. 151. West Virginia Central No. 41, Belington, 1902
Collection of William Metheny

Fig. 152. Builder's photo, West Virginia Central No. 42
Collection of the Railroad Museum of Pennsylvania

was not finished, Bretz thought the delivery should be delayed, but was convinced by Bower that they could be used as freight engines in the interim. The new 4-6-0's, Nos. 42 and 43, arrived on April 3 (Fig. 152).

Bretz was initially very impressed with the two new passenger engines, and reported that one had saved four minutes on the Blackwater grade with a four-car train, and would easily pull a five car train up the grade.

On April 1, it was noted that W. T. Blackiston had resigned as

superintendent of the Elk Garden mines and was replaced by Lee Ott, who had been superintendent at Thomas. The resignation had been forced by Davis who was still unhappy with the cost of production at Elk Garden.

April 6 was a bad day for wrecks on the West Virginia Central. Problems started when a freight train hauled by No. 39 stopped for water at Tub Run. When the train restarted up the grade, it broke in two, allowing the rear section to run back down the hill. It was reported to be doing about 40 miles per hour when it hit a curve and eight cars went over the bank. The caboose and one coal car kept on going for another mile when they both jumped the track. The conductor was in the wrecked caboose but escaped injury; a brakeman who also had been in the caboose had jumped clear before the wreck and was uninjured. A tramp, who had been riding the train, was killed. Later on the same day, a rockslide came down at Canyon Point and derailed the tender of a passing passenger train and knocked the front truck off a baggage car, causing a considerable delay to all traffic. Bretz estimated the cost of the runaway at $1,200. The Blackwater grade was to see many more devastating wrecks in the future.

On April 10, Davis authorized Bretz to construct a new depot at Harding at an estimated cost of $1,500 (Fig. 153).

Fig. 153. Depot at Harding

Davis also asked that the old depot at Thomas, which had been considerably expanded over the years, be removed and erected at Henry.

The Parkersburg Sentinel reported on April 11, that the Little Kanawha Railroad had been placed into the hands of receivers, and H. C. Jackson was appointed the general manager. The receivership was necessary, as $25,000 that had been expected to come from the new owners, did not materialize. In a statement issued by the Little Kanawha, it was noted that the "transfer system" at Parkersburg entailed a very heavy expense, and prevented the proper handling of freight and passengers. This

Fig. 154. Little Kanawha Railroad ferry at Parkersburg
Collection of John King

referred to the rather rickety ferry, which was used to move the trains across the Little Kanawha River at Parkersburg (Fig. 154). An earlier ferry had sunk on August 29, 1898 taking an engine with it. The railroad's maritime misfortunes continued in September 1901, when a transfer boat used at Palestine, the "C. A. Barney," exploded and burned, fortunately without loss of life.

Davis noted that the Little Kanawha Railroad had passed into the hands of the receivers and further noted that he expected that the parties involved would not now be able to pay for the options on the coalfield. Davis and Elkins had been offered some options at $8 per acre, but did not purchase any, as they expected the price to go lower.

In the middle of April, there was news that the Board of Public Works in Maryland would try to sell the C. & O. Canal when the trustees' lease on the property expired on May 1. Davis was encouraged to get involved if he thought that the B. & O. was not living up to its agreement of February 1899. Davis, however, did not get involved and eventually a judge allowed the B. & O. to continue to operate the canal.

News stories had been circulating since the beginning of the year of efforts to purchase the W. Md. At this time it was the Reading that was the reputed buyer, but again Davis decided not to get involved.

Work was progressing slowly on the C. & I. Moore reported to Davis on April 26 that Latrobe had given the contractors on Division No. 1 until June 15 to complete their work. Track laying would commence about this time. The masonry work on the 12th Street and the Tygart Valley River bridges was almost finished and the bridge erectors expected to put up the steel work on May 6 (Fig. 155).

Fig. 155. Tygart Valley River bridge, Coal and Iron Railway

The New York Times published a short note on April 29, to the effect that work would commence on the Chesapeake and Western Railroad and that the road would then be used by the West Virginia Central as an outlet to the Atlantic seaboard. This report provoked an immediate letter from Cassatt, who tersely demanded of Davis if there were any truth in the report. Davis responded he had indeed met with De Witt Smith, who had indicated to Davis that the C. & W. would connect with the West Virginia Central's C. & I. extension at Durbin. However, Davis claimed that he had not encouraged Smith, and he doubted the ability of Smith to complete the construction of the route. Davis mentioned that he was build-

ing the C. & I to meet the C. & O. at Durbin, and that the line traversed some excellent timberlands and iron ore deposits. Davis went on to say that he did have surveying parties out to the east of the C. & I, but implied that he was constructing a branch into the area. This satisfied Cassatt, who wrote back to say that he considered the C. & W. scheme to be a "wild one." He further noted that, "the advantage to you in being able to reach the large coal-consuming territory served by our lines and the B. & O. must outweigh any possible benefit you could derive from controlling an independent line to the seaboard." Davis later informed De Witt Smith that he could not encourage his line as it would disturb existing traffic arrangements with the present connecting lines.

John K. Cowan resigned as president of the B. & O. on May 27, resuming his old position of chief counsel to the railroad. He was replaced by Leonor F. Loree, who had been fourth vice-president of the Pennsylvania, confirming the Pennsylvania's domination of the B. & O.

Latrobe submitted a lengthy report to Davis on June 1, outlining the activities of the various survey parties. Latrobe was concerned about the activities of parties from the C. & W., who were at work in the same area. The C. & W. was reported to have four survey parties and two reconnoitering engineers in the field. Latrobe mentioned that one of his camps had been visited by one of the C. & W. men, who had expected to find the camp empty, and who was looking for maps and charts to try to find out what the party was doing. The intruder was chased off by one of Latrobe's men who had remained at the camp because of sickness. Latrobe asked Davis to find out what was needed legally to locate a line and protect it from encroachment by other railroads. Davis told Latrobe to ignore the efforts of the C. & W., to concentrate on the Franklin route and to get the best possible tunnel location through the Shenandoah Mountain.

By early June, Bretz was beginning to be concerned about the performance of engines Nos. 42 and 43. The engines were showing signs of excessive wear on the flanges and also tearing up the tracks. An engineer from Baldwin told Bretz that there was nothing wrong with the engines but the problem lay in the poor track and sharp curves. Bretz later became so upset with the performance of the engines when they started to jump the track, that he refused to make a payment due to Baldwin and asked if they could be exchanged for a pair of 4-4-0's. Baldwin still maintained that the problem was with the track although the company made some changes to the truck. Baldwin later made more changes to the engine truck bolster and swing links. After these changes were

Fig. 156. Ex-West Virginia Central ten-wheeler, circa 1908

made, the engines appeared to operate satisfactorily and there were no further complaints (Fig. 156).

The West Virginia Central was not alone in having problems with its engines at this time. The Dry Fork Railroad had purchased a 4-4-0 from the Pennsylvania Railroad, the engine becoming Dry Fork No. 4. The engine was perhaps ill suited for the poor track and weak trestles of the Dry Fork. On June 20, No. 4 was pulling a work train out of Hendricks when a flange on the engine broke as the train was crossing the bridge across the Dry Fork, near the mouth of the Laurel Fork. The engine fell from the bridge and into the river. The engineer and fireman were killed and also a supervisor, W. A. Booker. Later reports indicated that excessive speed may have contributed to the accident. The West Virginia Central was later called on for help in clearing the wreck.

In March, the maintenance-of-way engineer, Douglas, had complained about the state of the bridge at 21st. Bretz confirmed that the bridge was weak and poorly constructed but recommended waiting until the summer until it was replaced. On June 18, Bretz informed Davis that a replacement bridge had been ordered and would be completed in 90 days. Meanwhile, freight trains were restricted to four miles per hour when crossing the old bridge.

On June 18, Davis received a letter from an individual who owned coal lands near the North River Gap. Davis was asked if he was interested in purchasing 4,000 acres of the field, known as the Dora field. The C. & W. also owned a large coal acreage in the field, and the prospect of exploiting the coal had been one of the reasons for the C. & W. heading for the North River Gap. The coal was reported to be semi-anthracite but Davis was not interested in the field. Later reports indicated that the potential of the field had been vastly overstated.

Davis noted in his diary on June 24 that the C. & I. was progressing slowly, but should be finished by November. He also noted that the shaft at Henry and other improvements there were being pushed. The shaft eventually struck coal at a depth of 450 feet on September 12. The date on which the depot was

Fig. 157. Depot at Henry
West Virginia and Regional History Collection,
West Virginia University Library

transferred from Thomas and re-erected at Henry is not known but it would have been about this time (Fig. 157). The depot was reported to be in service in October. Davis noted that Henry "bids fair to be our principal mining place."

Davis informed Bretz on June 24, that he had secured a new company to build a tannery at Hambleton. The company, the Hambleton Leather Company, broke ground for the tannery on August 13.

Davis wrote to George Stevens, president of the C. & O. on July 3, noting that grading would not be finished on the C. & I.

before December, but that track laying would commence north of Durbin just as soon as that section was finished.

Latrobe wrote to Davis on July 8 on the three routes that had been examined from Harrisonburg to Hightown as follows:

1. Route by Dry River   80 miles
2. Route by Jennings Gap and Thorn Creek   88 miles
3. Route by Jennings Gap and Monterey   77.6 miles

The distance from Hightown to Durbin was an additional 23 miles.

Davis began to take an active interest in the Buxton and Landstreet stores at this time and told Buxton that an improvement was needed. He later decided that the West Virginia Central should own the stores and informed Kerens of this decision but was not sure what price to pay. In addition to the new store at Thomas, the company owned stores at Coketon, Elk Garden, Henry, Simpson (Harrison County) and Savage in Maryland. He later offered $20 per share cash or $25 per share in stock for Landstreet's interest in the company.

The Dry Fork Railroad did not seem to be having a very good summer. On July 18, the Parkersburg Sentinel reported that an immense rattlesnake had jumped through a window of a passenger car from a rock outcropping and "almost frightening the women and children in the car to death." The train was stopped and the reptile dispatched by the crew. The snake was reported to be some 13 feet long. Four women were reported to be in a state of shock and fear was expressed that they might never recover.

More important to the West Virginia Central were events that were taking place along the Little Kanawha Railroad. On July 13, J. T. Blair of Greenville, Pennsylvania and E. D. Fulton of Uniontown, Pennsylvania, signed an agreement with H. C. Jackson, A. B. White, V. B. Archer and H. B. Nye for a 90-day option to purchase the railroad. Fulton had been taking up options on coal lands in the Gilmer field for some months when he became associated with Blair, who had been the general manager of the Pittsburgh, Bessemer and Lake Erie Railroad for 20 years. Cartwright, who had been expected to rescue the railroad and the coal lands seems to have backed out of the deal by this time. On July 30, Newlon wrote to Camden to see if he was interested in the 25,000 acres. Newlon was careful to spell out the problem with Nease and the royalty payment, but for whatever reason, Camden was not interested.

Blair later met with President Joseph Ramsey, Jr., of the Wabash Railroad and Gould's trusted lieutenant (Fig. 158), who agreed to take over the options on both the coal lands and the Little Kanawha Railroad. Ramsey at this time was pushing the Wabash extension towards Pittsburgh in spite of the opposition by Cassatt, and possibly thought the Little Kanawha would be a useful start for a trunk road through West Virginia. Blair was instructed to act as Ramsey's agent in the mat-

Fig. 158. President Joseph Ramsey, Jr. of the Wabash Railroad
Collection of the Carnegie Library of Pittsburgh

ter, but not to disclose who was behind the deal.

Early in August, Davis ordered that all the coal lands purchased in Upshur, Barbour, Lewis, Gilmer and Braxton counties be put into a new company, the Washington Coal and Coke Company.

During the summer, there had been considerable talk about combinations of soft coal producers in West Virginia and Pennsylvania, which culminated in the middle of August in a report in the Baltimore Sun, that a combine was going to buy the West Virginia Central. However, at the Annual General Meeting of the West Virginia Central on August 13, Davis reported that the company had had a good year and that the railroad was definitely not for sale.

Early in September, Landstreet reported on a meeting with E. L. Fuller of Scranton, Pennsylvania, who had expressed an interest in purchasing the West Virginia Central. Davis's interest in the proposal was sufficient for him to ask Landstreet to find out exactly who Fuller was. According to Landstreet, Fuller had been an anthracite operator in Scranton, Pennsylvania, for 20 years and was also engaged in mining rock salt. He had been involved in the construction of the Delaware and Kingston Railroad, which became known as the Independent Anthracite Railroad. His worth, according to Landstreet's sources, was put at between $3 and $4 million. Landstreet concluded by saying that Fuller "... is in no sense a speculator, but a practical mining and railroad man..." and that he was about to dispose of his salt interests and was looking for a new investment for his money.

There was no indication that Fuller was acting for anyone other than himself and his immediate business friends.

Davis also asked Landstreet for any information he might have on the progress of the combinations in the soft coal industry. Landstreet thought that eventually there would be only two companies east of the Ohio River, one of which would be the Davis Coal and Coke Company. The community of interest would encourage the formation of combinations, as it would lead to stable rates.

On September 9, it was reported that an offer to purchase Baltimore's interest in the W. Md. had been received. The offer was for $8,000,000 but the identity of the purchaser was not disclosed. George D. Cook, a Baltimore banker, met with Rea of the Pennsylvania later in the month. He told Rea that the W. Md. could be purchased for $6,000,000 and that he would form a syndicate to purchase the road if the Pennsylvania approved. Rea told Cook that the Pennsylvania was not interested as it was thought that the returns of the W. Md. were inflated. Rea reported to Cassatt that as a terminal railroad in a port as important as Baltimore, the Western Maryland "is an invitation to base the promotion of new trunk lines, and was therefore something of a menace." This was a most perceptive statement, but the Pennsylvania did not pursue the matter.

On September 9, Fuller wrote directly to Davis expressing an interest in purchasing the West Virginia Central and its coal properties.

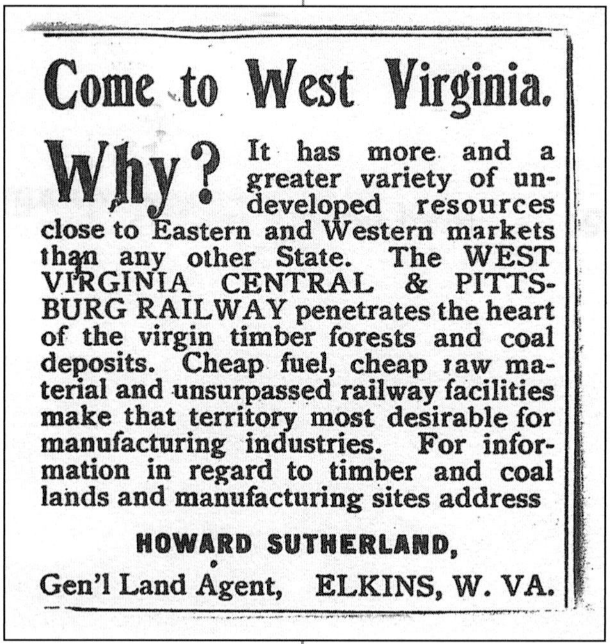

Come to West Virginia.

Why? It has more and a greater variety of undeveloped resources close to Eastern and Western markets than any other State. The WEST VIRGINIA CENTRAL & PITTSBURG RAILWAY penetrates the heart of the virgin timber forests and coal deposits. Cheap fuel, cheap raw material and unsurpassed railway facilities make that territory most desirable for manufacturing industries. For information in regard to timber and coal lands and manufacturing sites address

HOWARD SUTHERLAND,
Gen'l Land Agent, ELKINS, W. VA.

Fig. 159. West Virginia Central and Pittsburg Railway advertisement

The Sale of the West Virginia Central

12

The letter of September 9, 1901, from Fuller was not entirely unexpected given the earlier discussions with Elkins and Landstreet. Fuller acknowledged that he knew the West Virginia Central was not for sale, but he indicated that he had formed a syndicate that proposed to extend the lines of the West Virginia Central in several directions. The line would be extended from its current terminus in Cumberland to Cherry Run, West Virginia, which was the most westerly point reached by the W. Md. at this time. A second extension would run from Elkins across to the headwaters of the Little Kanawha River and hence down that river to Parkersburg on the Ohio River. A third extension was proposed to run from the C. & I. eastwards to tidewater. Fuller recognized that such extensions, when built, would increase the value of the West Virginia Central. However, if the road subsequently sold to unfriendly forces, it would render the extensions valueless. What Fuller wanted was first preference to purchase the West Virginia Central should it ever be sold, and that the sale price at that time would reflect the value without the extensions. Also both parties were to be fully protected by traffic agreements.

Davis does not seem to have acted immediately on this proposal, possibly because he had finally decided to go ahead and purchase the Braxton Coal Company's coal rights in Gilmer County. He recorded in his diary on October 10 that he had purchased the previous day, along with Elkins and Kerens, 25,000 acres of coal rights from the Braxton Coal Company and had also taken an option on the Little Kanawha Railroad. These decisions were to lead to some of the greatest problems ever encountered by Davis and his colleagues in their business careers. However, Davis was not to be directly involved in the resulting battles, as he departed for Mexico City on October 12. Davis was leader of the American delegation to the International Conference of the American States, which was a multinational group designed to promote a pan-American railroad, among other projects. He was to remain in Mexico until the middle of January 1902.

Two days before Davis purchased the Braxton Coal Company, Blair and Fulton assigned their options on the Little Kanawha Railroad and 40,000 acres of coal lands to Ramsey. Ramsey telegraphed Elkins on October 9, informing him of the sale, which suggests that in the month that had elapsed since the arrival of the Fuller letter, Davis and Elkins had become aware of the plans of Gould and the Wabash for West Virginia. Elkins, in his reply to the telegram on October 9, advised caution and doubted that 40,000 acres could be obtained with good coal measures beneath. Elkins's response is interesting because it gives the first suggestion that Elkins and Davis would be financially involved in some way with Ramsey and this purchase. Elkins also congratulated Ramsey on securing the Little Kanawha Railroad, and mentioned his and Davis's own 30-day option on the road. At this time, Ramsey had 60 days for the examination of the properties so that deal was not yet finalized. However, in accordance with the July 13 contract, Blair and Fulton paid $100,000 towards the purchase of the Little Kanawha Railroad on October 10.

On October 14, John T. Davis wrote to his father to say that he had reviewed the purchase of the Braxton Coal Company with Elkins and thought that Davis "was getting a great bargain." John T. Davis noted that he would inspect the field later in the week accompanied by Thomas B. Davis and Landstreet. On October 16, John T. Davis noted that he had received a telegram from Loree asking for a trip over the West Virginia Central on October 22. He noted that the telegram came from Philadelphia and assumed that Cassatt and the Pennsylvania were aware that something was going on.

When John T. Davis, Landstreet and Thomas B. Davis inspected the Braxton Coal Company coal lands they found the coal to be far superior to the best grades of Fairmont coal. The coal did not contain more than 1 percent sulfur or 5 percent ash, which compared well to the 2 percent sulfur and 7 percent ash typical of the Pittsburgh seam in the Fairmont area. A well drilled on the property showed a seam to be eight feet thick. However, the first problem with the contract appeared when C. B. Shaffer, of Ridgeway, Pennsylvania, claimed he had not approved of the sale and objected to allowing the Davis-Elkins interests to take only those portions of the field thought to contain worthwhile coal. This problem was eventually eliminated when Elkins agreed to take all or none of the field.

By now the newspapers were aware that something was going on and were full of wild conjectures. The Daily State Journal, published in Parkersburg, ran a story on October 19, claiming that the Little Kanawha Railroad had all but been purchased by the West Virginia Central, which would then be extended to a junction with the Little Kanawha at Palestine. Such an extension would give the West Virginia Central access to the Lakes by the Zanesville and Ohio River and the Wheeling and Lake Erie railroads, both roads being controlled by the Wabash. An eastward extension would join the West Virginia Central to the W. Md. to give a trunk line independent of the Pennsylvania.

President Loree and his wife, accompanied by General Manager Potter, and Haws his assistant, toured the West Virginia Central on October 22. Elkins, Kerens, John T. Davis, Landstreet and Bretz represented the West Virginia Central. Apparently Loree was not forthcoming about his reasons for the trip, although Mrs. Loree did drop a remark that the B. & O. was thinking of making an offer. John T. Davis reported that the B. & O. party was very impressed with the property, especially "its extent and physical condition."

Knowledge of the trip by the B. & O. party over the West Virginia Central prompted the Daily State Journal on October 23, to report that both the West Virginia Central and the Little Kanawha Railroad had been sold to the B. & O. The report was denied by Elkins and Landstreet, but the newspaper was not convinced.

Loree must have been somewhat uncomfortable during the trip because while it was in progress, other officers of the B. & O. were trying to break up the proposed sale of the Little Kanawha Railroad and the Braxton Coal Company. John T. Davis wrote to his father on October 23, that a contract satisfying Shaffer had been approved, but now H. C. Jackson was causing problems. Thomas Fitzgerald, the general superintendent of the B. & O., along with McGraw, had approached H. C. Jackson and told him that both the railroad and the coal company were worth much more than was being paid and convinced Jackson not to sign any contracts. Not only would Jackson not sign any of the contracts, he was, according to Kerens, determined to break up the railroad and coal deals.

John T. Davis sent his father a copy of the new agreement for the purchase of the Braxton Coal Company and also noted that he expected an offer from the Pennsylvania to purchase the road within two weeks. John T. Davis also noted that he could not get boxcars from the B. & O. to ship coal and coke west to Chicago although Weaver was able to get all he needed for his mines. It was obvious the community of interest was not going to be friendly to a company that it perceived as being allied to the Wabash. N. T. Arnold of the Belington and Northern Railroad, who was buying coal lands along the upper Little Kanawha River, also had expressed an interest in becoming involved in constructing a western extension of the West Virginia Central.

Elkins reported on October 27, that Fitzgerald and McGraw had offered Newlon $30,000 for his interest in the coal company and to throw the company into receivership, but he had refused. Elkins also noted that he had met with Camden, who was reported to be assisting the B. & O., but Elkins thought there was no truth to the rumor. Elkins also mentioned the offer of Arnold to build an extension west if the Davis interests would build to tidewater. Elkins mentioned these proposals to Ramsey and suggested that the West Virginia Central build to the Ohio River and meet the Wabash there. Elkins was concerned that if ever the Pennsylvania got control of the Wabash, it would effectively maroon the West Virginia Central. Ramsey suggested that the West Virginia Central and the Wabash join forces to build east and west.

John T. Davis wrote to his father on October 28, that the deal for the coal company was just about concluded, and that Camden and McGraw had led the fight against the West Virginia Central. The B. & O. now appeared to have given up the fight to block the sale of the coal company, but was still trying to disrupt the sale of the railroad by going after the 2,000 shares of stock held by Wood and Wirt counties.

With attention directed west to the Little Kanawha Railroad and the Braxton Coal Company, Fuller had not lost interest in trying to acquire the West Virginia Central. On October 29, Elkins reported that he had offered to sell Fuller the railroad and coal properties north of Elkins for $16,000,000. Fuller asked for a 30 day option but this was refused by Elkins who asked Fuller to make a counter offer.

John T. Davis's suspicions of Camden's role in the Little Kanawha affair were well founded. Camden was contacted by Loree on October 31 for any information he might have on the sale of the railroad, and what he thought its value might be. Camden replied on November 2, indicating that he personally knew little of the matter. He did advance the idea that because Blair had borrowed the $100,000 for the initial payment on October 10 from a St. Louis bank, that Kerens was behind the deal and that the Davis-Elkins interests would hold one third of the purchase and the Gould interests two thirds. He also indicated that grounds for litigation existed in the misuse of the stock owned by Wood and Wirt counties in the Little Kanawha Railroad. He also reported that the railroad was in a very dilapidated condition and only earning enough to cover expenses.

Camden concluded by encouraging the B. & O. to control the line and offered any assistance to achieve this outcome.

The Braxton Coal Company was finally sold to Kerens, acting for Davis and Elkins, on November 6 when $218,000 was paid. A final payment of $125,000 was due in December. The final payment of $250,000 for the Little Kanawha Railroad was made by Blair and Fulton on November 7. A last ditch effort was made by the B. & O. to buy the nearly 2,000 shares of Little Kanawha Railroad stock held by Wood and Wirt counties (out of 3,595 issued), but this was thwarted because public sentiment was firmly against the B. & O. and the Pennsylvania.

Elkins wrote to Davis on November 8, outlining discussions he had had with Carnegie, Twombley and others as to whether to build a trunk line or to sell out. Elkins and Landstreet also met with George Baer, president of the Reading, still an independent road at this time, and offered to sell him the West Virginia Central at $200 per share. Baer thought this was too expensive and proposed to lease the railroad for $600,000 per year for five years and then $800,000 per year thereafter. Elkins refused the offer as he thought a sale was preferable. He later met with Cassatt and informed him of these discussions, and was surprised at the decidedly negative view Cassatt held of the value of the West Virginia Central, which Elkins thought was due to the advice Cassatt was receiving from Berwind. Cassatt did allow Elkins to sell the stock in the West Virginia Central held by the Pennsylvania if a sale could be achieved. Elkins recommended to Davis that they sell to the Reading at $190 per share, but doubted if Baer would go above $175.

John T. Davis wrote to his father on November 9, wishing that the elder Davis were at home so that some definite steps could be taken. He thought that Elkins's "dickering with everybody is dangerous," and recommended that Davis acquire waterfront property at Yorktown, as other syndicates, including Rinehart, were doing in the region.

Not all the news at this time concerned the future of the West Virginia Central. Bretz received a telegram on November 11 informing him that between 75 and 100 houses had burnt down at Thomas the previous evening, including eight belonging to the Davis Coal and Coke Company. No damage was done to any railroad property. A great many people lost all their possessions and a subscription was taken up throughout West Virginia and Maryland to help the destitute. The railroad contributed $500 and Davis and Elkins each contributed a further $100 each. The West Virginia Central also provided free transportation for the victims who wished to go to stay with relatives or friends. Bretz later reported that seven "Italian shanties" had been destroyed but three more were being erected, "in mean time have them in box cars."

It was also announced that Wilson Kistler of Stock Haven, Pennsylvania, had purchased land in Elkins for the erection of a tannery. Work was expected to start in the spring of 1902 and to provide employment for up to 150 men when completed.

By November 12, even Elkins was becoming discouraged at the progress of the negotiations with the Reading. He reported to Davis that George Baer had materially changed his tactics and was now trying to depreciate the property. Elkins claimed that Baer originally offered $17,000,000 or was willing to rent the West Virginia Central for $800,000 per annum but now was unwilling to consider the price of $200 per share that Elkins wanted. Baer also stated that the coal lands were not as valuable as claimed. Since this was at about the same time that the Pennsylvania had expressed an interest in absorbing the Reading into the community of interest group, such a policy shift was not surprising, although this was not known to Elkins. He did suspect that the Vanderbilts had gone into the Reading, and by November 14 he was convinced that the "Vanderbilts, Reading and Pennsylvania have gotten closer together and reached a conclusion about our property, and as to which was to acquire it."

Because of such activities, Elkins swung round to John T. Davis's viewpoint and started to put together an underwriting to build east and west. Elkins proposed to construct a railway from the Lakes, at or near Cleveland, through Ohio, West Virginia and Virginia to tidewater, at or near Newport News. The road was to be called the West Virginia Trunk Line Railroad, with a capital stock of $45,000,000. The total length of the new railroad would be about 680 miles, of which 150 miles already existed in Virginia and West Virginia. The railroad would purchase 100,000 acres of coal lands and would also acquire the existing railroads. The following individuals signed up for the underwriting on November 12:

H. G. Davis and Brother	$2,000,000
(By John T. Davis)	
S. B. Elkins	1,500,000
R. C. Kerens	1,500,000
E. D. Kenna	1,500,000
F. S. Landstreet and associates	1,000,000

In addition, Ramsey and his associates were expected to subscribe $6,000,000, W. A. Clark, (a senator from Montana), $2,000,000, and various other parties, $5,000,000.

Elkins wrote to Davis on November 15, mentioning the underwriting and his indecisiveness as to whether they should join with Gould, or whether to go forward and build a line themselves. Elkins favored selling the West Virginia Central and "... taking some securities in a company formed to get from the Lakes to the sea." A couple of days later, Landstreet also advised Davis to consider building their own road east and west. In connection with the proposed new road, Elkins met with Rinehart of the C. & W., and was convinced by him that the North River Gap was the best possible way through the mountains to the Shenandoah Valley. He also talked to Spencer of the Southern who assured Elkins of fair treatment in Harrisonburg. Spencer, however, did not want to be directly involved for fear of upsetting the Pennsylvania.

Elkins continued to dicker with both Fuller, who offered $14,000,000 for the railroad north of Parsons, (Elkins wanted $16,000,000) and with Gould on a Lakes to the sea line. However, Elkins was convinced that if the Davis-Elkins interests joined Gould in some way, that the Pennsylvania might ultimately induce Gould to abandon West Virginia (by, for instance, allowing Gould to use the B. & O. east of Pittsburgh), and then the West Virginia Central would be even more isolated than at present. At one point he became quite paranoid and thought that Fuller was acting on behalf of the Reading.

Elkins did decide, because of a possible threat from the C. & O. obtaining possession of Jennings Gap and Dry River Gap, to order Latrobe to obtain rights of way through the two gaps to prevent the West Virginia Central from being bottled up. The importance of this move was emphasized when reports circulated that the C. & O. had

obtained control of the C. & W. At the same time, reports were received of survey parties operating in the vicinity of the Middle Fork. It was thought that these parties were from the B. & O., which was looking for a way to prevent a westward expansion of the West Virginia Central. It turned out later that they were working for N. T. Arnold and the Belington and Northern Railroad.

On November 19, Elkins was approached by two unnamed individuals, who hoped to interest the West Virginia Central in purchasing the W. Md. It was claimed that the City of Baltimore was only entitled to $8,000,000 for bonds and money advanced to the W. Md., rather than the $12,000,000 claimed by the city. Elkins reported to Davis that for an expenditure of $10,000,000 they could acquire the W. Md., finish the line to Curtis Bay and build a passenger station on the edge of Baltimore. Once again Latrobe was asked to review the route between Cumberland and Cherry Point. This line of action does not seem to have been pursued any further.

Loree contacted Camden on November 21 to ask about the stock of Wood and Wirt counties in the Little Kanawha Railroad, but was advised not to pursue the purchase of the stock until the excitement had died down. Camden recommended that the B. & O. employ, as an advisor, V. B. Archer, who was a large stockholder in the Little Kanawha Railroad and was also that company's attorney. In Camden's words, "Archer knows more about the inside of all this matter than anyone else ... and also shape things up for the purchase of the stock." Camden reported that Jackson, who had earlier tried to break up the sale, was in sympathy with the B. & O. and he would arrange a meeting between Loree and Jackson if Loree so desired. However, nothing seems to have come of these schemes.

Camden was not about to let his sympathies for the B. & O. stand in the way of his own business dealings. He wrote to Elkins on November 30, assuring him that the First National Bank of Parkersburg would loan him $10,000 (at five percent interest) to secure the purchase of the Braxton Coal Company.

The Parkersburg Sentinel, on November 22, carried an interview with Ramsey who claimed that the Wabash was not looking for a route east of Pittsburgh to the sea. He also claimed that a route to the coast through West Virginia would be too long. Ramsey went on to say that the Little Kanawha Railroad would provide a good coal producing route for the Wheeling and Lake Erie, but made no mention of its ownership.

However, on the ground, things were somewhat different. On November 23, the Little Kanawha Railroad was released by the receivers, Blair was appointed president and Ramsey's men appointed directors. Ramsey had been over the ground between Parkersburg and Zanesville and was convinced a line could be built cutting 26 miles off the present route via Marietta. Ramsey had survey crews out along the Little Kanawha River and he asked the West Virginia Central to survey a route from the head of the Little Kanawha River to a junction with the West Virginia Central. This action was more to John T. Davis's liking and he immediately sent a survey team, in charge of Moore, to the Middle Fork to survey a line to French Creek. By the beginning of December, the whole territory between Roaring Creek and the Little Kanawha River was being crisscrossed by survey parties.

Landstreet wrote to Davis on November 27, informing him that the barge "Davis" (previously the "Obed Baxter") had been sunk in a storm on November 23. The barge, along with two other barges, was being towed from Philadelphia to New England. When the storm struck, the tug took the crews off the other two barges, but the captain and crew of the "Davis" stuck to their posts and went down with the barge.

Gould's plans for the Little Kanawha Railroad became clear with the signing of the Little Kanawha Syndicate Agreement on December 2, 1901. The purpose of the Syndicate was to purchase the Little Kanawha Railroad and to extend it eastward, to purchase or build a railroad from Parkersburg to Zanesville and to purchase coal lands. The Syndicate was to raise $6,000,000 from its subscribers for these purposes and was to be managed by Gould, Ramsey and William. E. Guy. Davis and Elkins took an interest in the Little Kanwaha Syndicate but the date when they joined is not known. By far the largest individual subscriber was Gould himself. The underwriting was later increased to $8,000,000, with Davis and Elkins each taking $250,000; other individuals took all but $270,000 of this amount, giving (as per a report dated May 19, 1903) a total subscription of $7,730,000. Subscribers were asked to make partial payments whenever the Syndicate made a call (usually for five or ten percent) to ensure that sufficient funds were available for the work on the various projects. Among the names of the subscribers as listed on January 29, 1906 were the following:

George J. Gould	$1,635,000
J. T. Blair	50,000
Joseph Ramsey, Jr.	311,059
E. D. Fulton	20,000
N. T. Arnold	325,583
S. B. Elkins	176,149
H. G. Davis	175,437

On the same day that the Little Kanawha Syndicate Agreement was signed, Elkins telegraphed Davis saying that Fuller wanted a decision on the sale of the West Virginia Central. Elkins followed the telegram with a letter to Davis in which he again proposed the building of a new trunk road from the Lakes to the Atlantic. Elkins admitted he did not know what Gould or Ramsey thought of the proposition but was to meet with Ramsey in a few days.

On December 6, Elkins asked Davis whether they should sell the line north of Elkins for $15,000,000, and if so how the equipment should be divided. Fuller was getting impatient and again on December 7, Elkins telegraphed Davis for a decision, but by December 12, Elkins telegraphed to say that matters were in abeyance.

However, by December 16, a deal was finally struck with Fuller, and by December 27, details of the agreement began to emerge. The present owners would continue in control until the final payment was made. Davis would also have the option to buy back the extensions from Elkins if he wished to incorporate them into the Gould schemes or into a scheme of his own.

The contract for the sale of the West Virginia Central was signed on January 4, 1902, by T. B. Davis, Elkins, Kerens and Landstreet for the vendors, and by Fuller and the North American Trust Company for the purchasers. The agreed price per share was $170. The Davis interests controlled 89 percent of the outstanding stock of the West Virginia Central and agreed to sign over 94,340 shares on a payment

of $1,000,000 to be made on January 4. It was agreed that a further $2,000,000 (plus four percent interest) would be paid by April 1, 1902 and the balance by January 2, 1903. If the purchaser failed to make either the second or third payments, the amount paid would be forfeit. It was also agreed that the existing management would complete the C. & I., but that rights-of-way obtained east of the C. & I. and west of Belington were to be excluded.

A supplemental agreement was signed on the same day, which recognized that the vendors might wish to construct a line from the Ohio River to Pendleton or Pocahontas counties. In this event, Davis could buy back from the new owners, the C. & I., and the Huttonsville and Belington extensions for $2,000,000 and had until March 1 to make this decision.

Elkins met with Cassatt on January 8 and purchased the 3,000 shares held by the Pennsylvania Railroad in the West Virginia Central. Any comments Cassatt may have had on the sale were not recorded.

Reports of the sale appeared in the newspapers on January 7. The Parkersburg Sentinel noted that the road had been sold to the Pennsylvania for $17,000,000, although this was denied by officials of the Pennsylvania. The paper also carried a report that it had been sold to the Wabash. Other papers noted that a New York stockbroker named Fuller had been involved. On January 8, Thomas Davis confirmed that the road had been sold, but for more than $17,000,000, and that we "are well pleased with the sale." Elkins, however, denied that a sale had taken place. In a letter to Davis on January 11, he noted that the sale would not be complete until all the money had been paid, and that "it is really an option on which $1,000,000 payment has been made."

Davis was reported to have left Mexico on January 10, but even while he was still in Mexico he was plotting his next moves for the Roaring Creek and Gilmer coalfields. John T. Davis reported on January 11 that he had opened negotiations with Berwind for his Roaring Creek interests.

Hendley reported on the same day that the Virginia legislature had been approached to amend the charter of the Central Railway of Virginia to allow it to build to tidewater. Hendley noted that December had been a very stormy month and not much work had been done on the C. & I. It was expected that tunnel No. 1 would be ready for track by March 15.

Bretz resumed his reports to Davis on January 13, noting that Courtney had resigned as superintendent of motive power and had been replaced by I. N. Kalbaugh. Bretz also was looking for a maintenance-of-way engineer to replace Douglas, who had left in October 1901, but had not been successful. He noted that the Mount Vernon Bridge Company had commenced the erection of steelwork at the 21st bridge.

Davis returned from Mexico on January 15, 1902, and resumed his management of the West Virginia Central. He was informed by Sutherland, the general land agent, that the C. & O. had laid tracks to the river at Durbin and that it should be possible to get ties cut along the C. & O. delivered to the south end of the C. & I.

Davis began actively to seek a route to the west through his coal land on Roaring Creek and the Gilmer County field. Moore reported on January 27 on the earlier surveys that had been carried out between the head of Roaring Creek and the Middle Fork. At the same time John T. Davis reported that Berwind owned 25,000 acres along

Roaring Creek, 23 miles of railroad and three engines. Berwind was asking $1,000,000 for the property and claimed that an offer of $900,000 had already been refused. Davis asked Dailey to investigate the titles to Berwind's properties, as some were in dispute.

Moore did an actual survey of the route between Roaring Creek and the Middle Fork and on February 2, he reported that the route was impractical.

Davis met Gould and Ramsey on January 24 to discuss the coal lands situation in West Virginia. Ramsey was perturbed to learn that Jackson and White were trying to encourage the B. & O. to build to lands they owned in the Gilmer field and asked Davis to look into the matter. A further meeting was arranged for January 29 to divide up the field and, at Davis's suggestion, to confine Arnold to as small a section as possible. He later told John T. Davis that Gould and Ramsey were more likely to work in harmony with the Davis interests than was Arnold, but Arnold was to be treated fairly.

John T. Davis met with Fulton on February 5 to arrange a fair division of the Gilmer field. John T. Davis told his father that he thought Fulton had options on 60,000 acres, but this included only 4,000 acres of merchantable coal. John T. Davis thought Fulton was not to be trusted and would go back on his deal with Ramsey if he got a better offer.

Bretz, who had suffered an acute car shortage all fall due to the discrimination by the Pennsylvania and the B. & O., wasted no time in requesting approval for the purchase of new steel cars from the new owners. All such major purchases were to be approved by Fuller and the approval was granted on February 1. The Cambria Steel Company received the order for 500, 100,000 lb. steel cars to be delivered by October 1902. The total cost of the order was $612,500 and delivery of the cars was expected to start on April 15. Later in the year an additional 300 cars were ordered also from Cambria. Delivery of the new cars did not start until the middle of August; no reason for the delay was given. The new cars were numbered beginning with No. 5000, which is shown in Fig. 160.

Fig. 160. West Virginia Central hopper No. 5000. No. 5000 was the first of the Vanderbilt designed steel hoppers to be delivered to the West Virginia Central and the first steel car to be owned by the railroad
Collection of the Western Maryland Railway Historical Society

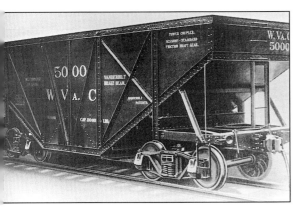

Bretz reported another wreck on the Blackwater grade on February 9. Engine No. 32 was pulling 17 cars loaded with lumber up the grade with No. 34 pushing at the rear, when a water stop was made at Tub Run. When the train restarted it broke into two parts and the rear section, including No. 34, rolled back down the grade. The engineer and fireman jumped to safety but the engine and cars wrecked on the bend at Big Run. The engine was not badly damaged but the cars were smashed.

Word of the sale of the West Virginia Central finally reached Railway Age, which reported on February 7 that "the opinion prevails that the purchase is virtually in the interest of the Gould system."

Davis wrote to Berwind on February 8, saying that $1,000,000 was too much for the Roaring Creek property as there was far less coal there than originally thought. However, by February 17 he informed John T. Davis and Bretz that he had purchased the property and expected to take possession in April. The price paid was reported by Davis to be $875,000. At the same time Davis reported that Gould had agreed to join them in building a line to tidewater and take an interest in the coal lands. He also received an encouraging report from Moore on the feasibility of a line from the Tygart Valley River to the Middle Fork. With the outline of a future trunk line through West Virginia beginning to take shape, Davis told Fuller on February 18 that he would repurchase the extensions south and west of Elkins. However, by February 20, he informed John T. Davis that he was not going to take the extensions because he had no written agreement with Gould and Ramsey on the new road.

The decision upset John T. Davis, who felt that not taking the branches and extending them would be a big mistake. He pointed out to his father that there was more lumber on the C. & I. than ever there was on the West Virginia Central, and that this lumber would have to move north. He also spelled out the vast amount of coal owned by the Davis-Elkins interests and that this could move over a road that was completed east and west. He also thought that Gould would have to join them in such an east-west line. John T. Davis also asked Bower for an assessment. Bower estimated that the Davis-Elkins interests owned approximately 1,200,000,000 tons of coal, which if moved at a rate of 5,000,000 tons per annum, would keep the line going for 240 years.

On the same day Davis informed Thomas B. Davis of his decision not to take the extensions. In this case, the decision was supported by his brother.

Davis's mind was made up and on February 24 he informed Fuller that he was not going to take the branches. Fuller wrote back saying, "it may be for the best, ultimately, and that all possible complications will be avoided by keeping the entire property together."

On the West Virginia Central, Bretz was having a particularly hard winter. He was able to report that the bridge at 21st had been finished on February 19 (Fig. 161), and was ordered by Davis to erect the old bridge at Chenowith Creek on the Huttonsville extension. Bretz reported on February 20 that it was 12 degrees below zero at Thomas and the low temperatures throughout the region soon froze the North Branch of the Potomac River. By February 26, Bretz was able to report that the ice was beginning to break up and that fortunately there was no damage to

Fig. 161. B. & O. (foreground) and W. Md. bridges at 21st circa 1911

the track. This optimism was to prove premature. The ice jams were followed by high water, which closed the road from February 26 to March 2. Bretz wrote to Davis that the weather during February was the worst he had ever encountered during his tenure on the West Virginia Central. The bad weather continued into early March when 18 inches of snow were reported at Elk Garden and ten inches at Elkins, which prevented work being finished on some of the damaged sections of the track. On February 8, Bretz reported that a pier on the bridge at Potomac had been undermined and a trestle would have to be built before permanent repairs could be made. When the situation returned to normal, Bretz requested that four new freight engines be purchased as well as two new passenger cars. Bretz was advised to wait until after April 1 to ensure that the new owners made the second payment.

On March 5, Davis wrote to Fuller outlining the work that still remained to be finished on the C. & I. This included the bridge crossing Shavers Fork and considerable work between Shavers Fork and the Greenbrier. Latrobe estimated that this work would be finished by July. Bretz reported tunnel No. 1 would be finished by the middle of March and asked permission to lay track as far as Shavers Fork. Davis arranged with Axtell for rails to be delivered at the south end of the line by the C. & O. so that work could proceed from both ends. Davis also reported meeting with Smith and Reinhart who still hoped to interest Davis in a joint project to build to tidewater, but Davis was noncommittal.

Davis now had decided to build west from a junction with the West Virginia Central in the vicinity of Roaring Creek over to the Middle Fork and Buckhannon, and asked Bower to look over the proposed route with Moore and John T. Davis.

At this time, Davis was committed to buying coal lands in both the Gilmer field and in the Kincheloe field further north for the Little Kanawha Syndicate. Problems continued with Fulton who also was supposed to be buying for the Syndicate but seemed to be in competition with Davis. Davis complained to Ramsey that all these conflicting efforts were driving up the prices of the coal lands and should be stopped. Ramsey later telegraphed that Davis was supposed to keep north of the Little Kanawha River and Fulton would keep to the south.

Since the beginning of the year, reports had circulated of Gould's interest in the W. Md. but these had been denied. Several parties had expressed an interest in buying the W. Md. from the city of Baltimore, but the mayor denied a secret sale would occur and said there would be a public offering. By March, Gould had decided to purchase the W. Md. and organized a syndicate known as The West Virginia Central and Western Maryland Purchase Syndicate to purchase the West Virginia Central from Fuller, and to purchase the W. Md. The Syndicate would also complete the W. Md. from Cherry Run to Cumberland, build tidewater terminals in Baltimore, and build from Belington to meet the Wabash. The Syndicate agreement was signed on March 12 and was to raise $20,000,000. Fuller wrote to Kerens on March 14 noting that Kerens had joined the Syndicate for $250,000 and had turned over his W. Md. stock to the Syndicate. Elkins reported to Davis on the Syndicate on March 16 noting that he had invested $200,000 but hoped that Davis would take half of this amount, which Davis later did. Elkins was pleased to see Gould's involvement in the Syndicate as this was what he had hoped to achieve during the negotiations for the sale of the West Virginia

Central. Elkins also noted that Landstreet had invested $500,000, and was to become highly involved in the activities of the syndicate. Elkins sent Davis a list of the Syndicate subscribers as of March 16, which included the following names:

George J. Gould	$1,000,000
Edwin Gould	500,000
Howard Gould	500,000
W. S. Pierce	500,000
E. L. Fuller	500,000
F. S. Landstreet	500,000
Myron T. Herrick	500,000
Cornelius Vanderbilt	500,000
R. C. Kerens	250,000

Eventually there were to be 155 subscribers to the Syndicate. Half of George Gould's subscription was later taken up by John D. Rockefeller.

On March 17, four bids for the W. Md. were opened by a committee of Baltimore City Council. The bids were from Hambleton and Company for $6,000,000 cash, the Fuller Syndicate for $8,509,819, and the Reading Railroad for $7,004,098. The fourth bid was somewhat of a mystery but was for $11,000,000 of which $3,000,000 would be cash. The successful bidder was expected to be announced on April 2, but on April 7 all the bids were rejected and the city was to advertise for new proposals. New proposals were received from the same four bidders on April 17; all the bids were increased from the initial bid. On April 29, Landstreet reported that the Fuller Syndicate had made progress with the council and that the only opposition was from one council member who was acting for the Reading. George Gould wrote to the mayor of Baltimore pledging his support of the Fuller bid and confirming that the new construction mentioned in the bid would be carried out. This seemed to be the crucial factor and the sale of the W. Md. to the Fuller Syndicate was announced on May 7.

Davis wrote to Landstreet on May 10, congratulating him on securing the W. Md. By now, Davis was definitely a lame duck president and his interest had shifted away from the West Virginia Central to his new road west to the Gilmer coalfield. This was known originally as the Midland Railway but on May 6 Davis sent an application for the incorporation of the Coal and Coke Railway proposed to run to Glenville. Construction of the new road was under the supervision of Bower, who had been "borrowed" from the West Virginia Central.

Davis was instructed by the new owners, on May 3, to purchase the New York mine at Simpson for the West Virginia Central under an option that expired on June 1.

Davis wrote to Fuller on May 12 mentioning that the repairs caused by the floods earlier in the year had been finished. He also reported that the air shaft at Henry was finished and some coal was being brought up and the main shaft was down 300 feet. Galbreath reported in July that 1.1/2 cars of coal per day were being shipped from Shaft No. 1 at Henry and work was being hurried to bring Shaft No. 2, which had been started in the fall of 1901, into production (Fig. 162). Galbreath complained that the coal seams in the vicinity of the shafts were very irregular; later reports showed that the coal seams in the vicinity of Henry were quite different from the seams in the remainder of the Thomas field. The new mines were also quite

Fig. 162. Shaft No. 1 at Henry, circa 1908

gassy; an explosion on December 2 injured three workers. For the year ending June 1903, production was 15,168 tons. Production peaked at 192,242 tons for the year ending June 1907 and declined to 93,599 tons for the year ending June 1921. The mine closed in the late 1920's.

Davis also mentioned that Bretz had requested that four new freight engines be purchased and an order was placed on May 11 with Baldwin, the price for each engine being $14,250. Bretz also requested that four new passenger cars be purchased, and this was approved by Winslow Pierce on June 11. The engines were delivered in early 1903. The last, No. 47, was delivered in April and is shown in its W. Md. days as No. 458 in Fig. 252 at Cumberland in the 1940's. The order for three cars was placed with the Pullman Company (Figs. 163 and 164); the combination baggage and passenger car was built at Elkins. The new cars were delivered in 1902.

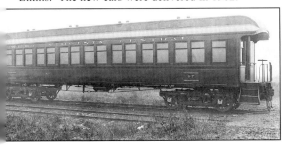

Fig. 163. Passenger Car No. 47 (exterior)
Collection of the Smithsonian Institution P6698

Fig. 164. Passenger Car No. 47 (interior)
Collection of the Smithsonian Institution P6699

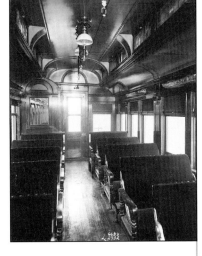

No. 7 on the passenger train was not derailed although the engine of the work train was knocked from the tracks. The engineer and fireman of the passenger train were both injured; the fireman later died of his injuries. The cause of the wreck was due to the watch of the engineer of the work train being 12 minutes slow. The rule was that work trains were to be out of the way of passenger trains ten minutes before they were due.

Davis notified Bretz that the Tygarts River Lumber Company expected to erect a large mill at Mill Creek and to put in a siding for the company. On May 1, the lumber company had purchased from the Mill Creek Coal and Lumber Company, a Davis holding company, the timber on 8766 acres for $30 per acre. The company erected a large mill, which is shown in Fig. 165, a few years later. Mill Creek was already the site of the mill operated by Hench, Dromgold and Shull and was to become an important shipping point for the West

Virginia Central. The company completed a new depot at the town during 1902 (Fig. 166).

Latrobe was instructed by Davis to close up the surveys east of the C. & I. by July 1, and to turn over all the profiles, blue prints and maps of the work. Latrobe reported at the end of July that the final report was almost ready and would be forwarded in a day or two. On September 11, Davis complained to Latrobe about the cost of the C. & I., which had now cost about twice the original estimate. Latrobe's reply is not known as he was reported to have died on September 19, at age 69 years.

Fig. 165. Mill of the Tygarts River Lumber Company, Mill Creek, (undated)

Fig. 166. Depot at Mill Creek

Bretz reported another head on collision on May 16, this time between a passenger train and a stopped work train. Engine

On July 1, Galbreath advised Davis that mines of the Davis Coal and Coke Company would no longer be referred to by name but would be given a number as follows:

Mine	Proposed Number	Coal
Elk Garden	6	Big Vein
Franklin	7	" "
Windom	8	" "
Hartmansville	9	" "
Buxton	17	Six Foot
Hampshire	18	" "
Montgomery Run	19	" "
No. 20	20	" "
Henry Thomas Seam	22	Upper Freeport or Thomas Seam
Thomas Drift	23	" "
Thomas No. 2	24	" "
Thomas No. 3	25	" "
Henry Davis Seam	33	Upper Kittanning or Davis Seam
Thomas Shaft	34	" "
Coketon No. 1	35	" "
Coketon No. 2	36	" "
Coketon No. 3	37	" "
New York	41	Fairmont or Pittsburgh Seam

The list includes all the mines that were to be included in the sale; the mines at Junior and Harding were specifically excluded.

The formal transfer of ownership of the W. Md. from the city of Baltimore to the Fuller Syndicate was completed on June 27. A temporary board of directors was constituted with a permanent board being constituted at a meeting on July 8. Winslow Pierce was the new president of the company and Landstreet vice-president and Fuller, Ramsey and George Gould were added to the board.

Discrimination by the Pennsylvania and the B. & O. in the distribution of cars continued to be a problem for the West Virginia Central throughout the summer. Landstreet noted that loaning the B. & O. engines to help them move freight cars had not brought any reciprocal consideration. Landstreet and Pierce met with President Loree of the B. & O. on July 8 and were told that the B. & O. could not favor the branch lines when equipment was needed on the mainline. Loree also said that the B. & O. would not consider a proposition for the use of its tracks between Cumberland and Cherry Run. This was a mistake as it gave the Gould interests the approval it needed to start planning its own track between these two points. The B. & O. responded by giving the W. Md. 30 days notice that traffic previously transferred to the W. Md. at Cherry Run, would be moved over the C. V. starting on September 1, 1902.

Bretz was contacted on July 17 by C. E. Doyle, general manager of the C. & O., to discuss building terminal facilities at Durbin. Bretz recommended that the C. & O. build a depot and the cost be split between the two companies. Davis wrote to Kerens on August 16 and told him that both tunnels were finished on the C. & I. and 15 miles of track laid from Elkins (Fig. 167). Two days later, Davis informed Pierce that the C. & I. should be finished in the fall and that track laying was proceeding at the rate of 1/4 mile per day.

Earlier, Davis had discussed with Pierce the contents of a report for the Annual General Meeting to be held on August 12. Davis noted that he had merged the profit of the Buxton and Landstreet stores into the figures for the Coal Department as, "It is not thought judicious to make public the profits of the stores, as they are a sensitive factor in all coal operations; and they are so closely allied to the coal and coke operations it was deemed appropriate that the profits should be credited to them."

It was reported on August 7 that the Weaver Coal Company had changed its name to the Weaver Coal and Coke Company following a large infusion of capital. It was announced also that the B. & B. C. depot in Belington was nearing completion (Fig. 168). A similar depot at Weaver was reported to be under construction at the end of the year and a large number of coke ovens also were being built (Fig. 169).

Belington was now an important railroad center with five different railroads entering the town. The bridge of the B. & N. across the

Fig. 167. East portal of tunnel No. 1, December 1917
Collection of the Western Maryland Railway Historical Society

Fig. 168. Belington and Beaver Creek Railroad depot, Belington, 1917
Collection of the Western Maryland Railway Historical Society

Fig. 169. Coke ovens at Weaver, circa 1910

Fig. 170. Tygart Valley River bridge of the Belington and Northern Railroad

Tygart Valley River was completed in November 1901 (Fig. 170), the tracks reaching the town in March 1902. It was anticipated also that the Wabash extension of the Little Kanawha Railroad, known as the Burnsville and Eastern Railroad, would enter the town. The B. & E. had been chartered in July 1902, and was planned to extend from Belington to Montrose on the West Virginia Central.

On September 21, it was announced that a new limekiln would commence operating on the Dry Fork Railroad about a mile from Hendricks. Coal and limestone had been discovered in 1898 by Richard Pearson, who had taken options on the land. Pearson interested Henry Weaver and the Weaver Coal Company in the property and Weaver furnished the capital to build two kilns. In 1902 a corporation, the West Virginia Lime and Cement Company was formed to operate the kilns, with Pearson as manager. This arrangement did not seem to suit Pearson who sued Weaver and the Weaver Coal and Coke Company in January 1903, to have the company placed into the hands of a receiver. The enterprise did not survive the legal battles, and by 1923 the site was reported to be derelict.

During 1902, there was considerable activity along the West Virginia Central involving the development of new mines by the Davis Coal and Coke Company and independent operators. Davis was contacted on April 16 by the Garrett County Coal and Mining Company, owner of 1,800 acres of coal lands in Maryland (Fig. 171), to arrange for a tipple at Gleason Flats above Harrison. The company had opened a mine at Dill, below Harrison, but wished to abandon it and expand at Gleason Flats. Eventually a small town, Dodson, developed on the Maryland side of the North Branch at Gleason Flats. In June, Bretz agreed to install a siding for the company about a mile above Harrison to serve two new mines, Dodson 1 and 2. Dill later became known as Potomac Manor and was the site of several coal operations. Early in July, the Monroe Coal Company purchased the plant of the Watson-Loy Coal Company, located at Barnum. The Watson-Loy Coal Company had been incorporated in May 1898, and owned 1,800 acres of coal lands on the Maryland side of the North Branch. A 216 foot cable bridge was constructed across the Potomac to deliver the coal to the West Virginia Central.

The West Virginia Central had commenced grading a spur from

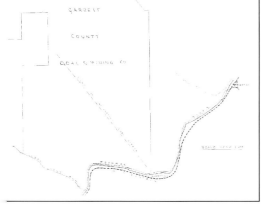

Fig. 171. Map of the coal lands owned near Harrison by the Garrett County Coal Mining Company
West Virginia and Regional History Collection,
West Virginia University Library

Switchback on the Elk Garden branch to Hartmansville, a distance of 3.1/2 miles, to a new mine at that point. The extension was due to be completed by October 1; the first coal was shipped over the extension on March 21, 1903.

Bretz reported on September 12 that A. Thompson of the Blackwater Lumber Company had purchased the mill of Thomas Burger and Son located at Douglas. Thompson wanted to haul logs from Douglas to Davis and hence extend the life of the Davis mill by six or seven years, and asked Bretz for a price for hauling 60,000 pound gondolas of logs on the West Virginia Central. Hauling logs did not prove to be successful and Thompson built a narrow gauge railroad from Douglas to Davis to deliver the logs. The mill at Douglas was closed and offered for sale in October 1903. The railroad was later extended along the north rim of the Blackwater Canyon and was know locally as the Limerock Railroad.

On October 15, McGraw wrote to Davis asking to purchase rails and ties that were currently stored at the south end of the C. & I. waiting to be laid. McGraw had incorporated a new railroad, the Greenbrier, Morgantown and Pittsburgh, to build along the East Fork of the Greenbrier from Durbin to the site of a new tannery. Unfortunately, the C. & O. had the same idea, and succeeded in laying track through The Narrows before McGraw, even though McGraw owned the land. Involved in the scheme with McGraw was Rease, which probably did not help McGraw's cause with Davis. Davis wrote to Rease on October 17 saying he was short of ties for the C. & I., and also had no spare rails. McGraw and the C. & O. engaged in the inevitable legal battle, but eventually the C. & O. completed a line to Winterburn, some five miles from Durbin.

On October 23, Davis noted in his diary that all the old directors of the West Virginia Central met with Winslow Pierce and had tendered their resignations. Gould had not waited for the January 2, 1903 deadline to complete the purchase of the West Virginia Central, but had launched a $25,000,000 bond issue on September 10 to pay for the properties. The new board consisted of George Gould, Howard Gould, Pierce, Fuller, Landstreet, Lawrence Greer, and H. C. Deming. Pierce was elected president and Landstreet became vice-president. Davis's connection with the West Virginia Central was not entirely severed, as he was still responsible for overseeing the completion of the C. & I.

The final statement for the purchase of the West Virginia Central is shown below as recorded by Davis in his diary:

| Stock deposited with Trust Co. | 103,497 shares |
| | $170 per share |

	$17,594,490.00
Less amount paid	3,000,000.00
	14,594,490.00
Interest due January 4 to October 20 (inc.)	470,266.90
Amount due	15,064,756.90
On hand, Davis Nat. Bank	47,470.92
	15,112,227.82
Amount to be paid Mr. Gorman	70,000.00
	15,042,227.82
Amount per share	$155.42

H. G. Davis & Bro.	21,102 shares @ $155.42			$3,279,672.84
H. G. Davis	14,246	"	"	"	2,214,113.32
T. B. Davis	8,765	"	"	"	1,362,256.30
S. B. Elkins	25,653	"	"	"	3,986,989.26
R. C. Kerens	12,428	"	"	"	1,931,559.76
H. G. Buxton	2,339	"	"	"	363,527.38
F. S. Landstreet	1,677	"	"	"	260,639.34

With the completion of the C. & I. expected soon, interest in the timberlands along the railroad increased. On October 16, Davis agreed to lease to W. S. Burger land for a mill site at Flint for $50 per year. Burger also purchased 1,700 acres of timber from Davis near Glady. A month later Davis reported selling the timber off lands along Shavers Fork to R. R. Rumbarger at $20 per acre.

The big news at the end of 1902 was yet another wreck on the Blackwater grade. This time, engine No. 41 (Fig. 172), with a 34-car

Fig. 172. Engine No. 41 and crew at Hendricks on December 1, 1902

Collection of the Western Maryland Railway Historical Society

train, left Douglas just after 4:00 P.M. on December 2, heading down the grade. The train gathered speed in spite of the application of the brakes and sand. The engineer, John T. Jankey, reversed the engine but to no avail, and by the time the train reached Tub Run it was doing between 35 and 40 miles per hour according to the fireman, L. Cross. Cross urged Jankey to jump before the train reached Big Run, but the engineer refused. Cross jumped before Big Run was reached but Jankey went over with the engine. Alva Wolfe, the front brakeman also jumped, and both he and Cross were slightly injured. The three remaining crewmen were at the rear of the train that remained on the track. Wreck crews were called from both Thomas and Elkins, but the body of the engineer was not found for 48 hours. Engine No. 41 was not returned to service until May 1903.

At the end of the year it was reported that work on the W. Md. extension to tidewater in Baltimore had commenced. This was in keeping with the Fuller Syndicate's promise to the city to build the extensions as rapidly as possible. It also was noted that Landstreet had been elected president of the Davis Coal and Coke Company and

L. F. Timmerman secretary.

One of the first items of business for President Pierce in 1903, was to send Davis annual pass No. 1 for use on the West Virginia Central in recognition of Davis's service. The two railroads retained their own passes initially, but later a combined pass was issued (Fig. 173). The contract for the sale of the West Virginia Central had included a clause requiring the issuance of annual passes to the vendors and their families, and also the free passage of their private cars when attached to scheduled passenger trains.

Several new coal companies were formed during 1903 to operate along the West Virginia Central. In January, the Glade Run Coal and Coke Company was incorporated; the first coal being shipped in 1906 from a mine near Schell. In June, the Wabash and Potomac Company was formed to operate near Blaine. The company produced 5,844 tons of coal in 1904, but then disappeared. During the second half of 1903 the Masteller Coal Company shipped the first coal from its mines near Hampshire, approximately one mile from West Virginia Central Junction. This company was to prove one of the longest lived along the West Virginia Central (Fig. 174).

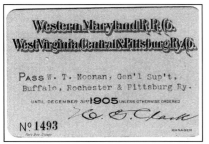

Fig. 173. Combined annual pass of the Western Maryland Rail Road and the West Virginia Central and Pittsburg Railway

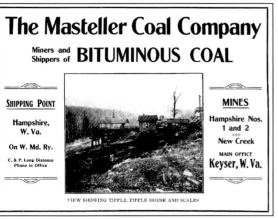

Fig. 174. Masteller Coal Company advertisement Western Maryland Railway Shippers' Guide 1911-1912 *West Virginia and Regional History Collection, West Virginia University Library*

Joseph Ramsey arrived in Elkins on February 11 on a tour of inspection and was quoted as saying the line between Cherry Run and Cumberland had not yet been fully surveyed and no contracts had been awarded. At about the same time Ramsey was elected president of the two railroads in place of Pierce.

Davis wrote to Pierce on February 14, and while recognizing that Pierce was no longer president, he thought that Pierce was the appropriate person to notify of the completion of the C. & I., except for the track laying, and its turnover to the operating department of the West Virginia Central. He noted that the contractors were two years behind schedule, which they claimed was due to improper classification and changes in plans and conditions. The cost of the extension was about twice what had been estimated originally and the contractors were to be assessed a $50 a day penalty for each day over the deadline. Davis proposed to make a tender to the contractors of the amount due to them, but he expected the contractors to sue for a large sum, possibly

$50,000. Davis was a little off in his estimate.

The contractor, Walton, Purcell and Moormen went into receivership, but the receiver sued the C. & I. in January 1911 and won an award of $240,000. The case was appealed to the federal circuit court, which sent the case back for a new trial in the district court. In September 1914 the jury awarded the receiver $159,840.

Changes in the management of the West Virginia Central were reported in April. Bower had tendered his resignation to go with Davis and the Coal and Coke Railway but was not appointed general manager of that road until May 31. Charles A. Steiner was appointed to succeed Bower. Bretz had submitted his resignation as early as February after declining to become general manager of the combined roads. Such a position would have entailed a move to Baltimore and as Bretz had developed other business interests in Cumberland, he elected to stay. His resignation became effective on August 1, and Alexander Robertson was appointed in his place. Robertson had been superintendent of the Middle Division of the Wabash before his appointment. Bretz later became general manager of the Cumberland and Pennsylvania Railroad effective June 1, 1904.

On June 4, in circuit court in Baltimore, a judge granted the W. Md. an order requiring the B. & O. to show cause as to why it should not be permanently enjoined from diverting freight away from the W. Md. The W. Md. claimed that 45,000 cars had been diverted between August 1, 1902 and May 1, 1903, causing a loss of $275,000.

The W. Md. and the B. & O. also came into conflict when the W. Md. filed plans with the Board of Public Works in Maryland for approval of its plans to cross the C. & O. Canal. The move was opposed by the trustees of the bondholders operating the canal, who were represented by Davis's old nemesis, Irving Cross. The board agreed to appoint an independent engineer to report on the plans.

George Gould paid a visit to his new properties on July 13. He was accompanied by Ramsey, Bretz, and officials of the Wabash and Missouri Pacific railroads. Gould arrived in Elkins on July 13, travelling over the B. & O. from Pittsburgh to Belington and then from Belington to Elkins over the West Virginia Central. The party then spent the night at Thomas before continuing to Cumberland. The following day, the party traveled to Cherry Run over the B. & O., and then transferred to the W. Md. for the trip to Baltimore.

Before leaving Pittsburgh, Gould gave a lengthy interview on his plans. The interview was widely reported on July 13. Gould noted that, "It is our purpose to weld the Wabash roads into one grand system before long that will reach from Ogden, Utah and El Paso at the Mexican border in the west, through Kansas City, Pittsburgh to Baltimore. We intend to make the latter city our seaport on the Atlantic. It is a magnificent one but has been neglected. We propose to develop it and make it a great port. We do not intend to go to New York. There is more eclat in a trunk line into the metropolis, of course, but it is too expensive as a freight exporting terminal. Baltimore is the best port of the Atlantic for the exporting of such commodities, as will make up our tonnage, coal, grain and packing house products. We have immense tracts of coal, but I do not think we shall mine it ourselves. Our business is operating a railroad and I believe that our plans will be to leave the tracts to operators and companies much as is done by the Flat Top Association in the Pocahontas region. We are after the tonnage and can secure it that way to a better advantage than if we were mining the coal ourselves. We bought the coal to ensure this tonnage."

Gould was not quite so sure of his position as the article implied. As early as September 1902, Gould had been negotiating with the Pennsylvania for the sale of the Little Kanawha and the Western Maryland Syndicates but the talks ended in failure. The talks resumed again in November 1903, with Cassatt offering to buy both Syndicates and to open up the B. & O. lines east of Pittsburgh to the Wabash. Cassatt adamantly refused to take any of the coal lands owned by the Syndicates and the negotiations collapsed.

Service finally started on the C. & I. on August 1, 1903. A train left Elkins at 8:00 A.M. and arrived at Durbin at 11:45 A.M. The return trip left Durbin at 2:15 P.M. and arrived at Elkins at 6:00 P.M. A freight service was started at the same time.

Work also started on the extension from Cherry Run to Cumberland at about the same time. It was expected that Hancock would be reached in six or seven months and the whole project finished in a year.

The Board of Public Works received the report of its engineer on the W. Md.'s plans to cross the C. & O. Canal in early September, and on September 10, agreed to allow the W. Md. to proceed. The approval was appealed immediately in court by the B. & O.

The W. Md. filed for a preliminary injunction against the B. & O. on September 21 in circuit court in Baltimore to prevent the diversion of freight from the W. Md. at Cherry Run. The case was decided against the W. Md. on February 27, 1904. The W. Md. then appealed the case to the court of appeals in Annapolis.

The trustees of the C. and O. Canal opposed the request of the W. Md. to cross the canal seven times between Cherry Run and Cumberland and the case was heard in October in Hagerstown. The case was decided in favor of the W. Md. on October 17, but was appealed to the Court of Appeals.

A new timetable went into effect on the C. & I. on October 1 (Fig. 175), which showed stops at the more important lumber camps that had sprung up. Stops were listed at Bowden, which had developed a limestone business, Fishing Hawk (later called Bemis), Glady and Burner. Depots were built at these points in the traditional West Virginia Central style (Fig. 176).

The fall of 1903 was marred by a number of serious accidents on the West Virginia Central. The first accident occurred on October 21 when engine No. 19, which had been in the Elkins shops for repairs, was being tested in the yards. At about 2:15 P.M. the engine exploded killing the three people on the engine and sending a shower of debris in all directions (Fig. 177). A piece of boilerplate crashed through a house a hundred yards away and killed Mrs. Agnes Rabbit. Two other individuals who were near No. 19 at the time of the explosion were injured.

On November 9, a passenger train approaching Hendricks hit a cow, knocking the engine off the tracks and into the river. The engineer was slightly injured but no injuries were reported to the passengers or the fireman.

A fire of mysterious origin destroyed the depot at Roaring Creek Junction on November 15. As part of a deal involving the use of the West Virginia Central tracks between the Junction and Elkins by trains of the Coal and Coke Railway, the West Virginia Central agreed to rebuild the depot and charge the C. & C. rental for its use. The new depot was completed during 1904.

At the end of December, it was reported that the right-of-way for the approaches to the tunnel through Knobley Mountain had been secured on the Cumberland extension.

The new year, 1904, did not start any better for the West Virginia Central when, on January 26, a passenger train crashed into the rear of a stationary freight train at Roaring Creek Junction. The fireman was slightly injured, but again no passengers were hurt.

A bill was introduced into the Maryland legislature on February 4 to allow the W. Md. to condemn strips of land along the C. & O. Canal in order for the railway to build bridges across the canal and the Potomac River. The bill was approved on March 4 without a dissenting vote, in spite of the opposition of the B. & O., and was signed by the governor. The last obstacle in the way of the W. Md.'s plans for its eastern extension was removed on June 8 when the Court of Appeals sustained the lower court's decision and approved the request of the W. Md. to condemn land along the C. & O. Canal.

The most serious incident, and perhaps the most unusual, occurred in July, when a freight train on the C. & I. stalled in the Cheat Mountain tunnel. The train, consisting of 30 cars of lumber, was hauled by No. 28 and was being pushed by No. 16, which had been cut into the train four cars from the rear. Just as the lead engine cleared the tunnel, the train stalled, leaving the rear engine and crew within the tunnel. The crew consisted of the engineer and fireman on No. 16, two brakemen and a flagman who were on the cars, and a conductor in the caboose. When the engineer, B. F. Phares, realized his predicament in the suffocating tunnel, he had the fireman, Elmer Townsend, cut the engine lose from the rest of the train. Thinking that Townsend would ride out on the front of the engine, Phares backed out of the tunnel only to find his fireman was still in the tunnel. The conductor started back into the tunnel to rescue the fireman

Fig. 176. Depot at Glady

Fig. 177. The remains of No. 19
Collection of the Western Maryland Railway Historical Society

(COAL AND IRON RAILWAY.)			
ward.	Stations.	Northward.	
07. No. 127.		t.8. No. 108	
a. m.		p. m.	p. m.
8 00	Elkins	f 4 45	2 16
f 8 14	Tunnel	f 4 30	1 58
f 8 18	McCauley	f 4 27	1 52
f 8 22	Meadows	f 4 23	1 46
f 8 27	Paulkner	f 4 17	39
8 29	Bowden	4 15	1 36
f 8 32	Harper	f 4 19	1 32
f 8 42	Woodrow	f 4 02	1 19
f 8 46	Pond Lick	f 3 58	1 18
9 00	Carl	f 3 44	12 57
f 9 10	River Siding	f 3 33	12 53
9 12	Morribell	f 3 31	12 29
f 9 15	Glady	f 3 29	12 09
f 9 41	Oxley	f 3 03	11 44
9 57	Kelley	f 2 48	11 23
f 10 03	Cove	f 2 42	11 15
s 10 06	Burner	s 2 37	11 09
f 10 14	Braucher	f 2 31	11 01
10 30	Durbin	2 15	10 40

f Flag Station; s, Regular Stop.
Daily.. †Daily except Sunday.
F. M. HOWELL,
ROBERTSON, Genl Passenger Agt
Manager,

Fig. 175. Coal and Iron Railway timetable, October 1, 1903

but was overcome by the fumes. Meanwhile, at the other end, No. 28 and eight cars were cut off from the rest of the train and the cars placed in a siding to allow No. 28 to pull more cars from the tunnel. No. 28 pulled two more cars from the tunnel but this allowed the remaining 17 cars in the tunnel to run back down the grade. One of the brakemen, who was unconscious, was on top of one of these cars. Phares on No. 16, saw the cars approaching and started his engine down the grade to minimize the impact. The cars struck the engine and pushed it down the grade before coming to rest at Faulkner, four miles from the tunnel. Phares had jumped before the collision and walked down to Faulkner. Here the unfortunate brakeman was removed from the top of the car and revived. The bodies of the dead fireman and conductor were later taken to Elkins on a relief train.

Vice-president Landstreet wrote to the governor of Maryland on July 20 offering to purchase the state's interest in the C. & O. Canal. At this time, the canal was still being operated by the trustees and the state, although having a large financial interest, had no say in operating the canal. The Board of Public Works could approve of the sale of the state's interest in the canal. Landstreet noted that the ownership of the state's interest would facilitate the W. Md. in acquiring rights-of-way over and along the canal. The governor called a meeting of the Board of Public Works on August 4 at which it was agreed to sell the state's interest. The Board met again on December 14 to consider the two bids that had been received, but deferred action. The bids, from the W. Md. and the Consolidation Coal Company, were for $155,000 and $151,000 respectively. The bids were low because of the accumulated debt and interest owed by the canal. The board, on December 22, finally agreed to accept Landstreet's bid.

A new coal company, the Gleason Coal and Coke Company, was incorporated on August 27 to mine on land approximately 1.1/2 miles from Harrison. A post office, which had originally been established at the mouth of Maple Run and known as Upper Potomac, was moved to Gleason siding and became Gleason in 1910. In 1905, the Gleason Coal and Coke Company was reported to have produced 1,500 tons of coal. Additional openings were made over the years, and by 1915 production had increased to 93,442 tons, making the mine the largest producer in Mineral County. The population of Gleason was estimated to be 500 in 1921. The hamlet of Upper Potomac later became known as Hubbard after the Hubbard Coal and Mining Company, which operated two mines on the Maryland side of the North Branch.

The end of 1904 found the work on the two tunnels nearest Cumberland (Knobley Mountain and Welton tunnels) to be almost finished except for the lining. Further east it was announced that trains would start running from Big Pool to near Hancock on December 19. Ramsey was quoted as saying that both the Cumberland extension and the tidewater terminals in Baltimore would be finished by October 1, 1905.

Ramsey had good reason to feel optimistic. The Wabash extension to Pittsburgh had been completed in June 1904, even though the contract between Carnegie and Gould had yet to be implemented. In West Virginia, work on the Little Kanawha Railroad extension had been abandoned in May 1903, in favor of pushing work on the route between Pittsburgh and Belington. This was to be accomplished in West Virginia by the construction of the Buckhannon and Northern Railroad and in Pennsylvania by the building of the Greene County Railroad. Gould's eastern railroads in 1905 are shown in Fig. 178,

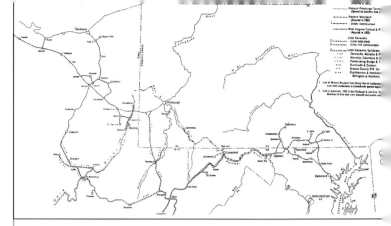

Fig. 178. The eastern railroads of George Gould in 1905 "Investigation of Railroads, Holding Companies and Affiliated Companies" Washington, 1940

although the Cumberland extension was not completed until 1906.

On January 10, 1905 the W. Md. and the B. & O. agreed to an out of court settlement of the freight diversion case which was due to start in the Maryland Court of Appeals. The settlement included a provision to reopen the Cherry Run gateway. Two weeks later, the canal trustees asked the court to approve the sale of land owned by the canal to the W. Md. On March 7, the sale was approved and the W. Md. ordered to deposit $500,000 with special trustees appointed by the court.

The new year, 1905, started much like 1904 with a massive wreck on January 24 near Piedmont involving three engines. Fortunately no one was injured although it was expected to take 24 hours to clear the tracks.

In February 1905, a newspaper report appeared that the West Virginia Central had purchased the Weaver Coal and Coke Company and the Belington and Beaver Creek Railroad. The report was true and the deal was finalized on April 8. Included in the purchase were 3,500 acres of coal lands, five mining plants and 251 coke ovens.

During March, heavy rains caused delays to all the trains in the Elkins area due to slides and washouts. The train from Durbin on the C. & I. on March 20 was six hours late in getting to Elkins due to a slide. Slides were to be a regular part of the C. & I.'s history (Fig. 179).

Fig. 179. Slide on the Coal and Iron Railway (undated)

Fires continued to play havoc in the area with two large fires being reported on April 10. The first fire occurred at the mill of the Condon-Lane Boom and Lumber Company at Horton, which was followed by a fire at the tannery at Elkins. In both fires the damage was extensive but both companies quickly rebuilt.

Robert Whitmer, owner of the mill at Horton, seemed to have been doing very well at this time apart from the fire. The Dry Fork Railroad had been operating two trains daily to Horton since April 1, 1903, and a year later the timetable still showed two trains each way daily (Fig. 180 and Fig. 181).

Whitmer, the company town adjacent to the mill at Horton, is

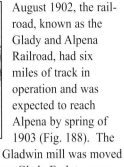

Dry Fork Railroad Co.

TIME TABLE No. 5.

In effect Wednesday, April 1st.

DAILY EXCEPT SUNDAY.

SOUTHWARD		STATIONS	NORTHWARD	
11	13	(W. Va. C.)	12	14
p.m.	a.m.		p.m.	m.
5.15	7.00 lv.	Cumb. ar.	7.15	12.00
a.m.	p.m.		p.m.	p.m.
7.00	2.15 "	Elkins, "	8.15	8.15
8.15	3.20 "	Hendricks "	12.15	7.05
8.29	3.34 "	Red Run f lv.	12.01	6.46
			a.m.	
8.32	3.37 "	Moore's Sidf "	11.58	6.43
8.35	3.40 "	Rich Ford f "	11.55	6.41
8.40	3.45 "	Mill Run f "	11.50	6.35
8.43	3.48 "	Elk Lick f "	11.47	6.32
8.49	3.54 "	Gladwin "	11.41	6.36
8.58	4.03 "	Flynn's Cros f"	11.32	6.17
9.00	4.05 "	Stover f "	11.30	6.15
9.03	4.08 "	Carrs f "	11.27	6.12
9.14	4.19 "	Dry Fork "	11.16	6.01
9.26	4.31 "	Harman "	11.04	5.49
9.35	4.40 "	Reynold's f "	10.55	5.40
9.43	4.43 "	Lower Dam f "	10.52	5.37
9.43	4.48 "	Job "	10.47	5.32
9.51	4.46 "	Gandy f "	10.39	5.24
9.54	4.59 "	Armentrout f"	10.36	5.21
9.58	5.03 "	Whitmer "	10.32	5.17
10.00	5.05 ar.	Horton "	10.30	5.14

f Stops only on signal or notice to conductor.

Fig. 180. Dry Fork Railroad timetable, April 1, 1904

Fig. 181. Dry Fork Railroad passenger train and engine No. 1

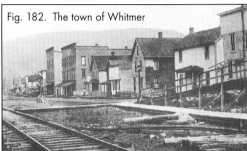

Fig. 182. The town of Whitmer

Fig. 183. Log train at the Condon-Lane Boom and Lumber Company millpond at Horton

Fig. 184. Whitmer-Lane company store at Horton

Fig. 185. Mill at Laneville on the Red Creek extension of the Dry Fork Railroad

Fig. 186. The town of Jenningston on the Dry Fork

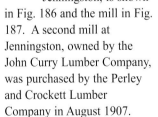

Fig. 187. The mill at Jenningston

shown in Fig. 182, a log train at the millpond at Horton in Fig. 183, and the company store at Horton in Fig. 184.

An extension to the Dry Fork had been built during 1903 along Red Creek to timberlands owned by the company, and although the extension was operated by the D. F., the railroad did not own it. The extension served a mill at Laneville (Fig. 185).

At the time of the April fire, Whitmer received good news when it was announced that the Jennings brothers of Pennsylvania were ready to construct a mill and town at the junction of Laurel Fork and the Dry Fork. The town, known as Jenningston, is shown in Fig. 186 and the mill in Fig. 187. A second mill at Jenningston, owned by the John Curry Lumber Company, was purchased by the Perley and Crockett Lumber Company in August 1907.

To the west of Laurel Fork, over on the east side of Middle Mountain, was Glady Fork, which was crossed at its upper end by the C. & I. on its way to the Greenbrier. T. W. Raine had agreed to purchase the timber on 1,016 acres on Glady Fork from Davis in February 1901 for $20 per acre. In March, Raine along with John Raine, F. L. Andrews and W. M. Andrews, incorporated the Raine-Andrews Lumber Company to cut timber on some 10,000 acres on Glady Fork. The company purchased a mill at Gladwin at the mouth of Glady Fork and commenced work on a standard gauge railroad up the Fork. By September, five miles were reported to have been graded and the first engine was delivered. A year later, in

August 1902, the railroad, known as the Glady and Alpena Railroad, had six miles of track in operation and was expected to reach Alpena by spring of 1903 (Fig. 188). The Gladwin mill was moved up Glady Fork to a new site at Evenwood in April 1905 (Fig. 189).

By 1905, the whole area served by the Dry Fork Railroad was covered with a network of logging railroads serving mills whose only outlet was over the Dry Fork to the West Virginia Central at Hendricks. The year 1905 was reported to be the first year in which the Dry Fork Railroad was profitable enough to start paying dividends. The year before, the railroad had purchased its first new locomotive from Baldwin, becoming the road's No. 6.

With so much lumber coming off the Dry Fork, Hendricks became something of a boom town, even having its own opera house (Fig. 190).

Whitmer's other venture, the Parsons Pulp and Paper Company, was reported to have started to manufacture paper in September 1905 (Fig. 191). An interior view of the mill is shown in Fig. 192. By 1907, the population of Parsons was reported to be 1,552, and the town supported five hotels and two opera houses (Fig. 193). A somewhat later view of the depot at Parsons is shown in Fig. 194.

On April 10, it was announced that Ramsey would resign as president of the Wabash due to differences with George Gould. The resignation was to take place on October 1, but was later changed to October 10. Ramsey had tried to secure money to complete the

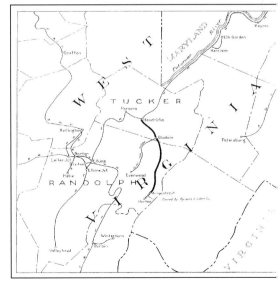

Fig. 188. Map of the Central West Virginia and Southern Railroad (ex-Dry Fork Railroad) and the Glady and Alpena Railroad in 1918

Fig. 189. Raine-Andrews mill at Evenwood

Fig. 190. Railroad scene at Hendricks

Fig. 191. Parsons Pulp and Paper Company mill at Parsons

Fig. 192. Interior view of the Parsons Pulp and Paper Company mill (undated)
Collection of the Tucker County Historical Society

Fig. 193. Street scene at Parsons circa 1908

Fig. 194. Western Maryland train at the depot in Parsons (undated)

Little Kanawha extensions but had been unsuccessful. He later entered into negotiations with the Pittsburgh and Lake Erie Railroad, and in June an agreement was signed for the sale of the properties. This had no impact on the West Virginia Central and Western Maryland Syndicate although Ramsey did resign as president of both roads and was replaced by Pierce.

Landstreet, still vice-president of both roads, visited Elkins on June 5, and told a meeting of business leaders that the shops and roundhouse at Elkins would be enlarged, and a new station constructed.

It was reported on August 2, that engine No. 25, used on the Davis branch, had been overhauled in the Elkins shops, and had emerged as Western Maryland No. 268. Whether this was the first West Virginia Central engine to be renumbered is not recorded. Several cabooses were under construction at Elkins at this time and they also received Western Maryland lettering.

Another disastrous wreck occurred on the Blackwater grade on August 10, and followed the same pattern as the December 1902 wreck that had killed Engineer Jankey.

Western Maryland engine No. 103 became unmanageable near Douglas and wrecked at Big Run (Fig. 195). The engineer, W. Watkins, and a brakeman, A. Spalding, were killed and four others injured. One car stayed on the track after the wreck and continued on down the grade until it crashed into a caboose at Hendricks. No. 103 was not re-railed until August 23 and then was taken to Elkins for repairs.

A special meeting of the stockholders of the West Virginia Central was called for October 16 to approve the sale of its properties to the W. Md. Three days later a similar meeting of the stockholders of the W. Md. was called to approve the purchase of the West Virginia Central, the Piedmont and Cumberland, the Coal and Iron and the Belington and Beaver Creek railways and several others. At the annual meeting of the stockholders of the W. Md. held the previous day, Ramsey had been removed as a director and was replaced by Frederick A. Delano, president of the Wabash. The action to unite all the railroads under one name was approved, and the West Virginia Central and Pittsburg Railway officially ceased to exist, becoming the West Virginia Division of the Western Maryland Rail Road Company.

The Fuller Syndicate officially went out of business on October 17 with a distribution to the subscribers of the Syndicate's W. Md. stock. At this time, the members had contributed 60 percent of their subscriptions, which for Davis amounted to $60,000. In return, the subscribers received W. Md. first mortgage bonds selling at $88, second mortgage bonds selling at $70 and stock selling at $28. For Davis, this amounted to $67,905 or a profit of $7,905. This was a little over four percent per annum, but even higher profits were expected in the future.

Fig. 195. August 10, 1905 wreck at Big Run
Collection of the Pocahontas County Historical Society

Fig. 196. "Dinky" at Upper Potomac, circa 1908

The Coal and Iron Railway and the lumber industry

13

Like its parent, the West Virginia Central, the Coal and Iron Railway also lost its identity, becoming the Durbin Branch of the W. Md. However, the name continued to be used locally for the next 30 years, and as this period coincided with the boom of the lumber industry along the line, the name will be used for this period (Fig. 197).

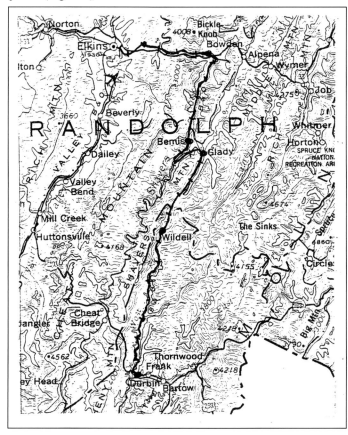

Fig. 197. Map of the Coal and Iron Railway

Logging had commenced on Shavers Fork probably as early as the 1880's with the logs being floated downstream to Point Marion in Pennsylvania. Sawmills at Lumber and Bowden were in operation by 1902; the mill at Bowden was reported to have burnt on May 28, 1903. However, it was the coming of the railroad that set off a land boom in the area.

A couple of weeks after the C. & I. opened on August 1, 1903, a correspondent of the Pocahontas Times took a trip over the new road and reported, "The road winds through a stately avenue of forest trees," and "the big spruce trees wall in the right-of-way" (Fig. 198). No settlements were reported on the 20 miles between Durbin and the Randolph County line, but at the mouth of Little River, the Pocahontas Lumber Company was installing a mill. The site became the town of Burner. The only settlement of note in Randolph County was at Fishing Hawk Creek where there was " a saloon, two houses and a barn." This became the site of the

mill town of Fishing Hawk. Sites for mills were being cleared at Glady and Oxley.

Fig. 198. The Coal and Iron Railway on the Randolph and Pocahontas county line

The same newspaper carried a report on December 22, 1904 in which the following companies were listed as operating along the C. & I. in Pocahontas County: Moore and Lawton at Oxley, Wildell Lumber Company at Wildell, F. S. Wise and Company at Gertrude, Pocahontas Lumber Company at Burner and W. S. Taylor at Braucher.

On June 22, 1905, 6,500 acres of lands along Glady Fork and the plant already there, were sold to J. R. Droney of New York for $130,000 or $20 per acre. A company, the Glady Lumber Company, was formed to operate the mill. The Glady Lumber Company was sold on October 1, 1905, the price now being $26 per acre plus the cost of improvements, for a total of $215,000. In February 1906, the Glady Lumber Company was sold again, along with its lands, mill and railroad to the Glady Fork Lumber Company for $358,000 or $40 per acre. The officers of the Glady

Fig. 199. The town of Glady

Fig. 200. The sawmill at Glady

Fork Lumber Company were E. Allen, president and also president of the Tygarts River Lumber Company, and Howard Sutherland, the vice-president. By 1912, two other companies were operating at Glady in addition to the Glady Fork company. At this time, the town of Glady is shown in Fig. 199, and one of the sawmills in Fig. 200. A scene in the woods at Glady is shown in Fig. 201 where a log loader rests in a ditch.

Fig. 201. A toppled log loader at Glady circa 1910

Some six miles from Glady at Fishing Hawk on Shavers Fork, where not much more than a saloon had been recorded in 1903, the Rumbarger Lumber Company had set up a mill, which was sold on January 1, 1906 to J. M. and H. C. Bemis.   Fishing Hawk achieved a degree of notoriety in September 1905, when it was reported that C. H. Harry, agent for both the C. & I. and the Adams Express Company, had taken "French leave." Some $600 was also reported to be missing. Neither Harry nor the money was ever found. A few weeks later a wreck at Fishing Hawk injured two men in the caboose of a freight train. A pusher at the rear of the train became detached and then proceeded to ram into the back of the train. The caboose was demolished.

The first order of business for the new owners of Fishing Hawk was to rename the town "Bemis." The mill is shown in Fig. 202; the lumberyards and mill workers' houses along the C. & I.

Fig. 202. Sawmill at Bemis

can be seen in Fig. 203. Fig. 204 shows a group of mill workers in July 1916. The mill at Bemis finally

Fig. 203. Lumberyard and workers' housing at Bemis

closed in 1921. During the night of June 3 and June 4, 1924, the general store at Bemis burned down following a gasoline explosion. The store had been constructed by J. M. Bemis and Son and was used by the W. Md. as an express and freight office. The store had been purchased earlier by the Pocahontas Supply Company to support operations by the West Virginia Pulp and Paper Company in the area. A new two story brick building was constructed which was later sold to the Davis Coal Land Company. The ruins of this building can still be seen by the track at Bemis.

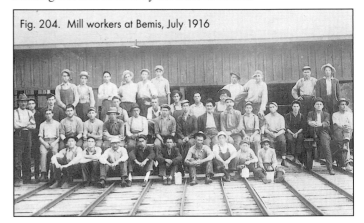
Fig. 204. Mill workers at Bemis, July 1916

North of Bemis was the third major lumber operation in Randolph County at Montes. A tract was purchased here in July 1904, by M. M. Brown who was later joined by several other family members and George Hill in forming the company, Brown and Hill, which constructed a mill in 1905. The mill burned in September 1908, but was rebuilt and continued to operate until 1911. The Brown and Hill mill and lumberyards are shown in Fig. 205 and Fig. 206 and the company store and office in Fig. 207. In October 1910, it was reported that an engine, two cars and a log loader had run away on a grade and had been wrecked. The engine was not identified, but Brown and Hill No. 1 and a log loader are shown in Fig. 208.

Crossing over into Pocahontas County, the first major mill town was at Wildell where a mill was operated by the Wildell Lumber Company. The mill was

Fig. 205. Brown and Hill mill, Montes
West Virginia and Regional History Collection,
West Virginia University Library

Fig. 206. Brown and Hill lumberyard, Montes
West Virginia and Regional History Collection,
West Virginia University Library

The mill burned in August 1909, was rebuilt and continued operations until 1915. The date the depot was constructed is not known (Fig. 211). Shays Nos. 1 and 2 of the Wildell Lumber Company are shown in Fig. 212.

Fig. 207. Brown and Hill company store and office, Montes
West Virginia and Regional History Collection,
West Virginia University Library

two illicit liquor dealers captured. The Pocahontas Times reported that the saloon had a bar "wide open, selling liquid damnation to all comers."

Fig. 208. Brown and Hill Shay No. 1 in the woods at Montes
West Virginia and Regional History Collection,
West Virginia University Library

Further south was the town of Gertrude where F. S. Wise operated a mill and five miles from Wildell was the town of May. The operation at May was started by the Hoover Brothers in 1904, later becoming the Hoover-Dimeling Company. This company

completed in early 1904 (Fig. 209), and a town of 40 houses shortly afterwards (Fig. 210).

Adjacent to Wildell was the rather unsavory town of Oxley where there was a small sawmill and a "famous pigs ear, gambling den and resort." This burnt on April 28, 1906 but in October a raid on another "pigs ear" was conducted and

Fig. 209. Mill at Wildell
West Virginia and Regional History Collection,
West Virginia University Library

was in turn purchased by Gilfillan, Neil and Company, which continued in operation until 1914. The mill is shown in Fig. 213 and Fig. 214. By 1907 it was reported that May had 1,200 inhabitants, a church, lodge, schoolhouse and "one of the largest stores that is found between here and the Mississippi River" (Fig. 215).

At Burner, the mill started by the Pocahontas Lumber

Fig. 210. Town of Wildell
Collection of the Western Maryland Railway Historical Society

Fig. 211. Depot at Wildell
Collection of Richard Dye

Company had developed into a large operation. The mill and millpond are shown in Fig. 216 in about 1911. A passenger train pulled by W. Md. No. 31, ex-West Virginia Central No. 36, is shown at Burner in an undated photograph (Fig. 217). The mill at Burner was reported to have burnt in 1911 and finally closed in

Fig. 212. Shays Nos. 1 and 2, Wildell Lumber Company
Collection of the Western Maryland Railway Historical Society

Fig. 213. Mill at May
West Virginia and Regional History Collection,
West Virginia University Library

Fig. 214. Another view of the mill at May
West Virginia and Regional History Collection,
West Virginia University Library

Fig. 215. May Supply Company's store, May

Fig. 216. Mill and millpond at Burner

Fig. 217. Western Maryland No. 31 (ex-West Virginia Central No. 36)
with a passenger train at Burner (undated)
Collection of William Metheny

Fig. 218. The town of Durbin. The C. & O. depot is
in the bottom right hand corner

1915 when all the available timber had been cut.

Three miles south of Burner was Braucher where lumber was hauled over an intervening ridge from a mill on Mountain Lick Creek using two inclined planes. The final mill town was Olive, three miles north of Durbin, where P. L. and W. F. Brown operated a mill until it closed in 1913. The mill was sold to the Mountain Lick Lumber Company, which operated until April 1919, when the mill was destroyed by fire.

Forty-seven miles from Elkins was Durbin and the junction with the C. & O. (Fig. 218).

A new timetable went into effect on November 19, 1905 (Fig. 219) that was not greatly different on the Cumberland to Elkins route, but did show a change on the C. & I. with one morning train moved to the early afternoon.

Railroad. The H. R. & A. ran from a junction with the West Virginia and Pittsburgh road at Holly Junction, down the Right Fork of the Holly River before crossing the divide over to the Elk River which was followed to Addison (Figs. 221 and 222).

Fig. 219. West Virginia Division timetable, November 19, 1905

Business appeared to be good for the new railroad. Ground was broken in Elkins for a new freight station in October and an agitation started among the citizens of Elkins for a new depot commensurate with the town's importance. By the end of the year, it was reported that the Elkins shops were working day and night and even a Sunday shift was instituted. Eighteen new 2-8-0 locomotives had been ordered from Baldwin and these appeared at the end of 1905. One of these engines, No. 510, is shown taking water at the Tub Run tower in the Blackwater Canyon in Fig. 220.

Early in January 1906 it was reported that the Kessler tunnel would be finished by the middle of January, and it was expected that passenger service over the new line would start in June. The first train from Hancock to Cumberland, a special hauled by No. 44, arrived in Cumberland on February 8 with Vice-president Landstreet and General Manager A. Robertson on board. Freight service over the new line commenced on March 14.

The W. Md. announced in March the purchase of 65 acres of land south of Ridgeley for another large yard. The yard, later known as the Knobmont yard, was needed to allow trains from the West Virginia Division to pass directly onto the new extension without having to reverse at Ridgeley.

Fig. 220. W. Md. Class H-5 locomotive No. 510 in the Blackwater Canyon (undated)
Collection of the West Virginia State Archives

On April 9, 1906 passenger train No. 4, due into Cumberland at 7:40 P.M., was detained by a slide near Dawson. A relief train was sent out from Cumberland to rescue the passengers but derailed just before reaching Dawson. The engine rolled down the bank killing the engineer and fireman.

At about this time, there was news of another railroad that would ultimately have an impact on the West Virginia Division. The railroad was the narrow gauge West Virginia Midland Railroad that had been chartered to take over the Holly River and Addison

The president of the H. R. & A. and the West Virginia Midland was John McGraw.

Fig. 221. West Virginia Midland train on the Clifton Trestle, circa 1905

Because of the presence at Addison of mineral springs, the name had been changed to Webster Springs and a large fashionable hotel built, which supplied the railroad with passenger traffic. It was reported that the line would be extended to Marlinton, but this did not happen.

Fig. 222. West Virginia Midland No. 10, at Webster Springs, August 1913

The first passenger train over the new extension was an excursion from Elkins to Gettysburg leaving on May 29 and returning on May 30. Regular service to Hagerstown commenced on June 18 with a connection to Baltimore. On September 30, a through service to Baltimore was inaugurated with one train in each direction making the trip. For the convenience of passengers, a parlor car was attached to the train. The service was further improved in October when vestibuled cars were used with a crew and engine change being made at Cumberland. The service was improved again in November when the number of stops between Elkins and Cumberland was reduced to speed up the service.

Passengers hoping to make a connection with the B. & O. at Belington did not fare so well when the B. & O. changed its schedule in November so that passengers leaving Elkins in the morning had to wait in Belington until the afternoon to catch a train.

Fig. 223. Western Maryland Shay No. 900
*West Virginia and Regional History Collection,
West Virginia University Library*

During November 1905, the West Virginia Central had ordered a Shay locomotive to serve as a pusher on the Blackwater grade. The engine was delivered in June 1906 as W. Md. No. 900. The locomotive was a 150-ton Class D Shay and is shown in Fig. 223. Although the engine was successful as a pusher, it took a long time to run back down the grade, creating a bottleneck. No. 900 only lasted four years in W. Md. service before being sold to a railroad in Mexico.

Another bad wreck occurred on Cheat Mountain on September 27. After the accident of July 1904, trains were cut into two before being taken up to the tunnel. On this occasion a train of 29 cars of lumber, bark and pulpwood was on its way from Durbin to Elkins. The first half was left standing in a siding near the tunnel while the engine went back down for the second half. On this particular day, the two parts of the train got away from the engine and careened down the hill towards Elkins, scattering lumber and demolishing cars as they progressed. Three brakemen were injured in the mishap.

By January 1907, the Gould interests still hoped to build a railroad linking the east and west coasts, and were reported to have surveyors in the field looking for a route between Cumberland and Pittsburgh. The way west from Cumberland lay through the Narrows, and to achieve this, the Georges Creek and Cumberland Railroad was purchased on January 17. By the end of the month negotiations had started with the Pittsburgh and Lake Erie for trackage rights between Connellsville and Pittsburgh in an effort to reduce the amount of construction required. The P. & L. E. would benefit from such an arrangement as it would eliminate a potential parallel track. Gould had tried to interest the Pennsylvania in the purchase of the W. Md. during 1905, but President McCrea, who had replaced Cassatt at the end of 1906, did not seem interested. Vice-president Rea was opposed to the purchase as he thought it would enable Gould to build east from Pittsburgh.

The new year, 1907, did not start auspiciously for the West Virginia Division. On January 22, there was a head-on collision near Harding in which one fireman was killed. A passenger train, which had left Elkins at 3:05 P.M., crashed into a freight heading towards Elkins. The engineer and fireman on the freight jumped in time to avoid injury. The engineer of the passenger train was trapped beneath the wreckage and severely injured; the fireman was killed. A baggage car went over the bank, but the passenger cars stayed on the track giving the passengers a severe shaking. A grand jury at Harding at the end of January failed to determine the cause of the wreck.

At about the same time, heavy rains did considerable damage along the C. & I. Most hard hit was tunnel No. 1, where a major slide occurred at the south end forcing passengers on an Elkins bound train to walk over the mountain. The road was closed for several days.

Davis had been very lucky during the years of his ownership of the Davis Coal and Coke Company to have avoided any major accidents although accidents involving one or two individuals were regrettably quite common. On February 4, at about 7:00 A.M., Mine No. 25 at Thomas exploded. The day shift was just entering the mine when the explosion occurred, otherwise the death toll would have been much greater. The final death toll was 25 men, including members of a rescue team that attempted to enter the mine. The mine had been considered gas free, although early reports indicated that the ventilation fans had not been operating over the weekend before the explosion.

Three days after the Thomas disaster, another explosion occurred. This time it was the ex-B. & B. C. No. 99 that exploded, while standing in the yard at Weaver. The night watchman had just been on the engine and noted that the water was low when the boiler exploded. Miraculously no one was hurt, but No. 99 was not rebuilt.

A month later a fire, on March 2, destroyed the shops of the Dry Fork Railroad at Hendricks causing an estimated $20,000 worth of damage.

On March 15, a W. Md. directors' meeting was held at which Pierce and Landstreet resigned as president and vice-president respectively of the railroad. Landstreet also resigned as president of the Davis Coal and Coke Company, but both men remained as directors. The new president of the W. Md. and the Davis Coal and Coke Company was B. F. Bush, who came from the Gould railroads in the west. No explanation of this change was given and Davis noted in his diary on March 18 that "much surprise was caused by the resignation of Pierce and Landstreet from the Western Maryland Railway." There was some speculation at the time that Landstreet would succeed Davis as president of the Coal and Coke Railway, but this was denied. Landstreet, along with E. L. Fuller, later incorporated the Landstreet Coal and Coke Company. The new company owned its own mines and also sold coal for other West Virginia mines. Galbreath became engineer of the new company after resigning from the W. Md.

It is of interest to note that the resignation of Pierce and Landstreet came two days after a collapse of the stock market which was to be the beginning of a period of financial problems that later became known as the Panic of 1907. Whether the resignations were connected to the stock market collapse is not known.

The new president, along with Landstreet and General Manager Robertson, made a trip over the railroad to Elkins on March 21. At Elkins, the party was met by a delegation from the local Board of Trade asking for a new depot, and by representatives of the West Virginia Saw Mill Association, who were concerned about a lack of cars to serve the mills.

A change was made in April to the organization of the Davis Coal and Coke Company when some offices were moved to Baltimore. In Cumberland the location of the offices was also changed to the building that had originally belonged to the Georges

Creek and Cumberland Railroad in Cumberland (Fig. 224). Changes were also in order at Davis when it was announced on May

Fig. 224. Offices of the Davis Coal and Coke Company in Cumberland.

Fig. 225. General view of the Thompson Lumber Company at Davis circa 1905

22 that the Babcock Lumber and Boom Company would take over the Blackwater Lumber Company and the Thompson Lumber Company. The Blackwater Lumber Company had become the Thompson Lumber Company in 1905. A general view of the Thompson plant at Davis is shown in Fig. 225.

Fig. 226. The Thompson Lumber Company loading dock at Davis
Collection of the Western Maryland Railway Historical Society

Fig. 228. The fire at Chaffey's mill, June 25, 1907
West Virginia and Regional History Collection, West Virginia University Library

Fig. 229. The new mill at William
West Virginia and Regional History Collection, West Virginia University

Fig. 230. The town of William and the millpond
West Virginia and Regional History Collection, West Virginia University Library

Fig. 231. Boarding house at William

Fig. 232. Shay No. 2 on the Chaffey logging railroad at William
West Virginia and Regional History Collection, West Virginia University Library

Fig. 227. The loading area and the depot at Davis in 1905
Collection of the Western Maryland Railway Historical Society

Two views of the company's loading dock area in Davis are shown in Figs. 226 and 227. The Babcock Lumber and Boom Company would continue to operate at Davis until 1924.

A disastrous fire occurred at William on June 25, when the Chaffey mill was destroyed (Fig. 228). This was the company's second mill at William, the first having been burnt on September 14, 1901. The mill was rebuilt and was expected to be back in business by December 1907 (Fig. 229). The millpond and the town of William are shown in Fig. 230 and the rather austere boarding house in Fig. 231. A scene on the Chaffey logging railroad is shown in Fig. 232 and a wood's crew in Fig. 233 and 234.

On July 17, heavy rains inundated the area around Elkins stopping all railroad traffic. The Tygart Valley River reached its highest level ever recorded and much of South Elkins was under water. Numerous slides were reported on the Blackwater grade and the C. & I., and trestles on the Huttonsville branch were washed out. On

Fig. 233. Crew at William
West Virginia and Regional History Collection, West Virginia University Library

Fig. 234. Lumber camp at William
West Virginia and Regional History Collection, West Virginia University Library

the C. & I. a slip at tunnel No. 1 was expected to take several weeks to clear. The Dry Fork Railroad was severely damaged with many bridges destroyed. At Glady, the Glady Fork Lumber Company lost 18 bridges on its logging road. Traffic between Cumberland and Elkins was restored on July 27; it is not clear how long the C. & I. was closed, certainly it was still closed on August 1. Traffic was restored by August 20 as a passenger train wrecked

Fig. 235. Depot at Belington, 1917
Collection of the Western Maryland Railway Historical Society

at Bemis. The mail car derailed, injuring the mail clerk but no passengers were hurt.

It was announced on August 22, that a new depot would be built at Belington with the cost to be shared by the B. & O., the C. & C. and the W. Md. Work started immediately and the depot was finished by April 1, 1908 (Fig. 235).

President Bush and Chief Engineer Barlow made their first visit to Elkins since the flood of July 17 on October 3. Barlow assured the citizens of Elkins that work would start on a new depot either in the fall or spring of 1908. In practice, ground was officially broken for the depot on April 20, 1908.

President Bush was back in Elkins a couple of weeks later accompanied by Vice-president Robertson and Chief Engineer Barlow. The party, along with John McGraw, went to Huttonsville and then by horseback to Webster Springs. They then examined the West Virginia Midland Railroad, returning to Holly Junction and then to Charleston over the C. & C. with Davis. This gave rise to much speculation that the W. Md. would purchase the W. Va. M. but nothing was to happen.

However, there was another railroad that was interested in this area. It was announced on October 31 that the narrow gauge Valley River Railroad would build from Mill Creek to Clover Lick on the C. & O.'s Greenbrier branch. W. A. Dromgold was president of the new road, and the Hench, Dromgold and Shull Lumber Company was behind the enterprise. Tracklaying for the new road reached Huttonsville by December 3, and Lee Bell by January 7, 1908.

Serious wrecks continued to plague the W. Md. during the fall. An eastbound freight hauled by engine No. 503 crashed into the rear of a stationary freight at Montrose at 12:15 A.M. on October 17. A pusher engine, No. 513, was being attached to the freight facing towards Elkins when the wreck occurred. Both engines were damaged and a caboose destroyed. The crew of the helper engine had time to jump clear; the crew of No. 503 was not so fortunate and the fireman was injured. On October 31, the coupling between an engine and its tender broke, allowing a fireman to fall between and suffering serious injuries. Engine No. 513 was back in service on November 15 after the Montrose wreck, when it jumped the tracks at Hendricks and blocked the main line for several hours.

In spite of the gloomy financial outlook, the W. Md.'s Annual Report for the year ending June 30, 1907 and published on October 31, showed an increase in both gross and net earnings.

Towards the end of November, the panic that had started in March was beginning to have an effect, when coke ovens in the Connellsville and Morgantown areas were closed down. The lumber business was also reported to be dull. The impact was felt by the W. Md., which laid off 50 men at the Elkins shops. This was followed by the total closure of the shops on December 23 for two weeks. When the shops reopened in January, it was on a four day per week schedule. The closures came at a bad time for the W. Md., as the local newspapers were quick to point out. The railroad continued to have wrecks, and the newspapers claimed that some of these were due to lack of maintenance.

The series of wrecks continued into 1908, starting on January 1, when a passenger train was wrecked near Parsons. Because of heavy snowdrifts on the C. & I. in early February, all passenger trains had to be double headed. On February 4, engine No. 263, the lead engine on a passenger train, derailed at Burner, but fortunately no one was hurt. A large snowplow was brought in to clear the C. & I. on February 6. It was then to go and clear the Davis branch where W. Md. No. 318 had been caught in drifts and stranded from February 1 to February 4 (Fig. 236).

Fig. 236. W. Md. No. 318 caught in drifts between Thomas and Davis, February 1 to February 4, 1908

On February 6, an engine, tender and three passenger cars left the track near Gorman at about 11:00 A.M. (Fig. 237). Two people were killed, including a passenger, and four seri-

Fig. 237. Wreck at Gorman, February 6, 1908
West Virginia and Regional History Collection, West Virginia University Library

ously injured. Twenty-two passengers and employees received minor injuries. The track was cleared by midnight and trains were able to pass the accident site. Although there was much snow at the time, the engineer, who examined the track immediately after the accident, reported that spread rails were the cause of the derailment.

The melting snow and heavy rains in the middle of February caused the inevitable landslides along the C. & I. and also on the Blackwater grade. Passenger train No. 2, which left Elkins at 7:50 A.M. on February 14, did not reach Thomas until 10:00 P.M. due to slides and washouts. The storm may have been the cause of a freight wreck near Blaine on February 19 when engine No. 516 and several cars went over a bank. A relief train had to be sent from Cumberland to rescue the passengers from a train trapped behind the wreck.

Bad news of a different sort occurred for the W. Md. on March

5 when the railroad passed into the hands of a receiver. This action was necessary as the railroad had maturing obligations on April 1 that it could not meet, even though both gross and net revenues had continued to increase through December 1907. The W. Md. was the second Gould railroad to go into receivership and was not to be the last. President Bush was appointed receiver by the U. S. Circuit Court.

The unsettled financial conditions did not prevent the W. Md. from starting work on the new depot at Elkins in April. The first step was to remove the old depot from the area of the new construction (Fig. 238). By July the brickwork of the first floor was finished.

Fig. 238. Removal of the old depot at Elkins, 1908
Collection of Rob Whetsell

Fig. 239. Clearing the wreck at Warnocks, April 14, 1908

On April 1, the morning passenger train to Elkins derailed at the Douglas tipple. The postal clerk on the train was seriously injured and required hospitalization. When the cars had been returned to the track and the train about ready to start, the engine derailed. This was followed on April 14, by a minor freight derailment near Warnocks, which delayed passenger trains but was soon cleared (Fig. 239).

Heavy rain in May caused a massive slide near Westernport delaying a passenger train for 12 hours. Two days later, a storm centered on the upper Tygart Valley River, washed out eight bridges on the Tolbard and Spiker lumber road near Mill Creek, but did no damage to the W. Md.

Two freight trains collided in the yard at Ridgeley on July 9 injuring the fireman of one of the engines. This was followed on July 18 by the wreck of a Baltimore to Elkins passenger train near Poland. The train consisted of a mail car, baggage car, passenger car, ladies' coach and a parlor car. Two cars were tipped over (Fig. 240) and six passengers and the baggage master slightly injured.

On November 16, the new depot at Elkins was opened temporarily due to severely cold weather, and one month later, the

Fig. 240. W. Md. wreck, July 18, 1908

Fig. 241. The new Western Maryland depot at Elkins

old depot was demolished (Fig. 241).

Big Run on the Blackwater grade was the scene of another wreck on November 23, when engine No. 503 running light down the grade, got out of control and went down the bank. Remarkably, neither the engineer nor the fireman was injured.

The Valley River Railroad commenced running passenger trains from Mill Creek, 8.1/4 miles up the Tygart Valley River to Stalnaker Bridge on December 21.

The winter and spring of 1909 seemed to have been fairly quiet on the West Virginia Division, the only excitement occurring on January 28 when an engine collided with three cabooses in the yard at Ridgeley in which a number of trackmen were asleep. Thirteen individuals received an assortment of injuries as a result of being thrown around in the cars. This was followed on April 10 by a fire, which destroyed the Elkins machine shop.

Ten new Pacific type engines were delivered by Baldwin to the W. Md. in the spring of 1909, becoming Class K-1 and numbered 151-160. One of these engines, No. 154 is shown in Fig. 242.

Tunnel No. 1 was the scene of near

Fig. 242. W. Md. Class K-1, 4-6-2, No. 154 (undated)

tragedy on May 21 when the engine of a passenger train hit a rock in the tunnel and brought down the lining timbers and tons of rock. The passenger cars were pulled from the tunnel by a following freight engine before any passengers suffocated, but it was feared that the engineer and fireman must have been killed. However they were able to dig themselves out and walk out of the tunnel.

A plan to reorganize the W. Md. was announced on July 16 in which stock would be issued to substitute for $18,000,000 of interest bearing bonds. A syndicate was formed to underwrite the plan and it was thought that John D. Rockefeller was a major player in the new syndicate. The plan put the W. Md. in a position to again think about the extension towards Pittsburgh.

The W. Md. was beset with problems during the second half of 1909. These started with heavy rains on July 30 causing considerable damage along the C. & I., particularly near Bowdon where the track was washed out. The Dry Fork Railroad was also heavily damaged. A head-on collision between a shifting engine, No. 209, and a freight engine, No. 512, occurred on August 9 in the cut north of Elkins. Fortunately no one was injured. The wreck caused a delay to a passenger train, the passengers having to walk into Elkins. This was followed on August 18 by two locomotives and

14 cars derailing near Shaw, severely injuring the fireman. A month later, on September 20, a freight train hit a slide near Morribel, derailing the engine along with seven cars, and injuring a brakeman. Another derailment occurred on September 30, when a passenger train from Elkins, approaching tunnel No. 1, hit a broken rail.

By October, freight was heavy on the C. & I. when 3,738 loads of lumber were transported, which was 583 more than was transported in the same time in October 1907. This showing was notable as the mill of one of the line's major shippers, the Wildell Lumber Company, had been destroyed by fire on August 24, and was not expected to resume production before January 1910.

On November 19, the W. Md. was auctioned to a reorganization committee of its bondholders for $6,500,000, and on December 1, the Western Maryland Railway was incorporated to succeed the Western Maryland Rail Road. Listed as directors of the new company were Bush, Pierce, George Gould, and Robertson, with Bush later being elected president and Robertson as vice-president and general manager.

The W. Md. and the P. & L. E. signed a traffic agreement on January 18, 1910, to allow the W. Md. to use the P. & L. E. tracks from Connellsville to Pittsburgh. The W. Md. proposed to start work on the Connellsville extension immediately.

A. M. Smith, the new general manager of the C. & C. met with Robertson on February 25 to try to improve the allocation of cars to the C. & C. Smith was told that the W. Md. would soon place an order for 500 steel hoppers and 400 steel underframe gondolas.

One of the longest locomotives in the World, weight 264 Tons, used on the Black Fork Grade out and of Hendricks, W. Va.

Fig. 243. W. Md. No. 957 at Hendricks, circa 1912

Robertson also mentioned that a couple of Mallet engines were to be purchased for pusher service on the Blackwater grade. One of these engines, No. 957, is shown in 1912 at Hendricks (Fig. 243).

The year 1910 did not seem to be a good year on the West Virginia Division with wrecks, fires and floods occurring regularly. Problems started on February 27 when engine No. 415 ran away from the yard at Douglas with a hostler on board who was unable to bring the engine under control on the Blackwater grade. Just before the engine derailed and rolled down the bank at Canyon Point, the hostler attempted to jump, but received injuries from which he later died. The engine was not recovered until March 21 when it was sent to Elkins for repairs.

The tannery at Hambleton was totally destroyed by fire on March 24 (Fig. 244). The local newspapers estimated the loss at $500,000 and 200 men were thrown out of work. The tannery was not rebuilt.

Another wreck occurred on April 13, when a mixed train of two passenger cars and seven freight cars, en route from Davis to

Fig. 244. The burning of the Hambleton Leather Company, March 24, 1910

Thomas, jumped the track. The two passenger cars went down an embankment, injuring eight passengers. The series of misfortunes continued into May, when two freight wrecks occurred within a couple of days of each other at Westernport and Gorman.

As if wrecks were not enough to keep the W. Md. crews busy, heavy rains in the middle of June caused damage to the railroad around Thomas and William and the Blackwater grade. The Dry Fork and Valley River railroads were also severely damaged.

Before the storm, a party of officials from the West Virginia Pulp and Paper Company had inspected the company's properties in Covington and Cass, and this had given rise to rumors that the company would soon extend its railroads into the Elk River valley. This was confirmed in October when a charter was issued to the Greenbrier, Cheat and Elk Railroad Company to build from Bemis to Webster Springs. The railroad was to become very important in the W. Md.'s future, quite apart from its connection with the C. & I. at Bemis.

During July 1910, the Davis Coal and Coke Company secured a long-term contract to supply coal to the Bethlehem Steel Company. The contract called for the Davis Coal and Coke Company to supply between 2,000 and 6,000 tons of coal per day

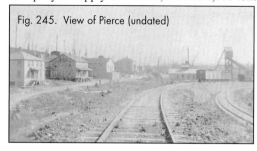

Fig. 245. View of Pierce (undated)

starting in May 1912, and this made it necessary to open additional mines. A new shaft mine, No. 38, was developed at Benbush on Snyder Run above Coketon, and two shafts, No. 39 and No. 40, were sunk at Pierce (Fig. 245). A branch, the Sand Run Branch, was built during 1910 and 1911 to connect the mines with the W. Md. at Sand Run Junction, one mile north of Thomas. All three mines were reported to be in production in 1911. To accommodate the miners and their families, the company was reported to be planning to build 100 double frame houses during the spring of 1912. A third mine at Pierce, No. 43, began production in 1914. The Sand Run branch also served the Fairfax Sand Company's quarry. A slope mine, No. 41, had been started in April between Thomas and Davis and was reported to be in production by February 1911. However, the mine only lasted until 1915 when it was closed due to low production. The mine at Benbush was also reported to be in production by February 1911. The new mines all produced coal from the Davis seam.

Fire destroyed the tipple of the Davis Colliery Company at Harding on September 15 (Fig. 246). The Junior Coal Company had not been included in the sale of the Davis Coal and Coke

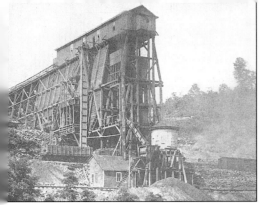

Fig. 246. Davis Colliery Company tipple at Harding

Company properties in 1902, and had been absorbed into Davis's new coal company, the Davis Colliery Company. Davis had tried to sell the Harding and Junior mines to the W. Md. in 1909 for $1,000,000, but a report (November 26, 1909) by C. H. Smith, assistant to Receiver Bush, put the value at $378,000 and recommended against the purchase. The report mentioned that 136 coke ovens were included in the property and that the output of both mines in 1907 was 206,000 tons of coal. Smith was critical particularly of the ventilation system in the Junior mine, which he claimed was inadequate and against state law. This observation was confirmed on February 4, 1911 when it was reported that the mine had been closed indefinitely by a state mine inspector for insufficient ventilation.

November was another bad month for wrecks on the West Virginia Division. Sixteen cars piled up at Schell on November 9, killing a brakeman. This was followed by a ten car pile up on November 21, and on November 26, the water tower at Poland collapsed causing a wreck involving W. Md. No. 509 and 11 cars. A new tower was reported to have been completed on December 8.

A report of the Cumberland coal trade for 1910 showed that the year had been good for both the Georges Creek and Upper Potomac fields, with production from the latter field being 3,384,961 tons. The new year did not start on an encouraging note as many mines were working less than full time and furloughs occurred on both the W. Md. and the B. & O. However, this did not deter the W. Md. from ordering new passenger cars and freight engines. Several of the new passenger cars were delivered at Cumberland in August. The engines were delivered from Alco-Richmond in November becoming the H7A class joining six similar H7 locomotives purchased from Baldwin a year earlier.

A second massive explosion occurred at a Davis Coal and Coke Company mine at 8:30 A.M. on April 24, 1911. The explosion occurred at Mine No. 20, sometimes referred to as the Ott Mine, located near Chaffee and penetrating under Elk Garden. Twenty-three miners were killed in the explosion. This was the second time that an explosion had occurred at this mine; the first time the mine had been empty. The death toll was less than it could have been had a full day shift of 200 men been at work. A coroner's jury later found that the explosion was due to a "blown out" charge igniting coal dust and that gas did not play a roll in the disaster. A grand jury in July brought in indictments for criminal negligence against the company and the mine foreman for allowing accumulations of dust and not having the fans working prior to the accident.

On April 20, following the resignation of President Bush, Alexander Robertson was elected president. At the same time, Steiner, the superintendent of the West Virginia Division was transferred to the Maryland Division at Hagerstown. H. H. Berry was appointed superintendent of the West Virginia Division.

The Davis Coal and Coke Company was in the news again in June when it completed a 160 foot tall concrete smoke stack at Thomas (Fig. 247). The stack was reported to be one of the tallest in the state at the time. The stack was part of a new power plant that had been started in the fall of 1910 to provide electricity for the mines around Thomas.

On July 26, there was another massive cave-in at tunnel No. 1, which was expected to take several weeks to clear. Passengers had to be transferred over the hill, and a reduction in freight traffic on the C. & I. of five percent during July was attributed to the closure. Work on the tunnel was slowed on August 5, when a number of laborers quit, claiming the work was unsafe.

Fig. 247. Davis Coal and Coke Company's new smoke stack at Thomas

On August 7, a Durbin to Elkins passenger train, No. 53, was delayed when it hit a bear 22 miles south of Elkins. The bear was finally dispatched with a rifle shot. This incident was followed by an excursion train striking a herd of cows, near Montes, on August 20. Two passenger cars were derailed, one turning over, but no passengers were injured.

The C. & I. was not the only branch experiencing a spate of distressing wrecks. The Belington branch was the scene of an accident to a passenger train on August 5, when train No. 44 was turned into a siding to avoid a freight train. Insufficient warning had been given to the engineer of the passenger train to enable him to slow down. The engine, No. 44, tender and two passenger cars piled up on some rocks. The passengers were severely shaken, but no serious injuries were reported.

For the W.Md., 1912 was to be an important year although January started badly when a fire destroyed the coaling tipple at Ridgeley. This was followed by the collapse of a crane that was being used by contractors to rebuild the Wills Creek bridge and which caused some delay to the work. The tipple at Ridgeley was rebuilt by the company's own forces; at the same time contractors were building a new coaling tipple at West Virginia Central Junction. Work on strengthening the Potomac River bridge at Cumberland was completed on April 14 when one of the W. Md.'s 700 class consolidations passed over for the first time. At the same time, work began on the construction of new shops and a roundhouse some two miles from Ridgeley at a point originally known as the Miller farm and later referred to as Maryland Junction.

An inspection train passed over the Connellsville extension on May 23, although regular freight service did not start until August 1 and passenger service on September 30. This extension gave the W. Md. an important role as a bridge route between the railroads of the Midwest and the eastern seaboard (Fig. 248).

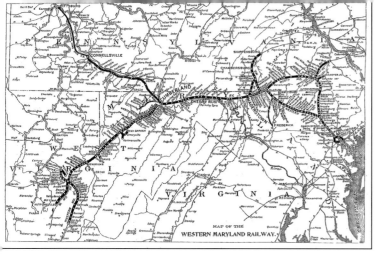

Fig. 248. The Western Maryland Railway in 1912
From the Western Maryland Railway Shippers' Guide, 1911-1912
West Virginia and Regional History Collection,
West Virginia University Library

There was a further delay in the Wills Creek bridge work when for a second time, a construction crane collapsed on July 1. The girder was placed on July 15 without incident and the final girder was placed on August 6. Work also started on a new bridge across the Potomac River to serve a new depot proposed for Cumberland. Approval for the construction of the depot was given by Cumberland City Council at the end of July. The depot was to be built near the original West Virginia Central depot on land purchased from the C. & O. Canal. The land included the Little Basin, (see Fig. 110), now reported to be "mosquito breeding cesspools" and full of decaying barges. The Tremont Hotel, a National Road landmark for over 100 years, was demolished also.

Fig. 249. Collision near Gorman, March 30, 1912
Collection of the Western Maryland Railway Historical Society

On the West Virginia Division, business continued much as before with the usual catalogue of fires, wrecks and floods. Fire destroyed the mill of the Tygart River Lumber Company at Mill Creek in March, and the sawmill of M. M. and D. D. Brown of Elkins in April. Two engines (Nos. 718 and 515) collided head on near Gorman on March 30 due to misunderstood orders (Fig. 249). Eighteen cars were damaged and an engineer injured. A second accident occurred at Gorman on July 17 when a passenger train derailed as it was entering a siding to allow another train to pass. Two cars went over a bank, but two others remained upright. Four passengers were seriously injured and several others received minor injuries.

The worst flood ever recorded to this time in Randolph County occurred on July 24 and 25 and did considerable damage to the West Virginia Division. A passenger train on the C. & I. reached tunnel No. 1 on its way to Elkins, but because of slides at both ends of the tunnel, had to reverse back down to Bowdon where the pas-

sengers had to spend the night on the train. Another train heading up the Blackwater grade got as far as Finley Run where a culvert had washed out. The passenger train, along with three following freight trains, had to back down the grade to Hendricks. On the Dry Fork Railroad, the bridge across the Blackwater River was washed out and ended up jammed against the Elk Lick bridge of the Otter Creek Boom and Lumber Company. Particularly hard hit was the Elk Garden branch between Harrison and Emoryville. At Harrison, several coal cars were swept into the Potomac River. The branch was expected to be closed for two weeks, but was not finally reported open until September 19.

The flood also destroyed the bridge across the Potomac River at Chaffee, which had been built in 1905 by the Three Forks Coal and Coke Company. This company had built a narrow gauge railroad up Three Forks Run in 1904 to the site of the new town of Vindex and mines in the vicinity owned by the company. The bridge was rebuilt in 1913 and the track converted to standard gauge at the same time.

In anticipation of the opening of the Connellsville extension, new engines, passenger cars and freight cars had been ordered. Six passenger cars from the Barney and Smith Car Company of Dayton, Ohio were scheduled for the Baltimore to Elkins service, and nine

Fig. 250. W. Md. Class K-2, 4-6-2, No. 209 at Cumberland, July 1952
Collection of Harold K. Vollrath

new Pacific engines, Class K-2, arrived from Baldwin for passenger service in early September (Fig. 250). Fifteen 2-8-0's had been ordered from Alco-Richmond and these arrived at this time becoming class H-7B and numbered 750-764 (Fig. 251). These differed from the H7 and H7A locomotives

Fig. 251. W. Md. Class H-7B, 2-8-0, No. 750 at Elkins, July 1950. Behind No. 750 is Class H8 No. 778
Collection of Harold K. Vollrath

as they were fitted with piston valves and superheaters.

A serious wreck occurred at Neffs, near Chaffee, on September 11, between a work train and an eastbound freight. The freight was hauled by W. Md. No. 458, which was one of the last engines deliv-

Fig. 252. W. Md. No. 458. Ex-West Virginia Central No. 47 at Cumberland, October 1940
Collection of Harold K. Vollrath

ered to the West Virginia Central (Fig. 252). The work train was pushing three cars of rails and a caboose in which the men were riding, when No. 458 plowed into the caboose. Two men were killed, including a track foreman, and 17 were injured.

In the fall of 1912, there was news of other West Virginia railroads of importance to the W. Md. The Greenbrier, Cheat and Elk Railroad announced that bids would be received until September 20 for the construction of ten miles of road to connect with the W. Md. near Bemis. In October, the Central West Virginia and Southern Railroad was incorporated to take over the Dry Fork Railroad. R. F. Whitmer remained the president of the new company. The reason for the change is not known, although the D. F. reached its maximum passenger and freight tonnage level during this time and then entered a period of decline.

Work started on a new freight depot, which was located on South Mechanic Street in Cumberland, on October 11. This was to be a three-story brick structure with stone trim, and was finished and ready for use by April 1913.

A new sleeping car service was inaugurated on October 26 between Baltimore and Elkins. The schedule called for a train to leave Baltimore at 9:00 P.M. with sleepers for Pittsburgh and Elkins. The Elkins car was detached at Cumberland at 2:20 A.M. and remained there until 7:00 A.M. when it left on Train No. 1 for Elkins arriving at 12:15 P.M. The return train (Train 4) left Elkins at 3:40 P.M., arriving in Cumberland at 8:55 P.M. It remained there until 1:45 A.M. when it left for Baltimore, reaching that city at 7:25 A.M.

Fire destroyed the roundhouse at Ridgeley on November 4. The 19-stall roundhouse contained eight locomotives at the time of which only three could safely be removed. The damage was estimated at $257,000. The company decided not to rebuild the roundhouse but to concentrate its resources on the new roundhouse being built at Maryland Junction. Two of the fire damaged engines were returned to service on November 14 after receiving repairs in the Elkins shops.

President Robertson resigned on November 7 due to ill health. He was replaced by J. M. Fitzgerald, who had been appointed vice-president in September, with responsibility for the railroad. Robertson was succeeded as director by J. D. Greene, who was closely associated with John D. Rockefeller. Winslow Pierce withdrew from the Board of Directors on January 21, 1913, leaving Rockefeller's representatives in the majority. Rockefeller, along with a couple of banks, was reported to control 60 percent of the W. Md.'s stock at this time.

A new schedule went into effect on the West Virginia Division on March 16. The most noticeable change was the reduction from two trains each way daily on the C. & I. to one train each way. The local newspapers claimed that the W. Md. had made no effort in the past to connect with the C. & O. at Durbin and this had led to the reduction in passenger traffic.

May was not a good month on the West Virginia Division on account of a number of wrecks. A wreck near Chaffee on May 16 caused the death of a painter who had been riding on a gondola, which derailed along with seven other cars. The road was closed for six hours and passengers on two trains were transferred round the wreck site. Two days later, an engineer was killed on the Haddix grade when his engine, No. 502, derailed and rolled down a bank. No. 502 was hauling nine cars up the grade heading towards Elkins, but had to cut the train in two parts to get up the hill. The engine was rolling back down the hill for the second section when it derailed.

On May 26, the kindling wood mill of the Keystone Wood Company at Hambleton burnt to the ground (Fig. 253). The mill

Fig. 253. Keystone Wood Company mill at Hambleton
West Virginia and Regional History Collection, West Virginia University Library

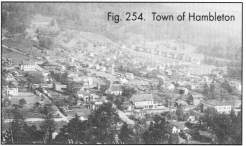

Fig. 254. Town of Hambleton

Fig. 255. Street scene in Hambleton
Collection of the Tucker County Historical Society

used scrap wood from the mill of the Otter Creek Boom and Lumber Company and because this mill was expected to close shortly, the kindling mill was not rebuilt. The Otter Creek plant closed on October 3, 1914. With two industries destroyed by fire and its last mill about to close, Hambleton entered a period of slow decline. Two views of the town in its heyday are shown in Fig. 254 and Fig. 255.

The Otter Creek mill belonged to the same owners as the mill of the Tygarts River Lumber Company at Mill Creek, which closed in July 1913. Mill Creek still remained a prosperous community for a few more years as three other companies operated in the area. The Wilson Lumber Company, now owners of the Valley River Railroad (Fig.

Fig. 256. Valley River Railroad No. 5 at Mill Creek, circa 1911
Collection of Harold K. Vollrath

256), operated a camp at Spangler, which the railroad reached in 1913. The Alton Lumber Company had taken over the operations of Hench, Dromgold and Shull, and D. E. Lutz and Sons operated a

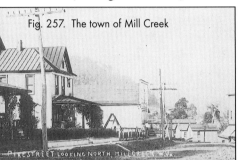

Fig. 257. The town of Mill Creek

logging railroad in the vicinity of Valley Bend. The town of Mill Creek (Fig. 257) had a population in 1913 of approximately 1,000. The depot, built by the West Virginia Central in 1902 at Mill Creek was shown in Fig. 166.

A new schedule went into effect on the W. Md. on June 15, which made some minor changes around Elkins. More important was a schedule announced for the same day by the C. & C. and the B. & O. in which through trains were to be run from Grafton via Belington to Elkins using the C. & C. tracks. This move upset President Fitzgerald of the W. Md. who claimed that the C. & C. was in violation of an agreement of September 1, 1911 allowing it to use the W. Md.'s facilities in Elkins. Fitzgerald refused to allow the service to continue after June 29. The deadline was extended for an additional ten days, and although there was some consideration by the C. & C. to building its own depot at Elkins, the service was discontinued.

On July 13, the mill of the Beaver Creek Lumber Company at Davis was destroyed by fire after having been closed in 1904 and standing empty since that time. This left three major industries in Davis, the West Virginia Pulp and Paper Company, the Babcock Lumber and

Fig. 258. Corner of Thomas Avenue and 5th Street, Davis

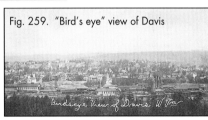

Fig. 259. "Bird's eye" view of Davis

Boom Company and the tannery. The population of Davis in 1910 was 2,615, and expanded for a few years after this but then commenced to decline. The town was reported to have two good hotels, seven churches and a "splendid business center." (Fig. 258).

A "birds eye" view of Davis is shown in Fig. 259 with the Babcock mill on the right, and the depot between the mill and the stone bank building in the center of the picture.

A close-up of the Babcock mill is shown in Fig. 260 and a panoramic view of the lumber yards and the town is shown in Fig.

Fig. 260. Babcock Lumber and Boom Company's mill at Davis

261. Babcock had extended its logging railroads along both sides of the Blackwater Canyon, and by 1912 most of the timber had been cut on the north side. The Babcock company used skidders on the north side to remove the timber

Fig. 261. Babcock lumberyards and the town of Davis

Fig. 262. Babcock Lumber and Boom Company skidder and log loader at work in the Blackwater Canyon

(Fig. 262), but by 1913, all three of the company's skidders were in use on the south side of the Canyon.

The skidders consisted of a mast, which could be as high as 75 feet to which was attached a cable nearly half a mile long. The other end of the cable was attached to a convenient tree. A truck was hauled along the cable, and to the truck were attached cables for dragging the logs. The skidders cleared the timber in a circular area before being moved to another site.

Babcock operated about 45 miles of logging railroads with six more under construction across Mozark Mountain

Fig. 263. Babcock Shay locomotive and woods crew

towards Dry Fork. Nine locomotives and four log loaders were in use on the railroads (Fig. 263). Typical company housing is shown in Fig. 264, with the town of Davis on the other side of the Blackwater River.

The new Potomac River bridge between

Fig. 264. Babcock Lumber and Boom Company housing at Davis
Collection of the Western Maryland Railway Historical Society

Fig. 265. The Western Maryland depot in Cumberland
Collection of the Western Maryland Railway Historical Society

Cumberland and Ridgeley was opened to traffic on July 3, the first train over being the eastbound Chicago Limited. At the end of the month the new passenger depot in Cumberland opened, replacing the old Central Station of the West Virginia Central (Fig. 265). The old building was demolished in August. The W. Md. also expected the new roundhouse at Maryland Junction to by open by August 1.

July 29 saw two wrecks on the W. Md., the first in the yards at Belington when a passenger train, already five hours late, hit some loaded coal hoppers. The engineer and fireman jumped before the crash and escaped injury, the passengers received the inevitable "shaking up." On the same day, the axle on the tender of a passenger engine on the Huttonsville branch broke, derailing the tender. The train continued across a trestle with the tender dragging along the ties, before it could be stopped. This time no one was injured or even shaken. A few days later, engine No. 153, pulling passenger train No. 1, ran into an open switch at Elkins and hit a string of four empty coal cars in a siding. Again the engineer and fireman escaped injury by jumping; the passengers, who were preparing to alight, were shaken and cut by flying glass.

Lee Ott, the general superintendent of the Davis Coal and Coke Company resigned effective August 1 to become a member, and later chairman, of the Public Service Commission of West Virginia. The Commission had been appointed earlier in the year by the governor, and had an oversight role of the operations of railroads and utilities in the state. Ott had started with the Davis Coal and Coke Company some 20 years earlier as a mule driver. President Fitzgerald announced in September that A. W. Galloway would become the new vice president and general manager of the coal company. Galloway was appointed also president of the Buxton and Landstreet Company in March 1914.

Complaints about service on the C. & I. continued throughout the summer and into the fall. Trouble reached a climax on November 3, when the morning train to Durbin left four hours late due to a shortage of engines. The W. Md. finally instituted a new schedule on November 16, in which two trains each way daily ran on the C. & I., and a similar service was instituted on the Huttonsville branch.

On November 10, the heaviest snowfall since 1908 hit the West Virginia mountains. At Davis, three feet of snow fell and drifts of six to ten feet deep were reported. As in 1908, a passenger train was marooned between Thomas and Davis, and three engines were reported to be stuck in a drift at Francis.

It was reported on December 25, that the lake at the new dam on Stony River was now full of water. The dam had been built by the West Virginia Pulp and Paper Company to ensure a steady flow of water down the North Branch for the mill at Luke. Work had commenced on the dam on June 14, 1912, but the contractor gave

up on March 12, 1913. The dam was finished by the Ambursen Hydraulic Construction Company of Boston, which had designed the structure. The dam was finished on July 23 and was 1,070 feet long and was a hollow reinforced concrete structure. A reporter for the Davis News visited the dam on its completion and noted that the only way the dam could fail was for the water to "soak through the bedrock" and come up under the dam. Even then only one or two sections of the dam would give way. Unfortunately this was exactly what was to happen. Although most of the dam was built on bedrock, some of it had been built on a layer of clay that overlay

Fig. 266. Stony River dam, circa 1918

a layer of sand. Water was noticed to be leaking on January 14, 1914 and a warning was issued to communities along the Potomac that a collapse was imminent. A section of the dam collapsed at 9:20 A.M. on January 15. Newspaper reports indicated a "wall of water 15 feet high" swept down the Potomac but the reports were grossly exaggerated and there was little damage and no loss of life.

The dam was rebuilt by June 1915, and served with no further problems (Fig. 266).

W. Md. freight depot at Elkins was destroyed by fire on January 29, 1914. A new building was commenced in September, but until this building was finished (Fig. 267), business

Fig. 267. New freight depot at Elkins, 1917
Collection of the Western Maryland Railway Historical Society

was conducted from an old passenger car.

An additional 20 freight engines arrived from ALCO in the spring. These became the H8 class and differed from the various H7 classes by having smaller driving wheels and a greater tractive effort. A member of this class, No. 785, is shown at Elkins in May 1953 (Fig. 268).

Fig. 268. W. Md. Class H8 No. 785 at Elkins in May 1953
Collection of Harold K. Vollrath

In January, it was reported that the W. Md. had lost money the previous year, in part because it could not move all the freight that it was offered. This led to the resignation of President Fitzgerald at the end of February and his replacement by Carl R. Gray who had been president of the Great Northern Railway. A few days after taking office Gray visited Elkins and toured the C. & I. and Huttonsville branches. He later was reported by the New York Times as saying that a large expenditure would be needed before the W. Md. could become profitable. The red ink continued to pile up in May and June but it was expected that a better showing would be made in the new fiscal year when the railroad completed

Fig. 269. Flood damage near Oakmont, June 1914

some major projects.

The loss of the Stony River dam caused problems for the mill at Luke during the summer of 1914, which was exceptionally dry. Because of low water in the North Branch, production had to be curtailed and workers furloughed. Problems also were encountered by the W. Md., when many of the gravity-fed water towers went dry. What rains did fall caused flash floods in Cumberland in June, and destroyed the tracks near Oakmont on the Elk Garden branch (Fig. 269).

An improvement in the coal business also was expected with the onset of war in Europe in August 1914. Mine No. 52 of the Davis Coal and Coke Company resumed work in August after having been closed for nearly three months. Traffic on the W. Md. was reported to be above normal in September with large shipments of coal and coke to eastern destinations, but by November conditions had again deteriorated. The mines around Junior were reported to have closed indefinitely and the mines of the Davis Coal and Coke Company were only working two days a week in December.

On November 11, a fire was reported to have destroyed one mill of the Babcock Lumber and Boom Company at Davis, but the mill was reported to be back in operation by the end of the year.

Fig. 270. Wreck at Big Run Curve, December 17, 1914
Collection of William Metheny

Fig. 271. Wreck train at work at Big Run, December 17, 1914. W. Md. crane No. 1651 is ex-West Virginia Central crane No. 3
Collection of William Metheny

Another wreck occurred on the Blackwater grade on December 17, when engine No. 511 with 33 cars got out of control and ran down the grade. The engineer and fireman jumped at Tub Run; the engineer broke a leg and the fireman suffered a fractured skull. The engine derailed at Big Run and all but two of the cars and the caboose left the track (Fig. 270). One brakeman, who had stayed with the train, was killed, and three other crewmen were injured. Wreck trains from Cumberland and Thomas worked at both ends of the wreck to clear the tracks (Fig. 271), but it was midday on December 19 before the line was open. Engine No. 511 was reported to be back in service by the end of January 1915.

Fig. 272. Mine No. 42 at Kempton in 1939
Collection of the Library of Congress

During the years 1912 and 1913, the Davis Coal and Coke Company had explored parts of Garrett County, Maryland, and had discovered workable quantities of Davis coal in the southwest corner. In 1913, work began on sinking a shaft mine, No. 42, and by 1914 the mine was producing coal (Fig. 272). The W. Md. completed a branch to serve the mine in 1914. A town, Kempton, developed around the mine, which by February 1915, had 48 houses and a large Buxton and Landstreet store.

In February 1915, it was reported that John D. Rockefeller had invested heavily in the Consolidation Coal Company. This led to the belief that shipments from the company's mines along Georges Creek would be diverted to the W. Md. By March, such shipments began, and an 11 percent increase in coal and coke traffic for the month was reported. The W. Md. was reported also to be considering extensions into Consolidation properties around Fairmont, West Virginia and Somerset, Pennsylvania.

On June 12, the Elkins Inter-Mountain reported that the Baldwin Locomotive Works had received an order for 250 locomotives to be supplied to Russia. This was part of a larger order, shared with the American Locomotive Company, to supply 2-10-0 decapod locomotives to Russia. With the collapse of Czarist Russia in 1917, some of these locomotives remained undelivered, and after re-gauging and other changes, were turned over to U. S. railroads. The W. Md. eventually received 10 of these engines, which became class I-1 and were numbered 1101-1110. These engines were to see service on the West Virginia Division.

A fire destroyed a section of the mill at Evenwood belonging to the Raine-Andrews Lumber Company on July 1. The fire did not seem to have upset operations too greatly as 70 cars per month of finished lumber were still being shipped in August. At about the same time the Parsons Pulp and Paper Company moved its hardwood mill from Laneville to Horton. The mill began sawing at its new location in March 1916.

W. Md. No. 92 (ex-West Virginia Central No. 43.) was wrecked on September 9 when it hit a broken rail near Roaring Creek Junction as it was pulling a train to Grafton. The baggage car also left the track and the engineer, fireman and a crewmember were injured.

During the summer, the mines along the W. Md. showed a considerable increase in production due in part to foreign orders. The Davis Coal and Coke Company resumed operations at mine No. 52 near Westernport, contemplated reopening the Buxton mine and opening new mines at Elk Garden. In September, the Davis Coal and Coke Company started work on a new mine on Beaver Creek near Davis. Coal shipments from the new mine started in May 1916.

Officials of the W. Md. met in October with the city commissioners of Keyser to discuss moving the depot from the town across the river to McCoole. This would avoid passenger trains having to reverse down the branch and hence save time. At the same time, a new con-

Fig. 273. Depot at Westernport in its new location, 1917
Collection of the Western Maryland Railway Historical Society

nection between the C. & P. and the W. Md. at Westernport was under construction to facilitate the passage of eastbound trains off the C. & P. This meant that the depot at Westernport had to be moved. This move was completed by December, and the building painted a dark gray with dark trim to give it a "very pretty appearance." (Fig. 273).

The Davis News announced in November that a new coal company was being organized to mine coal along Deep Run near Shaw. The new company, the Deep Run Big Vein Coal Company, announced that it would start shipping coal on February 1, 1916. By August 1916, the company was reported to have re-laid nearly two miles of standard gauge track along the old Mineville branch and to possess one Shay locomotive for the movement of cars. By June 30, 1916, the company had produced 21,527 long tons of coal; this increased to 34,0304 tons for the final six months of 1916. Other coal companies were also drawn to the area.

The new year, 1916, did not start well when a massive explosion occurred at the Kempton No. 42 mine on February 29. Seventy-one miners were in the mine at the time, fourteen were killed instantly; two more died of their injuries after being rescued from the mine. The mine was later inspected by the state mine inspector for Maryland who concluded that the explosion had been caused by a "blowout shot." This was the same cause as had been given for the Elk Garden explosion on April 24, 1911.

On April 7, the West Virginia Pulp and Paper Company announced that the plant at Davis would soon go to the eight-hour day, which was becoming the norm throughout the industry. How

Fig. 274. Remains of the mill of the Laurel River Lumber Company at Jennington
West Virginia and Regional History Collection, West Virginia University Library

the wages would be changed to avoid the workers taking a loss was not announced, although the company claimed to "pay the very highest wages prevailing."

Fire destroyed yet another mill along the C. W. Va. & S. on May 4, when the mill and machine shops at Jennington belonging to the Laurel River Lumber Company were lost (Fig. 274). This mill had originally been built by the Jennings Bros. Lumber Company in 1905 and sold to Laurel River in 1909. The planing mill was not destroyed and continued to operate; it was reported that the mill would be rebuilt. The new mill lasted until 1921 when advertisements for its sale appeared in the local newspapers. Included in the sale were one eight foot double band mill, one locomotive, one log loader and 50 houses.

The mill at Dobbin (Figs. 275 and 276) closed during 1916 and the town was rapidly deserted. By

Fig. 275. The mill at Dobbin (undated)
West Virginia and Regional History Collection, West Virginia University Library

Fig. 276. The boarding house and company houses at Dobbin circa 1908
West Virginia and Regional History Collection, West Virginia University Library

Fig. 277. Depot at Dobbin
West Virginia and Regional History Collection, West Virginia University Library

Fig. 278. Wreck at Durbin, July 15, 1916
Collection of the Western Maryland Railway Historical Society

1921, the population was estimated to be 75, the depot (Fig. 277) being down graded to a flag stop at about this time. Trains Nos. 1 and 4 ceased to stop at Dobbin altogether in 1929.

Wrecks plagued the W. Md. during the second half of 1916. Five passengers were injured when a passenger train derailed near Montrose on July 10. The engine and two passenger cars left the rails and turned over. No reason was given for the accident. Five days later, a wreck occurred on the C. & I. when a passenger train, that had just left Durbin, ran into an open switch. The engine crashed into a string of stationary cars and was derailed (Fig. 278). The engineer and fireman were uninjured but seven passengers received minor injuries. The engine of the train was reported to be No. 348 (ex-West Virginia Central No. 29), a freight engine that is shown in Fig. 310.

A more serious wreck occurred on October 12, when an excursion train from Westernport to Hagerstown ran head on into a work train in the Knobmont yard. Two railroad employees were killed and 16 others injured. The I. C. C. later reported that the crew of the excursion train was at fault for not following proper procedures when passing through the yard. The report noted also that, "there have been a number of accidents on the Western Maryland Railway which were due in large measure to bad operating practices and deficiencies in methods employed in train operation."

Proposed changes by the W. Md. to the schedule in November produced a storm of criticism from a business group in Elkins. The group wanted an improvement in the schedule to Cumberland and also on the C. & I. It was pointed out that the trip from Cumberland to Ronceverte could be completed in one day, but that the reverse journey required 1.1/2 days.

A reorganization of the W. Md. occurred in January 1917 when several of the subsidiary railroads, including the Georges Creek and Cumberland Railroad, were absorbed. In March, the Davis Coal and Coke Company was separated from the railroad to become an independent company with A. W. Calloway as president.

Spring floods in March 1917 were particularly devastating along the Tygart Valley River at Huttonsville and Mill Creek, where the lumber plants were reported to have been damaged. Service was suspended on the Huttonsville branch on March 12 because of the high water. Damage was also reported at Hendricks where the track was washed out.

A national railroad strike, in support of the eight-hour workday, was called for March 17. At this time, the nation was preparing to enter the war against Germany, and President Wilson was reported to find the idea of the strike at such a time, as "deplorable." In anticipation of the strike, the W. Md. commenced to build a fence around the yards at Port Covington, but the strike was averted when the railroads bowed to political pressure and gave in to the demands of the workers. The nation finally declared war on Germany on April 6.

Although a national railroad strike had been averted, a strike of machinists occurred at the W. Md.'s Hagerstown shops on March 20 when the company attempted to use machinist helpers to do the work of machinists. The strike quickly spread to Elkins and Ridgeley. The strikers were joined on April 5 by the boilermakers, blacksmiths, sheet metal workers and pipe fitters when the W. Md. announced that the striking machinists would be paid off. The strike finally ended on June 5.

A new company, known as the Blackwater Coal Company, was formed in April to take over the J. Calvin Cooper mine near Davis. This mine was the only mine in Tucker County that was owned by neither the Davis Coal and Coke Company nor the Cumberland Coal Company. During 1914, it was reported that the mine had produced 11,802 tons of coal. The new company supplied coal to the pulp mill at

Fig. 279. Tipple of the Blackwater Coal Company near Davis

Davis, but the mine closed at the end of May 1919 although it later reopened (Fig. 279).

During the first half of 1917, the Buffalo Creek-Cumberland Coal Company mine near Bayard closed after operating since 1904. A new company, the Emmons Coal Mining Company, started production from its mine, Culpepper No. 1, located one mile southeast of Bayard, in 1917. The company, which owned five other mining operations in Pennsylvania, seems to have been more successful than the old company. Bayard's population in 1920 was reported to have increased to 1,074 and the opening of a mine in Maryland by the West Bethlehem Coal and Coke Company, opposite Bayard, assured the continuing prosperity of the town. The Emmons Coal and Coke Company built a municipal building in Bayard housing its offices, the fire department, and an auditorium. The company operated a passenger train each morning from Bayard to its mine for its employees.

On May 24, in an effort to improve the movement of freight on the nation's railroads during the war, instructions were issued by a special war board to consolidate passenger train service and to eliminate trains that were not well patronized. This move was

expected to lead to a reduction in service in the Elkins area. These steps were not sufficient to reduce congestion on a number of eastern railroads including the W. Md. and the B. & O. President Wilson announced on December 26, that the railroads would be taken over by the government at noon on December 28 and operated by William G. McAdoo as director general of railroads.

The annual meeting of stockholders of the W. Md. was held in Baltimore on October 17, 1917. At the meeting, George Gould announced his retirement from the board of directors. Gould had had little influence on the affairs of the W. Md. since the takeover of the company by interests loyal to the Rockefellers.

In March 1918, the worst floods on the Tygart Valley River were recorded. Three bridges on the Huttonsville extension were washed out, and slides were reported on the C. & I. Service between Elkins and Cumberland was not affected, although other railroads in the central part of West Virginia, including the C. & O. and the C. & C., had to suspend service.

Six thousand miners in the Georges Creek and Upper Potomac fields went on strike on April 15 for better working conditions and recognition of the United Mineworker's union. The strike resulted in the loss of 20,000 tons of coal per day at a time when the country was hard pressed to meet its fuel needs. The men returned on April 17 after pressure from the secretary of labor and the union. The shortage of coal at this time prompted A. W. Calloway, who had been appointed director in charge of bituminous coal distribution for the federal government in February, to ask for production increases of between 5 and 6,000,000 tons per month. Calloway did recognize that problems on the railroads in moving freight limited the extra production that could be achieved.

The coal trade journal, the "Black Diamond," reviewed the activities of the mines along the West Virginia Division in its June 22, 1918 issue. Production in the Upper Potomac field by the Cumberland Coal Company was approximately 200,000 tons per year. The company also operated 135 coke ovens. The Davis Coal and Coke Company in Tucker County produced 1,128,292 tons of coal during 1916, the last year for which figures were available. During the same time, production from the company's seven mines in Mineral County was 265,774 tons.

In Garrett County, Maryland, the Aberdeen Coal Company had been formed to operate on 500 acres of land owned by the Steyer Coal Company and 500 adjoining acres owned by the Bayard Coal and Coke Company in order to operate both properties more efficiently. One of the mines is shown in Fig. 280.

At Oakmont, on the Elk Garden branch (Fig. 281), the Abrams Creek Coal and Coke Company was capable of producing 600 tons per day with a force of 150 men, but was only operating at 85 percent capacity because of a shortage of coal cars. The

Fig. 280. Mine at Steyer, Maryland (undated)
Collection of the Maryland State Archives, Robert G. Merrick Collection

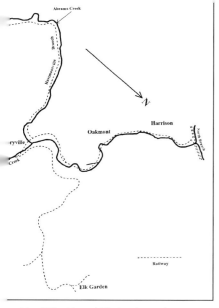

Fig. 281. Map of Elk Garden and
Hartmansville branches
Redrawn from the I. C. C. Valuation map
1919 with additions
from the 1923 Topographical Map of
Mineral County
Collection of the National Archives

Abrams Creek Coal and Coke Company had been organized in 1903 by S. D. Brady, and owned 500 acres of Upper Freeport coal lands.

By July 1, the yard, freight depots and engine facilities of the W. Md. and the C. & C. at Elkins were consolidated under one management. It was also noted that two W. Md. passenger trains between Cumberland and Connellsville would be discontinued, but that two B. & O. trains would be rerouted over the W. Md. tracks between these two towns. By the end of the month, the W. Md. and the B. & O. freight stations in Cumberland were also consolidated.

The war in Europe ended in November 1918 leading to speculation that the railroads would soon be returned to private ownership. The National Fuel Administration announced on January 1, 1919 that all price controls on coal would be lifted on February 1. At the time there was an abundance of coal and this led to mine closures, short work weeks and reductions in wages in the Upper Potomac and Georges Creek fields. Miners at the Emmons Coal Company in Bayard struck on February 11 when the company reduced the payment for each car loaded from $1.60 to $1.40. These problems led to a reduction in force on the W. Md. as coal shipments declined.

The mines and railroads were not alone in being beset by labor problems in 1919. On February 5, the West Virginia Pulp and Paper Company plant at Luke was closed in response to an effort by the men to unionize. The mill at Davis was also closed by a strike later in February.

In April 1919, the Davis Coal and Coke Company closed the mines at Davis on account of dirty coal. A month later, the company announced the end of its operations at Elk Garden, although the Dean Coal Company took over the lease held by the Davis Coal and Coke Company and commenced shipping coal. A year later, nearly 25,000 tons (long) had been shipped.

The Babcock Boom and Lumber Company at Davis announced a wage reduction on May 1 of between 12.1/2 and 20 percent, which led to a strike, although the company was able to continue production on a reduced basis. The tannery was also reported to be closed at this time.

More bad news occurred for the town of Davis on May 12, when the West Virginia Pulp and Paper Company informed the mayor that the company would no longer provide water for the town after July 31, 1919. The company had finally decided to close

Fig. 282. The West Virginia Pulp and
Paper Company mill at Davis (undated)
*West Virginia and Regional History
Collection,
West Virginia University Library*

the mill at Davis, which had now been shut down by the strike for 12 weeks. The company had expected to close the mill within the next couple of years because of the exhaustion of locally available timber supplies. The work of removing lead from the plant started on May 22 (Fig. 282); the remains of the plant and 40 acres of land were sold in November. The last trace of the plant was not removed until 1960 (Fig. 283).

A nationwide coal strike was called by the U. M. W. for November 1. District 16 of the union, which embraced the Georges Creek and Upper Potomac fields, joined the strike, which had an immediate impact on the W. Md. Fires were pulled in nine locomotives at Elkins and some employees were laid off. On November 8, a judge of the U. S. District Court of Indiana declared the strike illegal and the strike was called off by the union on November 11. Work resumed at both the Georges Creek and Upper Potomac mines on November 17, although the strike continued in

Fig. 283. Ruins of the pulp mill at
Davis (undated)
*West Virginia and Regional History
Collection,
West Virginia University Library*

the southern West Virginia coal fields and other states. Georges Creek and Upper Potomac miners walked off the job again on November 29 following the collapse of negotiations with the operators. It was reported on December 26, that some miners of the Davis Coal and Coke Company had returned to work, although most miners remained on strike. The strike led to the imposition of restrictions on the use of coal, which were even more stringent than had been applied during the war. This in turn led to a reduction by one third in passenger train service commencing on December 8. A proposal to end the strike was made by President Wilson on December 9; Wilson's proposal was accepted by the union and the strike ended on December 11. The W. Md. announced the restoration of all canceled trains to take effect at 12:01 A.M. on December 15.

A threatened nationwide strike by maintenance-of-way workers in February 1920, was also called off after an appeal by President Wilson. The railroads were finally returned to private ownership by the government on March 1, although there were many outstanding labor issues that threatened to erupt at any time. By the end of March, conditions on the railroads returned to normal, and the W. Md. and the B. & O. were able to report that the movement of freight was the greatest in three years. However the peace did not last long. Yard men on the B. & O. struck on April 12, which effected the W. Md.'s ability to move loads and essentially closed the railroad and the mines. Conditions returned to normal on April 17. Yardmen on the W. Md. at Hagerstown struck on June 26, although the men at Cumberland and Elkins continued to work. By the beginning of July, the strike had ended and the mines were reported to be receiving all the empty coal cars they needed.

At the beginning of November, the W. Md. announced that traffic over the road during the first ten months of the year was the heaviest ever. Hopes were expressed that 1920 would be a record year for the railroad. These hopes were threatened by a proposed strike of miners in the Georges Creek and Upper Potomac fields, scheduled for November 15, but the strike was averted at the last minute. It was reported that the Pennsylvania had laid off shopmen at Altoona in the middle of November due to a reduction in business, but both the W. Md. and the B. & O. denied that furloughs were imminent. However, by December, mines in the Fairmont region were closing down in response to poor demand for coal.

The first furlough of W. Md. shopmen at Hagerstown was announced on December 11. No furloughs were expected on the Elkins Division where the demand for coal continued.

Some changes affecting passenger service were announced in 1920. A new passenger train schedule went into effect on June 20, which eliminated the service on the Davis branch, but this was restored on August 18. In June, the W. Md. announced that the depot at Keyser would be removed and rebuilt at Keyser Junction across the river at McCoole in Maryland although no date for the move was given. Earlier in the year, on February 4, the depot at Blaine had been destroyed by fire and was replaced by a single story structure.

The business depression, which had started at the end of 1920, continued into 1921. It was announced at the end of January that 65 mechanics and 51 car repairmen at Maryland Junction would be laid off; at Elkins the force was reduced by 60 men. By February, the number laid off at Elkins had increased to 70 and it was reported that many of the smaller mines had closed and the larger mines were only working a couple of days each week. On February 25, notice was given by the W. Md. of its intent to reduce the wages of all employees, other than road and shopmen, effective March 27, 1921. As an additional economy measure, Sunday working was reduced as much as possible.

Fig. 284. W. Md. Class H9 No. 842 at Elkins, August 1949
Collection of Harold K. Vollrath

The recession did not stop the W. Md. accepting 40 new consolidation locomotives from Baldwin, the first of which, No. 801, was delivered at the beginning of March (Fig. 284). At the same time six old engines from the Elkins Division were sold to the Oklahoma Southwestern Railway.

The dullness of the coal trade continued throughout the spring. Senator Davis Elkins, son of Stephen B. Elkins, claimed that a "buyers' strike," caused by buyers hoping that the price of coal would drop before placing orders, was the reason for the lack of business. Elkins claimed that the wage increases given to the miners (the contract for which ran until April 1922), and the high freight rates charged by the railroads, contributed to the price of coal and these could not be changed. By the end of June, the con-

ditions in the coal industry were the worst since December 1920, and most mines were working only two days per week.

Complaints about passenger service in the area surfaced in June. It was claimed that the service between Cumberland and Elkins was the same as it was 30 years earlier, and that the sleeping car service to Baltimore, withdrawn during the war, had never been restored. Poor passenger service on the C. W. Va. & S. created trouble for the road from the West Virginia Public Service Commission and a new schedule, effective July 1, seemed to satisfy the public and the commission.

During August, coal traffic on the W. Md. was only 20 percent of normal. In the Upper Potomac field conditions of extreme poverty were reported to exist in the mining communities. The slump showed no sign of abating and continued into the fall. By early September a slight improvement in traffic was observed as the mines around Harrison and Blaine reopened with the miners accepting a reduced wage scale. The Garrett County Coal Company at Dodson also resumed on December 8 at the reduced scale. In the Georges Creek field, the Consolidation Coal Company closed most of its mines indefinitely throwing another 700 men out of work.

On December 12, the W. Md. reported that coal shipments from the Upper Potomac region had increased; 1000 cars were dispatched in a two-day period. This did not prevent an announcement on December 23 of more layoffs from the Elkins shops. An additional 40 men, including machinists, boilermakers and blacksmiths were discharged, bringing the employment in the shops to about 130 men.

At the end of December, it was reported that the Manor Coal Company, which had been formed in April 1920 to take over the operations of the Chaffee Coal Company at Vindex, would reopen the mines there on January 3, 1922. The mines at Vindex had been closed since the spring. The miners had agreed to a cut of between 25 and 30 percent in wages to enable the mines to reopen. Improvement in the traffic of coal and grain enabled the W. Md. to recall 20 furloughed firemen and brakemen at the end of January. The Davis Coal and Coke Company announced that its mines would close on February 1, 1922, but then reopened a few mines on February 17 at the reduced scale. By the middle of March, some picketing and violence were reported at Kempton and Thomas as some men held out for the old rate. At Bayard, the Emmons Coal Company evicted miners and their families from company housing if they had opposed the imposition of the reduced scale.

On January 12, 1922, the W. Md. announced that the shops and roundhouses in Baltimore would be operated by a contractor starting on January 16. A few days later, the W. Md. proposed to reduce the wages of all maintenance-of-way workers by 12.1/2 percent. The proposal was rejected by the union. This was followed on March 8 by an announcement that all maintenance-of-way work would also be placed with a contractor, the Dickson Construction and Repair Company. Maintenance-of-way employees would see their wages cut from 39.1/2 cents to 25 cents per hour and the workday increased from eight hours to ten. On March 16, the same company took over the W. Md. shops in Hagerstown, Cumberland and Elkins, again increasing the workday from eight to ten hours and reducing wages for all men. Machinists, for example, were reduced from 77 cents to 60 cents per hour and apprentices went from 42 cents to 20 cents per hour. A strike was called by the various unions for March 25, when the companies rejected a request to restore the wages to the previous level. On March 28, the W. Md. announced that the contractor would hire replacements for the striking workers. This created a tense situation when a trainload of strikebreakers arrived at the shops at Hagerstown on March 28 and was greeted by a mob of strikers. One striker was shot in the leg during the confrontation. On March 29, a dozen men were reported to be at work at Cumberland and the W. Md. claimed that it could operate almost normally on its Elkins Division. President Byers issued a statement on March 30 claiming that giving work to outside contractors was a necessary economy move, and permitted by the Transportation Act of 1920. The Railroad Labor Board had no jurisdiction in the matter, as the strikers were not employees of the railroad. The union position was that letting the work to outside contractors was a subterfuge to avoid decisions by the Railway Labor Board. A temporary restraining order was issued on March 31 by a federal judge in Baltimore, prohibiting the strikers from acts of violence against the W. Md.

A nationwide coal strike was called by the U. M. W. on April 1. The strike was effective in closing down the vast majority of mines in northern West Virginia and Georges Creek, although 16 mines were reported to be operating in the Upper Potomac region and a few small non-union mines continued to operate elsewhere. After a week it was reported that mines were working at Potomac Manor, Blaine, Thomas, and along the Chaffee and Elk Garden branches. The officials of the union, however, claimed that the shutdown was complete. In Davis, scene of several union demonstrations, city authorities passed an ordinance against loitering and unlawful assembly. Pickets were arrested at the Blackwater Coal Company mine near Davis, and the company was able to resume operations. By April 27, a steady return to work was reported in spite of the efforts of the union to keep the mines closed. On May 2 a demonstration by Reds in Thomas was feared, and a special train was used to bring five state policemen, armed with machine guns, from Elkins. The demonstration did not occur but "large quantities of literature of a Bolshevistic nature" were confiscated. By May 11, 28 mines were reported to be at work in the Upper Potomac territory. Several of the mines belonging to the Davis Coal and Coke Company were at work and a collapse of the strike seemed imminent. By May 17, production of coal in West Virginia exceeded that of the same week in 1920, when production was high, and also for the same week in 1921. The shaft mine at Thomas, No. 34, started work on May 22 when 40 men reported for work. The mines at Kempton, Benbush, and Pierce remained closed. Some 250 Georges Creek miners attempted to close the Luke mine of the West Virginia Pulp and Paper Company on June 5, but were dispersed by the sheriff.

On June 28, strikers at Thomas tried to prevent workers going to the mines and a near riot ensued. A large number of arrests were made of both strikers and their wives, and a special train was requested to take the prisoners to court at Parsons. Because of a lack of equipment, the W. Md. could only provide one car, No. 503, from the Davis branch, which was attached to the rear of a regular passenger train (Fig. 285). The wives of the strikers were placed in the regular ladies' car on the train. As the train was heading down the Blackwater grade, a flange on a wheel on the prisoners' car broke, and the car derailed and rolled down a bank. One man was killed and at least 50 were injured including two members of the National Guard who were escorting the prisoners. A relief train from Elkins brought a team of physicians and

Fig. 285. Striking miners and their wives boarding the train at Thomas, June 28, 1922
Collection of the Western Maryland Railway Historical Society

nurses to the scene and the injured were transported to local hospitals. Seventy-two lawsuits were eventually filed against the W. Md. for over $1,000,000 claiming the car was old, defective, and had been out of service for several years.

President Harding convened a conference on July 1 of operators and union representatives to try to reach an agreement, but the meeting was not a success. The president submitted a proposal to the conference on July 10 that the miners return to work at the old scale until August 10, by which time an arbitration panel would negotiate a new scale.

By now the strikers were becoming desperate as more men returned to work. On June 29, the Davis Coal and Coke Company tipple at Weaver was set on fire. This led the company to obtain an injunction preventing the strikers from gathering in groups anywhere near the company's mines. This had the necessary discouraging effect on the strikers, and by the middle of July, between 30 and 40 mines were in operation along the W. Md. producing some 20,000 tons of coal per week. By the middle of August, all the mines of the Davis Coal and Coke were running except No. 42 at Kempton. Mines on the Maryland side of the Potomac River did not reopen as readily as those on the West Virginia side because of intimidation by the strikers, which the Maryland authorities did nothing to prevent. The union was able to sign agreements with operators in several states on August 15 and by the end of August, 150 companies in northern West Virginia had signed an agreement with the union. The strike continued in the Georges Creek and Upper Potomac fields as the miners attempted to force the operators to recognize the union but without success. The result of the strike in West Virginia was to leave the union weaker than at the onset of the strike.

Although attention was focused on the miners' strike after April 1, the strike of the shopmen and the maintenance-of-way workers against the W. Md. continued. The W. Md. claimed on April 3 that normal operations were being conducted on the Elkins Division, and that ten men were being added to the shop forces each day. A day later it was reported that 27 engines would be taken out of service on the Elkins Division because of the reduced coal loadings. By the middle of April, the federal judge in Baltimore dissolved an injunction restraining the strikers from acts of violence and setting terms for the activities of the pickets. A few days later, a W. Md. assistant trainmaster was badly beaten by strikers, and a speeder was derailed by a thrown switch in the yards at

Ridgeley. Three employees were injured; one died of his injuries a couple of weeks later. These acts prompted the W. Md. to ask a federal judge in West Virginia to issue a temporary injunction again restraining the strikers, and the citizens of Thomas, from acts of violence and from interfering with the passage of trains. The judge obliged and the order was issued on April 22. Four days later, President Byers of the W. Md. announced that all locomotive repair work, formerly performed at Hagerstown, Ridgeley and Elkins would be transferred to Baltimore, eliminating 300 jobs at Ridgeley and 100 at Elkins. He also noted that 60 engines would be returned to Baldwin and the American Locomotive Company at Richmond for heavy repairs. The strikers received some support on May 10, when the Railroad Labor Board decided that contracting out shop work was in violation of the Transport Act and that provisions conflicting with the rules laid down by the Board were illegal. However, the railroads involved, including the W. Md., vowed to fight the ruling in court. The temporary restraining order issued on April 22, was confirmed by a federal judge in Wheeling on May 11.

On May 29, the Railway Labor Board announced a nationwide cut in wages for maintenance-of-way workers and cuts for other classes were expected to follow. The reductions led to a national strike of shopmen on July 1, involving approximately 400,000 men, which shut down the B. & O. entirely. The national strike was independent of the strike against the W. Md. where conditions remained the same. The Railroad Labor Board on July 20 awarded a total wage increase of $600,000,000 to the 2,000,000 railroad workers in the country but the strike continued. President Harding attempted to end the railroad strike on August 1, but by August 31 no progress was reported.

The Dickson Construction and Repair Company announced on July 5 an increase in wages for all its employees of 10 cents per hour. The company now employed 160 men at Elkins, 40 at Thomas and 300 at Maryland Junction. It was claimed that all the shops were filled with new employees and that the railroad was operating normally. President Byers issued a defiant statement on July 31, claiming that the W. Md. had no intention of giving up its contracting program.

On September 13, an end to the national strike appeared imminent when the union announced that the strikers could return to work on those railroads that accepted an agreement framed by the union. In West Virginia, the roads that signed included the B. & O., the C. & O. and the N. & W. The settlement did not include the W. Md., but by now the strikers were becoming discouraged and many returned to work with the Dickson company or joined the B. & O. Not all the strikers were willing to peacefully return to work; on September 15 a bridge near Cumberland was damaged by an explosion of dynamite.

President Byers again announced on October 3, that no progress was being made in settling the strike. Byers claimed that the W. Md. handled more coal in August 1922 than in any month in 1921 when there were no strikes, and in September, business was up 20 percent over August. Barracks that had been built to house the new workers at Elkins, Ridgeley and elsewhere, would be demolished, as the workers now had been assimilated into the communities.

At the beginning of November, more of the strikers at Hagerstown had given up, and secured jobs with the B. & O. By the middle of the month rifts occurred in the ranks of the remaining strikers, between those who wished to return to work and those wanting to continue the strike. On November 21, the Railroad Labor Board announced that the W. Md. contracts were merely a subterfuge to change wages and working conditions, and directed the railroad to reinstate the employees.

After the labor unrest of 1922, 1923 proved to be a very quiet year for the W. Md., although there was no end in sight to the strike against the mine operators in the Georges Creek and Upper Potomac fields, and the W. Md. shopmens' strike. President Byers announced in January his intention to take the decision of the Railway Labor Board to the courts, and meanwhile refused all efforts at mediation.

Shortage of coal cars in January caused a reduction in output from the mines of the Upper Potomac region, which received only 50 percent of empties required. By the beginning of February, the shortage had eased and 500 loads per day were being sent east from the Elkins Division. Falling demand later in February saw a reduction in the number of cars shipped to 400 per day, and by April only 50 percent of the normal tonnage of coal was being shipped east of Cumberland by the W. Md. and the B. & O.

A new timetable went into effect on June 17, which showed some minor changes to the schedule of trains on the Huttonsville branch (Fig. 286). The railroad promoted the new timetable, noting that if a passenger left Elkins at 7:10 A.M. he could arrive in Baltimore at 6:09 P.M. and then take the Pennsylvania Railroad to New York arriving there at 11:10 P.M. The citizens of Elkins were not entirely satisfied with the new arrangements as no trains on either the W. Md. or the B. & O. left the town after 3:00 P.M. The W. Md.

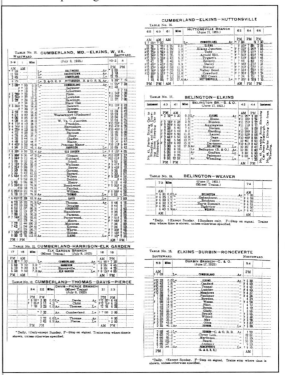

Fig. 286. Western Maryland Railway timetable, June 17, 1923

also asked the Public Service Commission for permission to discontinue trains on the Davis and Pierce branches as they were losing money. The P. S. C. granted approval to be effective July 8. The case was appealed and finally wound up in the West Virginia Supreme Court, which agreed with the W. Md.'s position on September 25.

By July, although shipments of coal were still only 50 percent of normal, the W. Md. was able to report record earnings for the first five months of 1923.

Only one serious wreck occurred during 1923. Passenger train No. 10, which had left Elkins at 7:10 A.M. on August 16, derailed between Shaw and Barnum. Engine No. 205, which was hauling a three car train consisting of a baggage and mail car (No. 180), a smoking car (No. 836) and a ladies' car, left the track, followed by the first two cars. The engine and cars rolled over, but although the ladies' car left the tracks, it remained upright. The engineer was killed and five crewmembers were injured. The fireman, who had been severely scalded, died later on a relief train taking him to hospital in Cumberland. Ten passengers also received minor injuries. The cause of the wreck was determined to be the excessive speed of the train.

The strike by union miners against the operators in the Georges Creek and Upper Potomac fields, was finally called off by the union on November 20. The strike had lasted 20 months. For some time, both fields had been operating at full capacity using non-union men.

During 1923, the West Virginia Geological Survey published its report on Tucker County in which it was reported by I. C. White that the "Davis" coal was not the Upper or Lower Kittanning as was originally thought, but actually the Upper Freeport seam. The "Thomas" coal, which was thought to be the Upper Freeport was reclassified as the Bakerstown coal.

In February 1924, a new company was organized, the Three Forks Lumber Company, which purchased 2,000 acres of timberlands near Vindex. The new company constructed a railroad to deliver its timber to Vindex for movement to the W. Md. by the Chaffee Railroad.

The W. Md. was hit by two devastating floods in 1924. The first, on March 29, was particularly damaging around Cumberland where the Potomac River went on a rampage. The floods caused all trains in and out of Cumberland to be canceled. At Piedmont the river was up to the C. & P. bridge across the Potomac. A W. Md. passenger train was marooned near Westernport; the clerk in the mail car staying at his post for five days before being rescued. To protect the Wills Creek and Potomac River bridges, the W. Md. placed cars loaded with limestone on the structures to weigh them down. This did not save the Potomac River bridge where two spans were washed away and several cars lost (Fig. 287). At Wills Creek, the W. Md. employed a crane to dislodge logs and debris from the bridge to prevent a dam forming. Two bridges, one at Shaw and the second at Harrison were washed out and considerable damage was done to the shops at Ridgeley. One of the worst hit towns was Kitzmiller in Maryland, across the river from Blaine. Relief supplies for the town had to be brought in by sled because of deep snow still remaining in the hills. It was also feared that the Stony River dam

Fig. 287. Potomac River bridge, Cumberland, March 1924

would again fail, but this fear proved groundless. Service between Baltimore, Cumberland and Connellsville was resumed on April 1, and trains also commenced running between Elkins, Thomas and Belington. Further south, the Blackwater River was reported to have reached its highest level ever. The C. W. V. & S. was also damaged but trains began running again on April 5. To compound the problems of repairing the damage, the Potomac flooded again on April 7, but this did not delay the start of traffic scheduled for April 8.

At its meeting in Hagerstown on April 9, the Maryland and District of Columbia Federation of Labor offered to help mediate the W. Md.'s shopmens' strike, which was now entering its third year. The offer was spurned by President Byers, leading to a call for a boycott of the W. Md.

Nearly a month after the flood, only ten mines out of 35 had resumed operations between Piedmont and Thomas. Demand for coal was slow, and the miners of the Davis Coal and Coke Company voluntarily agreed to accept a 25 percent cut in wages to ensure the mines stayed open.

On May 1, it was announced that the stockholders of R. F. Whitmer and Company had determined to dissolve the company and a certificate of dissolution was issued on July 9, 1924. The Parsons Pulp and Lumber Company had passed into the hands of a receiver in 1923. These actions did not affect the C. W. Va. & S., although the amount of lumber carried was considerably reduced from the peak year of 1912.

The second major flood of the year hit Cumberland on May 12. Traffic on the W. Md. was canceled early in the morning as water covered the tracks at the station in Cumberland, and slides were reported on the line to Elkins. Trains on the Durbin branch also had to be annulled because of slides. Both the B. & O. and the W. Md. were able to restore service on May 14. A report published in October 1925, placed some of the blame for the March and May floods on the W. Md.'s Wills Creek bridge and the embankment through Ridgeley, although this was denied by the company. Little action was taken on the report's recommendations.

On May 19, the city engineer of Cumberland reported that the Market Street bridge across the W. Md. tracks, which had been

Fig. 288. W. Md. Class I-1, 2-10-0, No. 1103 at Ridgeley, May 1947
Collection of Harold K. Vollrath

opened in February 1901 (Fig. 141), was too light for present use and was in a dangerous condition.

During an inspection tour of the Elkins Division by officials of the W. Md. on December 10, it was announced that business on the Division had never been better. To accommodate even more business, three of the "Russian Decapods," W. Md. Class I-1, (Fig. 288), were sent to Elkins on December 11, and by early January 1925, all ten were in service out of Elkins.

The new year, 1925, found the W. Md. optimistic about the

future freight loadings from the West Virginia Division and an increase in the Elkins shop force from 150 to 210 men was noted.

The W. Md. and the B. & O. were in trouble with the P. S. C. when the two roads discontinued a parlor car service between Elkins and Wheeling at the end of 1924 without giving the required notice. The service was reinstated at the beginning of April but both railroads filed in July to discontinue the service. The P. S. C. gave approval for the discontinuance effective August 15.

The spring of 1925 again found the coal industry in a slump. Wages along Georges Creek were reduced ten percent effective April 1, but by early June coal loadings had picked up sufficiently for the W. Md. to pull 415 cars from storage. By July, the W. Md. was able to report that revenue from the transportation of coal and coke was nearly back to 1924 levels. It was also reported that the mines on Abrams Creek had resumed operations for the first time since January 1. Coal shipments continued to increase into September, aided in part by a strike of miners in the anthracite fields. The increased demand for coal prompted the Emmons Coal Mining Company to grant a wage increase on September 1.

In the fall, the engineers and firemen of the W. Md. were upset that a pay increase granted by the Railroad Labor Board to Class 1 railroads had not been implemented by the W. Md. and there was a growing possibility of a strike. The W. Md. denied that it had been ordered by the Labor Board to award an increase and started advertising for replacement workers should a strike occur. Meetings between the unions and management proved futile. On October 7, the W. Md. issued a statement that men who failed to report for duty would be considered to have left the company's service and would lose seniority if they returned. The company also asked on October 12 that employees sign an agreement accepting new working rules commencing October 16. President Byers claimed on October 13 that the railroad had offered the men a 5.1/2 percent increase if the men would agree to a revision of the work rules. This the unions had refused and hence the new rules would go into effect without the increase. Byers concluded by saying, "The men must be punished." Prior to the deadline, employees who refused to sign the new agreement were dismissed prompting the unions to call a strike for 6:00 A.M. on October 15. Byers reported on October 16 that passenger service was being maintained and some freight trains were being operated with new employees. By October 21, Byers claimed that service on the railroad was near normal and thus the stage was set for a prolonged strike.

At the end of the year, an announcement was made that a contract had been let by the West Virginia Midland to extend from Webster Springs to Bergoo, the terminus of the Greenbrier, Cheat and Elk Railroad. The lumber

Fig. 289. Tannery at Gormania in the early 1920's

industry continued to decline in 1926 as the tannery at Gormania (Fig. 289) closed down its boilers leaving only a night watchman at the plant. Like so many other towns along the North Branch,

Fig. 290. The town of Gormania circa 1909

Gormania began a steady decline from its heyday in the early 1920's (Fig. 290). The tannery buildings were dismantled in the fall of 1938.

Early in 1926, the W. Md. announced plans for the construction of 1,800 new boxcars, part of which would be built at the Elkins shops. By April, the shops were completing 30 new cars per month, but this was later increased to 50 cars per month. Elkins was also expected to benefit from an increased movement of coal shipped through Durbin from the C. & O. By February, coal traffic on the Durbin branch had increased from 25 to 45 cars per day but this decreased later in the month due to the settlement of a strike in the anthracite coalfield.

For some time, rumors had circulated of significant coal deposits along the Durbin branch. The first report of interest in the area by coal operators was in August 1924 when a 42-inch seam of coal was found near Flint. The coal was claimed to be the Sewell seam, which was considered to be a desirable smokeless fuel. Plans were made in March 1926 to open a mine near Montes by the Thompson Coal Company, but it was to be September before the W. Md. made a start on a bridge across Shavers Fork to the proposed mine. The delay was due to the W. Md. wanting to use the bridge from Parsons for the proposed crossing, as the Parsons structure was being replaced as part of a program to strengthen all the bridges on the West Virginia Division. By the end of 1926, a second company, the Walkers New River Mining Company, was contemplating opening a mine near Flint.

A bad slide occurred on the Durbin branch on April 22, which closed the road for five days to freight traffic although passengers and mail were transferred round the slide causing a two hour delay.

At the end of the year it was announced that the Whitmer interests had virtually completed logging in the Dry Fork area and were proposing to close the mill at Horton. At about the same time, the Three Forks Lumber Company announced that it was going to cease business after only two years of operations. The end of large scale lumbering in West Virginia was only a matter of time, as it had been reported earlier that only 200,000 acres of virgin forest remained of the 15,000,000 acres that had originally existed in the state.

The strike by locomotive engineers and firemen continued into 1926. Attempts to involve John D. Rockefeller, Jr. proved unsuccessful, as did mediation efforts by local businessmen. The 1922 strike of W. Md. shopmen also continued into 1926. One hundred and thirty two of the shopmen had filed suit against the W. Md. in 1925 claiming back wages, one test case finally reaching trial in May 1926. The W. Md. claimed there was insufficient evidence to support the claim; the judge agreed there was no binding contract and directed the jury to find for the company. Various legal appeals by the shopmen culminated in an appeal to the U. S. Circuit Court of Appeals in Richmond, Virginia, in June 1942. Again the position of the railroad was upheld by the court. The U. S. Supreme Court declined to hear the case in October 1942. The strike by the engineers and firemen also was never settled. Two engineers, both originally with the West Virginia Central, were reported to be still on strike in 1949, 24 years after the strike started.

President Byers did not comment publicly on the result of the May 1926 trial. He did report that traffic on the W. Md. was "holding up splendidly," and that coal traffic was up 34 percent over the same period for 1925. Although there was some decline in coal production during the summer, output reached record levels in West Virginia during the fall. This led the Davis Coal and Coke Company to restore the wages of its workers to the 1920 level, an increase of about 40 percent, effective November 1. The Emmons Coal Mining Company had also increased wages on October 16 and later restored wages to the 1920 level. To accommodate the increased traffic, employment at the Elkins shops increased in November to a record 400 men.

It was announced on February 8, 1927, that the B. & O. had purchased 144,000 shares of W. Md. stock sold by the Rockefeller interests. This purchase, plus shares purchased in the open market, gave the B. & O. about 35 percent of the stock, but the company denied any intention of controlling the W. Md. The purchase was part of an effort at this time to affect a consolidation of the eastern railroads.

On March 17, the car and carpenter shops at Elkins were destroyed by fire. The fire started in a boxcar in the shops for repairs and may have been due to a cigarette. The company announced that the shops would be rebuilt but meanwhile work on repairing cars continued in the yards. In spite of efforts of business groups in Elkins, no decision was made by the W. Md. to rebuild the shops during the year.

The towns of Whitmer and Horton received a new lease on life in March, when a new company, the Spears Lumber Company, took over the Whitmer interests in the area. Spears announced plans to build additional logging railroads to reach new sources of timber. The mill at Horton reopened in August.

The only serious wreck of the year occurred on April 3, when the engine of a freight train derailed near Schell and rolled over. The engineer, Fred Wilson, was trapped in the cab and severely scalded. It was three hours before he could be removed, but he died the next day.

In April it was reported that the W. Md. had filed an application with the I. C. C. to take over the G. C. & E. The G. C. & E. filed an application on July 7, 1927 with the I. C. C. to acquire the 39 miles of railroad from Cheat Junction to Spruce, which although owned by the same interests, was not part of the G. C. & E. Approval for the purchase of the G. C. E. was announced on December 8; the W. Md. issued $1,585,000 in bonds to pay for the 74 miles of new road. The G. C. E. gave the W. Md. access to the coal and lumber of the Curtin interests at Bergoo.

The Parsons Pulp and Paper Company mill at Parsons closed on July 17. The facility was dismantled during 1935, the final act being the dynamiting of the 170-foot high water tower on September 10, 1937.

The W. Md. received good news for its Durbin branch, when the first car of Sewell seam coal was shipped on August 11 by the Walkers New River Mining Company. By the end of 1927, the Walkers New River Mining Company had shipped 5,825 tons of coal. A second company, Monserrat and Company, shipped its first car of coal from Bemis on October 1.

The new coalfield attracted considerable attention from other mine operators including John T. Davis. John T. Davis had retained the right to use the name "Davis Colliery Company" after the death of his father in 1916 and the sale of the Coal and Coke Railway and its coal interests to the B. & O. in 1917. The Davis heirs owned about 1,200 acres of coal land near Bemis, and John T. Davis was sufficiently impressed by the coal mined by nearby Monserrat and Company, to order five openings made to test the quality of the coal on his land. A new company, the Davis Coal Land Company, was incorporated by John T. Davis to mine the coal.

Demand for coal in early 1928 was very poor, and coal traffic on the W. Md. was much below normal. Miners of the Davis Coal and Coke Company agreed to accept a reduction of five cents per ton for coal mined in an effort to keep the mines from closing. The stagnant market did not affect the mines along the Durbin branch as the demand for smokeless coal remained high. New tipples were erected by the Walkers New River Mining Company, and 25 acres of land at Flint were purchased for the erection of houses for additional miners. In early April, with the market for coal still depressed, 22 cars of coal were shipped from the Cheat Mountain field in one week, which was considered remarkable under the circumstances.

The W. Md. officially took over the operation of the G. C. & E. on March 15; the first freight train left Elkins for Bergoo on April 4 initiating a weekly service. The W. Md. was reported to have a large force of men at work on the track in June replacing ties and putting in ballast. The Pardee-Curtin Lumber Company's mill at Bergoo commenced operations in June. Pardee-Curtin later leased 600 acres of coal lands near Webster Springs to a new company, the Point Mountain Mining Company, which planned to develop an old mine known as the McGraw mine.

The W. Md. and the B. & O. were granted approval by the P. S. C. to discontinue the sleeping car service between Elkins and Fairmont that the two companies jointly operated. There was no public opposition to the move and the P. S. C. noted that the service was poorly patronized.

The remainder of 1928 continued to see an increasing demand for the Cheat Mountain coal with improvements being made to the mines of the Walkers New River Coal Company and the Monserrat and Company. Production by these two companies in 1928 was 25,199 tons and 11,927 tons respectively. The Davis Coal Land Company also shipped coal during 1928, with the total for the year being 7,348 tons. Demand for coal generally had improved during the second half of the year and many mines in northern West Virginia had reopened.

In January 1929, at the annual meeting of the Spears Lumber Company, it was announced that the timber in the Dry Fork region was almost exhausted and that the mill at Horton would soon close and the C. W. Va. & S. would be abandoned. The mill closed on February 18 and an attempt was made to sell the railroad to the W. Md. When this failed, an application was made to the I. C. C. on May 15, 1929 to abandon the road. The I. C. C. granted approval for the abandonment on July 23, 1929, to take effect in 30 days, but it was to be November before operations finally ceased.

The first coal shipped from the Point Mountain Coal Company's mine passed over the W. Md. in early March. A month later, a second company, the Minds Coal Mining Corporation, was chartered to mine coal in the Point Mountain field. Interest in the Cheat Mountain field extended to the west side of the mountain when it was announced in March that the Sewell seam had been found near Mill Creek.

As the coal industry expanded, the remnants of the lumber industry continued to disappear. The pulp mill at Parsons was sold on April 12 for $36,500 for its scrap value.

Fig. 291. Deep Run Railroad Shay engine at Deep Run tipple. The name of the original owner, the Greenbrier, Cheat and Elk Railroad, is partly visible on the tender *Collection William Metheny*

During 1929, the W. Md. purchased several small railroads, which would help to build up its coal traffic. The first was the Deep Run Railroad, which was purchased from the Deep Run Big Vein Coal Company in March. The railroad ran for about two miles from Shaw and used a Shay locomotive to move coal from the tipple to the W. Md. (Fig. 291). With the purchase by the W. Md., the Shay was replaced by regular road engines, and stored at Cumberland.

The W. Md. announced in June changes to its passenger schedule starting with the elimination of passenger service on the Elk Garden branch on June 1. The company had made a request to the P. S. C. on March 10, 1929, to be permitted to discontinue passenger service on the branch, but the P. S. C. ordered the company to retain the service between Harrison and Emoryville. The W. Md. again appealed to the P. S. C. to discontinue these trains; this time the P. S. C. agreed and the trains were discontinued at the end of July. On June 11, trains Nos. 1 and 4 were speeded up with the elimination of stops at Pinto, Gerstall, Franklin, Gleason, Hubbard, Dobbin and Gilman.

In July it was reported that engineers of the W. Md. were at work in Webster County with a view to extending the railroad beyond Bergoo towards the coalfields around Webster Springs. Engineers of the B. & O. were also looking at the region with the idea of building up the Elk River to tap into the same coalfield. On July 29, the G. C. & E. filed an application with the I. C. C. to take over 12 miles of standard and narrow gauge track from Bergoo to Webster Springs owned by the W. Va. Midland. Also included were two miles of narrow gauge track down the Elk River and four miles of track up the Back Fork of the Elk. The cost of the purchase was $650,000; the W. Md. would then lease the new trackage. At this time, coal was being hauled from Bergoo using the engines of the lumber company, the grades being too steep and the curves too sharp for regular road engines. By November, three companies were operating in the Webster County field, namely the Point

Mountain Coal Company, the Golden Ridge Coal Company and the Pardee-Curtin Coal Company.

The W. Md. applied to the I. C. C. on July 12 to purchase the Chaffee Railroad. The purchase was approved by the I. C. C. on November 8. The W. Md. continued to operate the Chaffee with two Shays; the ex-Deep Run Railroad Shay being used as a backup engine and becoming W. Md. No. 3.

The stock market crash of October 29 did not have an immediate impact on coal production. Demand for the smokeless coal of Randolph and Webster counties continued to exceed the demand for bituminous coal from the remainder of the northern West Virginia fields, with between 20 and 26 cars per day passing through Elkins. By the end of December, bad weather reportedly caused a surge in demand for all grades of coal.

Throughout the year, the eastern railroads had floated various plans for consolidation into four or five major systems, but it was not until December that the I. C. C. announced its own plans. This involved the consolidation of the W. Md. with the Wabash, partially fulfilling George Gould's ambitions of 25 years earlier. The B. and O. was ordered by the I. C. C. to divest itself of its holdings in the W. Md. by July 1930, later extended to January 1931.

At the end of the year, the W. Md. filed with the P. S. C. for permission to take four trains off the Huttonsville branch. The trains, Nos. 63 and 64 operated daily, and Nos. 65 and 66 operated on Sundays. Because of improved highways and bus services in the area, the passengers carried by these trains were few in number. The P. S. C. authorized the removal of the trains beginning April 1, 1930

Although 1930 was the first full year of the Great Depression, smokeless coal from the Sewell seam continued to be in demand. The first coal from the Mill Creek mine, operated by the Elkins Sewell Coal Company, was moved from the mine to Mill Creek in the middle of January for local use; the first two cars shipped over the W. Md. passed through Elkins on February 20. In Webster County, the Pardee-Curtin company announced in April the opening of another mine with a potential capacity of 1,500 tons per day. In March, the Davis Coal Land Company took over the operations of the neighboring Monserrat and Company. This plant had been closed since the end of 1929 due to the death of its owner.

Early in May, the Valley River Railroad filed to abandon operations from Mill Creek to Valley Head. The railroad was owned by the Wilson Lumber Company, which had almost completed the cutting of its timber along the Tygart Valley River. Passenger service was abandoned in February 1931, and the rails removed in December of that year. In September, the West Virginia Midland Railroad was authorized to abandon its line from Webster Springs to Diana.

The effect of the various additions and abandonments of the past few years was reflected in the W. Md.'s route map for West Virginia, and is shown in Fig. 292. Fig. 292 is a segment of the map from a passenger timetable of a few years later.

In August, about 25 cars per day were being shipped from the Point Mountain field and from the Bemis and Flint region. By September, this had increased to 40 cars per day. To accommodate the increasingly heavy traffic from the Durbin and Elk River branches, the W. Md. commenced in September to rebuild the

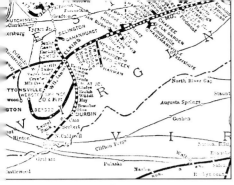

Tygart Valley River bridge south of Elkins serving the two branches. The bridge in use was the one built in 1901 for the C. & I. (Fig. 155), and a weight limit restricted the bridge to use by the I-1 class decapods. The steel work for the new bridge was installed in December.

An era ended for the W. Md. in a bizarre way on September 23 when President Byers was fatally shot by Dudley Gray, vice president for traffic, who then turned the gun on himself. No reason for the killing was established although the two men had disagreed on policy. George Bagley was elected president of the company on October 10.

On December 1, the C. W. Va. & S. announced that passenger and freight service would resume between Hendricks and Harman. The new timetable showed two trains daily each way (Fig. 293), although it was probably a Mack bus, which had been in service since about 1922, that was used (Fig. 294). The new service lasted almost six years, but by November 1936, it was reported that the tracks were being torn up for scrap.

By the end of 1930, 50 cars of smokeless coal from the Randolph and Webster fields were being moved through Elkins daily. In addition, the Elkins Sewell Coal Company at Mill Creek was loading six cars each week.

The depression continued to affect the coal industry of northern West Virginia throughout 1931, although the smokeless coal

Time Table No. 1.

Central West Virginia & Southern Railroad Company

TRAIN SERVICE

IN EFFECT 12-01 A. M.
Sunday, Dec. 7, 1930
EASTERN STANDARD TIME

Subject to change without notice

A. S. LINDSEY,
General Manager

SOUTHBOUND   (All Trains daily except Sunday.)   NORTHBOUND

FIRST CLASS				FIRST CLASS	
No. 13	No. 11	Distance from Hendricks	STATIONS	No. 12	No. 14
P. M.	A. M.	0.0	..HENDRICKS...	A. M.	P. M.
3.15	8.40	0.0	..HENDRICKS...	11.45	6.00
3.28	8.52	3.7	f....RED RUN...	17.4	11.34	5.48
3.39	8.56	4.8	f.MOORE'S SIDING.	16.3	11.30	5.44
3.36	9.00	6.0	f ..RICHFORD..	15.1	11.26	5.40
3.42	9.06	7.5	f ..MILL RUN..	13.6	11.20	5.34
3.45	9.10	8.3	f ..ELK LICK..	12.8	11.17	5.31
3.52	9.16	9.9	...GLADWIN...	11.1	11.10	5.24
4.03	9.27	13.0	JENNINGSTON.	8.1	10.59	5.13
4.10	9.34	15.0	f SCOTT'S SIDING.	4.1	10.54	5.06
4.16	9.41	17.0	RED CREEK JCT.	4.1	10.46	5.00
4.32	9.56	21.1	...HARMAN....	0.0	10.30	4.44
P. M.	A. M.			A. M.	P. M.

f. Stops on signal or notice to Conductor.
Takes connections with W. M. Ry. No. 10 and No. 4 East and No. 9 West.

Fig. 293. Central West Virginia and Southern Railroad Time Table No. 1, December 7, 1930

Fig. 294. Central West Virginia and Southern Railroad Mack bus
Collection of the Western Maryland Railway Historical Society

was still in demand. New coal companies continued to be chartered to operate in the field; at the end of January the Red Oak Smokeless Coal Company was incorporated to operate near Bergoo. The company owned land about 1.1/2 miles from Bergoo and began shipping coal in July. This may not have been the best of times to open a new mine even in the smokeless field as a month earlier Pardee-Curtin had released 150 miners because of poor demand.

The B. & O. asked the I. C. C. in June for more time to dispose of its W. Md. stock. Because of the depressed state of the stock market, the I. C. C. ordered the B. & O. to place the stock in trust thus allowing the W. Md. to continue as an independent railroad for another 30 years.

News reports in July indicated that the W. Md. had terminated its contract with the Dickson Construction and Repair Company. The reports were premature, as the W. Md. did not terminate the contract until January 31, 1934. After this date employees of the shop and track departments were carried on the W. Md.'s payroll.

By October, the W. Md. was able to report an increase of traffic on both the Durbin and Elk River branches, and in November, the W. Md. commenced to use its own engines to move coal from Bergoo. A new cut-off was built in November to give a better connection with the Elk River branch and the Durbin branch, and in February 1932, a contract was let for the construction of a new cut-off at Spruce.

The year 1932 followed a similar pattern to 1931 with reduced working in most mines along the W. Md. except for the smokeless field.

On February 4, the worst floods since 1896 hit the Elkins area causing delays in train services from Elkins to Durbin and Cumberland. At Hendricks, 700 feet of track were washed out, which led to passengers being transferred by motorcar between Thomas and Hendricks. The Davis Coal and Coke Company suspended operations at several mines due to the flood. At Mine No. 23, Pendleton Run was reported to have broken into the mine and flooded the workings. By February 14, the W. Md. was back to normal operations and moved 100 cars of coal through Elkins that had accumulated at the mines.

The mines around Thomas were reported to be back in operation by the beginning of March, although a month later it was noted that the mines were only working one day per week. In early June the mines around Thomas and Davis closed down entirely, throwing 400 men out of work.

Two new mines were reported to be under development in the smokeless field during the year. The first at Monterville in Webster County, operated by W. R. Minds, was announced in April. In June, W. H. Green, who had been involved with several mines along the Coal and Coke Railway, announced plans to begin a new mine near Bemis, although it would be a year before operations commenced.

Early in July, severe flooding occurred in southern West Virginia reaching as far north as the upper reaches of the Elk River. Flooding in the Slaty Fork region of Pocahontas County caused washouts between Bergoo and Laurel Bank on the G. C. & E.

At the end of October, the W. Md. was shipping between 65 and 70 cars daily through Elkins from the Elk and Cheat fields. This represented an increase in tonnage as the mines increased production. At Flint, the miners were working a full week; in the Webster County field, four days per week was normal. By December, mines in the Upper Potomac field were reported to be working only two or three days per week.

Early in January 1933, the Pardee-Curtin Coal Company commenced work on opening a new mine, No. 4, near Bergoo, indicating a continued confidence by the company in the demand for its coal. This seemed to be justified, as by July, a recovery in demand occurred. During July, the W. Md. hauled a train of 93 cars from the Elk and Cheat fields, through Elkins, and over the Blackwater grade. Five engines were required on the grade, which at that time was considered unusual. The demand remained high throughout the remainder of 1933 with up to 100 cars passing through Elkins daily. The demand did not help the mine at Mill Creek, which had reorganized in March, but which declared bankruptcy in September.

Fig. 295. Entrance to Pardee-Curtin's Bergoo Mine No. 3 in 1934
West Virginia and Regional History Collection,
West Virginia University Library

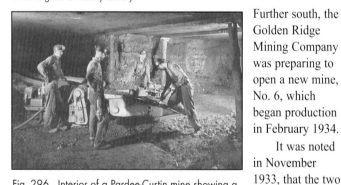

Fig. 296. Interior of a Pardee-Curtin mine showing a coal loader and the immense thickness of the Sewell seam (undated)
West Virginia and Regional History Collection,
West Virginia University Library

Further south, the Golden Ridge Mining Company was preparing to open a new mine, No. 6, which began production in February 1934.

It was noted in November 1933, that the two biggest producers of coal in northern West Virginia were the Consolidation Coal Company and the Pardee-Curtin Coal Company. For Pardee-Curtin, which had only been in the coal business a few years, this was a remarkable achievement. Exterior and interior views of Pardee-Curtin's mines are shown in Figs. 295 and 296.

An increased demand for coal at the beginning of 1934 prompted many northern West Virginia mines to return to a 40-hour week. Demand was particularly heavy for the Sewell coal leading to production increases in Randolph and Webster counties. On

April 1, 14,000 miners in northern West Virginia went on strike when the union contract expired and the operators refused to accept a new contract. The strike extended to both Randolph and Webster counties reducing the activities of the W. Md. A new wage structure was proposed by the National Recovery Administration and President Roosevelt, on April 23, appealed to the miners to return to work. A general return to work occurred on April 24. By the fall, demand for smokeless coal had again increased, with about 100 cars per day passing through Elkins in the middle of October.

The P. S. C. on June 6, 1934, granted the W. Md. permission to discontinue its Sunday trains, Nos. 1 and 4, between Elkins and Ridgeley. The railroad had also asked to discontinue trains 61 and 62 on the Huttonsville branch, but this request was denied by the Commission.

Production of coal at Bemis by the Davis Coal Land Company increased steadily during the early 1930's, reaching 23,877 tons in 1934. However, production ceased in 1935 with the death of John T. Davis on June 27. This ended the direct involvement of the Davis family in the mining business in West Virginia.

The P. S. C. finally allowed the W. Md. to withdraw the Huttonsville passenger trains in an order issued on May 15, 1935. The service ended a few days later. It appeared to be only a matter of time before service would be eliminated entirely from the southern end of the branch, as only one car of freight in each direction moved over the line daily. The mine at Mill Creek was not operating, although its purchase by new owners at the end of the year gave hope for its reopening. The lumber industry in the area was a shadow of its former self, the Wilson Lumber Company having moved its operations to Bergoo.

The W. Md. improved the yards at Elkins during 1935 by installing a new turntable and enlarging and rebuilding the roundhouse. It was also rumored that new yards would be built at Bergoo to handle the increase in output expected from two new Pardee-Curtin mines, Nos. 5 and 6. Heavy coal traffic through Elkins during the winter of 1936 kept the yards and shops busy.

Severe floods hit the mid-Atlantic region in March 1936; the Cumberland area being particularly hard hit. Heavy rains caused Wills Creek to flood much of downtown Cumberland and the W. Md. tracks on March 17. Train service on all railroads entering Cumberland was curtailed, a train from Elkins getting as far as Blaine before being stopped by floods. The

Fig. 297. Aftermath of the March 1936 flood in Cumberland. The wrecked bridge crossed Wills Creek from City Junction on the W. Md. to the B. & O. The white arrow marks the highest point reached by the floodwaters

crest of the flood, higher than had ever been recorded before, was reached at midnight. The damage from the flood was reported to be more extensive and costly than had been the case in 1924, particularly along Wills Creek (Fig. 297). The W. Md. was able to get a train through to Cumberland from The Narrows at noon on the 20th, but more flooding on the Potomac on March 24, destroyed the newly repaired track at Rawlings. The service to Elkins was not fully restored until March 26.

To meet the decline in passenger traffic due to the increased use of buses and private cars, the I. C. C. on February 28, 1936 ordered the railroads to reduce passenger fares to two cents per mile beginning June 2. On the W. Md. the reduction led to a four-fold increase in passengers on trains to and from Elkins, producing an increase of 68 percent in passenger revenues during the month of June.

The increased demand for coal at the end of 1936 produced heavy traffic through Elkins from the coal fields of Webster and Randolph counties. Overall during 1936, there had been an increase in demand for coal from West Virginia of 17 percent compared to 1935. Coal loadings continued to be high into 1937, with the Hickory Lick mine near Monterville loading a record 60 cars in one day on April 23. Such activity attracted the attention of other railroads. In May, the West Virginia Midland Railroad petitioned the P. S. C. to be allowed to reopen the old West Virginia Midland Railway. The petition was opposed by the W. Md., which claimed that the new line would capture the business that it had built up. During the second half of 1937, coal loadings from the Webster County field slumped with only the Hickory Run mine working full time, most other mines working only three days per week.

Cumberland, which had been devastated by the "Great Flood" of 1936, was hit again on April 26, 1937. The flood did not reach the levels of 1936, being some five feet lower in Ridgeley. The B. & O. was forced to divert its Baltimore to Pittsburgh trains over the Pennsylvania Railroad, but the W. Md. escaped serious damage. Service between Cumberland and Elkins resumed on April 27.

The W. Md. was not so lucky on October 28, when a storm dumped 2.1/2 inches of rain on the upper Potomac region. Tracks between Cumberland and Piedmont were washed out disrupting service for several days. Particularly hard hit were Shallmar, where the tracks to the mine were washed out, and Kitzmillar, where several houses were washed off their foundations.

As a result of the depression and the closure of many mines along its lines, the W. Md. began to eliminate underused trackage in West Virginia and Maryland. First to go was the branch up Deep Run to Nethkin from Shaw. One of the last mines to close near Nethkin was the Jaffy mine, which closed in October 1937. The track along Deep Run was reported to have been removed in May 1938. The W. Md. then filed an application with the I. C. C. on March 18, 1939 to abandon a section of the G. C. & C between the Narrows and Midland.

The W. Md. asked the P. S. C. on April 20, 1938, for permission to downgrade the agency station at Junior to non-agency status. The P. S. C. approved the request on June 8, 1938.

Cumberland escaped serious flooding in 1939 although heavy rains in early February caused problems for the W. Md. Trains to Elkins were canceled on February 4 due to washouts between Westernport and Luke and a major landslide at Douglas. Service was not restored until February 7.

Another nationwide coal strike began on April 3, 1939 leading to furloughs on the coal hauling railroads including the W. Md. An agreement to end the strike was signed on May 13. The mines were expected to reopen starting on May 15; the Walker Coal Mining Company at Bemis expected to reopen on May 16 with between 80 and 100 men reporting. By June 5, the W. Md. reported heavy shipments of coal and an additional 100 men were recalled to work at Elkins.

The W. Md. and the B. & O. asked the P. S. C. for permission to abandon W. Md. trains Nos. 42 and 43 (B. & O. trains Nos. 32 and 33), which the companies operated jointly between Elkins and Grafton. Although there was public opposition to the request, the P. S. C. agreed with the companies, and the last trains ran on August 25.

The start of the Second World War in Europe on September 3 was expected to lead to an increased demand for coal and indeed by the end of September, mines in the Georges Creek and Upper Potomac areas were working a five day week. Much of the demand was due to the normal stocking up for winter and recovery from the

Fig. 298. Armour Leather Company, Parsons, circa 1941

April strike, but it led to the mines at Elk Garden and Hartmansville, which had not worked for months, being reopened. The increase in coal traffic was welcome news to the W. Md., which reported its highest net income for ten years in the month of October.

The tannery at Parsons was reported to have been sold on November 27, 1939, to the meat packing concern, Armour and Company, becoming the Armour Leather Company (Fig. 298).

The W. Md. filed with the I. C. C. on May 22, 1940, to abandon the old West Virginia Central line between Elkins and Roaring Creek Junction, a distance of 5.81 miles. The B. & O. and the W. Md. had been operating jointly a single line between Elkins and Belington since 1931, with the B. & O. abandoning the old Coal and Coke line along the west side of the Tygart Valley River. The I. C. C. approved the abandonment on August 14, 1940. The W. Md. then applied to abandon the line between Emoryville and Oakmont in November 1940. Permission was granted on January 6, 1941 and the tracks were removed in May 1941.

Expiration of the miners' contract on March 31 let to a nation-wide strike in spite of an appeal by President Roosevelt as the nation geared up its defense industries. Although an agreement was reached by the end of April, confusion remained as to the new wage scale and most area mines remained closed. It was not until the middle of May that there was a complete resumption of work. With coal shipments returning to normal the W. Md. announced a recall of 100 furloughed workers starting June 5.

W. H. Green, who had begun a new mine near Bemis in 1932, announced on June 23, 1941, that the mine had been sold to the Glady-Sewell Coal Company. However, when the new owners failed to pay the balance due on the purchase, Green was appointed receiver of the company in January 1942. The Randolph County

Circuit Court decreed that the mine be sold at public auction and it was repurchased by Green on April 24, 1942. The mine was finally abandoned in November 1942, because of a scarcity of labor.

The Pardee-Curtin band mill at Bergoo was destroyed by fire on August 14, 1941, causing a loss of about $200,000. The planing mill and lumber in the yards were not destroyed and work started on rebuilding the mill immediately. At this time, the Pardee-Curtin mill was one of the three largest in the state.

An explosion at the Davis Coal and Coke Company's mine No. 23 at Thomas on November 10 killed three men and seriously injured one other. The explosion was apparently caused by gas but did no damage to other sections of the mine, which was able to reopen the following day.

On November 17, miners at the "captive" mines, i.e. those mines owned by the steel companies, went on strike and were quickly joined by miners from the commercial mines. In the Upper Potomac and Georges Creek fields, the shut down was complete by November 21, but on November 23 the mines reopened. Miners at the Davis Coal and Coke Company had voted two days earlier to return to work.

The W. Md. announced plans in September 1942, to reduce the service between Cumberland and Elkins to one train each way per day, and to eliminate the passenger service, trains 53 and 54, to Durbin. Because of strong public opposition, the proposals were rejected by the P. S. C. on October 27, even though the Commission agreed that the trains operated at a loss. The W. Md. then asked the P. S. C. that it be permitted to operate trains 53 and 54 as a mixed train, and this was approved by the commission. The W. Md. fared better with the I. C. C. when it applied to abandon the line between Daily and Huttonsville, a distance of 7.58 miles. The I. C. C. set February 12, 1943, as the date for the abandonment. Rails on the Davis branch were removed during 1942, although they were re-laid in 1948 to serve a strip mine at Child. The tracks were later extended to Davis to serve another mine, the new line being known as the Francis Branch.

The year 1943 was to be a tumultuous year for the coal industry and for the railroads, steel industry and consumers that depended on it. Trouble started in January with strikes in the anthracite fields. The contract for the miners in the soft coal industry expired on March 31, but a 30- day extension ensured no immediate strike. Negotiations were not successful and on April 28, mines in northern West Virginia began to close down. A nationwide strike commenced on May 1, leading to a government seizure of the mines on the same day. The miners agreed to return to work on May 4 for two weeks, later extended to June 1, when the mines again closed. After an appeal by President Roosevelt the miners resumed work on June 7 until June 20. With no new contract in sight, mines began closing on June 19, and on June 21, the 5,000 miners in District 16 (Allegany, Garrett, Tucker, Grant and Mineral counties) joined the walkout. The W. Md. announced more furloughs for trainmen as it had been forced to do during the earlier closings. The miners were ordered back by the union on June 23 but it was to be June 29 before full production resumed as many miners still refused to work without a contract. The union agreed to continue working without a contract until October 31; the government returned the seized mines to their owners prior to the end of

October. As the deadline approached, the miners again grew restless and sporadic closings occurred. The Minds Coal Mining Company at Monterville closed on October 27 and by October 29 several mines on Georges Creek were closed. All union mines closed on November 1 leading again to a government seizure. A

Fig. 299. W. Md. DS3 No. 105 at Port Covington, November 1942
Collection of the Western Maryland Railway Historical Society

new contract was agreed to on November 3, but it was to be November 9 before conditions returned to normal.

In November, the W. Md. placed a new diesel engine into yard service at Elkins in response to complaints about smoke from steam engines. The new engine, No. 105 (Fig. 299), was one of three built by Baldwin in 1942, and was one of the second batch of diesels ordered by the W. Md.

At the end of the year, the W. Md. filed an application with the I. C. C. to purchase the Cumberland and Pennsylvania Railroad. The I. C. C. gave approval for the purchase on May 3, 1944. The W. Md. also reported that, in spite of the numerous miners' strikes, 1943 had been its best year ever.

Fig. 300. Montrose after the June 23, 1944 storm

On June 23, 1944 a severe storm struck much of northern West Virginia and parts of Pennsylvania and Maryland. The storm spawned five separate tornadoes, one of which destroyed the town of Montrose and its depot (Fig. 300).

Fig. 301. Thomas after the same storm

A second tornado, described as minor, hit Thomas, damaging the town and the depot (Fig. 301 and 302.). The depot at Thomas was rebuilt without its awning and characteristic rounded end to the passenger section.

The W. Md. announced plans to withdraw two trains from the Cumberland to Elkins service on March 1, 1945. This was in accordance with a directive from the Office of Defense Transportation, which required passenger trains to meet a 35 percent occupancy or be canceled. In spite of public opposition, Trains Nos. 1 and 4 were taken off on March 1. The O. D. T. can-

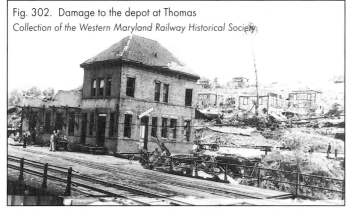

Fig. 302. Damage to the depot at Thomas
Collection of the Western Maryland Railway Historical Society

celed its order in late August at the end of the war, and Trains No. 1 and 4 were reinstated on August 27.

A walkout by mine foremen, seeking recognition for their union, caused many mines to close at the beginning of October. One of the first to close was the Point Mountain operation of the Minds Coal Mining Company. A few days later, Pardee-Curtin's Bergoo No. 2 was forced to close. By the middle of the month, 340 mines in West Virginia were closed and 40,000 men were idle. By October 17, the strike was called off and the men returned to work.

On April 1, 1946, a nationwide miners' strike was called by the union with some 400,000 men being idled. By April 4, coal traffic was down to ten percent of normal but the W. Md. did not expect to furlough any workers. On April 17, a cut in the length of the work week was announced. At the end of the month, W. Md. trainmen were only working two days per week, and 35 engines on the Elkins branch were out of service. Layoffs started in the maintenance-of-way department. Complying with a directive from the Office of Defense Transportation, the railroad again canceled Trains Nos. 1 and 4, and the Durbin train ran only on alternate days starting May 10. By this time the number of furloughed workers had reached 1,200 of which 200 were on the Elkins Division. A truce was called in the strike on May 10 for two weeks, but during the truce, a nationwide railroad strike was called. The W. Md. was not a party to the strike and normal schedules were maintained. When the truce ended in the miners' strike and no contract had been signed, the mines were seized by the government on May 22. However, the mines at Point Mountain and Vindex remained closed. The W. Md. reported on May 24 that no mines were working between Westernport and Thomas. An agreement ending the coal strike was signed on May 29 and by June 3, the mines were back in production, and the W. Md. was able to start recalling furloughed workers.

A second nationwide walkout occurred on November 21, which again led the O. D. T. to order a 25 percent reduction in passenger service to preserve coal stocks. On the W. Md. Trains Nos. 1 and 4 were once again canceled, and trains on the Durbin branch operated only on Tuesdays, Thursdays and Saturdays. One hundred workers were to be furloughed from the Elkins shops effective December 10. The miners' strike was called off on December 7.

Perhaps because the earlier O. D. T. directive reducing passenger service had affected only those trains drawn by steam engines, the W. Md. experimented with diesel haulage on a Cumberland to Elkins passenger train on December 20, and its return to Cumberland on December 21. The diesel used was not identified

other than it was a demonstrator owned by Baldwin.

EMD delivered two F3A freight diesels to the W. Md. in June of 1947. These were later rebuilt as F7A units, joining 26 F7A's and nine F7B's delivered in 1950 and 1952. One of the rebuilt locomotives, No. 51, is shown at Bayard in 1972, preceding two RS3 units (Fig. 303).

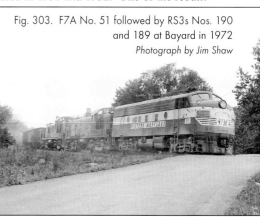

Fig. 303. F7A No. 51 followed by RS3s Nos. 190 and 189 at Bayard in 1972
Photograph by Jim Shaw

Following the labor unrest of 1946, 1947 was to prove a relatively quiet year. After a massive explosion at a mine in Illinois, which killed 111 miners, a memorial work stoppage was called for April 1. It was expected that the miners would return on April 7, but the union refused to send the miners back until all the mines had been inspected. Although the Minds Coal Mining Company mine at Point Mountain opened, most mines remained closed until about April 14. The W. Md. was able to report normal coal shipments by April 15. Another walkout started on June 23, when Congress approved the Taft-Hartley labor law. This was followed by the ten-day miners' vacation. The mines, which were still under government control after their seizure on May 22, 1946, were due to be returned to their owners on June 30, and it was not known if the miners would return. The vacation impacted the W. Md., which reported that coal shipments through Cumberland were down 15 percent on July 1. With a new contract signed, miners began a return to work on July 9, and by July 10, the W. Md. reported that normal coal movement was expected by the next day. Movement of coal was reduced during the summer due to a persistent car shortage, which led to the mine at Point Mountain having to close one day per week for two months. To alleviate the shortage, the W. Md. announced in November the purchase of 1,000 new coal cars and two new diesels to be built by EMD.

The Davis Coal and Coke Company opened a new coal washing plant near Bayard on August 1. This had cost the company $1,200,000 and was designed to wash the coal from all of the company's mines. A spur to the plant was constructed by the W. Md. In 1949, the residents of Bayard were complaining about fumes from a burning pile of waste. The company attempted to douse the fire but was unsuccessful. By 1951, the residents continued to report health problems and that white paint on their houses was turning black. Although the Davis Coal and Coke had sold the plant to a strip mine operator, it continued with its efforts to control the fire.

It was reported on September 30 that the Bethlehem Steel Company had purchased the Minds Coal Mining Corporation giving the steel company control of the Point Mountain mine. At this time, the mine employed between 500 and 600 men.

Unrest in the coalfields commenced again on March 15, 1948, when an unofficial strike started over the issue of miners' pensions.

The Davis Coal and Coke Company mines at Thomas, Pierce and Kempton were among the first to close. The strike spread to the mines at Vindex, Point Mountain and to the Masteller mine, all of which closed on March 16. The W. Md. reported on March 18 that 80 percent of the mines along its lines were closed. Trains Nos. 1 and 4 were, as usual, canceled on March 22 for the duration of the strike. No furloughs had occurred on the W. Md. one week after the strike started, but train crews were on reduced hours and furloughs were expected at the shops in a matter of days. A federal judge ordered the union to end the strike on April 4 but to little effect. The continuation of the strike finally led to the furloughing of 65 men from the W. Md. yards at Elkins. The miners began a return to work on April 13 but it was far from complete. Mines around Elkins were reported to have reopened and on April 14 the W. Md. restored the trains 1 and 4. The W. Md. reported on April 16 that most mines were now working. When a federal judge fined the miners' union for criminal contempt, the miners again walked off the job but returned on April 22. Miners at Thomas and Vindex, who had led the most recent closures, were reported to be at work. By the end of April, with a return to normal loadings, furloughed workers were being recalled.

Peace did not last long; on July 6 the Point Mountain mine closed again as miners of the "captive" mines went on strike. At this time the "captive" mines were mining about ten percent of the nation's coal. The steel companies had not been signatories to the agreement that had ended the strike earlier in the year, but signed an agreement with the union on July 13; work resumed the following day.

More furloughs occurred for W. Md. crews in March 1949 as a result of a two week work stoppage called by the UMW. In the Elkins area, 30 train crews were laid off and at Maryland Junction, 70 men were furloughed. The miners returned to work on March 28. The W. Md. reported coal shipments to be near normal by April 5. The mineworkers' union called a one week stoppage beginning June 13 in an effort to reduce coal stocks and increase the demand for coal. This led to furloughs on most coal hauling railroads, but the W. Md. hoped to be able to avoid furloughs by cutting the workweek by 40 percent. After a week back at work the miners went on a two week vacation during which time their contract expired. Until a new contract was signed the miners worked only a three-day week beginning July 5. The closings and the resulting three-day week led to a drop in earnings from coal shipments by the W. Md. of 48 percent during July compared to July 1948. The three-day week continued until September 19 when a nationwide walkout of miners occurred. The W. Md. announced

Fig. 304. EMD F7A No. 58 leads F7A No. 239 and an unidentified Alco through Gorman in 1971. No. 239 was one of 12 F7A's delivered in 1952
Photograph by Jim Shaw

plans to furlough 150 workers if the strike did not end in a few days. By October 5, the railroad announced further furloughs including one third of the force on the Elkins Division. Once again, in response to an order from the I. C. C., the W. Md. withdrew trains Nos. 1 and 4 from the Cumberland to Elkins service on October 26. The miners were ordered back to work by the union on November 9. On November 17 coal traffic on the Elkins Division was back to normal. Recall notices were issued to 200 furloughed W. Md. employees in the Elkins area, and passenger trains 1 and 4 were reinstated on November 21. The peace did not last long as the miners went on a three-day week commencing December 1 leading to more furloughs on the W. Md.

National attention was focussed in December on the town of Shallmar across the North Branch from Harrison. Because of the closing of the Wolf Den mine in March, the town had been plunged into poverty. The mine had employed about 100 men and produced 300 tons of coal each day. Lack of orders was the reason given for the closure.

During December, perhaps in response to the continuing strife in the coalfields, the W. Md. announced plans to purchase 20 new diesel freight engines and diesel switchers from EMD and Alco for delivery in 1950. The EMD order was for eight F7A's, four F7B's and four GP7's; four RS2 units were ordered from Alco. One of the F7A's, No. 58, is shown at Gorman in 1971 in Fig. 304.

During the 1940's, the W. Md. had remodeled several of the depots between West Virginia Central Junction and Thomas in an effort to make them more functional and economical to operate. One of the first to be rebuilt was at Westernport, which was reported to be under construction in October 1945. The single story freight building was removed at the same time. The remodeled depots included those at Shaw (Fig. 305), Blaine (Fig. 306), Harrison, and Bayard (Fig. 307).

Fig. 305. Remodeled depot at Shaw

Fig. 306. Depot at Blaine after remodeling

Fig. 307. Depot at Bayard

The miners were reported to have returned to work on January 3, 1950 after the New Year's holiday. However, isolated strikes occurred in West Virginia and Pennsylvania leading to passenger train cancellations as coal supplies dwindled. The W. Md. withdrew trains Nos. 1 and 4 from the Cumberland to Elkins service on January 9. A nationwide strike began on February 6, closing mines in Tucker and Garrett counties. More train cancellations were ordered by the I. C. C.; trains on the Durbin Branch were reduced to alternate days and furloughs occurred on the W. Md. The strike continued until March 6 when production resumed. The W. Md. recalled 400 of the 1,750 furloughed workers and trains Nos. 1 and 4 were reinstated. On March 20, it was reported that the W. Md. had filed with the P. S. C. to withdraw the two trains permanently. The request was heard by the P. S. C. in April, but it was to be May 31, 1951 before the P. S. C. announced it had denied the application.

On March 15, 1950, it was announced that the last major mine on the Chaffee branch, Manor Mine No. 3, would close on March 31 due to a lack of orders. The Davis Coal and Coke Company mine at Kempton closed in April 1950, and the tracks removed a couple of years later. The mine, producing 1,200 tons per day, was the largest mine in Maryland at the time. Loss of eastern markets, due to high production costs, was the stated

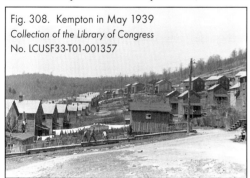

Fig. 308. Kempton in May 1939
Collection of the Library of Congress
No. LCUSF33-T01-001357

reason. The Buxton and Landstreet store was also closed at the same time. With no other sources of employment, Kempton began a long period of decline as families moved away (Fig. 308).

During the spring of 1950, fears were expressed by coal industry representatives of more mine closings, curtailed production and spreading unemployment as customers substituted other fuels for coal. These fears were echoed by E. S. Williams, president of the W. Md., but who thought the impact of reduced production would not affect the W. Md. too severely as traffic from the "captive" mines was expected to continue at a high level.

During 1950, the W. Md. consolidated several of its operations in West Virginia. On the G. C. & E. branch, all operations at Spruce and Bergoo were consolidated at Laurel Bank. In June, the W. Md. announced that the facilities at Thomas would be moved to Elkins along with eight locomotives and 29 workers stationed there.

The W. Md. announced plans in July 1951, to build 1,200 coal cars at Elkins. Although this was good news for Elkins, the town was not so pleased when the W. Md. again asked the P. S. C. for permission to discontinue trains Nos. 1 and 4. The P. S. C. granted permission for the withdrawal of the trains on March 25, 1952 with the cancellation scheduled to take effect on May 17. The decision was appealed, and on May 5, the Commission ordered the W. Md. to continue the trains temporarily. The trains were finally withdrawn on June 21 after a further P. S. C. hearing. The schedule for trains Nos. 1 and 4 in 1949, is shown in the September 1949 timetable (Fig. 309).

Unofficial strikes plagued the steel industry during May 1952 leading to furloughs on the B. & O. The W. Md. furloughed 70 men at Elkins on May 22 but planned to recall them on June 9. An official steel strike was called on June 2 and lasted 55 days. This led to the closure of the "captive" mines, including Bethlehem Steel's mine at Monterville, on June 4. About 100 W. Md. employ-

ees were furloughed at Elkins on June 12; by July 9 a total of 700 W. Md. workers had been laid off. An agreement to end the strike was signed on July 26, and by July 31 traffic on the W. Md. was about 70 percent of normal. Recall of all the furloughed workers was delayed by a week long memorial holiday called by the U. M. W. on August 25, but the W. Md. recalled 650 men, including 135 at Elkins, on August 29.

A walkout of workers at the West Virginia Pulp and Paper mill at Luke occurred on August 29 and lasted until November 17, but more serious for the W. Md. was the threat of a nationwide coal strike. A pay increase for miners was included in a contract signed by the U. M. W. and the operators in September, but the amount was reduced by the Wage Stabilization Board on October 18. This led to a nationwide coal strike beginning on October 20 leading to furloughs on the B. & O., N. & W. and other coal hauling railroads. Although the W. Md. reported that practically no coal was being mined along its lines, no furloughs were expected. The strike ended on October 28, with 70 percent of the mines along the W. Md. back in operation the same day.

On December 2, the first diesel hauled freight train arrived in Elkins from Cumberland on a trial run. The three EMD F7 units hauled 102 empty cars and seven loaded cars and returned to Cumberland the next day with a loaded coal train. W. Md. officials

CUMBERLAND TO ELKINS
WESTWARD

Miles	STATIONS	★ 9	★ 1
		AM	AM
0.0	Lv....Baltimore....	f 8 30	
86.8	"....Hagerstown...	11 55	
165.8	Ar.....Cumberland	2 30	
0.0	Lv....Cumberland....	f 2 45	f 7 01
5.4	"....Seymour....		f 7 15
11.9	"....Rawlings....	f 3 08	f 7 19
15.0	"....Black Oak....		f 7 30
16.8	"....Gerstell....	3 18	
21.5	"..McCoole (Keyser)..	3 27	f 7 44
26.8	"....Westernport....	3 36	7 51
27.8	"....Luke....	3 40	7 55
28.2	"..W. Va. C. Junction..	f 3 43	f 7 58
29.6	"....Hampshire....	f 3 46	f 8 01
34.9	"....Barnum....	3 57	8 11
37.5	"....Shaw....	4 00	8 14
41.4	"....Chaffee....	f 4 10	f 8 21
44.7	"....Blaine....	4 18	8 31
46.4	"....Harrison....	4 22	8 36
57.1	"....Steyer....	f 4 44	f 8 57
59.1	"....Gorman....	4 47	9 02
61.5	"....Bayard....	4 54	9 08
64.0	"....Wilson....	f 4 59	
66.7	"....Henry....	f 5 05	f 9 17
71.0	"....Beechwood....	f 5 14	f 9 26
74.9	"....William....		f 9 33
77.0	"....Thomas....	5 27	9 40
78.8	"....Douglas....	f 5 34	f 9 45
87.0	"....Hendricks....	5 59	10 08
87.8	"....Hambleton....	6 01	10 10
90.3	"....Parsons....	6 06	10 16
92.7	"....Porterwood....	f 6 13	f 10 22
94.2	"....Moore....		f 10 25
100.4	"....Montrose....	6 28	10 37
104.7	"....Kerens....	6 35	10 45
106.8	"....Whyte....		f 10 50
112.1	Ar.....Elkins....	6 50	11 00
		PM	AM

ELKINS TO CUMBERLAND
EASTWARD

Miles	STATIONS	★ 10	★ 2
		AM	PM
0.0	Lv.....Elkins....	f 7 25	f 1 55
5.3	"....Whyte....	f 7 36	f 2 05
7.4	"....Kerens....	7 40	2 09
11.7	"....Montrose....	7 46	2 15
17.9	"....Moore....	f 8 00	
19.4	"....Porterwood....	f 8 03	
21.8	"....Parsons....	8 06	2 35
24.3	"....Hambleton....	8 13	2 42
25.1	"....Hendricks....	8 15	2 44
33.3	"....Douglas....	8 38	3 08
35.1	"....Thomas....	8 43	3 13
37.2	"....William....	f 8 49	
41.1	"....Beechwood....	f 8 59	f 3 27
45.4	"....Henry....	f 9 09	f 3 37
48.1	"....Wilson....	f 9 15	
50.6	"....Bayard....	9 18	3 46
53.0	"....Gorman....	9 27	3 53
55.0	"....Steyer....	f 9 29	f 3 57
65.7	"....Harrison....	9 51	4 19
67.4	"....Blaine....	9 55	4 24
70.7	"....Chaffee....	f 10 01	f 4 31
74.6	"....Shaw....	10 09	4 39
77.2	"....Westernport....	f 10 12	f 4 45
82.5	"....Hampshire....	f 10 27	
83.9	"..W. Va. C. Junction..	f 10 29	f 4 56
84.3	"....Luke....	10 31	4 59
85.3	"....Westernport....	10 34	5 02
90.6	"..McCoole (Keyser)..	10 45	5 13
95.3	"....Gerstell....	f 10 55	
97.1	"....Black Oak....		f 5 24
100.2	"....Rawlings....		
106.7	"....Seymour....	f 11 13	f 5 40
112.1	Ar.....Cumberland	11 30	5 55
112.1	Lv....Cumberland....	11 45	
191.1	Ar....Hagerstown..	2 03	
277.9	Ar....Baltimore....	5 05	
		PM	PM

ELKINS TO DURBIN
WESTWARD

Miles	STATIONS	■ 153
	(Mixed Train)	AM
0.0	Lv.....Elkins....	f11 15
2.9	"....Canfield....	f11 22
6.1	"....Lumber....	f11 27
7.7	"....Meadows....	f11 30
9.5	"....Faulkner....	f11 35
10.2	"....Bowden....	f11 37
13.1	"....Weese....	f11 42
15.7	"....Flint....	f11 49
17.0	"....Walker....	f11 53
18.8	"....Bemis....	11 59
21.8	"....Cheat Jct....	f12 09
25.3	"....Glady....	12 18
27.9	"....Beulah....	f12 28
31.2	"....Wildell....	f12 38
36.4	"....May....	f12 54
44.8	"....Olive....	f 1 22
47.1	Ar.....Durbin....	1 30
0.0	Lv....Durbin–C&O....	f1 40
24.5	"....Clover Lick....	3 03
39.5	"....Marlinton....	3 03
98.6	Ar....Ronceverte(C&O)	5 15
		PM

DURBIN TO ELKINS
EASTWARD

Miles	STATIONS	■ 154
	(Mixed Train)	AM
0.0	Lv.Ronceverte(C&O)..	f9 05
59.1	"....Marlinton....	11 23
74.1	"....Clover Lick....	f12 00
98.6	Ar....Durbin–C&O....	1 15
0.0	Lv.....Durbin....	f 2 00
2.3	"....Olive....	f 2 08
10.7	"....May....	f 2 36
15.9	"....Wildell....	f 2 52
19.2	"....Beulah....	f 3 02
22.6	"....Glady....	3 12
25.3	"....Cheat Jct....	f 3 21
28.3	"....Bemis....	3 31
30.1	"....Walker....	f 3 37
31.4	"....Flint....	f 3 41
34.0	"....Weese....	f 3 48
36.9	"....Bowden....	3 56
37.6	"....Faulkner....	f 4 00
39.4	"....Meadows....	f 4 03
41.0	"....Lumber....	f 4 08
44.2	"....Canfield....	f 4 19
47.1	Ar.....Elkins....	4 30
		PM

THE FASTEST TRAINS CARRY RAILWAY EXPRESS

America's High Standard SHIPPING SERVICE

RAILWAY EXPRESS AGENCY

NATION-WIDE SERVICE

Fig. 309. W. Md. passenger timetable, September 1949

accompanying the train pronounced themselves satisfied with the performance of the diesels. At this time the railroad operated 67 diesels, mostly east of Hagerstown and expected to add more during 1953 to be used east of Cumberland.

Fig. 310. W. Md. No. 348 (ex-West Virginia Central No. 29)

Collection of William Metheny

Coincidentally, the last West Virginia Central engine operated by the W. Md. that had been purchased during the Davis years, was scrapped in October 1952. The engine, No. 348, ex-West Virginia Central No. 29 (Fig. 310), had finished its days as a yard engine at Elkins.

Conversion from steam to diesel on the W. Md. continued in 1953 with diesels being used between Cumberland to Connellsville in January. At the same time, enginemen from the Elkins Division were being trained at Ridgeley to operate the new engines. President Grotz was able to claim in his annual report in March that diesels were saving the company money and indeed layoffs of boilermakers, blacksmiths, machinists and others had already occurred. Because of these economies, Grotz was able to report near record revenues in 1952 in spite of the steel and coal strikes.

The W. Md. announced in April, that some of the ten new diesel locomotives expected to be delivered during the May would be used in the Cumberland and Elkins area. The engines were the RS3 model built by Alco, with two more added in December 1953, and a final two added in September 1954. These were numbered 185-198; No. 187 is shown in Fig. 311 at Montrose in 1970. Two other members of the group No. 189 and No. 190 can be seen behind F7A No. 51 in Fig.

Fig. 311. RS3 No. 187 at Montrose in 1970

Photograph by Jim Shaw

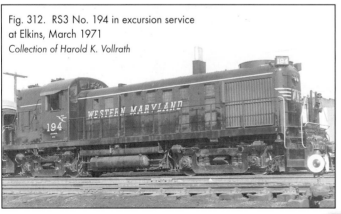

Fig. 312. RS3 No. 194 in excursion service at Elkins, March 1971

Collection of Harold K. Vollrath

303. Four of the RS3's were fitted with a steam generator for passenger service. This installation changed the profile of the short hood as can be seen on No. 194 in Fig. 312. Trials were also underway in April of a diesel multiple unit on the G. C. and E. branch where single units had already been tried. The first diesel hauled passenger train on the Elkins Division left Cumberland for Elkins on June 15, although the locomotive used was not identified. The success of diesels throughout the W. Md. meant the rapid demise of steam. The last West Virginia Central engine, No. 455, ex-West Virginia Central No. 44, was scrapped in June 1953. The last steam locomotive in use on the W. Md. dropped its fire for the last time on July 20, 1954.

During the 1950's, the impact of the private automobile on the railroads' passenger traffic became pronounced, leading to many cancellations of service. It was reported in November 1952, that the W. Md. planned to petition the P. S. C. of Maryland to eliminate all passenger service in Maryland. A hearing was held before the P. S. C. in January 1953 where it was claimed that an average of only three passengers used each train and that the company was losing $400,000 per year on passenger trains. On May 13, the P. S. C. granted the W. Md. permission to discontinue its Cumberland to Hagerstown passenger service but not the service between Hagerstown and Baltimore. The last passenger train to leave Cumberland for Hagerstown did so at noon on May 30; the service between Baltimore and Hagerstown was withdrawn in June 1957.

The continued decline in coal mining along Georges Creek and an increase in the use of trucks to move coal, prompted the W. Md. to ask the I. C. C., in October 1953, for permission to abandon some of the ex-C. & P. trackage. Included in the request was the bridge across the North Branch between Westernport and Piedmont, and also the notorious grade crossing in Westernport that had started the Cookerly Farm affair. Permission to abandon the trackage was given in November, but the Commission deferred a decision on the bridge.

In 1954, production of coal from the last mine of the Davis Coal and Coke Company, No. 36 at Coketon, had dropped to less than 3,000 tons and the mine closed. The Davis Coal and Coke Company itself had been taken over in 1952 by the Compass Coal Company, which ended production at the only other mine operated by the company, No. 40 at Pierce, the same year. Production of coal also ended in 1954 by the Cumberland Coal Company at Douglas.

The P. S. C. granted approval to the W. Md. on April 29, 1954 to change the mixed train to Durbin from a day to a night schedule (Fig. 313). Train No. 153 would leave Elkins at 6:30 P.M. for the 2.1/2 hour trip to Durbin and would leave Durbin at 9:25 P.M. Minor changes were made to the Cumberland to Elkins schedule to allow for a connection with the Durbin train. The W. Md. also announced that the Durbin train would be diesel hauled in the future. The new schedule took effect on May 3.

Additional diesel locomotives were delivered by EMD during the spring of 1954. These were the first of 21 GP9 units acquired by the W. Md. One of the original group, No. 28, is shown at Montrose in 1966 (Fig. 314).

The remnants of Hurricane Hazel deluged the Cumberland area on October 15. Floods and landslides delayed traffic on both the

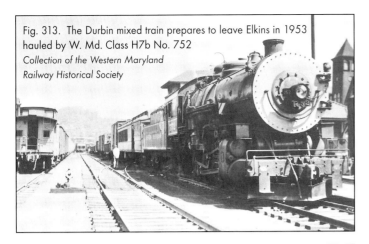

Fig. 313. The Durbin mixed train prepares to leave Elkins in 1953 hauled by W. Md. Class H7b No. 752

Collection of the Western Maryland Railway Historical Society

Fig. 314. EMD GP9 No. 28 at Montrose in 1966. The GP9 is followed by Alco RS3 No. 188

Photograph by Jim Shaw

W. Md. and the B. & O. between Cumberland and Connellsville although the hardest hit line was the Thomas subdivision between West Virginia Central Junction and Bayard. So extensive was the damage due to washouts that it was to be October 21 before the line was reopened. Also hard hit was Kitzmiller where construction for a new road bridge across the North Branch had cut an embankment and allowed floodwaters to swirl through the town.

Many of the steam servicing facilities were removed during 1955 including the massive coal tipple and roundhouse at Maryland Junction. The coal tipple had been built to replace one that had been destroyed by fire in February 1945.

On the Chaffee branch, the line from Trout to Vindex was finally removed in 1955, five years after the closing of the Manor mine. The lower section of the line still remained in use.

The annual ten day vacation for coal miners started on June 30, 1956 leading to furloughs for 87 employees on the Elkins Division. A nationwide strike by steel workers started at the same time, which increased the number of furloughs on the Division to 120 by July 8. When the miners at the "captive" mines returned to work on July 10, they also joined the ranks of those idled by the steel strike. The strike ended on July 29 and the mines reopened.

In January 1957, the W. Md. filed with the P. S. C. to abandon the last passenger trains between Cumberland and Elkins. The company maintained that it was loosing money on the service, and the loss had been increased when it lost the contract to carry mail between the two towns. Permission was granted for the removal of the trains by an order dated December 24, with the last trains scheduled for January 4, 1958. The last train from Elkins, hauled by an unidentified RS3, arrived in Cumberland at 11:30 A.M. and

was scheduled to return to Elkins at 7:00 P.M. Although an appeal was made to the West Virginia Supreme Court, the Court declined to hear the case and the service was not reinstated.

Two months later, on March 5, 1958, the company asked the P. S. C. for permission to discontinue service between Elkins and Durbin. The W. Md. reported that it had lost $41,000 on the service in 1957. The P. S. C., in a decision on July 28, 1958, allowed the railroad to reduce the service to three days per week. This service is shown in the last passenger timetable issued by the W. Md. on August 11, 1958 (Fig. 315). The decision by the P. S. C. did not satisfy the W. Md., which appealed to the West Virginia Supreme Court. The Supreme Court, on February 24, 1959, agreed with the railroad, and ordered the P. S. C. to issue a new order allowing the W. Md. to discontinue the service completely. Passenger service was scheduled to finish on April 10, 1959. The last train, which left Elkins at 7:15 P.M., was crowded with 125 passengers for its trip to Durbin. The train on the return trip consisted of 72 loaded coal cars and 14 empty freight cars, in addition to the two passenger cars, and was hauled by six diesels. The train arrived at Elkins at 2:45 A.M. on April 11, and was the last regularly scheduled passenger train into Elkins.

In March 1959, a flood control project in Cumberland was completed. Work had commenced in 1949 and by 1954 improvements to upper Wills Creek were finished. The final phase of the work, at the lower end of Wills Creek, involved rebuilding the W. Md. bridge. Trains were diverted over a temporary wooden trestle in December 1957 and the new bridge completed a year later. At the same time a new bridge was being built south of the station to a connection with the B. & O. The new connection was completed in October 1958, and this then allowed for the removal of the much rebuilt West Virginia Central bridge across the Potomac. Although not part of the flood control project, the W. Md. also began the demolition of its freight shed on South Mechanic Street in August 1958.

Also in March 1959, the W. Md. was reported to be building a spur from Wilson, two miles south of Bayard, across the North Branch. The spur was to serve an area containing an estimated 25,000,000 tons of coal. A tipple, owned by the Buffalo Coal Company, was being built and it was expected that 1,000 tons of coal would be shipped daily. The project had been initiated by the Mineral and Timber Land Department of the W. Md., which had been set up by the railroad to develop land owned by the railroad

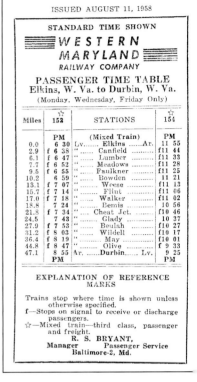

ISSUED AUGUST 11, 1958

STANDARD TIME SHOWN

WESTERN MARYLAND RAILWAY COMPANY

PASSENGER TIME TABLE
Elkins, W. Va. to Durbin, W. Va.
(Monday, Wednesday, Friday Only)

Miles	153	STATIONS	154
	PM	(Mixed Train)	PM
0.0	6 30	Lv......Elkins......Ar.	11 55
2.9	f 6 38	"......Canfield.........	f11 44
6.1	f 6 47	"......Lumber.........	f11 33
7.7	f 6 52	"......Meadows.........	f11 28
9.5	f 6 55	"......Faulkner.........	f11 25
10.2	6 59	"......Bowden.........	11 21
13.1	f 7 07	"......Weese.........	f11 13
15.7	f 7 14	"......Flint.........	f11 06
17.0	f 7 18	"......Walker.........	f11 02
18.8	7 24	"......Bemis.........	10 56
21.8	f 7 34	"......Cheat Jct.......	f10 46
24.5	7 43	"......Glady.........	10 37
27.9	f 7 53	"......Beulah.........	f10 27
31.2	f 8 03	"......Wildell.........	f10 17
36.4	f 8 19	"......May.........	f10 01
44.8	f 8 47	"......Olive.........	f 9 33
47.1	8 55	Ar. ......Durbin..... Lv.	9 25
	PM		PM

EXPLANATION OF REFERENCE MARKS

Trains stop where time is shown unless otherwise specified.
f—Stops on signal to receive or discharge passengers.
☆—Mixed train—third class, passenger and freight.
R. S. BRYANT,
Manager   Passenger Service
Baltimore-2, Md.

Fig. 315. Western Maryland passenger timetable, August 11, 1958

under the name of the West Virginia Central and Pittsburg Railway.

Considerable disruptions occurred to the W. Md.'s traffic during the second half of 1959. The two week miners' vacation at the beginning of July had caused furloughing of 250 W. Md. employees around Cumberland. A strike by steel workers began on July 15 and lasted until November 7. This caused the furloughing of an additional 250 workers throughout the system in August.

With no passenger traffic between Elkins and Cumberland, the W. Md. had no further use for the passenger and freight depot at Luke. This depot had been built in January 1913, replacing an earlier structure. The building was demolished in January 1960, and was replaced by a brick freight office to serve the Luke mill.

The winter of 1960 was very severe in the mountains of West Virginia and Maryland. On February 23, six cars of an eastbound freight derailed at Canyon Point. Deep snow hampered the wreck crew and it was the next day before the line could be reopened. A diesel engine and snowplow, attempting to reopen the Francis Branch, derailed and became snowbound on February 29. It took a crew 30 hours to dig out the engine and return it to the rails.

Another link with the past was broken when it was announced that the West Virginia Central office building in Elkins (Fig. 100) would be demolished in July 1961. The building was usually referred to as the Coal and Coke building in its later years, after the West Virginia Coal and Coke Company, which had purchased the building from the W. Md. The coal company sold the building in 1946 to a fraternal organization and it later housed a variety of businesses.

In 1960, the Virginia Electric and Power Company (VEPCO) announced plans to build a coal fired power station on the Stony River near Bayard. Construction started in April 1963, and the plant, officially known as the Mount Storm Power Station, was finished in August 1966. A new 17.1/2 mile long branch from Bayard was constructed by S. J. Groves and Sons for the power company to haul construction materials and coal to the power station. The branch was leased to the W. Md. in September 1963 when it was completed. Several new mines were opened, both along the Stony River Subdivision and in adjacent areas of West Virginia and Maryland A spur was built along Elk Run, near Henry in 1963 to serve a new mine, the Alpine mine, which shipped its first coal in November 1967. This mine provided coal for power plants in southern Maryland and the Bethlehem Steel plant near Baltimore in addition to Mount Storm. On the Stony River Subdivision, the North Branch Coal Company's new mine began shipping coal in October 1964. Both mines were operated by the Maust Coal and Coke Corporation but were sold in August 1969 to the Island Creek Coal Company of Cleveland. In 1962, 2.4 miles of track were relaid on the Kempton branch in anticipation of a new deep mine being opened, which did not occur. The branch served several strip mines before being closed again in 1976.

Throughout the 1960's and 1970's, the W. Md. sought approval from the P. S. C. to downgrade freight depots to non-agency status, which generally allowed for the handling of carload freight only. These downgrades included Shaw (1962), Durbin (1972), Thomas (1975), Belington (1976), Parsons (1977) and Bayard in 1979. During the same period, many of the non-agency stations were abandoned.

Fire destroyed the tipple and head-house of the mine at Monterville on November 10, 1961, leading to concerns that the mine would close permanently. Employment at the mine was down from 500 to 130 men and it had only worked three or four days a week for some time. Bethlehem Mine Corp. finally announced the closing on November 15.

Approval was given on June 25, 1962 for a new dam on the North Branch of the Potomac River, above Bloomington, that had been requested by the Corps of Engineers to enhance water supplies, provide flood control and recreational opportunities. Construction of the dam required moving 11.6 miles of the W. Md. from the West Virginia side of the river to the Maryland side, and flooding the village of Shaw. The first contract for work on the dam was awarded on May 21, 1971 to S. J. Groves and Sons for relocating 6.4 miles of the railroad. Work started in June 1971 and was completed by September 1974. A second contract for the remainder of the work was let in July 1972 to the Green Construction Company and was scheduled to be completed in May 1975. A third contract for moving approximately 8/10 of a mile of the spur along Three Forks Run was awarded in June 1974. All the railroad work was completed by October 1976; trains were expected to use the new route starting in November. The dam was completed in July 1981, and in 1987 it was renamed the Jennings Randolph Lake in honor of the West Virginia senator. A short length of approximately 3/4 of a mile of the old line remained to serve the mine of the Masteller Coal Company at Hampshire.

In 1973, the Chessie System took over management of the W. Md. although the separate identities of the railroads remained. This was the culmination of a series of maneuvers involving the C. & O., B. & O. and the W. Md., which were first discussed in January 1958. A tentative agreement for a merger between the B. & O. and C. & O. was not reached until March 1960. A request for approval for the merger was filed with the I. C. C. on June 14, 1960. While this request was being considered, the president of the B. & O. announced in November 1961, that the W. Md. would also be part of the merger as the B. & O. owned 42 percent of the W. Md. stock and the C. & O. owned about 14 percent. Although the proposed merger was opposed by other railroads, the I. C. C. gave approval on December 31, 1962. The railroad unions took the case to the U. S. Supreme Court, which cleared the way for the merger on December 9, 1963. A request by the B. & O.-C. & O. system to control the W. Md. was made to the I. C. C. on June 24, 1964, approval being granted on March 6, 1967. The B. & O.-C. & O. was expected to take control of the W. Md. on March 29, 1968. Because of various legal challenges, the takeover was deferred until early 1969 when three C. & O.-B. & O. officers were elected to the W. Md. board. On August 31, 1972, the B. & O.-C. & O. announced a new corporate name for the combination; the "Chessie System."

In 1973, with the Chessie System firmly in control, requests to abandon duplicate lines commenced. The W. Md. in June asked the I. C. C. for authority to abandon 124 miles of track and to obtain trackage rights over 184 miles of B. & O. tracks. Permission was granted in 1975 for the abandonment. Included was the line from Tonoloway, near Hancock, to Connellsville and the ex-P. & C. line between Ridgeley and West Virginia Central Junction. In both

Fig. 316. CSX GP38 No. 2111, still in Chessie System blue, yellow and orange paint, heads east from Westernport on the old West Virginia Central main line in 1996

cases, some segments of the lines were left in place to serve existing customers, for example, the Westvaco plant at Luke (Fig. 316). Westvaco was the new name of the West Virginia Pulp and Paper Company after March 1969. Consolidation of train operations of the W. Md. and the B. & O. occurred on January 5, 1976. Among the changes occurring was the transfer of yard operations from Knobmont to the B. & O.'s yard in Cumberland.

The C. & O. filed with the I. C. C. in March 1975 for permission to abandon the Greenbrier branch from North Caldwell to Durbin. The track between Durbin and Bartow would be leased to the W. Md. for operation to serve a tannery at Frank. Final approval for the abandonment of the Greenbrier branch was given by the I. C. C. in August 1978, with the branch slated for closure in December 1978.

MAPCO Inc., a Tulsa, Oklahoma energy company, announced plans in May 1976 to construct a large mining complex in Garrett County to produce metallurgical quality coal for steel mills in Japan. Production at the mine was expected to reach 2,000,000 tons per year using non-union labor. The mine, known as the Mettiki mine, was located some two miles up the South Fork of Sand Run from Wilson. The mine was reached by extending the spur serving the Buffalo Coal Company. The new mine was officially opened on October 5, 1978.

Even while construction was progressing at the new mine, it was the focus of attention for union pickets during a prolonged miners' strike that began on December 6, 1977. By the end of the year, 400 Chessie System workers around Cumberland were idled. The strike lasted until March 25, 1978. Chessie began recalling furloughed workers on March 27.

The Chessie System and the Seaboard Coast Line merged on November 1, 1980 into the CSX Corporation. The last corporate trace of the W. Md. disappeared in 1983 when it was absorbed by the B. & O. In 1986, a new division of CSX, CSX Transportation (CSXT) was formed with responsibilities for CSX's railroad operations. The B. & O. finally disappeared into the C. & O. in 1987, the C. & O. in turn being absorbed by CSXT.

Another miners' strike scheduled to commence at midnight on

March 26, 1981, was expected to be short but it was June 8 before work resumed. The Mettiki mine operated throughout the strike in spite of the efforts of pickets to close down the operation. Damage to power lines by strikers caused a temporary closure. The Chessie System, which lost an estimated $16,000,000 because of the strike, recalled workers on June 12.

Fire destroyed the W. Md. roundhouse at Elkins on November 28, 1981. Also destroyed in the fire were eight freight cars, three cabooses and a crane. Two days after the fire, 79 of the 90 car workers at Elkins were furloughed, although the railroad hoped to be able to resume repair work. Servicing locomotives continued in the open air.

When the C. & O. abandoned its Greenbrier branch, it was expected that there would be an increase of traffic on the W. Md. from Durbin to Elkins. This did not occur, and in June 1983, application was made to the I. C. C. to abandon the line from Durbin to Greenbriar Junction. Approval for the abandonment was announced by the I. C. C. on December 6, 1983, with service ending on February 15, 1984.

The last train up the Blackwater Canyon ran on September 30, 1983 although the line was not immediately abandoned. The Chessie System then announced on April 24, 1984 its intention to file with the I. C. C. for permission to abandon the line between Elkins and Hendricks, a distance of 24.58 miles. The Chessie claimed that it lost $100,000 on the line in 1983 and that operation of the line was hazardous in winter. The I. C. C. agreed and authorized the abandonment for December 15, 1984. The abandonment came at a fortuitous time as floods in November 1985 caused considerable damage. The rails were removed during 1987. In April 1986, the Chessie System requested permission to abandon the remaining 1.19 miles of the Thomas Subdivision from the junction in South Elkins through the station yard to just beyond the Rt. 33 bridge. This meant that the station at Elkins was now isolated from the remaining Chessie System lines in the area. To make the isolation total, the bridge across the Tygart Valley River was removed in 1992.

In 1993, CSXT decided to abandon 122 miles of track from Tygart Junction to Bergoo, but in January 1994 the plan was scrapped as an increase in coal traffic was expected. When this did not materialize, and CSXT was able to claim a loss of $845,000 on the line between January 1992 and September 1994, the plan was refiled with the I. C. C. Protests were made by West Virginia's two senators and by coal and lumber interests along the route. The I. C. C. agreed with the shippers and asked CSXT to consider operating the section of the route between Elkins and Tygart Junction. This decision was appealed by CSXT in July 1995.

The West Virginia State Railroad Authority (W. V. S. R. A.) purchased the line from CSX in 1997. The W. V. S. R. A. already operated another ex-B. & O. branch, the South Branch Valley Railroad, but decided not to operate the new line. Bids were requested for the operation of the new acquisition and a new company, the West Virginia Central, was inaugurated in May 1998 to provide service on the road.

On January 1, 1997 the contracts held by Consolidation Coal and Mettiki to supply coal to the Mount Storm generating station were due to expire, and a new contract for a ten year period was

Fig. 317. Loading cars at the Mettiki mine, October, 2000

awarded by Virginia Power exclusively to non-union Mettiki. This led to the closure of the mines around Bayard and Henry and the carrying of coal to the plant by road. By 1999 Mettiki was producing 105,000 tons of coal per week and employed nearly 200 underground workers. Some coal is still shipped by rail from the Mettiki mine to the Indian River power station in Delaware. This traffic currently amounts to approximately two 80-car trains per month during the summer and fall. Empty cars are brought in by CSXT and left at the mine for loading (Fig. 317). The diesels

Fig. 318. CSX No. 415 (GE CW44AC) and No. 762 (EMD SD70AC) wait in the yard at Bayard, September 27, 2000

then wait in the yard at Bayard (Fig. 318), and then haul out the loaded cars the next day (Fig. 319). This traffic appeared to be insufficient to justify the branch, and it was rumored that CSX was trying to sell the last major remnant of the West Virginia Central and Pittsburg Railway that it owns.

During the winter of 2001 and 2002, CSX refurbished the line to Mount Storm and in the spring of 2002 some coal was transported from the Gatzmer mine to the Lehigh Cement Company's plant at Union Bridge, Maryland. This business soon ceased but was replaced by coal trains going to Mount Storm from the Coastal Coal Company's Whitetail mine near Kingwood, West Virginia. The most recent movements over the subdivision occurred in

Fig. 319. Last train for the 2000 season leaves the Mettiki mine EMD SD70AC No. 722 leads No. 726, October 10, 2000

January 2003, when trains left the Mettiki mine bound for Curtis Bay or the Chalk Point Generating Station in Prince George's County, Maryland. Whether this diversification of traffic will be sufficient to ensure the continued operation of the subdivision remains to be seen.

Equipment of the West Virginia Central and Pittsburg Railway

The First Report of the West Virginia Central and Pittsburg Railway, published on January 1, 1882, showed the company possessing the following standard gauge equipment: two locomotives, seven gondola and flat cars, ten iron hoppers and one passenger and baggage car. In addition, one narrow gauge locomotive was in use at Elk Garden. Very little new information on the locomotives was gleaned from the Davis papers. The roster below is taken from the list prepared by Raymond Hicks for Railroad History (No. 113, 1965), with corrections suggested by Robert Brendel.

Table 3
Locomotives of the West Virginia Central and Pittsburg Railway

No	Builder	C/N	Date	Type	Cyls.	DD	WM No.	Remarks
1	NJLW		1856	4-4-0	16x22	60		Ex-P&R 367 (Catswissa 14) Rec'd 1881. Cost $4,251.37. Scrapped 1889.
1	Baldwin	3316	1873	4-6-0	18x22	50		Ex- PRR 540. Rec'd 1/1889. Cost $2500. Originally No. 16. Sold October, 1899. $1,800.
1	Rogers	5406	1899	2-6-0	19x28	54	209	From #37. Ren'd W.M. #1000. Sold Medusa Cement Co. 3/1928. Sc. 1944.
2	Danforth	1100	1881	2-8-0	20x24	51	253	Sc. 1914
3	Mt. Savage		1882	2-8-0	20x24	50	253	W.M. No. assigned but not used. Sc. about 1905.
4	Cooke	1405	1882	2-8-0	20x24	51	254	Sc. 1908
5	Baldwin	7336	1884	2-8-0	20x24	50	255	Sc. 1914
6	Baldwin	7614	1885	4-4-0	17x24	62	28	Sold Valley Fuel Co. 1920
7	Baldwin	8637	1887	4-4-0	17x24	62	29	Sc. 1914
8	Baldwin	8640	1887	2-8-0	20x24	50	256	Sc. 1915
9	Baldwin	9181	1888	2-8-0	20x24	50	257	So. Reliable Junk Co. 1916
10	Baldwin	9185	1888	2-8-0	20x24	50	258	" " "
11	Baldwin	9301	1888	4-4-0	17x24	62	30	Sc. 1014
12	Baldwin	9458	1888	2-8-0	20x24	50	269	So. Reliable Junk Co. 1916
13	Baldwin	9713	1889	2-8-0	20x24	50	259	" " "
14	Baldwin	9788	1889	2-8-0	20x24	50	260	Sc. 1914
15	Baldwin	9787	1889	2-8-0	20x24	50	261	So. Reliable Junk Co. 1916
16	Baldwin	10453	1889	2-8-0	20x24	50	262	" " "
17	Baldwin	9905	1889	2-8-0	20x24	50	203	Sc. 1916
18	Baldwin	9956	1889	4-4-0	18x24	62	45	Sc. 1923
19	Baldwin	10454	1889	2-8-0	20x24	50	–	Dest'd in boiler expln. Elkins, 1903
20	Baldwin	10844	1890	2-8-0	20x24	50	264	Sc. 1914
21	Baldwin	11102	1890	2-8-0	20x24	50	265	So. Reliable Junk Co. 1916
22	Baldwin	11328	1890	2-8-0	20x24	50	266	" " "
23	Baldwin	11828	1891	0-6-0	20x24	50	1001	Sc. 1923
24	Baldwin	11899	1891	2-8-0	20x24	50	267	Sc. 1914
25	Baldwin	11935	1891	2-8-0	20x24	50	268	Sc. 1912
26	Baldwin	12465	1892	0-6-0	20x24	50	1002	Sc. 1927
27	Baldwin	12467	1892	2-8-0	20x24	50	301	So. Reliable Junk Co. 1916.
28	Baldwin	12794	1892	2-8-0	19x26	50	347	So. Va. Cent. #347 1929. Sc. 1938
29	Baldwin	12803	1892	2-8-0	19x26	50	348	Ret'd 10/16/52. Sold as scrap.
30	Baldwin	14390	1895	2-8-0	21x26	50	351	So. H. & B. T. M. #40. 9/16/47.
31	Baldwin	14555	1895	2-8-0	21x26	50	352	Sc. 1924.
32	Baldwin	14556	1895	2-8-0	21x26	50	353	Sc. 1927.
33	Baldwin	15838	1897	2-8-0	21x26	50	354	Sc. 1924.
34	Baldwin	15872	1898	2-8-0	21x26	50	355	Sc. 1924.
35	Baldwin	15873	1898	2-8-0	21x26	50	356	Sc. 1928.
36	Rogers	5366	1899	4-4-0	17x26	62	31	So. Reliable Junk Co. 1916.
37	Rogers	5406	1899	2-6-0	19x28	54		Ren'd 1, then W.M. 1000. Sold Medusa Cement Co. 1928. Sc. 1944.
37	Baldwin	17431	1890	2-8-0	21x26	50	357	Sc. 1925
38	Baldwin	17731	1900	2-8-0	22x28	50	451	Sc. 5/1950.
39	Baldwin	17732	1900	2-8-0	22x28	50	452	So. Vang Const. Co., 1929
40	Baldwin	18720	1901	2-8-0	22x28	50	453	Sc. 1928.
41	Baldwin	18731	1901	2-8-0	22x28	50	454	Sc. 12/26/47.
42	Baldwin	18810	1901	4-6-0	19x26	62	91	Sc. 1924.
43	Baldwin	18811	1901	4-6-0	19x26	62	92	Sold for Scrap, 1927.
44	Baldwin	21696	1903	2-8-0	22x28	50	455	" " 6/1953.
45	Baldwin	21738	1903	2-8-0	22x28	50	456	Sc. 12/31/46.
46	Baldwin	21978	1903	2-8-0	22x28	50	457	Sc. 1/20/47.
47	Baldwin	22009	1903	2-9-0	22x28	50	458	Sc. 12/26/47.

By 1903, when the West Virginia Central had been sold to the Fuller Syndicate, The Official Railway Equipment Register listed the following freight and passenger equipment for the railroad. The only addition to the roster after the sale would have been the 800 steel hoppers.

Table 4
Freight Equipment

Kind of Cars	Numbers	Outside Dimensions			Capacity	No.
		Length	Width	Height		
Caboose	1 to 17	16	8	12.4		17
Crane, M. of W	1, 2, 3	35.4	10	15.10		3
Steam Shovel, M of W	205					1
Flat	300 to 313	28	8	3.11	40000	14
Flat	314 to 324				50000	11
Carpenter, M of W	350	39.6	9.4	8.8		1
Scale	351					1
Box	400 to 449	124.9	8.3	12.3	80000	50
Box	450.451	34	8.2	17.1?	90000	2
Box	452 to 499	34	8.3	7.1?	80000	48
Gondola, Solid bottom	500,501	30	8	6.5	60000	2
" " "	503,506	30	8	6.5	60000	2
" " "	504,505	30	8	6.5	40000	2
" " "	507 to 544	34	8	5.5	50000	26
" " "	545	34	8	6.5	60000	1
" " "	546 to 566	34	8	6.5	50000	21
" Drop Bottom	567 to 699	31	8	6.6	60000	133
Box	700 to 703	28	8.7?	11	50000	4
"	704 to 729	31	8.7?	12	50000	26
"	730 to 779	34	8.7?	11	60000	50
"	780 to 799	34	8.8	12.4	60000	20
Hopper Gondola	800 to 1599	26	9	8	60000	600
Wooden Coal Hoppers	1600 to 1975	25.8	8	9.5	60000	376
Gondola, Drop Bottom	2000 to 2081	34	8	6.5	60000	82
" Coke	2082 to 2442	34	8	11.5	60000	361
" Drop Bottom	3001 to 3185	34	8	6.5	60000	186
" "	3186 to 3285	36.10?	9	7	90000	100
Steel Hoppers	5000 to 5799				100000	800
Total						3171

Table 5
Passenger Equipment

Combination..........1, 2, 3, 4, 5, 16, 17, 18, 19, 20, 21		11
Passenger coaches....36, 37, 38, 39, 40, 41, 42, 43, 44, 45, 46, 47, 48, 49		14
Officers' car, "West Virginia."		1
Total........		36

Fig. 320. Shooting marbles. Unidentified West Virginia Central combination car
Herman and Stacia Miller Collection, City of Cumberland

Brown, D. D. Collection of notes and photographs of logging activities in Randolph and neighboring counties. West Virginia and Regional History Collection. West Virginia University Library, Morgantown, West Virginia.

Browning, Art. *Up from Mill Creek on the Valley River Line*. Journal of the Mountain State Railroad and Logging Historical Association. Vol. 8. No. 3. (Summer 1991) pp 6-12.

Callahan, James Morton. *Semi-Centennial History of West Virginia*, West Virginia: Semi-Centennial Commission 1913.

Camden, Johnson Newlon. Papers. West Virginia and Regional History Collection. West Virginia University Library, Morgantown, West Virginia.

Carpenter, Charles. Papers. West Virginia and Regional History Collection, West Virginia University Library, Morgantown, West Virginia. Contains some material dealing with the West Virginia Central and Pittsburg Railway.

Clarkson, Roy B. *Tumult on the Mountains. Lumbering in West Virginia, 1770 - 1920*. Parsons, West Virginia: McClain Printing Company. 1964.

Davis, Henry Gassaway. Diary, April, 1867 - February, 1916. A single volume kept by Davis.

Davis, Henry Gassaway. Papers. West Virginia and Regional History Collection, West Virginia University Library, Morgantown, West Virginia. A large volume of papers dealing with Davis's interests in coal, lumber, railroads, politics and charitable activities. Although some papers have been categorized as "Railroads" (A & M 13 Series 9, Box 155 - Box 165) several years are missing and are scattered elsewhere. The material includes daily letters from the general managers and other employees on the happenings of the West Virginia Central and the Coal and Coke railways.

Eckman, David L. *The Chaffee Railroad*. The Blue Mountain Express. Western Maryland Railway Historical Society. Vol. 21. No. 1. (Winter 1991-1992) pp 12-19.

Eckman, David L. *The Belington and Beaver Creek Railroad*. The Blue Mountain Express. Western Maryland Railway Historical Society. Vol. 22. No. 2 (Summer 1993) pp 15-20.

Elkins, Stephen B. Papers. West Virginia and Regional History Collection, West Virginia University Library, Morgantown, West Virginia.

Fansler, Homer Floyd. *History of Tucker County, West Virginia*. Parsons, West Virginia: McClain Printing Company, 1962.

Fizer, George A. *Early Problems of the Thomas, West Virginia, Coal Industry*. The Blue Mountain Express. Western Maryland Railway Historical Society. Vol. 24. No. 3 and 4. (Fall/Winter 1995-1996) pp 3-10.

Fizer, George A. *Short Trains and Stiff Grades-The Western Maryland's Chaffee Branch*. The Log Train. Journal of the Mountain State Railroad and Logging Historical Association. Vol. 3. No. 4/Vol. 4. No. 1. (January 1986, April 1986), pp 3-24.

Fizer, George A. *The Cumberland Coal Company*. The Blue Mountain Express. Western Maryland Railway Historical Society. Vol. 24. No. 3 and 4. (Fall/Winter 1995-1996) pp 11-28.

Fizer, George A. *The Dry Fork Railroad Company*. The Blue Mountain Express. Western Maryland Railway Historical Society. Vol. 21. No. 3 (Summer/Fall 1992) pp 3-16.

Fizer, George A. *The Kempton Branch*. The Blue Mountain Express. Western Maryland Railway Historical Society. Vol. 25. No. 2. (Summer 1996) pp 2-22.

Fizer, George A. *The Lumber Industry at Bemis, West Virginia*. The Blue Mountain Express. Western Maryland Railway Historical Society. Vol. 26. No. 3 and 4. (Fall and Winter 1997) pp 20-33.

Fizer, George A. *The Tanning Industry on the West Virginia Central*. The Blue Mountain Express. Western Maryland Railway Historical Society. Vol. 23. No. 2 and 3. (Summer/Fall 1994) pp 31-41.

Fizer, George A. *The Western Maryland's Mexican Connection*. The Log Train. Journal of the Mountain State Railroad and Logging Historical Association. Vol. 3. No. 4, Vol. 4. No. 1. (January 1986, April 1986), pp 26-28.

Fizer, George A. *The West Virginia and Pittsburgh Railroad*. The Log Train. Journal of the Mountain State Railroad and Logging Historical Association. Vol. 7. No. 3. (October 1989), pp 3-9.

Ghost Towns of the Upper Potomac. The Garrett County Historical Society. Oakland, Maryland. 1999.

Griffin, Sam. *West Virginia Central and Pittsburg Railway*. Indianapolis, Indiana. 1899.

Guthrie, Keith. *Blackwater Canyon*. The Log Train. Journal of the Mountain State Railroad and Logging Historical Association. Vol. 10. No. 3. (Fall 1993) pp 6-12.

Guthrie, Keith. *By Rail to Stony River Dam*. The Log Train. Journal of the Mountain State Railroad and Logging Historical Association. Vol. 11. No. 4. (Winter 1995) pp 8-14.

Guthrie, Keith. *Logging in Canaan*. The Log Train. Journal of the Mountain State Railroad and Logging Historical Association. Vol. 14. No. 3. (Summer 1998) pp 4-20.

Guthrie, Keith. *The Logging Era on the Elkins-Durbin Line*. The Log Train. Journal of the Mountain State Railroad and Logging Historical Association. Vol. 13. No. 1. Pp 4-16.

Guthrie, Keith. *Water under the Dam*. The Log Train. Journal of the Mountain State Railroad and Logging Historical Association. Vol. 11. No. 3. (Fall 1994) pp 6-11.

Hicks, W. Raymond. *The West Virginia Central and Pittsburg Railway*. Railroad History. The Railway and Locomotive Historical Society. No. 113. 1965. Pp 6-31.

Investigation of Railroads, Holding Companies & Affiliated Companies. Report of the Committee on Interstate Commerce. Railroad Combination in the Eastern Region. Part I (Before 1920). Washington: United States Government Printing Office, 1940.

Lambert, Oscar Doane. *Stephen Benton Elkins*. Pittsburgh, Pennsylvania: University of Pittsburgh, 1955.

Little Kanawha Railroad Company. A Report of the Investigation by the Interstate Commerce Commission of the Ownership, Management and Control of the Little Kanawha Railroad Company. Washington: 1915.

Markle, Robert R. *Breaking up the Western Maryland. Part 1.* The Blue Mountain Express. Western Maryland Railway Historical Society. No. 16. (April 1979) pp 5 and 6.

Markle, Robert R. *Breaking up the Western Maryland. Part 11.* The Blue Mountain Express. Western Maryland Railway Historical Society. No. 18. (October 1979) pp 2 and 3.

Markle, Robert R. *Breaking up the Western Maryland. Part 111.* The Blue Mountain Express. Western Maryland Railway Historical Society. No. 20. (April 1980) pp 16.

McFall, D. A. *The Stations at Thomas, West Virginia.* The Blue Mountain Express. Western Maryland Railway Historical Society. Vol. 25. No. 1 (Spring 1996) pp 24-31.

McFall, D. A. and Cline, D. *Western Maryland Railway Stations South of Cumberland.* The Blue Mountain Express. Western Maryland Railway Historical Society. Vol. 27. No. 1 and 2. (Spring and Summer 1998) pp 3-48.

McNeel, William Price. *The Durbin Route.* Charleston, West Virginia: Pictorial Histories Publishing Company. 1995.

Mellander, Deane E. *Rails to the Big Vein.* Potomac Chapter, National Railway Historical Society. 1981.

Oertly, William J. *The West Virginia Midland Story*. The Log Train. Journal of the Mountain State Railroad and Logging Historical Association. Vol. 3. No. 2. (July, 1985) pp 3-16.

Oertly, William J. *Western Maryland Railway; 1900-1920, The Gould Years.* The Blue Mountain Express. Western Maryland Railway Historical Society. No. 28. (April 1982) pp 4 and 5.

Pepper, Charles M. *The Life and Times of Henry Gassaway Davis.* New York, New York: The Century Co. 1920.

Price, Charles Grattan, Jr. *The Crooked & Weedy.* Being a Very Informal, Illustrated History of Virginia's Most Un-Common Carrier: Chesapeake Western Railway. C. G. Price, Jr. 1992.

Reger, David B. *West Virginia Geological Survey. Mineral and Grant Counties.* Morgantown, West Virginia: Morgantown Printing and Binding Company. 1924.

Reger, David B. *West Virginia Geological Survey. Randolph County.* Morgantown, West Virginia: Morgantown Printing and Binding Company. 1931

Reger, David B. *West Virginia Geological Survey. Tucker County.* Morgantown, West Virginia: Morgantown Printing and Binding Company. 1923.

Rice, Donald L. *Randolph County 200. A Bicentennial History of Randolph County.* The Randolph County Historical Society, 1987.

Rice, Donald L. *The Elkins Centennial Album, 1890 - 1990.* Parsons: West Virginia. McClain Printing Company, 1990.

Sparks, Richard. *Rod Type Locomotives of the Greenbriar, Cheat and Elk Railroad.* The Log Train. Journal of the Mountain State Railroad and Logging Historical Association. Volume 2, Number 2, (October 1983) pp 16, 17.

Sypolt, Larry and Kemp, Emory. *The Little Kanawha Navigation.* Canal History and Technology Proceedings. Vol. X (March 23, 1991) pp. 49-93.

Teter, Don. *Goin' up Gandy.* Parsons, West Virginia: McClain Printing Company. 1977.

The Western Maryland Railway. Shippers' Guide. The Freight Traffic Department, Baltimore, Maryland. 1911-1912.

The West Virginia Central and Pittsburg Railway Company. First Mortgage and Deed of Trust. July 1, 1881.

Thompson, George B. *A History of the Lumber Business at Davis, West Virginia. 1885-1924.* Parsons, West Virginia: McClain Printing Company. 1974.

West Virginia Central and Pittsburg Railway. Statement, Engineer's Report, Charter, Contracts, and Other Documents.

West Virginia Central and Pittsburg Railway Company. Annual Reports. January 9, 1883 to August 13, 1901.

West Virginia Central and Pittsburg Railway Company. First Report. January 1, 1882.

Williams, John Alexander. *West Virginia and the Captains of Industry.* Morgantown, West Virginia: West Virginia University Library, 1976.

Workman, M. E., Salstrom, P., and Ross, P. W. *"Northern West Virginia Coal Fields."* Morgantown, West Virginia: Institute for the History of Technology and Industrial Archaeology, West Virginia University, April 1994.

In addition to the materials listed above, use was made also of the collection of newspapers on microfilm held by the West Virginia and Regional History Collection at West Virginia University Library. These included the Charleston Gazette, the Elkins Inter-Mountain and the Randolph Review. Also the Cumberland Evening Times, on microfilm at the McKeldin Library of the University of Maryland, provided much useful information particularly on the early years of the Western Maryland.

Fig. 260. Babcock Lumber and Boom Company's mill at Davis

Fig. 265. The Western Maryland depot in Cumberland
Collection of the Western Maryland Railway Historical Society

Fig. 275. The mill at Dobbin (undated)
West Virginia and Regional History Collection,
West Virginia University Library